The diplomacy of decolonisation

Manchester University Press

Key Studies in Diplomacy

Series Editors: J. Simon Rofe and Giles Scott-Smith

Emeritus Editor: Lorna Lloyd

This innovative series of books examines the procedures and processes of diplomacy, focusing on the interaction between states through their accredited representatives, that is, diplomats. Volumes in the series focus on factors affecting foreign policy and the ways in which it is implemented through the diplomatic system in both bilateral and multilateral contexts. They examine how diplomats can shape not just the presentation, but the substance of their state's foreign policy. Since the diplomatic system is global, each book aims to contribute to an understanding of the nature of diplomacy. Authors comprise both scholarly experts and former diplomats, able to emphasize the actual practice of diplomacy and to analyse it in a clear and accessible manner. The series offers essential primary reading for beginning practitioners and advanced level university students.

Previously published by Bloomsbury:

21st Century Diplomacy: A Practitioner's Guide by Kishan S. Rana
A Cornerstone of Modern Diplomacy: Britain and the Negotiation of the 1961 Vienna Convention on Diplomatic Relations by Kai Bruns
David Bruce and Diplomatic Practice: An American Ambassador in London, 1961–9 by John W. Young
Embassies in Armed Conflict by G.R. Berridge

Published by Manchester University Press:

Reasserting America in the 1970s edited by Hallvard Notaker, Giles Scott-Smith, and David J. Snyder

The diplomacy of decolonisation
America, Britain and the United Nations during the Congo crisis 1960–1964

Alanna O'Malley

Manchester University Press

Copyright © Alanna O'Malley 2018

The right of Alanna O'Malley to be identified as the author of this work has been asserted by her in accordance with the Copyright, Designs and Patents Act 1988.

Published by Manchester University Press
Altrincham Street, Manchester M1 7JA, UK
www.manchesteruniversitypress.co.uk

British Library Cataloguing-in-Publication Data is available

ISBN 978 1 5261 1626 0 hardback
ISBN 978 1 5261 1662 8 paperback

First published by Manchester University Press in hardback 2018

This edition published 2019

The publisher has no responsibility for the persistence or accuracy of URLs for any external or third-party internet websites referred to in this book, and does not guarantee that any content on such websites is, or will remain, accurate or appropriate.

Typeset by Out of House Publishing

For my parents, Geraldine and Peter

It is by imitation, far more than by precept, that we learn everything; and what we learn thus, we acquire not only more efficiently, but more pleasantly. This forms our manners, our opinions, our lives.
          (Edmund Burke, Irish orator, philosopher and politician, 1729–1797)

The Congo was the one place where we could, at that time, have had a beginning of a new world order.[1]
          (George McGhee, US Under-Secretary of State for Political Affairs, 1962)

Note

1 Dag Hammarskjöld Library, United Nations, New York. Yale-UN Oral History Project, Ambassador George C. McGhee interviewed by James S. Sutterlin, 9 May 1990, New York, p. 33.

Contents

Acknowledgements		viii
List of names		x
List of abbreviations		xii
	Introduction	1
1	A challenge for humanity	11
2	The Dag factor	38
3	Fighting over Katanga	73
4	'After Dag – what?'	114
5	'A nice little stew'	138
6	The Stanleyville hostages and the withdrawal of the UN, 1964	166
	Conclusion	197
Index		202

Acknowledgements

This book is based on my doctoral dissertation, which was defended at the Department of History and Civilisation at the European University Institute (EUI) in Florence on 27 April 2012. It was revised into its current form at Leiden University and the University of Sydney.

Surrounded by the rolling landscape of Tuscany and the wonders of the Renaissance city of Florence, the EUI is truly a unique place in which to produce a thesis. It was a great privilege to spend six years in the rich academic environment and I am grateful to Richard Aldous and Maurice Bric from University College Dublin for supporting my PhD application. The rigour of the intellectual community at the EUI cannot be overstated and this project has in particular benefitted from debates and discussions with my doctoral supervisor, Kiran Patel, Sebastian Conrad, Federico Romero, and Dirk Moses. My EUI colleagues, in particular the veritable 'band of brothers' provided a constant source of inspiration and support. Jannis Panagiotidis proved an excellent sparring partner from day one, with Mats Ingulstad in the role of academic nemesis. Martin Muller was always on hand to offer a selection of piercing insights and silver-tongued witticisms both inside and outside the classroom. Pablo Del Hierro sportingly read drafts and proved an ample companion for long stints in the archives. Thomas Cauvin, Lucas Lixinski, Veera Mitzner and Frank Gerits also provided thoughtful remarks and remain excellent friends.

The diversity of the EUI community has yielded a plethora of happy memories and wonderful life-long friends including Basia and Matthew, Chris, Conor and Constanze, Eugenio, Heko and Miluska, Ilze, Katherine and Jacob, Keiva, Karolka and Marija. I would like to thank the committee of Bar Fiasco for the experience of political management that has since proven a useful skill in navigating an academic career.

Beyond the EUI, the process of transforming this manuscript into a book benefitted from advice and support from a range of friends and colleagues including Jeffrey S. Ahlman Nigel Ashton, Lindsay Black, Ananda Burra, Meike de Geode, Andre Gerrits, Alessandro Iandolo, Ryan Irwin, Simon Jackson, John Kent, Nivi Manchanda, Anne-Isabelle Richard, Maria Weimer and Herbert F. Weiss. I am particularly indebted to Marilyn Young who served as a member of my thesis defence committee and was been a formidable advisor and a most ardent supporter of my career. She was a real source of inspiration as a scholar and as a woman in academia and her recent passing is a great loss to the historical profession.

Without the financial support of the Irish Government, the EUI, Leiden University and the Gerda Henkel Stiftung, this book may never have come to fruition. The opportunity to spend a semester at New York University in 2009 was invaluable for the time it afforded me to spend in the United Nations Archives in New York. The Institute for History at Leiden University funded additional archival research trips to the United States and generously granted me sabbatical leave from February–August 2017, to finish the manuscript. The Society for Historians of American Foreign Relations (SHAFR) supported research for the final chapter by granting me the William Appleman Williams Junior Faculty Research Grant to travel to the National Archives at College Park, Maryland in 2014. Another research grant from the Gerda Henkel Stiftung in 2015 facilitated archival trips to the George Padmore Research Library, the Public Records and Archives Administration Department of Ghana in Accra and the National Archives of India in Delhi, which was very helpful in supplementing the dissertation research. In particular at the Padmore Library I'd like to thank the archivist James Nasbah, and his research assistants Eric and Felix, for facilitating an extremely productive research trip and finding all the files I requested. The staff of the EUI Library in Florence and the Peace Palace Library in The Hague were also very helpful during the long years of writing this book.

Finally, a Kathleen Fitzpatrick Visiting Fellowship at the Laureate Research Programme in International History at the University of Sydney from April to June 2017 was fundamental in providing me a thoughtful intellectual space with which to bring the final manuscript together. I am indebted to Glenda Sluga, Natasha Wheatley and Jamie Martin for their inspiration, hospitality and generosity of spirit.

My wonderful siblings Thomas, Geoffrey and Camille kept me on track, particularly at moments when I was struggling with the manuscript.

Meeting my husband, Joris Larik, at the EUI enhanced even more the fundamental impact of my time in Florence on my career and my life. His love and unremitting support has reminded me that it is possible to achieve what sometimes seemed impossible and my love for him knows no bounds.

Names

Adoula, Cyrille. Prime Minister of the Congo, 1961–1964.

Ball, George. Under-Secretary of State for Economic Affairs, February–December 1961. Under Secretary of State, November 1961–1966. Kennedy's 'Point Man' on the Congo crisis.

Bomboko, Justin. Foreign Minister of the Congo, June–September 1960, also 1961–1964. Part of the Congo UN Delegation.

Bowles, Chester B. Under-Secretary of State, January–December 1961. Afterwards, President's Special Advisor on African, Asian and Latin American Affairs until May 1962.

Bunche, Ralph J. UN Under Secretary-General for Special Political Affairs, 1958–1971. Special Representative of the Secretary-General in the Congo, July–August 1960.

Bundy, McGeorge. US National Security Advisor, January 1961 to February 1966.

Cleveland, J. Harlan. Assistant Secretary of State for International Organization Affairs, February 1961–September 1965.

Cordier, Andrew Wellington. Executive Assistant to Dag Hammarskjöld, 1952–1961. UN Representative in the Congo, September 1960.

Dayal, Rajeshwar. Indian diplomat and Special Representative of the Secretary-General in the Congo, September 1960 to March 1961.

Dean, Patrick. Permanent Representative of the United Kingdom to the United Nations, 1960–1965. British Ambassador to the US, 1965–1969.

Diallo, Telli. Guinean Ambassador to the US and the UN, 1959–1964.

Foot, Hugh (Lord Caradon). British Minister of State for Foreign and Commonwealth Affairs, 1964–1968. British Permanent Representative to the United Nations, 1964–1970.

Gbenye, Christophe. Minister of the Interior in the Congo, July–September 1960. Leadership of the CNL in 1964 and supporter of Gizenga and Lumumba.

Gizenga, Antoine. President of the Parti de la Solidarite Africaine and former Deputy-Prime Minister of the Congo. Leader of the pro-Lumumba regime in Stanleyville, 1960–1961.

Gullion, Edmund. US Ambassador to the Congo, 1961–1964.

Hammarskjöld, Dag. UN Secretary-General 1953–1961. Killed in the Congo, September 1961.

Harriman, Averell. W. 'Ambassador-at-large' in Kennedy's administration, 1961–1963.

Home, Alec Douglas. British Foreign Secretary, 1960–1963.

Kanza, Thomas. Congolese representative to the UN under Lumumba and Ambassador to Britain under Adoula. Negotiated for the rebels during the 1964 hostage crisis in Stanleyville.

Kasavubu, Joseph. ABAKO founder and president. President of the Congo, 1960–1965.

Linner, Sture. Chief of the UN civilian operation until September 1961. Afterwards, Officer-in-Charge of UN operations, May 1961 to February 1962.

Lumumba, Patrice. Founder of the MNC and first Congolese Prime Minister until September 1960. Assassinated, January 1961.

Mobutu, Colonel Joseph. Chief of Staff of the Congolese National Army (ANC). Head of the College of Commissioners September 1960 to March 1961. Ruler and dictator over the Congo 1965–1997.

Mulele, Pierre. Congolese rebel and leader of the Simba rebellion 1963–1964.

Nehru, Jawaharlal. First Prime Minister of India, 1947–1964.

Nkrumah, Kwame. First President of Ghana, 1960–1966. Ally of Patrice Lumumba.

O'Brien, Conor Cruise. Irish Diplomat and Special Representative of the Secretary-General in Katanga, 1961.

Rusk, Dean. US Secretary of State, January 1961–1969.

Stevenson, Adlai E. US Ambassador to the UN, 1961–1965.

Timberlake, Clare H. US Ambassador to the Congo, July 1960 to March 1961.

Thant, U. UN Secretary-General 1961–1972.

Tshombe, Moise. 'President' of Katanga, July 1960 to January 1963. Prime Minister of the Congo, 1964–1965.

Williams, G. Mennon ('Soapy'). Assistant Secretary of State for African Affairs January 1961 to March 1966.

Abbreviations

ABAKO	Association des Bakongo pour l'Unification, l'Expansion et la Défense de la Kikongo (Congolese political party)
ANC	Armée Nationale Congolaise
CAC	Congo Advisory Committee
CAF	Central African Federation
CNL	Conseil National de Libération
CRO	Commonwealth Relations Office
EEC	European Economic Community
FLN	Front de Libération Nationale
ICJ	International Court of Justice
MNC	Mouvement Nationale Congolais. A nationalist political party in the Congo created by Patrice Lumumba, Cyrille Adoula and Joseph Ileo.
NSA	National Security Agency
ONUC	Operations des nations unies au Congo (the first UN peacekeeping force in the Congo)
PAFMECA	Pan-African Freedom Movement of East and Central Africa
PSA	Parti Solidaire Africain
SGB	Société Générale de Belgique
TANKS	Tanganyika Concessions Limited
UAR	United Arab Republic
UMHK	Union Minière du Haut Katanga
UNEF	United Nations Emergency Force (peacekeeping mission to Suez 1956–1967)
USAID	US Agency for International Development
USUN	US Mission to the UN

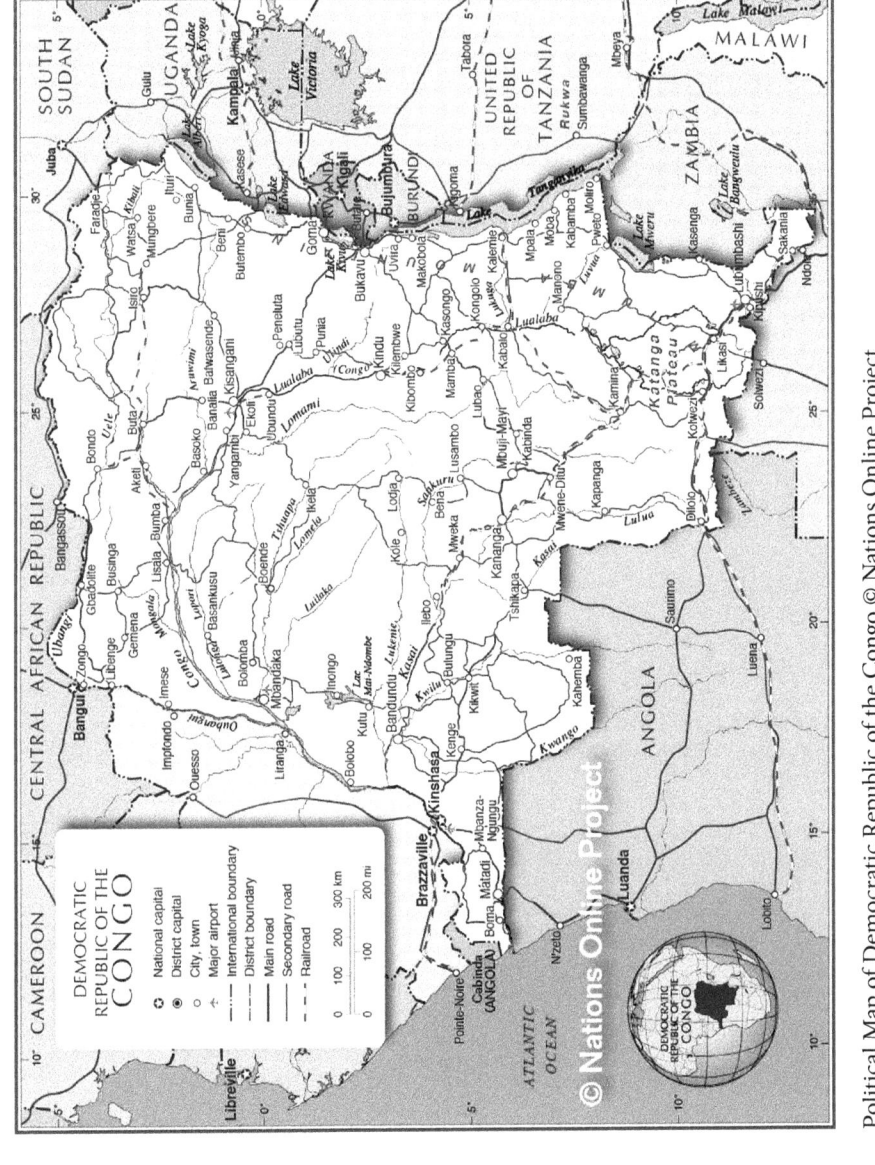

Political Map of Democratic Republic of the Congo © Nations Online Project

Introduction

[The Congo] is the place where the American Ambassador found an alligator in his garage, where two more (alligators, not ambassadors) swam into the Congo-flooded generating plant at Stanleyville, where yet a fourth is believed to have eaten the West German Ambassador in November (he was wading near the bank with a tow-rope; nothing of him was seen again but his panama hat).[1]

Writing in 1962, *The Economist* deemed the Congo the world's leading surrealist country, a place where, upon independence from Belgium on 30 June 1960, logic and reason quickly gave way to chaos and anarchy. Despite the orientalist undertones in this view, the Congo was catapulted into the international consciousness as the scene of conflict and confusion when a civil and constitutional crisis erupted just a week after the independence ceremony. The conflict amplified a constellation of internal rivalries, dubious and competing claims of provincial sovereignty, implicit and explicit outside intervention into Congolese politics, competition over natural resources and a corrupt political system which continues to hinder the development of the country today.

The breakdown of law and order began when the Congolese army, the Force Publique, mutinied against their Belgian officers, leading to violence and chaos on the streets of the capital Léopoldville (now Kinshasa). In response, the Belgians sent paratroopers into their former colony to protect the remaining European community and their economic interests, an act that was widely interpreted by the Congolese people as a signal that Belgium would try to regain control of the country. The newly elected Congolese Prime Minister Patrice Lumumba and President Joseph Kasavubu appealed to the United Nations (UN) to intervene in order to defend the sovereignty of the Congo from what they perceived as an aggressive act of Belgian imperialism.

Upon receiving the request, the UN Secretary-General Dag Hammarskjöld immediately set about arranging a meeting of the Security Council to consider the problem. Hammarskjöld viewed the unfolding crisis in the Congo as an important moment in the ongoing process of global decolonisation and, therefore, an event which required a swift and unprecedented response from the UN. From the creation of ground-breaking peacekeeping mandates to the formation of specific groups such as the Special Committee on Decolonisation (the Committee of 24) and the instrumentalisation of others such as United Nations Fourth Committee (Special Political and Decolonisation Committee), the myriad challenges of the Congo crisis quickly served to condition the ways in which the UN henceforth approached the challenges associated with decolonisation. This book reinterprets the role of the organisation in this conflict by presenting a multidimensional view of how the UN operated in response to the crisis. As the United States (US) and Britain were directly involved with formulating UN Congo policy, through an examination of the Anglo-American relationship, the book analyses how the crisis became positioned as a lightning rod in the interaction of decolonisation with the Cold War, and wider relations between North and South.

By scrutinising the ways in which the various dimensions of the UN came into play in Anglo-American considerations of how to respond to the Congo crisis, the book investigates how and why the Congo question reverberated in the wider ideological discussions about how decolonisation should evolve and what the role of the UN would be in managing this process. The UN itself became a contested battleground for different ideas and visions of world order as the newly independent African and Asian states sought to redress the inequalities rendered by colonialism and the US and Britain tried to maintain the status quo ante. Hammarskjöld, until his untimely death in September 1961, and his successor, the Burmese diplomat U Thant, tried to reconcile these two contrasting views and, thereby, carve out a more activist role for the UN in global politics.

The UN enjoyed an unprecedented and unique moment of influence in the late 1950s and early 1960s, due to the advent of many African and Asian nations to the world stage as they gained independence from colonial rule. A former Swedish diplomat with a cosmopolitan worldview, Hammarskjöld fostered a particular vision of the UN as an activist and interventionist organisation which should prevent the spread of the Cold War to the newly independent African and Asian nations, by providing them with a safe haven which would guarantee their sovereignty. This was a view shared by Thant, who continued to foster this vision of the role of the UN when he took over as Secretary-General in October 1961. For their part, newly independent countries seized upon this initiative. In 1960 alone, seventeen former African colonies joined the growing membership ranks of the UN, consolidating the influence of the Afro-Asian bloc in the General Assembly. Their numerical majority and self-declared 'neutral' or 'non-aligned' status diluted the traditional power base of the Western bloc and gave them a position from which they sought to rapidly advance the agenda for decolonisation. The altered power structure within the organisation soon manifested itself in the political support the Secretariat gave to the Afro-Asians; the actions of the peacekeeping and civil missions in the Congo and the wider relationship between the UN, the US and Britain.

The UN context highlighted the incongruity in American and British Congo policies and, as the crisis unfolded, served to change their assessment of the organisation and its role in managing the decolonisation process in Africa. For the first time, this book identifies three dimensions of the UN: a public forum or stage on which representatives of Britain and the US tried with limited success to formulate joint positions on aspects of the UN Congo policy; a socialisation space in which the actors negotiated their strategies with other countries; and as an actor in its own right in the Congo with the peacekeeping operation and civil support mission. This perception of the UN differs from other accounts, such as those which focus mostly on the peacekeeping operation,[2] or those that explicitly examine the role of the Secretary-General.[3] Rather, my book takes an expansive view of the UN across these three levels, looking at how they interacted to create and execute UN policy in the Congo and highlighting the agency the organisation had in shaping the outcome of the crisis.

First, the public nature of discussion and debate at the UN became critical for Britain and the US. This was particularly prevalent as the crisis escalated through 1961 and public debates revealed the differences in American and British Congo policies. This lack of unity, which soon undercut the whole Western bloc, was damaging to the overall position of both countries at the UN given the reinvigoration of the General Assembly due to the aforementioned rise of the Afro-Asian bloc. Combined with different responses to the activism of the UN in the Congo, the heated context of colonial debates led by the Afro-Asians and the desire to thwart the spread of Soviet influence with new member-states, the UN environment had a particular constellation which served to condition American and British policies towards the Congo.

For Britain, international prestige and the fear of rebellion and instability from the Congo spreading east to neighbouring British colonies led to concerted efforts to keep the Congo off the UN agenda and impose a moratorium on public debates. The US was primarily concerned with preserving the solidarity of the Western bloc and therefore initially adopted a largely passive position. As the crisis escalated, in practice this had the effect of drawing criticism from the Afro-Asian bloc, especially when the Congo debate spilled over into discussions on other colonial questions. Over time, attempts to keep the disparity between American and British Congo policies out of public view failed, most notably when the US supported UN military action in the Congo in December 1962 against British objections. The public debates also exposed the negative impact of the legacy of British colonialism on relations with African countries and revealed the diminishing influence Britain had on colonial issues.

Second, in light of the broader context of the Cold War, Hammarskjöld and Thant carved out an innovative role for the UN in launching the largest peacekeeping mission up to that date: Operation des Nations Unies au Congo (ONUC). The initial activism of the organisation in the mandates for the mission proved problematic for the Western powers when UN Congo policy ran contrary to their objectives. For Britain, ONUC's activities, and in particular the military campaign against the breakaway province Katanga, threatened economic interests and strategic concerns in Central Africa. The US, however, supported military action to end the secession in order to ensure that Congolese uranium in the province, which had been used to create the first atomic bomb in 1945, would not fall into Soviet or Communist hands. As the peacekeeping mission became gradually mired in political and financial turmoil, the campaign against Katanga escalated tensions with the Soviet Union and set America and Britain at odds over the question of the use of force by UN troops.

Third, this book conceives of the corridors and meeting rooms of the UN as a socialising space in which American and British statesmen and women were increasingly required to interact with representatives from newly independent African and Asian countries who dominated discussions on the Congo and linked them to wider debates on colonial questions. These dialogues frequently involved criticism of British decolonisation policies and tested the veracity of American anti-colonial sentiments, creating further tensions in the Anglo-American relationship. As a result of their often fruitless efforts to reach agreement on how to steer UN Congo policy, especially during the early years of the crisis, it emerged that America and Britain had different perceptions of the utility of the UN.

Positioning the UN as a lens through which to examine American and British policies, it is apparent that the Congo became a microcosm of wider interacting global tensions, and a crisis which shaped the broader contours of the relationship between the West and the emergent Afro-Asian world. During this period, British officials increasingly regarded the UN as an organisation that obstructed and upended their plans for decolonisation in Africa as colonial debates exposed the negative impact of Britain's imperial legacy. As the British position in the General Assembly became marginalised, there was little that representatives could do but try to encourage moderation and stall UN efforts to monitor the process of transforming the former British Empire into the Commonwealth. The cacophonous critiques of African and Asian leaders, combined with the UN campaign in the Congo, which proceeded in direct contrast to British objectives, exasperated officials. Just a year into the crisis in 1961 Lord Robert Salisbury, former Secretary of State for Commonwealth Relations, complained: 'What an *awful* body the UN have become!!'[4]

In contrast, the US regarded the UN as an increasingly useful instrument with which to shape a liberal order across the decolonised world. As State Department officials became concerned about the erosion of America's traditional support base in the General Assembly, policies towards the UN were revised and revitalised. At the centre of this strategy was an attempt to thwart the spread of Communist influence in newly independent countries by sponsoring modernisation programmes designed to create liberal democracies and building relations with African and Asian leaders while downplaying their criticism of the colonial record of America's European allies. The nature of negotiation at the UN proved to be quite taxing in this regard as American representatives often found themselves caught between the campaigners for decolonisation on one side and the resilient capitalist networks of European colonialism on the other. The Congo crisis combined these challenges, destroying the delicate reciprocity that had previously existed whereby Britain supported American Cold War objectives at the UN, and the US abstained in votes on colonial questions. Although the earlier conflict over the Suez Canal in Egypt in 1956 had already exposed how American and British internationalism could differ in the context of decolonisation, this book argues that the contested nature of the UN mission in the Congo led to the crisis becoming a fundamental turning point of the decolonisation process.[5]

The key question that this book considers is how the decolonisation dimensions of the crisis reverberated in wider debates on colonial issues, damaging relations between the Anglo-American powers and the Afro-Asian world.[6] The conflict in the Congo erupted in the milieu of ongoing wars of independence in Algeria from 1954 to 1962 and Angola from 1961 to 1974. In the background, the campaign against apartheid and the question of the status of South-West Africa (now Namibia) dominated discussions in the Trusteeship Council and General Assembly since 1947, creating an atmosphere of distrust and disillusionment as Afro-Asian statesmen and freedom fighters tested the limits of sovereignty. Scholarship from Jeffrey James Byrne, Matthew Connolly and Ryan Irwin, among others, has focused on examining how anti-colonial nationalism interacted with the Cold War, presenting a Third World view of the two major processes of post-war international relations.[7] By examining 'South–South' connections, this book for the first time positions the Congo crisis as an important moment of African and Asian solidarity, drawing out Afro-Asian perspectives of, and reactions to, Western policies towards the Congo. Crucially, it highlights the agency of African and Asian actors in shaping UN Congo policy, and their efforts to resist the hegemonic influence of America and Britain over the Congo by utilising their authority in the UN. Attempts to direct the UN mission led to the creation of permanent mechanisms and structures within the UN system, through which they used the Congo as a paradigm to determine the course and the pace of decolonisation. Therefore, this book reconsiders both the importance of the Congo crisis as an episode of decolonisation and the role of the UN therein, differentiating it from existing literature on the crisis, which is dominated by the Cold War perspective, but also from literature on decolonisation.[8] It argues that the crisis should be considered as a moment that consolidated the impact of decolonisation as not just a process that transformed the world of empires into nation-states, but one which elucidated a wider Third World critique of neo-colonialism and imperial internationalism.

Central to this argument is my analysis of the role of the UN, and how the Congo mission increased the organisation's mandate in monitoring the process of decolonisation, due to the involvement of African and Asian members. Their development of the UN system and the activism of the Secretariat diversified what decolonisation represented from questions of self-determination and sovereignty, into a wave of political, social and economic changes which challenged the inequality inherent in relations between North and South. The UN and its predecessor, the League of Nations, have lately received revived attention from historians working to reassess the role of global institutions in shaping such wider patterns of relations. Many of these efforts have arisen in the wake of historian Mark Mazower's work, which traces the evolution of global governance and the growth of the UN over time. Others, such as Susan Pedersen, Patricia Clavin and Paul Kennedy, have fortified this emerging field with excellent multi-archival studies that connect the history of these institutions with the wider development of ideologies, ideas and normative practices.[9] Emerging scholars have followed in this vein, producing fascinating individual histories of specific aspects of institutions, policies and processes.[10] Thanks to the work of Glenda Sluga and Sunil Amrith, the history of our global institutions has evolved steadily both as a way to chart the evolution of different internationalisms but also in viewing the UN as a lens which reveals the dynamics of states and peoples.[11] This book contributes to the field by analysing the role of the UN in the Congo as a way of highlighting different visions of world order as it transformed the way decolonisation was henceforth managed by challenging the policies of America and Britain.

This book also moves beyond existing literature on the crisis, which casts the Congo as a proxy struggle for power during the Cold War. While the Cold War dimensions have been expertly outlined by Madeline Kalb, Lise Namikas and Stephen R. Weissman, this book argues that American Cold War strategy was often at odds with British and Belgian efforts to maintain colonial networks of power and control of the region's vast natural resources.[12] John Kent and David N. Gibbs have long maintained that the Congo crisis reached global dimensions precisely because of the competition over strategic materials between European capitalists and American business interests.[13] This element of the crisis brought up questions of state-building and development politics which further exposed differences between America and Britain.[14] The Foreign Office tried repeatedly to maintain control over economic interests by implicitly resisting the UN operation, which led to British Congo policy being interpreted as neo-colonialist. In a different way, the US also came to be viewed as a neo-colonialist power as the State Department sought, in an increasingly explicit manner, to use the UN mission to modernise the Congo in the image of the West in order to prevent Soviet infiltration of Central Africa.[15] Cold War concerns certainly securitised the economic dimensions of the crisis, therefore, but the characterisation of the Congo exclusively as a Cold War struggle tends to flatten the distinction between the intersecting levels of the crisis in which the dynamic agency of the UN and Third World actors comes into focus.

Finally, although this book does not focus explicitly on the role of the Congolese actors, it adds to the existing field by evaluating their interaction with the UN and, at times, with the Afro-Asian bloc.[16] In the selection of actors for this book I chose not to include Belgium, given the wide array of literature which already exists on Belgium and the Congo.[17] From time to time, Belgian politicians do appear in the narrative, particularly at moments when Britain and the US sought to coordinate their Congo policies. Similarly, although the role of the Soviet Union is recorded at certain junctures, this book contributes only in a tangential manner to the work of scholars such as Sergey Mazov and Alessandro Iandolo who focus more explicitly on Soviet policies towards the Congo.[18]

The next six chapters, arranged chronologically, follow the way the Congo crisis unfolded at the UN in New York, and in the field missions in Léopoldville and Elisabethville (now Lubumbashi), the provincial capital of Katanga. The first chapter establishes why, in 1960, the outbreak of the Congo crisis and its successive internationalisation through UN intervention was an important question for Anglo-American relations. It provides an outline of what the crisis itself was and the format of the UN response. The chapter sketches the broader context of Anglo-American relations, as well as establishing the nature of the partnership, as it existed between President Dwight D. Eisenhower and British Prime Minister Harold Macmillan, and afterwards with President John F. Kennedy. The chapter lays out American and British relations with the UN and looks at how the two countries responded to the decision to intervene in the Congo.

The second chapter highlights the changing nature of the UN from 1960 to 1961. It focuses on the emergence of a new US policy in New York, identified as the first decisive moment that the US tried to steer the course of UN policy in the Congo. It highlights the opposing views of Britain, framing the implementation of the Afro-Asian resolution of February 1961 as the first example of the infighting that was to characterise their relationship over the Congo.

Building on the fissure that emerged over the February Resolution, the third chapter focuses more explicitly on the role of ONUC and explains why military incursions into Katanga in September, and again in December of 1961, proved damaging to the Anglo-American relationship. It is revealed that there was a break in the efforts to formulate a joint Congo policy due to the British refusal to sanction further military action against the breakaway province.

The fourth chapter focuses on the invigoration of the Secretariat as it is shown how Hammarskjöld, and later his successor U Thant, adapted the UN policy in the Congo towards the demands of the Afro-Asian bloc. This chapter presents some of the wider debates which were at play during the Congo crisis, highlighting the role of African and Asian states at the UN and repositioning their importance in the crisis as a whole.

Continuing in this vein, the fifth chapter examines how the US continued to transpose itself at the UN by increasing its efforts to court members of the Afro-Asian bloc in a bid to circumvent their influence with the Secretary-General and pilot UN Congo policy more decisively. This chapter argues that the final round of UN military action, codenamed Operation UNOKAT, sealed the rift in positions between Britain and the US.

The final chapter examines efforts, particularly by the US, to construct a Western-friendly regime in the Congo up to and following the withdrawal of the UN force in 1964. It looks at the airlift of European hostages out of the city of Stanleyville in 1964 as an episode which highlights imperialist approaches towards the potential spread of Communist influence in Africa.

By framing the Congo crisis as a key turning point in the process of decolonisation, this book highlights the agency of the UN and the Afro-Asian bloc in accelerating the anti-colonial campaign and attempting to reshape the relationship between North and South. The UN environment served to condition American and British policies towards the Congo, challenging the conduct of imperial internationalism and recasting the image of the organisation as a nexus for engagement with the Third World.

Notes

1 George Padmore Library, Accra (hereafter GPL), BAA/RLAA/690, 'Republic of Congo': Newspaper Clippings (Congo), Jan 1962, Bureau of African Affairs, Special Correspondent, 'Congo complexities, report from an uncountry', *The Economist* (16 December 1961).

2 A. Lee Burns and N. Heathcote, *Peace-Keeping by UN Forces, from Suez to the Congo* (New York: Frederick A. Praeger, 1963); T. Findlay, *The Use of Force in UN Peace Operations* (Oxford: Oxford University Press, 2002); E.W. Lefever, *Crisis in the Congo: A United Nations Force in Action* (Washington, DC: Brookings

Institution, 1965); N. MacQueen, *Humanitarian Intervention and the United Nations* (Edinburgh: Edinburgh University Press, 2011); G. Abi-Saab, *The United Nations Operation in the Congo, 1960–1964* (Oxford: Oxford University Press, 1979).
3 B. Firestone, *The United Nations Under U Thant, 1961–1971* (Plymouth: Scarecrow Press, 2001); R. Lipsey, *Hammarskjöld: A Life* (Ann Arbor: University of Michigan Press, 2013); P. Heller, *The United Nations Under Dag Hammarskjöld, 1953–1961* (Lanham: The Scarecrow Press, 2001); C. Stahn and H. Melber (eds), *Peace Diplomacy, Global Justice and International Agency, Rethinking Human Security and Ethics in the Spirit of Dag Hammarskjöld* (Cambridge: Cambridge University Press, 2014); B. Urquhart, *Hammarskjöld* (New York: Norton, 1994). S. Williams, *Who Killed Hammarskjöld? The UN, The Cold War and White Supremacy in Africa* (London: Hurst Publishing, 2011).
4 The Monday Club was a lobby group within the Conservative Party created in January 1961 in order to protect British interests and white minority regimes during the process of decolonisation. National Archives, London (hereafter NAL), FO 371/155107, Letter from Chairman of the Monday Club Robert 'Bobbety' Salisbury, to British Foreign Secretary Lord Home, 26 November 1961. Emphasis in the original. For further see A. O'Malley, ' "What an awful body the UN have become!!" Anglo-American UN relations during the Congo crisis, February–December 1961', *Journal of Transatlantic Studies*, 13:4 (2016), 26–46.
5 S. Dockrill, *Britain's Retreat from East of Suez: The Choice between Europe and the World?* (Basingstoke: Palgrave Macmillan, 2002); P.L. Hahn, *The United States, Great Britain and Egypt, 1945–1956: Strategy and Diplomacy in the Early Cold War* (Chapel Hill: University of North Carolina Press, 1991); R. Takeyh, *The Origins of the Eisenhower Doctrine: The US, Britain and Nasser's Egypt, 1953–57* (New York: St. Martin's Press, 2000).
6 On the UN and decolonisation see M. Berger, 'After the Third World? History, destiny and the fate of Third Worldism', *Third World Quarterly*, 25:1 (2004), 9–39; S. Jensen, *The Making of International Human Rights: The 1960s, Decolonization and the Reconstruction of Global Values* (Cambridge: Cambridge University Press, 2016); W.R. Louis and R. Robinson, 'The imperialism of decolonization', *Journal of Imperial and Commonwealth History*, 22:3 (1994), 462–511; W.R. Louis, 'Public enemy number one: Britain and the United Nations in the aftermath of Suez', in Martin Lynn (ed.), *The British Empire in the 1950s: Retreat or Revival?* (New York: Palgrave Macmillan, 2006), pp. 186–213; M. Terretta, ' "We had been fooled into thinking that the UN watches over the entire world": Human rights, UN Trust Territories and Africa's decolonization', *Human Rights Quarterly*, 34:2 (2012), 329–360; O. Turner, ' "Finishing the job": the UN special committee on decolonization and the politics of self-governance', *Third World Quarterly*, 34:7 (2013), 1193–1208; M. Thomas (ed.), *European Decolonization* (Burlington: Ashgate, 2007).
7 J.J. Byrne, *Mecca of Revolution, Algeria, Decolonization, and the Third World Order* (Oxford: Oxford University Press, 2016); M. Connelly, *A Diplomatic Revolution: Algeria's Fight for Independence and the Origins of the Post-Cold War Era* (Oxford: Oxford University Press, 2002); M. Connelly, 'Taking off the Cold War lens: visions of North-South conflict during the Algerian War for Independence', *American Historical Review*, 105, 3 (2000), 739–769; R.M. Irwin, *Gordian Knot, Apartheid and the Unmaking of the Liberal World Order* (Oxford: Oxford University Press, 2012); L. James and E. Leake (eds), *Decolonization and the Cold War: Negotiating Independence* (London: Bloomsbury Academic, 2015); C.J. Lee (ed.), *Making a World after Empire: The Bandung Moment and its Political Afterlives* (Athens: Ohio University

Press, 2010); R. Vitalis, 'The Midnight Ride of Kwame Nkrumah and Other Fables of Bandung (Bandoong)', Humanity: An International Journal of Human Rights, Humanitarianism, and Development, 4, 2 (2013), 261–288. O.A. Westad, *The Global Cold War: Third World Interventions and the Making of Our Times* (Cambridge: Cambridge University Press, 2012).

8 J.M. Haskin, *The Tragic State of the Congo: From Decolonization to Dictatorship* (New York: Algora, 2005); A. Hochschild, *King Leopold's Ghost: A Story of Greed, Terror and Heroism in Colonial Africa* (Boston: Houghton Mifflin Harcourt, 1999); C. Hoskyns, *The Congo Since Independence, January 1960-December 1961* (Oxford: Oxford University Press, 1965); E.W. Lefever, *Crisis in the Congo, a United Nations Force in Action* (Washington, DC: The Brookings Institute, 1965); E.W. Lefever, 'The U.N. as a foreign policy instrument: the Congo crisis', in R. Hilsman and R.C. Good (eds), *Foreign Policy in the Sixties: The Issues and the Instruments; Essays in Honour of Arnold Wolfers* (Baltimore: Johns Hopkins University Press, 1965); C. Legum, *Congo Disaster* (London: Penguin Press, 1961); R.D. Mahoney, *J.F.K: Ordeal in Africa* (New York: Oxford University Press, 1983); C. Young, *Politics in the Congo: Decolonization and Independence* (Princeton: Princeton University Press, 1965).

9 P. Clavin, *Securing the World Economy: The Reinvention of the League of Nations, 1920–1946* (Oxford: Oxford University Press, 2013); A. Iriye, *Global Community: The Role of International Organizations in the Making of the Contemporary World* (Berkeley: University of Berkeley Press, 2004); R. Jolly, L. Emmerij and T.G. Weiss, *UN Ideas that Changed the World* (Bloomington: Indiana University Press, 2009); P. Kennedy, *Parliament of Man: The United Nations and the Quest for World Government* (London: Penguin, 2007); M. Mazower, *No Enchanted Palace: The End of Empire and the Ideological Origins of the United Nations* (Princeton: Princeton University Press, 2009); M. Mazower, *Governing the World: The Rise and Fall of an Idea* (New York: Penguin Press, 2012); S. Pedersen, *The Guardians, the League of Nations and the Crisis of Empire* (Oxford: Oxford University Press, 2015); B. Reinalda, *Routledge History of International Organizations: From 1815 to the Present Day* (London: Routledge, 2013); A. Roberts and B. Kingsbury (eds), *United Nations, Divided World: The UN's Roles in International Relations* (Oxford: Oxford University Press, 1993); S. Schlesinger, *Act of Creation: The Founding of the United Nations* (New York: Basic Books, 2003).

10 S. Jackson and A. O'Malley (eds), *The Institution of International Order: From The League of Nations to the United Nations* (London: Routledge, 2018); M.B. Jerónimo and J.P. Monteiro (eds), *The Pasts of the Present: Internationalism, Imperialism and the Formation of the Contemporary World* (London: Routledge, 2017); J. Pearson Patel, *The Colonial Politics of Global Health: France and the United Nations in Postwar Africa, 1945–1960* (Cambridge, MA: Harvard University Press, forthcoming 2018); A.I. Richard, 'Competition and complementarity: civil society networks and the question of decentralising the League of Nations', Journal of Global History, 7:2 (2012), 233–256.

11 S. Amrith and G. Sluga, 'New histories of the U.N.', Journal of World History, 19:3 (2008), 251–274; P. Clavin and G. Sluga (eds), *Internationalisms: A Twentieth-Century History* (Cambridge: Cambridge University Press, 2017); M.R. Garcia, L. Kozma and D. Rodogno (eds), *The League of Nations Work on Social Issues: Visions, Endeavours and Experiments* (New York: United Nations Publications Office, 2015); G. Sluga, *Internationalism in the Age of Nationalism* (Philadelphia: University of Pennsylvania Press, 2013).

12 M. Kalb, *Congo Cables: The Cold War in Africa from Eisenhower to Kennedy* (New York: Macmillan, 1982); L. Namikas, *Battleground Africa: Cold War in the Congo*

1960–1965 (Stanford: Stanford University Press, 2013); S.R. Weissman, *American Foreign Policy in the Congo 1960–1964* (Ithaca, NY: Cornell University Press, 1974).

13 D.N. Gibbs, *The Political Economy of Third World Intervention: Mines, Money and U.S. Policy in the Congo Crisis* (Chicago: University of Chicago Press, 1991); J. Kent, *America, the UN and Decolonisation: Cold War Conflict in the Congo* (London: Routledge, 2010); A.S. Gijs, 'Fighting the red peril in the Congo: paradoxes and perspectives on an equivocal challenge to Belgium and the West (1947–1960)', *Cold War History*, 16:3 (2016), 273–390.

14 E. Borgwardt, *A New Deal for the World: America's Vision for Human Rights* (Cambridge, MA: Belknap Press of Harvard University Press, 2005); J.M. Carter, *Inventing Vietnam: The United States and State Building, 1954–1968* (New York: Cambridge University Press, 2008); H.K. Jacobson, 'ONUC's civilian operations: state-preserving and state-building', *World Politics*, 17:1 (1964), 57–107; M.B. Jerónimo and A.C. Pinto (eds), *The Ends of European Colonial Empires: Cases and Comparisons* (Basingstoke: Palgrave Macmillan, 2015); S. Kunkel and C. Unger (eds), *International Organizations and Development, 1945–1990* (Basingstoke: Palgrave Macmillan, 2014); A.D. Rietkerk, 'In pursuit of development: the United Nations, decolonization and development aid, 1949–1961' (PhD dissertation, London School of Economics, 2015); G. Rist, *The History of Development* (London: Zed Books, 2010).

15 See: N. Gilman, *Mandarins of the Future: Modernization Theory in Cold War America* (Baltimore: Johns Hopkins University Press, 2003); L. Grubbs, *Secular Missionaries: Americans and African Development in the 1960s* (Amherst: University of Massachusetts Press, 2010); M.E. Latham, *Modernization as Ideology: American Social Science and 'Nation Building' in the Kennedy Era* (Chapel Hill: University of North Carolina Press, 2000); B.I. Kaufman, *Trade & Aid: Eisenhower's Foreign Economic Policy, 1953–1961* (Baltimore: Johns Hopkins University Press, 1982); P. Muehlenbeck, *Betting on the Africans: John F. Kennedy's Courting of African Nationalist Leaders* (Oxford: Oxford University Press, 2012); K.C. Statler and A.L. Johns (eds), *The Eisenhower Administration, the Third World and the Globalization of the Cold War* (Lanham: Rowman & Littlefield, 2006).

16 T. Hovet, *Africa in the United Nations* (Evanston: North Western University Press, 1963); W.W. Nyangoni, *Africa in the United Nations System* (Rutherford: Associated University Presses, 1985); G. Nzongola-Ntalaja, *The Congo from Leopold to Kabila: A People's History* (London and New York: Zed Books, 2002); D. Van Reybrouck, *Congo: The Epic History of a People* (London: Fourth Estate, 2014); C. Coquery-Vidrovitch, A. Forest and H. Weiss (eds), *Rébellions-Revolution au Zaire (1963–1965)*, tome 1 (Paris: Editions L'Harmattan, 1987); H. Weiss (introduction), *Congo 1965, Political Documents of a Developing Nation* (Princeton: Princeton University Press, 1967).

17 P. Davister, *Katanga: Enjeu du Monde: recits et documents* (Bruxelles: Editions Europe-Afrique, 1960); L. de Witte, *The Assassination of Lumumba*, trans. A. Wright (London: Verso, 2001); G. Vanthemsche, *Belgium and the Congo, 1885–1980*, trans. A. Cameron and S. Windross (Cambridge: Cambridge University Press, 2012).

18 I.V. Gaiduk, *Divided Together: The United States and the Soviet Union in the United Nations, 1945–1965* (Stanford: Stanford University Press, 2012); A. Iandolo, 'Beyond the shoe: rethinking Khrushchev at the fifteenth session of the United Nations General Assembly', *Diplomatic History*, 41:1 (2017), 128–154; S. Mazov, *A Distant Front in the Cold War: The USSR in West Africa and the Congo, 1956–1964* (Stanford: Stanford University Press, 2010); P. Muehlenbeck, *Czechoslovakia in Africa, 1945–1968* (Basingstoke: Palgrave Macmillan, 2016).

1
A challenge for humanity

When the Congo crisis erupted in the heart of Africa in June 1960, it was not the first time that the country had been thrust into the international spotlight. The former Belgian colony, and once personal treasure trove of King Leopold II from 1885 to 1908, had been the focus of international attention since the journalist Edmund Dene Morel delivered a damning report of atrocities committed by Leopold's regime in 1900. A British journalist, Morel wrote a series of lurid accounts of the abuse of the Congolese people as part of Leopold's brutal exploitation of the country's natural resources, at the time primarily rubber and ivory. Campaigning for human rights he created the Congo Reform Association in 1904 following a British House of Commons Resolution condemning Leopold's actions. The British diplomat Roger Casement was dispatched to verify Morel's claims, which he did in a 1904 report that compounded Morel's story with accounts of similar humanitarian abuses.[1] The Congo Reform Association soon received support from a variety of public intellectuals including writers such as Joseph Conrad, Arthur Conan Doyle and Mark Twain, who depicted the Congo as a dark and mysterious place at the centre of the African continent in which appalling and unimaginable crimes were committed.[2] However, in the imagination of international policymakers, the Congo represented more than a blank space on the map. Even at the beginning of the twentieth century, the economic potential of the country's vast resources and the struggle to control them, alongside its strategic location, foreshadowed that the independence of the Congo, and the transfer of control of its vast mineral deposits to the Congolese people, would have a significant impact on international relations, particularly on the process of decolonisation.

Up to the moment of gaining sovereignty from Belgium on 30 June, the Congo, in each of its incarnations as the Congo Free State from 1885 to 1908, and Belgian Congo between 1908 and 1960, was a place in which other states were interested. The country's immense natural resources from rubber and ivory in the nineteenth century, to diamonds, cobalt, copper and gold (among many more) in the twentieth century, lured prospectors, explorers and conquerors from around the world, keen to gain a share in the booty. As a result, the history of the territory is marred by conflict and adversity, but it is also marked as a place where the exposition of the limits of human struggle produced a surge in ideas about freedoms and rights, even under colonial regimes.[3] In the case of the Congo, this discourse was led by Morel's Congo Reform Association with the aim of activating a sense of international consciousness and responsibility to end Leopold's destructive regime. The Congo, therefore, became one of the first cases in which human rights and native rights were articulated in the context of colonial governance.[4] The collapse of Leopold's Congo Free State and the establishment of the Belgian Congo in 1908 did little to change the plight of the Congolese people, whose country continued to be used as a source for materials during both World Wars and later supplied the uranium for America's first atomic bomb. By 1945, the Congo, still with a significant portion of its resources intact, was poised to be an important pawn in the Cold War. From Leopold's efforts to define the international project and shape the international system with the Congress of Berlin in 1878, to Morel's campaign for the prevention of atrocities against the Congolese people, to Casement's condemnation of standards and practices of Belgian colonial governance, the Congo continued to be perceived as a testing grounds for ideas about how to manage relations with Africa and policies defining internationalisms towards the region.

Therefore, the independence crisis that erupted in the Congo in 1960 had its roots in the longer history of exploitation of the people and their resources by successive regimes, the destruction of the original tribal system and the damaging effects of Belgian colonial rule. The conflict which broke out in 1960 was exacerbated by both conniving European strategic involvement in protection of their interests in the region, and the clash of provincial and tribal hostilities as various groups vied for power. As one UN official described it:

> What made the Congo problem so particularly intractable was ... the political setting was explosive in the highest degree: to other African states their new found independence seemed at stake in the fate of the Congo; to the USSR this was a heaven-sent opportunity to intervene in the name of anti-colonialism; to other Western states a valuable economic-strategic interest was involved in the big copper mines of the Union Minière of the province of Katanga.[5]

The road to Congolese independence was relatively short. Political associations were illegal in Belgian Congo, with the exception of those created by tribal groups in rural areas, which were not recognised by the administration. For the small number of Congolese students who were educated in schools run by Christian and Jesuit organisations, political activities were carefully monitored by the authorities. A turning point came when Patrice Lumumba, a young, charismatic postal worker, created the Mouvement Nationale Congolais (MNC), a nationalist party which called for independence in 1958. The MNC drew its strength and popularity by bringing together a range of Congolese politicians, including Cyrille Adoula, a trade-union leader, and Joseph Illeo, a politician who had been vocally asserting Africans' right to self-rule since 1956. Even though their politics on other questions differed, Congolese politicians agreed on the question of imminent independence. This was fundamental to the party's appeal as it was able to transcend divisions and helped to create a sense of the

Congo as a nation, despite the wide array of tribal groups, ethnic divisions and internal identities which could be found across the vast territory.

In December 1958, Lumumba and a small delegation travelled to Accra in Ghana for the All-African Peoples' Conference, organised by Ghanaian Prime Minster Kwame Nkrumah. This was an important turning point in solidifying plans to push for Congolese independence, as the group was introduced to a range of leaders from the independent African states, including Ethiopia, Ghana, Guinea, Liberia, Libya, Morocco, Tunisia and the United Arab Republic. Moreover, among the 300 delegates were a range of other embattled independence leaders from Angola, Algeria, Cameroon and Zambia. The noted Kenyan Pan-Africanist and independence activist, Tom Mboya, was the elected Chairman of the conference. For the first time, Congolese leaders thereby had the opportunity to exchange views with a wide range of African independence leaders, from those who governed newly independent states, to others who were actively engaged in violent struggles against former colonial powers.[6] As Nkrumah later described it, 'It was at this memorable conference that the Congolese nationalists had their baptism as apostles of the impending struggle for African's liberation'.[7] Similarly, Thomas Kanza, later Lumumba's Chief Representative at the UN, described Lumumba's visit to Accra as critical in creating the impression among outsiders to the Congo situation (including the Americans) that he was pro-Communist because he was known to have met with leaders such as Julius Nyerere of Tanzania and Sékou Toure of Guinea.[8] Upon his return to Léopoldville, Lumumba organised a mass meeting on 31 December at which he proclaimed, with 'fiery oratory', that there should be immediate independence for the Congo. The effect on the assembled crowd of 3,000 was electrifying and supporters immediately adopted independence slogans. The following week, on 4 January, riots broke out in Léopoldville when Belgian authorities tried to subdue a crowd chanting 'Independence immédiate!' as they gathered for a public lecture on independence from the other main Congolese party, the Association des Bakongo pour l'Unification, l'Expansion et la Defence de la Kikongo (ABAKO).[9]

ABAKO, led by Joseph Kasavubu, was formed in the late 1950s in defence of the Kikongo language and culture, with the aim of restoring the ethnic kingdom of Kongo. The party was strongly opposed to Belgian colonial rule and, through tribal and religious organisations at the local level, was also able to command widespread support, especially in lower-Congo among the Bakongo ethnic group. Following the Belgian authorities' brutal treatment of the Congolese demonstrators on 4 January 1959, in which forty-nine Congolese were killed, the push for independence surged through supporters of both parties, and others organised along tribal lines, including the Bangala of the Equatorial Province and the Balubas of Kasai and Katanga.

Denounced by the Belgian press as 'the bloodiest ever in Léopoldville', Brussels responded to the riots by immediately convening an emergency session of the Belgian Parliament, and organising a commission of enquiry. The colonial administration, meanwhile, arrested 300 Congolese, including Kasavubu, charging him with 'exciting racial hatred'.[10] On 13 January the Belgian Government announced plans for independence, including the extension of elections at the local level, the organisation of a national election the following year, the abandonment of all forms of discrimination and the establishment of a Congolese Parliament. Local government reform had already been initiated by the Belgian Government in 1945 with the establishment of a Burgomaster (mayoral) system in the largest towns, each divided into several communes. In the December 1957 elections, ABAKO candidates had secured the majority of the positions in Léopoldville, giving them effective control of the Burgomasters in the capital, which created unease amongst the Belgian population and had led to discussions of independence, well before the riots took place. With a remarkable lack of foresight, announcing the plans to extend the democratic system nationwide, the Minister for the Congo Maurice Van Hemelryck told the Belgian Parliament 'We have skirted catastrophe'.[11]

It should be noted that the automatic appeal of the idea of rapid independence among Congolese people was not solely a desire for self-determination but also a reaction to the deteriorating economic situation in the Congo. Since 1957, falling asset prices in commodity markets, created in part by the aftershock of the Suez crisis and balance of payments problems in the Belgian economy, had created significant unemployment in the Congo, especially in the industrial regions of the larger cities, leaving many disenfranchised workers to roam the streets.[12] These individuals quickly succumbed to Lumumba's charismatic charm, and his promise of a free and prosperous Congo. Therefore, while the economic predicament was an important primer in advancing the idea of independence for the Congo among Belgian politicians and among the Congolese people, it loaded the vision of independence with impossible dreams of wealth and prosperity. This would add to the sense of disillusionment and chaos that prevailed after independence, as the reality of everyday life for many Congolese remained largely similar to their experience under colonial rule.

With Kasavubu and the other leaders of ABAKO imprisoned, it was left to Lumumba to continue to agitate for a rapid timetable towards independence. He organised a series of meetings with other political parties in Elisabethville and his hometown of Stanleyville in the Orientale province, protesting the proposed timetable for emancipation. After announcing his intention to end cooperation with Belgium in September, which incited a further series of riots in Stanleyville in October, Lumumba too was arrested.[13] At this point the remaining leaders of the ABAKO, MNC and the newly formed Partie Solidaire African (PSA) were invited to Brussels to discuss how to proceed towards independence. They agreed to a roundtable conference in January 1960 on the condition that Lumumba was released in time to attend. In response to the staunch alliance among the Congolese parties on this question, the Belgian authorities agreed to his release and Lumumba was flown directly from prison to the roundtable conference amid much excitement to discuss the formation of the Congo independent state. His dramatic arrival overshadowed Kasavubu who, although had earlier been arrested, had never been charged or jailed. In order to demonstrate his dissatisfaction at being upstaged by his rival, Kasavubu walked out of the conference.[14] As the solidarity with which the Congolese politicians approached the question of independence started to crumble, they were confronted with even more significant challenges when the Belgian delegation, led by Prime Minister Gaston Eyskens, presented their proposal for independence.

The Belgian Government had organised the roundtable to take place in two parts. The political questions such as the Congolese constitution, separation of powers and the timetable towards independence was discussed in January. Later, in April, the economic plan was to be laid out. In the first stage, the Congolese politicians were surprised at the speedy timetable presented by Belgian officials, which proposed 30 June 1960 as the date of independence. National elections were scheduled for May, after which the Congolese Parliament and the Congolese Senate would appoint the President and the Prime Minister. The conference continued for over a month, at the end of which the delegates agreed on a series of resolutions called the 'Loi Fondomentale', which served as the basic constitution for the new state. Lumumba and many of the other politicians, including Jason Sendwe, leader of the Katanga Baluba Association, and Moise Tshombe, President of the Confederation of Katanga Associations (Conakat), interpreted the results of the first roundtable as a victory. Commenting on the outcome in the final session, Lumumba promised a friendly relationship with Brussels, but warned: 'We shall also fight against every attempt to dislocate our national territory. The greatness of the Congo is based on the preservation of its political and economic entity.'[15]

Lumumba's emphasis on economic sovereignty was indicative of the importance that both the Congolese and the Belgians placed on the Congo's strategic assets. During this period, Congolese politicians met with numerous financiers and business representatives to negotiate deals regarding access to the Congo's resources. However, at the economic roundtable in April, they were informed that with control of the Congolese economy, they would inherit a crippling public debt of £350 million.[16] The debt had been accrued, according to the Belgians, by development work in the Congo and by a reduction in the value of the country's main exports, copper in particular.[17] The debt burden threatened to jeopardise the liquidity of the country upon independence, but also created tension between the Belgians and the Congolese when it emerged that Belgian companies, which controlled a large part of the country's portfolio, would retain their assets after independence. This meant that a large amount of the country's wealth potential would remain in Belgian hands, a realisation which planted the seeds of discord between Brussels and Léopoldville. Additionally, it was later estimated that 60 per cent of Congolese politicians were collaborating with the Belgian secret services, effectively spreading Belgian influence inside Congolese political circles too.[18] As Cleopophas Kamitatu, the provincial President of the PSA who led his party's delegation to Brussels, remarked, 'they let go of [Congo] with one hand, hoping they could get hold of it again with the other'.[19]

Against this uneasy backdrop, the national elections took place in May, returning the MNC as the largest party, Kasavubu as President and Lumumba as Prime Minister. While the hastily constructed national political system revealed a tapestry of national, provincial and tribal associations and loyalties, a clear feature was the resounding defeat of parties that openly embraced Belgium, with the exception of Tshombe's Conakat party in Katanga, which drew large financial support from European mining companies in operation there.[20] This produced a situation the French Philosopher Jean-Paul Sartre defined as 'the moment when the whites were no longer in command but continued to administrate, and when the blacks were in power but not yet in command'.[21] By the time independence loomed on 30 June, the stage was set for a quarrel which began almost immediately when the Belgian King Baudouin delivered a biased, condescending speech at the independence ceremony in which he hailed the achievements of Belgium in civilising the country and made disparaging remarks about the inexperience of the Congolese to govern themselves. Ironically, given that Belgium would be the frontrunner in continuing to exploit the country's resources, he also warned the new Congolese Parliament of the dangers of 'the attraction which some of your regions can have for foreign powers which are ready to profit from the least sign of weakness'.[22] In response, Lumumba gave an impromptu address in which he launched a scathing attack on Belgium.[23] He denounced the colonial yoke Brussels had imposed on the Congolese people for eighty years and that had involved colour barriers, racial discrimination across social and political life, and the despoliation and exploitation of Congolese land and resources. 'The struggle', he argued, 'involving tears, fire and blood, is something of which we are proud in our deepest hearts, for it was a noble and just struggle, which was needed to bring an end to the humiliating slavery imposed on us by force'.[24]

Hence, from the beginning, the relationship between Léopoldville and Brussels, which was lukewarm at best, soon deteriorated rapidly. The fundamental problem at the heart of the Belgian–Congolese split was that Belgium failed to recognise Congolese independence formally beyond rhetorical assurances, particularly with regard to the economic and foreign policies of the newly formed Central Government.[25] At the same time, the Congo remained dependent on Belgian civil administrators and existing personnel in the Congo, as there were not enough trained Congolese ready to take over the administration of the country. As the *Hindu* newspaper remarked, 'Mr. Lumumba seems uncertain how to deal with the Belgians. At the inaugural function he launched out a bitter attack on them – and he has also requested them to stay and help him!'[26] This tension at the political level was mirrored in civil turmoil as violence erupted on the streets of Léopoldville. The issue that the Belgians claimed 'forced' them to intervene directly was the mutiny of the Congolese army, the Force Publique, on 8 July 1960.

In 1960 the Force Publique comprised of 24,000 soldiers and non-commissioned officers, all of whom were Congolese, and about 1,000 officers, all of whom were Belgian.[27] This structural inequality was maintained after independence by blocking the upper cadres of the army from Congolese troops.[28] On 6 July, the Congolese soldiers mutinied and incarcerated their Belgian officers after it was announced by the commander, General Emile Jassens, that independence would have no bearing on either the structure of the military or the service conditions of the troops.[29] The Belgians were keen to stamp out the rebellion quickly and the Belgian Prime Minister Gaston Eyskens responded by dispatching paratroopers into Léopoldville, immediately violating the Congo's sovereignty. This action effectively precipitated the crisis and prompted Lumumba to appeal to the UN for international assistance to protect his country's sovereignty, thereby immediately catapulting the crisis on to the international stage.

The breakdown of law and order in Léopoldville soon started to spread rapidly across the Congo, giving Tshombe the opportunity to declare the secession of the province and the creation of the 'independent' state of Katanga on 11 July. In 1960, Katanga had a considerable European population, especially around the provincial capital Elisabethville. While in total it contained only 12 per cent of the entire population, it produced 60 per cent of total Congolese revenue, which meant that it was the wealthiest region in the country, and that the rest of the Congolese economy relied on its resources. The anti-apartheid activist and journalist Colin Legum has equated the effect of the secession as being equal to 'taking the Ruhr out of Germany or the Midlands out of Britain'.[30] The majority of Katanga's resources were extracted and processed by a financial group called Société Général de Belgique (SGB), which was an umbrella organisation for a number of other companies. The largest of these was the Union Minière du Haut Katanga (UMHK), a Belgian company that owned concessions over 13,000 square miles of Katanga. The SGB conglomerate gave the Belgians a pretext for, and a structure through which to support Tshombe's regime, thereby undermining the authority of the Central Government in Léopoldville. Having already bequeathed an enormous debt to the new Congolese government, Belgium added insult to injury by supporting Tshombe's provincial Government with financial and technical assistance. In addition, the secession of Katanga had global reverberations. In 1960 alone, the province produced 69 per cent of the world's industrial diamonds, 49 per cent of its cobalt and 9 per cent of its copper. These strategic materials were largely controlled by the UMHK, which had a 75 per cent stake, with the remainder in the hands of the Tanganyika Concessions group (TANKS), a British company run by Captain Charles Waterhouse a Tory MP.

UMHK was heavily intertwined in economic and political aspects of mining in the Congo, managing an output of around 8,431 metric tons of cobalt and 280,403 metric tons of copper annually, and had granted large support to Tshombe's party since 1959.[31] The company also had controlling interests in a range of enterprises from railways, cement works, flourmills and insurance companies to cattle ranches, hospitals and schools.[32] The power and wealth of the group is illustrated by its remarkable profit margins. For example, from 1950 to 1959, UMHK recorded a total net profit of 31 billion Belgian francs.[33] It has been argued that plans for the secession of Katanga were already underway in Brussels since 1959 but had been delayed until after independence due to 'pressure from the USA and other international powers'.[34]

Certainly, the political and economic support Belgian financiers and companies gave Tshombe's Conakat party, and the willingness with which Brussels had suddenly offered independence to the Congo, indicate that, at the very least, arrangements were made to preserve Belgian business interests. Belgian politicians in the Congo had also warned Brussels through 1959 that the 'extremist' activities of ABAKO would lead to a deterioration of the situation in Katanga where the 'authentic Katangese' declared their intention to differentiate themselves from the Bakongo people. Some even went as far as recommending that a split in the ABAKO be engineered in order to prevent the marginalisation of minority groups in Katanga, such as the white European population.[35] There were also allegations circulating that Belgium deliberately engineered the secessions of Katanga and the province of Kasai with the aim of creating a federation with the eastern province of Kivu and Ruanda-Urundi to protect major economic interests in the region.[36]

The economic roundtable in April 1960 had given the Belgians an opportunity to develop relations with representatives of Katanga, a process, as Herbert Weiss has argued, that essentially resulted in their 'predilection for secession'.[37] The April meeting also strengthened ties between Belgian leaders and a set of Léopoldville politicians who became known as the 'Binza Group'. The Binza Group, so called because they often met in the Binza district of Léopoldville, was centred around Colonel Joseph Desire Mobutu, (later Chief of Staff of the Congolese army and Congolese President from 1965 to 1997) Victor Nendaka, who had split from Lumumba and the MNC in March 1960; Albert Ndele, later the head of the Congo National Bank; Justin Bomboko, later Congolese Foreign Minister; and Damien Kandolo who had been the highest ranking Congolese civil servant before independence.[38] The Group initially developed very close relations with the Belgians and, soon after independence, with American, British and UN officials, as they later sought to remove Lumumba and his representatives from power.

This variety of political links underscored the importance of the contribution of Katangan resources to the Belgian economy. From 1955 to 1960 the extraction of resources produced profits of £464 million for Belgian and European shareholders. Given the strategic role played by TANKS in this economic architecture, Britain also adopted a conservative position towards the Congo from the beginning, which had at its core the preservation of UMHK and, thereby, the protection of British investments. British interests and shareholdings were concentrated in three companies: Tanganyika Concessions and the Anglo-Dutch companies, Shell and Unilever.[39] Waterhouse, the CEO of TANKS, enjoyed close relations with the British Foreign Secretary Alec Douglas Home and other members of the Conservative Party Foreign Affairs Committee.[40] Throughout the crisis, directors created influential pressure groups in the British Parliament and lobbied for protection of Katanga and British economic interests in Central Africa.[41] Dividends paid to TANKS shareholders in 1960 amounted to £3 million and the group connected Belgian and Anglo-American financiers. In addition, although the company headquarters was transferred to Salisbury in 1960, the British Government retained the final option in the case of the sale of the company's interests in UMHK or the Bengula railway system, which was the main artery for the export of minerals from the Congo. By the end of 1958, Britain had £1,000 million invested in Southern Africa while TANKS directors such as Waterhouse, Lord Selborne and Lord Salisbury continued to promote racist dogma. Lord Robins of the British South Africa company, who chaired a board including these British peers, had been quoted as asking in 1962, 'Why should it be supposed that a black African, just because he washes, speaks English, and wears European dress, must of necessity be accepted into the society of white men of the top grade?'[42]

Both UMHK and TANKS were part of the Anglo-American Corporation of South Africa, headed by the multi-billion dollar gold and diamond magnate, Harry Oppenheimer. The Corporation controlled the mining of gold, diamonds, copper, platinum, uranium, vanadium and a vast array of other strategic materials, including pulp, paper, coal, potash and beer, while also maintaining direct control over hundreds of thousands of employees, producing profits of £7.4 million in 1958. Representatives enjoyed 'special relations' with the governments in the territories where they operated across Central Africa from the Congo to Angola to South Africa and even asserted substantial influence over the international markets for their products. Through the Corporation, millions of pounds were loaned to Anglo-American subsidiaries operating in Katanga, including UMHK and TANKS. Another group, called 'Union Corporation', was linked to the Anglo-American Corporation, producing almost £2 million profit in 1958 for its shareholders, among whom were Charles Hambro, a director of the Bank of England, and several prominent British peers.[43] In view of the interwoven nature of this financial architecture which underpinned relations between the Congo, Britain and the US, it is hard to overstate the importance of the influence of the Anglo-American group in trying to preserve the political and economic status quo in Central Africa. As one UN report summarised it: 'In addition to mining, there is hardly any field in which British companies and their subsidiaries are not engaged ... The western powers are involved in Southern Africa up to their necks.'[44]

In addition to this wide range of investments, the strategic position of Katanga was important to the efficiency of the copper-belt in Central Africa, which straddled the Northern Rhodesian border and affected British authorities in nearby colonies of Tanganyika, Uganda and the Federation of Rhodesia and Nyasaland or Central African Federation (CAF). The protection of colonial economies was important as, while in 1959 British colonies in Africa provided only 3 per cent of imports and absorbed less than that in British exports, Britain's financial position was dependent on the value of sterling assets held by colonies, which in 1958 had been valued at £1.45 billion.[45] Crucially, 60 per cent of British overseas capital was invested in Commonwealth countries, including those in Central Africa that gained independence from 1960 onwards.[46] Between 1959 and 1969, British exports to Africa fell from 12.2 to 9.9 per cent, whereas imports increased from 9.9 to 12.1 per cent and investments grew from £325 million to £408 million. As William Minter has described it: 'The British capitalist ... still had some confidence in former colonies.'[47] This was precisely what the British Government had been planning for since the Colonial Development Organisation (now the Commonwealth Development Corporation or CDC) had been launched in 1948. In cooperation with the Colonial Office, economic development plans in British colonies in Africa initiated development by colonial administrations in order to attract private investors.[48] However, civil strife and the breakdown of law and order affected the operation of Shell and UMHK mining facilities, as they became sites for anti-colonial demonstrations as the crisis progressed. As the perception of instability fused with the volatile politics of nationalism in the Congo, there was an increasing fear of capital flight among investors and industries in newly independent states. In trying to diversify colonial economies, British plans for decolonisation and post-colonial development in Central Africa and, by extension, British Congo policy, centred around how independence and nationalism would impact upon the security of private firms, their operating environment and the continuity of access to raw materials.

Part of the importance of securing access to resources and investments in Katanga was also to keep the infrastructure of neighbouring British Commonwealth members in Africa intact, and maintain British control over local industries. For this reason, the secession was viewed as directly impacting British economic interests, an impression that was verified when members of the UMHK, and later Unilever, lobbied the Foreign Office to recognise an independent Katanga.[49] Historians such as John Kent have dismissed the idea that Britain was caught off guard by the secession. He has argued that the arrival of Belgian troops in Elisabethville, the provincial capital, just one day before the secession was announced, points to the fact that Katanga's 'independence' was in fact orchestrated by European, neo-colonial interests. Whether or not the secession was masterminded by European actors, Belgian and British policies towards the Congo highlight the role of financial groups and white minority leaders influencing government policy in Brussels and London, towards perpetuating the economic and political status quo of pre-independence African countries, especially the Congo.

Chief among the supporters of the secession of Katanga was the Prime Minister of the neighbouring Federation of Rhodesia and Nyasaland, Roy Welensky. The Federation, which bordered the Congo and Katanga, was governed by a white-minority regime. Welensky was opposed to the advance of black majority rule in Africa, and believed that the secession of Katanga was advantageous to British interests in the region. From July 1960 onwards, he supported Tshombe's administration with financial and political aid, and lobbied the Foreign Office to recognise the independence of Katanga. Welensky had long been a vocal critic of Colonial Office policies regarding African political advancement and the divisions between black and white rule inherent in the political infrastructure of former British colonies, which had the effect of politicising the masses.[50] His open support for Katanga highlighted his disagreement with the Foreign Office on this issue.[51] During parliamentary questions in July 1960, when asked why there was such a disparity between London and Salisbury on the Congo question, the British Foreign Secretary Selwyn Lloyd was evasive, pointing out that the external relations of the Federation was a matter for their own Government, although the 'affairs in the Congo are of deep concern to both Governments'.[52] In the short term, fears about the impact of the secession on the stability of the Federation, which was viewed as a useful middle ground between the 'extremes of African nationalism and apartheid', dominated Britain's response to the crisis.[53] British Prime Minister Harold Macmillan weighed in personally on the disagreement with Welensky, declaring that nothing should be done to 'prejudice' the interests of the Federation as it 'could make a very important contribution to the maintenance of our position in Central Africa'.[54] Much of Britain's Congo policies were influenced by this conviction and the hesitancy to challenge Welensky, whose support for Katanga was shared by the right-wing Tories in the Conservative Party. More broadly, the disagreement with Welensky and the support for Katanga within Macmillan's own Cabinet highlighted broader issues regarding the dissolution of the British Empire.[55]

During his tour of Africa in 1960, Macmillan gave his now infamous 'Winds of Change' speech, in which he referred to the changing nature of African politics and the growth of nationalist sentiment throughout the continent. But Macmillan himself had also foreshadowed this fabled statement in 1957 when he warned that nationalism, 'which a few years ago was but a ripple, has become a tidal wave surging from Asia across the ocean to the shores of Africa ... Of all the political forces, the new rise of nationalism is the most powerful ... it can be led but it cannot be driven back'.[56] The challenges of the rise of African nationalism had already been made clear to the British Foreign Office with the outbreak of violence in Nyasaland in 1958. Nationalist leader Hastings Banda led a protest against the Federation, calling for the inclusion of more black Africans in the Federation's Legislative Council. The violent response of the Nyasaland police to the protest resulted in the death of fifty-one people and the internment of over 2,000 others. In response, the British Government launched the Devlin Commission, which produced a report in 1959 that criticised the excessive use of force during the protests and branded the country a 'police state' for its suppression of African nationalists. The Colonial Office and Secretary of State for the Colonies, Alan Lennox-Boyd, responded angrily to the report, accusing its lead investigator, Judge Patrick Devlin, of using it as an opportunity for personal revenge since he had been recently passed over for the position of Lord Chief Justice. Despite the protestations, the report, and the later the findings of Monckton Commission, which was set up in 1960 to advise the Government on the future viability of the Federation, spelled the death-knell for the initiative. In addition, the reports pointed to some of the deeper problems with British decolonisation policies in Africa.

As Martin Thomas has recently argued, independence in Ghana had revealed to British officials that adapting British preferences rather than a real engagement with 'constructive nationalism' allowed for the creation of post-colonial development projects which retained elements of the colonial system.[57] Up to 1960, British decolonisation had unfolded across Africa, following Indian independence in 1947, with the emergence of Libya in 1951, Sudan in 1956, Ghana in 1957 and Somalia in 1960. The brutal response of British colonial officials to the Mau Mau rebellion in Kenya in 1952 served to raise public criticism of British colonial policies and echoed the horrors of the Belgian regime in the Congo, hardening public opinion in Europe against the continuation of colonialism.[58] The transformation of the British Empire into the Commonwealth system had at its core the promotion and protection of British economic and financial interests and networks. The main aim was to ensure that Communism did not spread among the newly independent former British colonies while at the same time, guaranteeing Britain continued access to resources and trade markets.[59] Macmillan believed that this was a workable model for decolonisation, a process in which the colonies could gradually be moved from self-rule towards independence under the Commonwealth system.[60] As John Darwin has described, London's plans did not involve a renunciation of British power and influence in Africa; rather, 'rationalisation and reappraisal were the order of the day'.[61] The Commonwealth therefore provided a means by which Britain could have an informal empire, adapting the benefits of colonial rule in a post-colonial world without the financial burden of dependencies and, in the process, securing the importance and prestige of Britain's world role.[62]

The Commonwealth was an attempt, similar to that of France, to convert the colonial world into a more representative system under which states had autonomy but whereby British and French international power and prestige was sustained through a coherent sphere of influence. In 1958 Paris offered French African colonies autonomy within a French community or full independence without French financial support, as a path towards self-government. Adopting the Françafrique policy, many former French African colonies, including Central African Republic, Chad, Congo (Brazzaville), Dahomey, Gabon, Côte d'Ivoire, Malagasy Republic, Mauritania, Niger, Senegal, Mali, Sudanese Republic and Upper Volta, opted for independence from, but the maintenance of, close ties to France. The 'France Afrique' project had very similar aims to the Commonwealth, being focused on deterring the spread of Communism while maintaining French political influence and access to economic resources in former colonies. However, Britain and France did not seek to coordinate efforts to transform their empires, despite both countries facing similar difficulties with the process of decolonisation. As Lennox-Boyd remarked by 1960, it was 'fifty years too late to coordinate colonial policies'.[63]

In response to their decolonisation policies, Britain and France also faced similar crises in Africa with the eruption of violence in the Algerian war of independence from 1958 to 1961 and in South Africa in 1960. In March 1960, sixty-seven black demonstrators were shot dead at Sharpeville and the South African Government banned the African National Congress and Pan-Africanist Congress parties in an effort to suppress a black African nationalist uprising. At the same time independence loomed in Nigeria, Tanganyika, Sierra Leone, Kenya, Tanzania and Uganda.[64] It was into this context that the Congo crisis erupted and the ways in which it evolved from the beginning soon led to a realisation among British officials that the struggle had the potential to ignite conflict in their remaining colonies. It was a three-fold problem; alongside the Katanga question and the preservation of British economic interests in the region, there was the potential for wider geopolitical fallout from the crisis that would impact not only the stability of the Commonwealth but British decolonisation policy as a whole.[65] In addition, there was a considerable tension with American Congo policy.

An 'ambiguous partnership'

> It is becoming increasingly apparent that Anglo-American differences in the conduct of Congo policy are as serious as any since the Suez crisis.[66]
> *The Times*, 14 December 1961

In the years leading up to the Congo crisis, the relationship between the US and Britain was being 'rebuilt against a background of distrust',[67] after the fallout from the Suez Canal conflict in 1956; one of the most dramatic breaks in diplomatic relations between the two countries. The British decision to back an Israeli attack on the Egyptian canal in order to guarantee its own interests in the region was deliberately concealed from its American allies due to the belief that even though the American attitude towards the issue had been ambiguous, the Atlantic Alliance, as a whole, was strong enough to withstand any potential conflict.[68] However, British Prime Minister Anthony Eden's gamble backfired when the Americans condemned British actions. The result, James Mayall has argued, was that it 'finally exposed the fiction of the "Special Relationship," that being, the reality of British dependence on, rather than influence over, the United States'.[69]

While the Suez debacle undoubtedly exposed the disparities in power between the US and Britain, it also became a departure point for the reinvigoration of relations and a movement towards joint Anglo-American planning in the post-colonial world.[70] In the immediate aftermath former British Prime Minister Winston Churchill urged President Dwight D. Eisenhower to preserve the 'special' nature of the Anglo-American relationship.[71] Successive conflicts in the Middle East and Africa, struggles with decolonisation across the globe, and growing tension between the US and the Union of Soviet Socialist Republics (USSR), all contributed to an emphasis on reinvigorating relations. Eisenhower, while serving as an American general during the Second World War, had previously worked together with Macmillan, who worked in North Africa as the official representative of the British Government in 1942.[72] Their close personal relationship became an important conduit for the development of good Anglo-American relations. The growing intimacy towards the end of Eisenhower's presidency is evidenced by the signing in 1958 of the Agreement for Cooperation on Uses of Atomic Energy for Mutual Defence Purposes. John Baylis has described the deal as 'one of the most important peacetime agreements ever arrived at between the two countries'.[73] While Britain gained a whole new armoury of the most advanced nuclear weapons being created, the US enhanced its own nuclear research with British expertise.[74] By the beginning of the 1960s, therefore, Anglo-American relations in key areas such as nuclear and defence cooperation were increasingly close. However, as American Cold War plans began to interact with British plans for decolonisation, Africa emerged as a contested space for the development of joint Anglo-American policies.

Although the US traditionally proclaimed itself to be an anti-colonial nation, the American stance towards European decolonisation up to 1960 was ambivalent at best.[75] Stephen Ambrose has argued that when Eisenhower took office in 1953, 'he had been eloquent in telling Churchill that old-style European colonialism, especially in Africa, could not and should not last'.[76] Despite its overtly anti-colonial stance, American policy on decolonisation amounted to little more than rhetoric about the importance of self-determination as the emphasis on preserving relationships with European allies like Britain and France took precedence over an activist American agenda for decolonisation.[77] However, even before the crisis in the Congo had erupted, Joseph Satterthwaite, Assistant Secretary of State for African Affairs, noted that events in Africa had moved too quickly for the State Department to keep up and that Africa now needed to be considered as a major policy area.[78] This was not just the view of the African Affairs Bureau. In March 1959, US Ambassador to the UN, Henry Cabot Lodge, reported from New York that 'Scarcely a day goes by without my contact at UN vividly impressing me with rapidly evolving revolution in Africa'. He urged that while the US should continue to exert a moderating influence on Britain and France, a more visible policy was now needed.[79] As the crisis developed, increasingly more overt American actions at the UN reflected a deeper shift in views on how decolonisation should take place.

As early as 1955, the international relations scholar Hans Morgenthau had articulated the idea that the UN should internationalise the process of decolonisation more fully than simply overseeing it with the Trusteeship system.[80] This was a view echoed by Chester Bowles who, in 1959, was member of the US House of Representatives but later became President Kennedy's Special Representative and Adviser on African, Asian and Latin American Affairs in 1961. He pointed out that American support for European colonial regimes in Africa only had the effect of increasing resentment and rebellion among native populations and actually undermined the influence and image of the US abroad. Rather, he maintained that the US should assert its influence in Africa on its own terms, instead of stabilising European regimes, and in the process develop a more 'Afrocentric' approach to US foreign policy in Africa. Although Bowles' influence within the State Department waned even before Kennedy was assassinated in 1963, his ideas did augur a shift in American attitudes towards Africa over time. Key among them was the theory that the US should avoid being identified with 'stagnant or repressive policies' of the metropolitan powers and, rather, seek to influence former colonial powers to abandon or modify such policies.[81] By the end of the Congo crisis, the State Department pursued this policy in an overt manner and had come to consider European influence in Africa as a destabilising force.

The Congo question also related to issues of race and the domestic resonance of American foreign policy towards Africa among civil-rights activists in the US.[82] Kennedy appointed Gerhard Mennen Williams as his Assistant Secretary of State for African Affairs to run the new African Bureau in 1961, nicknamed 'Soapy' due to his family's fortune in the soap and toiletries industry. He appeared to represent a new opportunity for improved relations with African states after he was incorrectly paraphrased by the press as supporting the idea of 'Africa for the Africans', following a comment during a press conference while touring the continent in 1961.[83] But as Steven Metz has noted, the shift in American attitudes towards decolonisation was gradual and progressed at a glacial pace, rather than being a dramatic change.[84] Although the rhetoric appeared to shift drastically between Eisenhower and Kennedy, since the latter launched a policy initiative to engage non-aligned leaders and abandoned the former's policy of automatically abstaining at the UN on colonial questions, their actual policies remained largely similar. Although it took almost one year before the State Department crafted a coherent position on the Congo, from the beginning it was clear that the rolling back of empire was a necessary condition to sustain the solidarity of the West.[85] Until the middle of 1961, however, the hesitancy to be identified as a neo-colonial power among the other African countries, and the importance of maintaining a united Western position, led the US to adopt a passive stance. As the crisis deepened, increasing domestic pressure from civil rights activists, who equated the American attitude towards the Third World with racial segregation in the southern American states, combined with the escalating Cold War tensions to sharpen and direct US policy more forcefully.

The third dimension of US policy in the Congo was focused on the modernisation and development of the country under a stable Western-friendly government. From June 1960 onwards, the US increasingly influenced the political constellation in Léopoldville, through direct diplomacy, the CIA and bilateral aid. The growing importance of Africa as a sphere of American foreign policy through the 1950s had led to a focus in the State Department on theories and practices of development and modernisation through market-based economies and the fostering of liberal ideas in the mould of the New Deal which, if successfully executed, would reduce the attraction of Soviet aid and socialist models among newly emergent states. The New Deal was a development programme launched in 1933 to help the American economy recover by structuring reform in three social areas: relief for the underdeveloped sections of society; recovery of the economy; and reform of the financial sector to prevent another depression such as that induced by the crash of 1929. Walt Rostow, an American economist, rose to prominence with a model of development which advocated free trade, liberal markets and the efficacy of a capitalist system to deter the spread of Communist and socialist ideology among newly independent states.[86] His theories resonated with Kennedy, in particular, who appointed him Deputy National Security Advisor in 1961, and later also with Lyndon B. Johnson who promoted him to National Security Advisor in 1966. However, Rostow's model of modernisation proved rigid in its application and became a point of contention during negotiations with India, Ghana and Egypt, where the State Department attempted to implement it most vigorously. As Latham points out, in contrast, the Soviet development funds and socialist models that created a strong role for the state and a nationalised economy based primarily on industrial development became attractive to post-colonial leaders. The static nature of the American model in comparison, and the preference for technological development, diversifying exports and the creation of market-based economies, led to a gradual rather than rapid transformation that post-colonial states tended to prefer.[87] Negotiations over the implementation of American modernisation strategies led to a debate among policymakers and post-colonial leaders about 'both the *forms* and *purposes* of development'.[88] This debate was not limited to the interaction with post-colonial leaders, however, because although the American liberal trade thesis was compatible with the basic tenets of British development policies, the forms though which it was developed threatened the role of European colonial networks in Africa. With the expansion of free-market economics and trade liberalisation across Africa, the stability of the British trade network in Africa was threatened.

The State Department directed efforts towards modernising the Congolese economy, which was a reflection of its broader strategies for Third World development. The 'new liberals' of the State Department included economists such as Rostow, Bowles and Adlai E. Stevenson.[89] As Rakove has argued, 'Rostow sought to articulate a particularly American vision of development that could be pursued in the developing world'.[90] What was important about Rostow's views was not just their influence in guiding the policies of the State Department but also that he considered that democracy was not an 'absolute condition' for development. Bowles and Stevenson similarly believed in the importance of engaging African nations in an open and cooperative manner, which they hoped would distinguish the American approach to Africa as anti-colonial rather than neo-colonial. They advocated for the development of African economies through expansive aid programmes and the opening of markets in order to encourage the American private sector to invest more across the continent.[91] Although Bowles and certainly Stevenson had a more limited influence on State Department policies than Rostow, they formed an important part of the liberal lodestars who rose to prominence in the Kennedy administration and had a lasting effect on how the US approached Africa.[92]

It was also during these years, in 1961, that the United States Agency for International Development (USAID) was created to manage the flow of aid to the developing world, and to promote social and economic development.[93] Alongside these structural and institutional changes, the US also sought to diversify its approach to African development in particular. Rostow promoted the creation of what was termed a 'community of free nations', whereby the industrialised countries of the world, including the European states, Japan and the US, would direct investment and provide technical assistance to Third World countries, thereby staving off the influence of Communism.[94] This was not just a plan for modernisation but a vision of world order which was designed to transcend the North/South divide both in terms of race and wealth. In order to realise this vision, the State Department sought close cooperation with Britain, noting that 'the UK … has a huge direct stake in the area'.[95] Despite the common interests between them, however, one key factor hindered cooperation and forestalled the potential creation of the 'community of free nations' and that was the role of private companies.

It has already been shown that preservation of the traditional position of private companies in the Congolese economy and in other former colonies was at the heart of British approaches, but for the US, expanding the role of American business in these newly opened markets also proved an important consideration of Cold War policy. As Thomas has described it, 'in the business of decolonization, as in its politics, the trend towards Americanization was irresistible'.[96] The links between both Eisenhower and Kennedy's administrations and private business interests in the Congo were intricate and intertwined. Eisenhower's Secretary of State (until 1959), John Foster Dulles, and CIA director, Allen Dulles, had connections with the AMAX mining company that operated in Katanga and one of Stevenson's law firm's biggest clients was the diamond trading company, Leon Tempelsman and Son, which had extensive operations across the country. Gibbs has argued that not only did Stevenson use his influence to allow this company to expand its activities in the Congo after independence, but also encouraged the US Government's policy of stockpiling Congolese diamonds. Templesman positioned itself as a middleman for this process and in exchange the Congolese were promised American agricultural commodities.[97] The Rockefeller Foundation, which in the early 1960s was interested in expanding its activities in Africa, was also well-connected to the Africa Bureau through Bowles, who was a former trustee, Kennedy's Secretary of State Dean Rusk, who was a former president of the organisation, and, most importantly, Deputy Assistant Secretary, J. Wayne Fredericks, who Gibbs describes as 'a major architect of the policy that eventually crushed Katanga'.[98] This impression of the architecture of US Congo policy gives an important insight into the role and influence of private interests in shaping approaches towards the execution of modernisation strategies. At the centre of this were not just the attempts to formulate and develop African economies to prevent the spread of socialist ideas but also to expand American business interests to compete with the European monopolies and control of natural resource extraction. Arguments about Cold War imperatives and anti-Communist ideologies provided a convenient shield with which to achieve both aims in one stroke.

The US approach to the Third World was an important element of the global context of the Cold War strategy of the State Department, at the roots of which was a particular vision of liberal internationalism. The tension in the State Department between the various groups that crafted foreign policy, including the National Security Council and the CIA came to the fore in policy towards the Congo. The State Department from Eisenhower, through Kennedy to Johnson remained split between several rival factions who brought different opinions to bear on the development of Congo policy and the relative importance of Africa and the Third World as a sphere of American interests.[99] Among the first group, referred to as the 'Africanists' or the 'Liberals', were Williams, Stevenson and Bowles, who believed that decolonisation required engagement with African and Asian states, supported the campaign for civil rights for African-Americans and approached development and modernisation as a moral, as much as a utilitarian, cause. The second faction were the 'Europeanists', among them Rusk and Under-Secretary George Ball (who later became Kennedy's 'point man' on the Congo). This group tended to view decolonisation and Africa through the lens of relations with Europe, with the preservation of the stability of NATO as key. In between these two groups were what Rakove terms 'the pragmatists', including National Security Advisor McGeorge Bundy, Under-Secretary of State for Political Affairs George McGhee and officials from the International Organizations Bureau who tended to be sympathetic towards their UN colleagues, many of whom were from former colonies.[100] These advisors tended to take the middle ground, balancing the idealism of the liberals with the realism of the Europeanists. What these groups did agree on was that the Cold War was the overriding challenge of American foreign policy.[101] Africa, therefore, soon became regarded as a space in which the demands of decolonisation needed to be balanced against the testing of different experiments in nation-building, the protection of American economic interests and the ways in which America's global mission could be realised. The structural and conceptual differences between these groups prevented the US from formulating a coherent and balanced policy towards the Congo until the middle of 1962.

By 1960, though the American dependence on Congolese uranium ores had decreased, there was still an economic cooperative framework with Britain and Belgium to develop the ores as a source of commercial energy power, crucial to the Belgian atomic energy programme.[102] Although American atomic technology was no longer solely reliant on Congolese uranium, it was important that the Soviet Union did not seize the opportunity to gain control over these or any of the other resources of the Congo. When the Congo gained independence, although the American share of all Congolese investment was between 1–2 per cent, control over these resources remained essential to the US economy.[103] Even by 1965, the United States Interdepartmental Stockpile Committee still viewed the Congo as of primary importance in the sourcing of borty (low quality powdered diamond, used in industries) and diamonds.[104] Alongside the protection of specific resources, and the increasing amount of investment, by 1962 alone, the US Government had contributed more than $85 million in bilateral aid to the Central Government. In addition, the State Department had allegedly spend $200,000 in an information campaign to gather support for the Central Government alongside, as one historian describes it, 'unknown millions more for CIA payments to Congolese politicians'.[105] Following along the lines of earlier Cold War strategies, the CIA played an important role in executing American Congo policy by trying to subvert perceived Communist influences within the Central Government. From the outset, the US was keen to avoid any direct intervention into the Congo and thereby came to rely quite extensively on the CIA and on European allies Britain and Belgium acting through the UN.

On 12 July, US Ambassador in Léopoldville, Clare L. Timberlake, cabled the State Department requesting that American troops, under a UN banner, be dispatched to the Congolese capital in order to prevent a complete breakdown in law and order following the rebellion of the Force Publique.[106] Eisenhower may have expressed surprise at the amount of political activity in the Congo before the election in 1960 since 'he did not know that many people in the Congo could read', but correspondence between the State Department and the Belgian Foreign Ministry reveals that the US had long been aware of the potentially precarious nature of Congolese independence.[107] From the beginning of the crisis, however, the US ruled out even sending a token force to the Congo, insisting that any and all assistance be channelled through the UN, in order to avoid a confrontation with the Soviet Union and because the attention of the State Department was focused on Vietnam.[108] The State Department was of the opinion that the Belgians should take the lead in the Congo but was also aware that the Belgian troops in the capital and tacit British support for Katanga was broadly perceived as neo-colonialist, and drew criticism from other African states. This position reflected the deeper tension in American Congo policy between its proclaimed anti-colonial posture and the maintenance of relations with former colonial powers.[109] The solution was to go to the UN. Eisenhower's remarks to Secretary of State Christian Herter in response to Timberlake's appeal reflected this sentiment more precisely when he stated: 'we are always willing to do our duty through the UN but we are not going to unilaterally get into this'.[110]

While generally positive about the potential of the UN to manage decolonisation, the US had grown disillusioned about the value of the organisation as a venue for foreign policy due to its increasingly tense atmosphere. The branding of American foreign policy as imperialist during debates on the US intervention in Guatemala in 1954 had heightened tensions with the Soviet Union and led to an attack on American neo-colonialism by members of the General Assembly.[111] In dispatching a military force to overthrow the Arbenz Government, the US flaunted UN conventions on sovereignty and intervention, but had as a consequence been firmly branded as a neo-colonialist power. Eisenhower lamented the predicament of handling the environment at the UN. In a letter to Churchill he reflected that 'under the cover of all those international agreements for peace, small nations ... could do the most outrageous things'.[112] This frustration was echoed by others in his administration, including Dulles, who complained to Belgian Foreign Minister Pierre Wigny in 1958 that 'the admission of these newly-independent, but unprepared nations into the UN with the same vote as older and greater powers debased the concept of independent nations exercising self-responsibility in international affairs'.[113]

The cynicism in American views of the UN was also convenient, facilitating more overt actions in US policy in Vietnam and with the Bay of Pigs intervention in Cuba in 1960, without attention to international scrutiny. When the US was challenged on these violations of international law at the UN, representatives offered dubious explanations such as the Communist threat posed by Castro's regime in Cuba. However, the Congo question was different. Primarily the State Department believed that the crisis was a Belgian responsibility but also recognised that the optics and racial dimension of the question were important to the African states. The disappointment with the UN as a forum for discussion was not immediately connected with its burgeoning role in peacekeeping, which, after the success of UN peacekeeping in Suez, had led to a public motto of 'let Dag do it'.[114] While the interventionist attitude of the Secretary-General and the activist tenure of the organisation seemed to initially serve US interests by taking the lead in the Congo, the actions of the peacekeeping force exacerbated the broader dilemmas around the issue of Katanga. This was part of the deeper problem with the ad hoc nature of US Congo policy and created what McGhee referred to as 'cross-currents of distrust' between US representatives and the UN officials, many of whom were anti-colonial.[115] In addition, disillusionment with the UN soon turned into despair when the crisis accelerated and it was precisely the newly independent nations of the General Assembly who seized upon the Congo to launch a wider challenge to Anglo-American internationalism. The US far underestimated the ways in which the Afro-Asian bloc would respond to the crisis and the rambunctious meeting of the General Assembly in September 1960 revealed the limits of common ground with Britain and the lack of room to manoeuvre at the UN.

Notes

1 E.D. Morel, *Red Rubber: The Story of the Rubber Slave Trade Flourishing on the Congo for Twenty Years 1890–1910* (Manchester: The National Labour Press, 1906).
2 A. Conan Doyle, *The Crime of the Congo* (London: Hutchinson & Co., 1909); J. Conrad, *Heart of Darkness* (London: Blackwoods, 1902); M. Twain, *King Leopold's Soliloquy: A Defence of His Congo Rule* (Pamphlet, Leftward Books, 1905).
3 Regarding the internationalisation of imperial affairs see: A. Anghie, *Imperialism, Sovereignty and the Making of International Law* (Cambridge: Cambridge University Press, 2007), pp. 32–114; F. Cooper and J. Burbank, *Empires in World History* (Princeton: Princeton University Press, 2010); M. Koskenniemi, *The Gentle Civilizer*

    of Nations: The Rise and Fall of International Law, 1870–1960 (Cambridge: Cambridge University Press, 2002), pp. 98–178.
 4 For further see: K. Grant, *A Civilised Savagery: Britain and the New Slaveries in Africa, 1884–1926* (London: Routledge, 2005); Hochschild, *King Leopold's Ghost*; M.B. Jerónimo, *The 'Civilising Mission' of Portuguese Colonialism, 1870–1930* (Basingstoke: Palgrave Macmillan, 2015); S. Miers, *Slavery in the Twentieth Century: The Evolution of a Global Problem* (Walnut Creek: Altamira Press, 2003).
 5 H.G. Nicholas, *The United Nations as a Political Institution* (Oxford: Oxford University Press, 1975).
 6 Immanuel Wallerstein argues that the effect of the AAPC conference was important in mobilising public opinion and spreading political awareness. I. Wallerstein, *Africa: The Politics of Unity* (New York: Random House, 1967), pp. 34–35.
 7 Public Records and Archives Administration Department, Accra (hereafter PRAAD), Special Collection Bureau of African Affairs (SC/BAA), RG 17/1/415, 'Osagyefo's Book on the Congo'.
 8 Thomas Kanza, 'The Congo crisis, 1960–1961: a critical oral history conference', *Transcript* (Washington, DC: Woodrow Wilson Centre, 2004), p. 18.
 9 PRAAD, RG 17/1/149, General Congress of Union of African Trade, Special Collection Bureau of African Affairs (SC/BAA), Background information on the recent events in the Belgian Congo, Information Bulletin on African Affairs.
10 *Ibid.*
11 *Ibid.*
12 International Monetary Fund, *Annual Report of the Executive Directors for the Fiscal Year Ended April 30, 1958* (Washington, DC: International Monetary Fund, 1958).
13 Haskin, *Tragic State of the Congo*, pp. 18–19.
14 Kanza, 'The Congo crisis', p. 28.
15 Speech of Patrice Lumumba at the closing of the Belgo-Congolese Round Table Conference, 20 February 1960, in T. Schmidt, *The Belgo-Congolese Round Table Conference* (Brussels: C. Van Cortenbergh, 1960), pp. 43–44. See also J. Gerard-Libois, *Katanga Secession*, trans. R. Young (Madison: University of Wisconsin Press, 1966); J. Gerard-Libois and B. Verhaegen, *Congo 1960*, Vols I and II (Brussels: Centre de Recherche et d'Information Socio-Politiques, 1961).
16 Haskin, *Tragic State of the Congo*, p. 19.
17 The value of copper exports had been falling since 1958 as the US reduced its strategic stockpiling programme. L.J. Butler, *Copper Empire, Mining and the Colonial State in Northern Rhodesia, c. 1930–64* (Basingstoke: Palgrave Macmillan, 2007), p. 233.
18 Jean Omasombo, 'The Congo crisis', *Transcript* (Washington, DC: Woodrow Wilson Centre, 2004), p. 43.
19 Cleophas Kamitatu, 'The Congo crisis', *Transcript* (Washington, DC: Woodrow Wilson Centre, 2004), p. 26.
20 GPL, BAA/RLAA/502, 'Special Committee on the Implementation of 1514 (1962) Vol. IV', Verbatim records of the Committee, 2 August 1962, Chapter 6, Tshombe's Katanga.
21 P. Lumumba, *La Pensee Politique de Patrice Lumumba, Textes recueillis et presentes par Jean Van Lierde* (Brussels: Presence Africaine, 1963), p. 43.
22 G. Arnold, *Africa: A Modern History* (London: Atlantic Books, 2017), p. 22.

23 The extent to which the speech was truly impromptu is contested by participants in 'The Congo crisis', *Transcript* (Washington, DC: Woodrow Wilson Centre, 2004), pp. 67–71.
24 NAL, FO 371/146639, Extract from a speech by Patrice Lumumba given at the inauguration ceremony in the Congolese capital Léopoldville to mark the official beginning of Congolese independence on 30 June 1960.
25 Legum, *Congo Disaster*, pp. 59–60.
26 Archives de Ministere de Affaires Etrangeres, Bruxelles (hereafter AMAE), Dossiers Diplomatique, AFI-1 Juliette 1960, Editorial in the *Hindu* (2 July 1960).
27 A. James, *Britain and the Congo Crisis, 1960–1963* (Basingstoke: Palgrave Macmillan, 1996), p. 42.
28 E. Nwaubani, 'Eisenhower, Nkrumah and the Congo crisis', *Journal of Contemporary History*, 36:4 (2001), 599–622.
29 *Ibid.*, p. 607.
30 Legum, *Congo Disaster*, p. 121.
31 J. Hillman, 'Chartered companies and the development of the tin industry in Belgian Africa, 1900–1939', *African Economic History*, 25:1 (1997), 1–230.
32 Hoskyns, *The Congo Since Independence*, p. 17.
33 Conor Cruise O'Brien, *To Katanga and Back: A UN Case History* (New York: Simon & Schuster, 1962), p. 173.
34 Kanza, 'The Congo crisis', p. 72.
35 GPL, BAA/RLAA/692, 'Congo-I'- Correspondence (Congo, Ghana), Report of F. Scheller to the Minister of the Belgian Congo and Ruanda-Urundi, undated.
36 National Archives, Delhi (hereafter NAD), CPD-14/60- AFRII, 1960, Vol. 1, Developments in Congo (formerly Belgian), Ministry of External Affairs, Telegram from the Indian Embassy in Brussels to Foreign, New Delhi, 19 July 1960.
37 H. Weiss, 'The Congo's independence struggle viewed fifty years later', *African Studies Review*, 55:1 (2012), 113–114.
38 Nzongola-Ntalaja, *The Congo from Leopold to Kabila*.
39 Gibbs, *The Political Economy of Third World Intervention*, p. 61. N.J. Ashton, *Kennedy, Macmillan and the Cold War: The Irony of Interdependence* (Basingstoke: Palgrave Macmillan, 2002), p. 113.
40 GPL, BAA/RLAA/691, 'Republic of Congo': Newspaper Clippings (Congo), Jan 1963, Bureau of African Affairs, 'Africans must solve the Congo problem, the imperialists are doing their worst', Fenner Brockway, *Ghanaian Times* (10 January 1963). See also P. Murphy, *Party Politics and Decolonization: The Conservative Party and British Colonial Policy in Tropical Africa* (Oxford: Clarendon Press, 1995), p. 94.
41 GPL, BAA/RLAA/502, 'Special Committee on the Implementation of 1514 (1962) Vol. IV', 6, Verbatim records of the Committee, 2 August 1962, Chapter 6, Tshombe's Katanga.
42 GPL, BAA/RLAA/502, 'Special Committee on the Implementation of 1514 (1962) Vol. IV', 6, Verbatim records of the Committee, Chapter 6, Tshombe's Katanga, United Nations Memo, 2 August 1962, p. 8. See generally on Conservative members' links to Central Africa, Murphy, *Party Politics and Decolonization*.
43 GPL, BAA/RLAA/502, 'Special Committee on the Implementation of 1514 (1962) Vol. IV', 6, Verbatim records of the Committee, 2 August 1962, Chapter 6, Tshombe's Katanga.

44 *Ibid.*, pp. 7–8.
45 William Minter, *King Solomon's Mines Revisited: Western Interests and the Burdened History of Southern Africa* (New York: Basic Books, 1986), p. 165.
46 By 1962, however, diversification of interests and the emergence of the question of EEC membership began to challenge the idea that British wealth was solely predicated on controlling Commonwealth assets and markets. Martin Thomas, *Fight or Flight: Britain, France and their Roads from Empire* (Oxford: Oxford University Press, 2014), pp. 276–278.
47 Minter, *King Solomon's Mines Revisited*, p. 178.
48 Thomas, *Fight or Flight*, p. 278.
49 J. Kent, 'Anglo-American diplomacy and the Congo crisis, 1960–63: the not so special relationship', in J.W. Young, E.G. Pedaliu and M.D. Kandiah (eds), *Britain in Global Politics: From Churchill to Blair, Volume 2* (Basingstoke: Palgrave Macmillan, 2013), p. 122.
50 D.G. Boyce, *Decolonisation and the British Empire* (Basingstoke: Palgrave Macmillan, 1999), p. 212.
51 NAL, FO 371/146772, Question from Mr. Callaghan to the Secretary of State for Foreign Affairs, Mr. Selwyn Lloyd, Parliamentary Questions, 20 July 1960.
52 NAL, FO 371/146772, Questions from Mr. Gaitskell for the Prime Minister, 14 July 1960. It was noted that any incursion into the Congo of Federal troops would be a matter of the international responsibility of the British Government but that both were closely consulting on the matter.
53 L.J. Butler, 'Britain, the United States, and the demise of the Central African Federation, 1959–63', *The Journal of Imperial and Commonwealth History*, 28:3 (2000), 131–151.
54 Boyce, *Decolonisation*, p. 212.
55 In fact, some of the more right-wing members of the party even founded the Monday Club in protest which was aimed at commemorating 'Black Monday', 3 February 1960, the day Macmillan made his 'Wind of Change' speech. Such virulent opposition is a firm reflection of the perceived importance of the colonies to Britain in 1960, and also of the underlying sentiment that pervaded the party. For further see S. Ball, *The Guardsmen: Harold Macmillan, Three Friends and the World They Made* (London: Harper Perennial, 2005), pp. 344–360; R. Blake, *The Decline of Power, 1915–1964* (Oxford: Oxford University Press, 1985), p. 398.
56 Macmillan's speech delivered in Bedford in July 1957, as quoted in D. Horowitz, 'Attitudes of British Conservatives towards decolonization in Africa', *African Affairs*, 69:274 (1970), 109–115.
57 Thomas, *Fight or Flight*, pp. 261–262.
58 On the Mau Mau rebellion see D. Anderson, *Histories of the Hanged: The Dirty War in Kenya and the End of Empire* (New York: Norton & Co., 2005); C. Elkins, *Imperial Reckoning: The Untold Story of Britain's Gulag in Kenya* (New York: Henry Holt/Jonathan Cape, 2005).
59 N.J. White, *Decolonisation: The British Experience Since 1945*, second edition (London: Routledge, 2014), p. 94.
60 P.E. Hemming, 'Macmillan and the end of the British Empire in Africa', in R. Aldous and S. Lee (eds), *Harold Macmillan and Britain's World Role* (Basingstoke: Palgrave Macmillan, 1995), p. 97. See more generally A. Husain, *Mapping the End of*

Empire: American and British Strategic Visions in the Postwar World (Cambridge, MA: Harvard University Press, 2014), p. 267.
61 J. Darwin, *Britain and Decolonisation: The Retreat from Empire in the Post-War World* (Basingstoke: Palgrave Macmillan, 1988), p. 288.
62 For more on Britain and the Commonwealth see S.R. Ashton and W.R. Louis (eds), *East of Suez and the Commonwealth, 1964-1971* (London: The Stationery Office, 2004); S.R. Ashton, 'British government perspectives on the Commonwealth, 1964-71: an asset or a liability?' *Journal of Imperial and Commonwealth History*, 35:1 (2007), 73-94; A. Bosco and A. May (eds), *The Round Table: The Empire/Commonwealth and British Foreign Policy* (London: Lothian Foundation Press, 1997); G.L. Goodwin, 'The Commonwealth and the United Nations', *International Organization*, 19:2 (1965), 678-694; T.B. Millar, 'The Commonwealth and the United Nations', *International Organization*, 16:4 (1962), 736-757; P. Murphy 'Britain and the Commonwealth: confronting the past – imagining the future', *The Round Table: The Commonwealth Journal of International Affairs*, 100:414 (2011), 267-283.
63 As quoted in Hemming, 'Macmillan and the end of the British Empire in Africa', p. 112.
64 This was a particularly tense moment in South Africa where Nelson Mandela and 155 other African nationalists were on trial for treason. R. Lamb, *The Macmillan Years, 1957-1963: The Emerging Truth* (London: John Murray Publishers, 1995), p. 246; A. Porter and A. Stockwell, *British Imperial Policy and Decolonization*, Vol. II (Basingstoke: Palgrave Macmillan, 1989), p. 64; Darwin, *Britain and Decolonisation*, pp. 287-288.
65 James, *Britain and the Congo Crisis*, pp. 4-10.
66 As quoted in A. Holt, 'Lord Home and Anglo-American relations, 1961-1963', *Diplomacy & Statecraft*, 16:4 (2005), 699-722.
67 J. Dumbrell, *A Special Relationship: Anglo-American Relations from the Cold War to Iraq* (Basingstoke: Palgrave Macmillan, 2006), p. 55.
68 'The British government was convinced in some strange way that the US would ultimately back it and that allied action would somehow force Washington to support what persuasion did not accomplish. Eden and his foreign minister [Selwyn Lloyd] rendered that the choice was clear for Washington if it had to take sides between Egypt and its European allies.' T. Risse-Kappen, 'Collective identity in a democratic community: the case of NATO', in P.J. Katzenstein (ed.), *The Culture of National Security: Norms and Identity in World Politics* (New York: Columbia University Press, 1996), p. 381.
69 J. Mayall, 'Africa in Anglo-American relations', in H. Bull and W.R. Louis (eds), *The 'Special Relationship': Anglo-American Relations Since 1945* (Oxford: Oxford University Press, 1986), pp. 321-340.
70 For the shift in British foreign policy after Suez with regard to the creation of a post-colonial role see Dockrill, *Britain's Retreat from East of Suez*; W.S. Lucas, *Divided We Stand: Britain, the US and the Suez Crisis* (London: Sceptre, 1991); P. Darby, *British Defence Policy East of Suez, 1947-1968* (Oxford: Oxford University Press, 1973).
71 Winston Churchill wrote a personal letter to Eisenhower about the re-establishment of links between the two great countries, stating: 'I do believe, with unfaltering conviction, that the theme of the Anglo-American alliance is more important today than at any time since the war. You and I had some part in raising it to the plane of

which it has stood. Whatever the arguments adduced here and in the United States for or against Anthony's action in Egypt, it will now be an act of folly, on which our whole civilization may founder, to let events in the Middle East come between us.' J. Baylis, *Anglo-American Defence Relations 1939-1980: The Special Relationship* (Basingstoke: Palgrave Macmillan, 1981), p. 89.

72 General Eisenhower had served as Supreme Allied Commander of the Allied Expeditionary Force in Europe during the Second World War, and, based partly in London, had established a good working relationship with Macmillan who served in the wartime coalition in the Ministry of Supply and the Colonial Ministry before being sent, in 1942, to North Africa as the British Government representative to the Allies in the Mediterranean. Baylis, *Anglo-American Defence Relations*, p. 92.

73 *Ibid.*, p. 90. This was, however, before the fall-out over the Skybolt affair in 1961, which resulted eventually in the agreement to give the Polaris missile to the British in 1964. It should be mentioned here that the McMahon Act, which had previously kept all US military development secret from Britain and other allies, had basically been repealed by this point.

74 Dumbrell, *A Special Relationship*, p. 55.

75 W.R. Louis, 'American anti-colonialism and the dissolution of the British empire', in H. Bull and W.R. Louis (eds), *The 'Special Relationship': Anglo-American Relations Since 1945* (Oxford: Oxford University Press, 1986), pp. 261–283.

76 S.E. Ambrose, *Eisenhower, Volume Two: The President, 1952-1969* (New York: Simon & Scheuster, 1984), p. 587.

77 C. Bowles, *Africa's Challenge to America* (Berkeley and Los Angeles: University of California Press, 1956).

78 'United States Assistance to Sub-Saharan Africa'. Memorandum from the Assistant Secretary of State for African Affairs (Satterthwaite) to the Under Secretary of State (Dillon), 30 March 1960. H.D. Schwar and S. Shaloff (eds), *Foreign Relations of the United States, 1958-1960, Volume XIV, Africa* (Washington, DC: United States Government Printing Office, 1992), p. 100. Hereafter, *FRUS*.

79 Telegram from Lodge, Mission at the United Nations to the Department of State, 17 March 1959, Schwar and Shaloff, *FRUS, 1958-1960, XIV, Africa*, p. 44.

80 H.J. Morgenthau, 'United States Policy Towards Africa', in C.W. Stillman (ed.), *Africa in the Modern World* (Chicago: University of Chicago Press, 1955), pp. 317–328.

81 'Statement of U.S. Policy toward South, Central and East Africa', National Security Council Report, 19 January 1960. Schwar and S. Shaloff, *FRUS, 1958-1960, XIV, Africa*, p. 82.

82 On the connection between race and civil rights see C. Anderson, *Eyes off the Prize: The United Nations and the African American Struggle for Human Rights, 1944-1955* (Cambridge: Cambridge University Press, 2003); T. Borstelmann, *Cold War & the Color Line: American Race Relations in the Global Arena* (Cambridge, MA: Harvard University Press, 2003); M.L. Dudziak, *Cold War Civil Rights, Race and the Image of American Democracy* (Princeton: Princeton University Press, 2000); R. Romano, 'No diplomatic immunity: African diplomats, the State Department, and civil rights, 1961–1964', *Journal of American History*, 87:9 (2000), 546–580.

83 T.J. Noer, *Soapy: A Biography of G. Mennen Williams* (Ann Arbor: University of Michigan Regional, 2006), pp. 223–225.

84 S. Metz, 'American attitudes towards decolonization in Africa', *Political Science Quarterly*, 99:3 (1984), 515–533.
85 J.F. Ade Ajayi, 'Peace, stability and legitimacy in Africa: the factor of colonialism and neo-colonialism', in G. Lundestad (ed.), *The Fall of Great Powers: Peace, Stability and Legitimacy* (Oslo: Aschehoug AS, 1994), pp. 215–235.
86 For further detail see W.W. Rostow, *Politics and the Stages of Growth* (Cambridge: Cambridge University Press, 1971); K.C. Pearce, *Rostow, Kennedy and the Rhetoric of Foreign Aid* (East Lansing: Michigan State University Press: 2001).
87 M.E. Latham, *The Right Kind of Revolution: Modernization, Development, and US Foreign Policy from the Cold War to the Present* (Ithaca, NY: Cornell University Press, 2010), p. 88.
88 *Ibid.*, p. 89.
89 For an overview of how these figures among others shaped the State Department's approach to modernisation and Africa under the Kennedy administration, see Robert B. Rakove, *Kennedy, Johnson and the Non-Aligned World* (Cambridge: Cambridge University Press, 2013), pp. 41–55.
90 *Ibid.*, p. 42.
91 For further see Bowles, *Africa's Challenge to America*.
92 For example, the African bureau in the State Department was created only in 1958 but remained an important repertoire of Rostow's planning through the 1960s.
93 Provision of aid should not be viewed as a solely altruistic endeavour. The World Bank identified this practice as essential to the expansion of overseas markets for American exports, the development of markets of US companies, and the overall expansion of the free trade system, which was directly beneficial to the US economy. V. Prashad, *The Darker Nations: A People's History of the Third World* (New York: The New Press, 2007), p. 71. See also F. Gerrits, 'Hungry minds: the Eisenhower administration and cultural assistance in sub-Saharan Africa (1953–1961)', *Diplomatic History*, 41:3 (2017), 594–619.
94 Rakove, *Kennedy, Johnson and the Non-Aligned World*, p. 43.
95 Paper prepared in the Department of Defense, 'The Strategic Importance of Africa', Working Paper for Discussion Group Meeting May 25, 1963. N.D. Howland (ed.), *FRUS, 1961–1963, Volume XXI, Africa* (Washington, DC: United States Government Printing Office, 1995), p. 332.
96 Thomas, *Fight or Flight*, p. 279.
97 On Templesman, see Gibbs, *The Political Economy of Third World Intervention*, pp. 107–112.
98 Gibbs also points out the Fredericks went on to become a Vice-President at Chase Manhattan bank 'where he probably helped arranged Congo's commercial loans'. *Ibid.*, pp. 113–114.
99 D. Rothchild, 'Engagement versus disengagement in Africa', in A.M. Jones (ed.), *US Foreign Policy in a Changing World* (New York: McKay, 1973); V. McKay, *Africa in World Politics* (New York: Harper & Row, 1963); D. Horowitz, *The Free World Colossus* (New York: Hill and Wang, 1971); G. Kolko, *The Roots of American Foreign Policy* (Boston: Beacon Press, 1969); W.A. Williams, *The Tragedy of American Diplomacy* (New York: Delta, 1969); S. Amin, *Neo-Colonialism in West Africa* (New York: Monthly Review Press; 1973); S. Amin, 'Underdevelopment and dependence in black Africa: origins and contemporary forms', *Journal of Modern*

African Studies, 10:4 (1972), 503–552; T.M. Shaw and C.M. Newbury, 'Dependence or interdependence: Africa in the global political economy', in M.M. DeLancey (ed.), *Aspects of International Relations in Africa* (Bloomington: University of Indiana 1979).
100 McGhee, Yale-UN Oral History, p. 6.
101 Rakove, *Kennedy, Johnson and the Non-Aligned World*, p. 29.
102 There was in fact a significant tension between Britain, the US and Belgium over the financing of the projected Belgian atomic energy programme since the 1944 Tripartite Agreement which agreed to pay the Belgian Government, rather than the extracting firm, for Congolese uranium. Britain and the US were unwilling to continue to finance the project unless it was tied to specific plans whereas the Belgians wanted funding more in the form of compensation for training Belgian researchers in America and 'just damages for the wrong [we] Belgians have had to suffer'. They believed the source of this funding should be a surtax on Congolese uranium which would make it more expensive for the American programme. J.E. Helmreich, *United States Relations with Belgium and the Congo, 1940–1960* (Delaware: University of Delaware Press, 1998), pp. 134–135.
103 Namikas, *Battleground Africa*, p. 56.
104 Averell Harriman Papers, Library of Congress, Washington DC (hereafter AHP), Subject Files, Congo, Special Files: Public Service, Kennedy/Administrations, 1958–1971, Folder 5, Subject File Congo (1), Box 448, Inter-departmental Memo, 15 October, 1965.
105 GPL, BAA/RLAA/690, 'Republic of Congo': Newspaper Clippings (Congo) 1963, Bureau of African Affairs, *Chicago Tribune* Editorial (24 February 1963). Quote from Minter, *King Solomon's Mines Revisited*, p. 150.
106 Telegram from the President's Assistant Staff Secretary (Eisenhower) to the Staff Secretary (Goodpaster), at Newport, Rhode Island, 12 July 1960. Schwar and Shaloff, *FRUS, 1958–1960, XIV, Africa*, p. 295.
107 National Security Council (NSC) meeting, 5 May 1960, Editorial Note. Schwar and Shaloff, *FRUS, 1958–1960, XIV, Africa*, p. 274.
108 See M. Bradley and M. Young, *Making Sense of the Vietnam War* (Oxford: Oxford University Press, 2008); M.P. Leffler, *For the Soul of Mankind: The United States, the Soviet Union, and the Cold War* (New York: Hill and Wang, 2008); F. Logevall, *Embers of War: The Fall of an Empire and the Making of America's Vietnam* (New York: Random House, 2014); A.J. Rotter, *The Path to Vietnam: Origins of the American Commitment to Southeast Asia* (Ithaca, NY: Cornell University Press, 1989); M. Young, *The Vietnam Wars, 1945–1990* (New York: HarperCollins, 1991).
109 As Eisenhower instructed the National Security Council (NSC) in 1958: '[I] would like to be on the side of the natives for once … We must believe in the right of colonial peoples to achieve independence … [but] if we emphasized this right too strongly, we created a sense of crisis in relations with the mother countries.' From NSC Memorandum of Discussion, 7 August 1958. Schwar and Shaloff, *FRUS, 1958–1960, XIV, Africa*, p. 20.
110 Memorandum of telephone conversation between President Eisenhower and Secretary of State Herter, 12 July 1960. Schwar and Shaloff, *FRUS, 1958–1960, XIV, Africa*, p. 296.

111 On Guatemala see N. Cullather, *Secret History: The CIA's Classified Account of its Operations in Guatemala, 1952–1954* (Stanford: Stanford University Press, 2006); M.T. Gilderhus, 'The Monroe Doctrine: meanings and implications', *Presidential Studies Quarterly*, 36:1 (2006); P. Gleijeses, *Shattered Hope: The Guatemalan Revolution and the United States, 1944–1954* (Princeton: Princeton University Press, 1992); R.H. Immerman, *The CIA in Guatemala: The Foreign Policy of Intervention* (Austin: University of Texas Press, 1982), pp. 5–16; W. LaFeber, *Inevitable Revolutions: The United States in Central America* (New York: W.W. Norton & Company, 1993); S. Schlesinger, S. Kinzer, J.H. Coatsworth and R.A. Nuccio, *Bitter Fruit: The Story of the American Coup in Guatemala,* revised edition (Cambridge, MA: David Rockefeller Center for Latin American Studies, 2005); J.W. Young, 'Great Britain's Latin American dilemma: the Foreign Office and the overthrow of "Communist" Guatemala, June 1954', *The International History Review*, 8:4 (1986), 573–592.
112 A. Horne, *Macmillan: The Official Biography* (London: Pan Macmillan, 2008), p. 429.
113 Memorandum of conversation between Pierre Wigny, Belgian Foreign Minister, Secretary of State John Foster Dulles and others. Schwar and Shaloff, *FRUS, 1958–1960, XIV, Africa*, p. 252.
114 Lipsey, *Hammarskjöld*, p. 308.
115 McGhee, Yale-UN Oral History, p. 28.

2

The Dag factor

I must do this. God knows where it will lead this Organisation and where it will lead me.
                        (United Nations Secretary-General Dag Hammarskjöld, 1960)[1]

By the first week of July 1960, looting and civil disorder on the streets of Léopoldville, and sporadic incidents of violence against Belgian troops and the European population, led Lumumba and Congolese President Joseph Kasavubu to appeal to the UN for help. Decades before the rhetoric of the 'responsibility to protect' entered into international discourse during the 1990s, Hammarskjöld responded to the Congolese request by immediately declaring that the UN had an obligation to protect the sovereignty of the Congo from Belgian incursion. The dramatic statement above has been attributed to him as he set about arranging a meeting of the Security Council to consider the problem. On 15 July 1960, the first peacekeepers from ONUC arrived into the Congo, signalling the beginning of the largest UN peacekeeping mission that had ever been launched. ONUC consisted of over 19,000 troops and civilian assistants at its peak, costing in the region of $100 million.[2] In terms of size and scope, another mission on this scale would not be launched again until the end of the Cold War. By the middle of August 1960, there were more than 14,500 troops on the ground from India, Ireland, Sweden and some African states.[3]

    Hammarskjöld's main objective was to contain the crisis by ensuring that all aid and support for the Congo came through the UN, thereby preventing the superpowers from drawing the conflict into the Cold War.[4] Many of the members of the Afro-Asian bloc in the General Assembly, including the strongest opponents of colonialism such as Algeria, India, Ghana, Mali and Morocco, viewed the spread of the Cold War into Africa through the Congo as a major threat to peaceful decolonisation. The role of the Afro-Asian bloc was central to UN Congo policy from the beginning and many African leaders viewed the independence of the Congo as a process in which the UN would be inherently involved. Indeed, the Congolese themselves had viewed their independence in tandem with the UN from the beginning.

Even in 1959, leaders envisioned the assertion of their right to self-determination in a situation under the supervision of the UN.[5] Upon receiving the request for intervention from Lumumba and Kasavubu in July 1960, therefore, Hammarskjöld had closely consulted with African representatives who agreed that the Congo required international intervention and urged for the 'Africanisation' of the crisis, by using only African peacekeepers.[6]

From the beginning, the Secretary-General adopted a 'hands on' approach, evoking, for the first time, Article 99 of the UN Charter on 13 July. This provision allowed the Secretary-General to 'bring to the attention of the Security Council, any matter which in his opinion may threaten the maintenance of international peace and security'.[7] By calling for an immediate meeting of the Security Council, Hammarskjöld directly inscribed the crisis on the global security agenda. In his opening statement to the Council on 13 July he recommended that the UN accede to the request from the Government of the Congo for military assistance in defending their independence following the dispatch of Belgian troops to the Congo.[8] This was, as described by *The Economist*, 'a task that has no precedent'.[9] Never before had the UN been asked to intervene in a sovereign country to protect its independence. By invoking his powers under Article 99, Hammarskjöld further defined the nature of his tenure in the Secretariat as activist and interventionist. In addition, the adoption of the resolution by eight votes to none with three abstentions superseded the usual division between the West and the Soviet Bloc.[10]

Hammarskjöld's vigorous and swift response was an extension of his earlier efforts to carve out a more activist role for the UN. The success of the peacekeeping mission in Suez in 1956 had demonstrated the value of neutral intervention, although similar missions in Lebanon and Korea had also raised concerns about the long-term impact of peacekeeping in producing a sustainable resolution to conflict. Until Hammarskjöld's election as Secretary-General in April 1953, Chapter VII provisions of the Charter, which had foreseen a role for the organisation intervening in a conflict, had not been tested by his predecessor, Trygve Lie. Much attention has been paid, even in recent years, to portraying Hammarskjöld as a monkish intellectual who viewed the role of Secretary-General as one that required moral integrity and visionary leadership.[11] Hammarskjöld was more than this, however, he was also an astute politician and he recognised the shifting balance of power within the UN and the necessity to respond to it. In his public statements and press conferences, he referred to the use of 'non-publicized diplomacy' as one of the ways in which negotiations could continue when traditional diplomatic methods such as public diplomacy and conference diplomacy failed. In promoting the role of the UN in fostering an atmosphere for non-publicised diplomacy (or quiet diplomacy) he described the value as being 'the mediating influence of the participation of all those who are vitally interested in peace, while free from an immediate involvement in the issues at stake in terms of prestige or national interest'.[12] Before the outbreak of the crisis, in 1955 Hammarskjöld had been successful in using his methods of quiet diplomacy and his good offices to negotiate the release of eleven US pilots who had been captured by China during the Korean War.

When he consulted with the African states on 12 July before his first statement on the Congo to the Security Council the following day, it was the first time that all the African UN members had met with the Secretary-General in an informal atmosphere, i.e. outside the General Assembly. It was also the first time the Secretary-General created an informal advisory group on a specific conflict in Africa. As the crisis progressed, the Secretary-General continued to meet frequently with members of the African group in an informal setting, which quickly became known as the 'Congo Club'.[13] Outlining to the representatives of Ethiopia, Ghana, Guinea, Liberia, Libya, Morocco, Sudan, Tunisia and the United Arab Republic that the UN would launch a technical assistance programme and a peacekeeping intervention, Hammarskjöld stressed that even though the Congo was not a UN Trusteeship, its political difficulties were the responsibility of the UN. This represented an extension of the ways in which the Secretary-General had up to that point used the powers of his office to deal with special aid requirements for Trust Territories. In earlier speeches to the General Assembly and the UN Economic and Social Council (ECOSOC), Hammarskjöld already signalled his intention to expand the role of the UN to also address other newly independent states when he declared 'I would like to stress, and stress emphatically, that in our approach in this secretariat and in my approach in the report, there is no such priority' [for Trust Territories].[14] With a tacit mandate from ECOSOC and on the basis of a telegram addressed to him from the Addis Ababa Conference of African States on 20 June, Hammarskjöld had in fact been preparing the UN response to the request for intervention, before having ever received it from Lumumba and Kasavubu.[15]

A key feature of Hammarskjöld's plan for the Congo was not just a strengthening of the UN role but also active participation for the African states themselves. He had long believed, and reiterated in his first meeting with the Africans, that 'Africa [was] the best part of the world to take care of its own problems'.[16] This was in fact part of his broader vision for the development of the UN in line with the requests and demands of the Afro-Asian bloc, a view he repeated in further meetings with the African representatives, referring to 'an identity of interests between myself and the cause of the Congo and the cause of Africa'.[17] By drawing together the African states from the beginning of the crisis, Hammarskjöld set about changing the way the UN responded to the challenges of decolonisation, strengthening the capacity of the organisation to respond effectively but also realising his vision for a more activist role for the UN on these questions. In the process, this presented an opportunity for the Afro-Asian countries to coordinate their positions and design cohesive policies and draft resolutions for the Security Council on the Congo question and other issues related to decolonisation. This was an expansion of their position at the UN, moving beyond earlier efforts of actors such as the Front de Libération Nationale (FLN), who used public diplomacy to wage a campaign against French colonialism.[18]

The Africans responded generally positively to Hammarskjöld's Congo plan on 12 July, noting that the Congo was a matter 'of very grave concern' to the African community.[19] African and Asian leaders exercised public and private influence with Congolese leaders and UN officials, such as Ralph J. Bunche, who was Hammarskjöld's Special Representative in Léopoldville. In the early months of the crisis they negotiated with

Lumumba to work closely with the UN in Léopoldville in order to implement resolutions more fully. In New York, a host of Afro-Asian leaders, including Ghanaian Prime Minister Kwame Nkrumah and Indian Premier Jawaharlal Nehru, used the public debates of the 15th session of the General Assembly to influence the Secretary-General to formulate UN Congo policy with attention to the objectives of the Afro-Asian bloc. Going beyond the UN as a mere platform for diplomacy, leaders now used the networks and instruments such as the Congo Club and the Congo Advisory Committee (CAC) that Hammarskjöld created to construct UN Congo policy, as a funnel through which their objectives for the Congo, and Africa more broadly, could be realised. While the FLN intervention at the UN in 1958 harnessed the power of public diplomacy, the African Group now sought to transmogrify this influence to reshape international norms and it was during the Congo crisis that this became a formalised process.[20] Now, Hammarskjöld offered the Afro-Asian bloc the instruments but also the political support of the Secretariat to achieve their aims.

The most effective instrument Hammarskjöld granted to Afro-Asian opinion during the crisis was the creation of the CAC, which he established in July shortly after the passing of the first Security Council resolution on the Congo. An expanded version of the model which was first used in 1956 when an advisory committee was created for the United Nations Emergency Force (UNEF) during the Suez crisis, it was composed of representatives from the countries that had contributed troops to ONUC. The meetings were designed to advise him, through regular deliberations, on the best course of action in the Congo. The creation of the committee and the Congo Club, which met in Hammarskjöld's office once a week (or more frequently when required) to discuss the Congo question over dinner, was indicative of how the Secretary-General sought to activate the instruments of the UN, and the Secretariat, granting it limited agency throughout the crisis. During the initial meetings of the CAC, he assured its members of the open atmosphere he promoted, highlighting that although the committee would have an 'open door policy', there was no outside interference: 'Any time anybody can give us information or advice, we are happy to get it. For that reason there are no closed doors, there is nothing that is definitive … under these circumstances I think that you are fully safeguarded.'[21]

More broadly, the newly independent states, that were now members of the Afro-Asian bloc, had a wide agenda of global reform from decolonisation to development and poverty reduction. As Bernard Firestone has argued, they 'were determined to wrest control of the UN's agenda from its founders'.[22] This led to sweeping debates during these years on the meaning of sovereignty, and the nature of anti-colonial internationalism and the format of post-colonial development. In accordance with Hammarskjöld's efforts to bolster the position of weaker countries within the international system, the CAC gave the Afro-Asian bloc a direct channel to Hammarskjöld as they consulted on the development of ONUC policy but also on a wide range of other economic and developmental questions relevant to the Congo mission as they arose. Indeed, in his statement before the Security Council explaining the role of the CAC, Hammarskjöld declared that the contributing countries would advise him on both the military and civilian aspects of the mission, allowing them to influence directly the state-building process in the Congo. Following the UNEF model, the host country was not represented on the committee, which, as the Congo crisis deepened, created tensions with the Congolese and some members such as Ethiopia and India who believed that the Congo should be represented. Crucially, committee members were also in a position to advise the Secretary-General on the application and therefore the interpretation of Security Council mandates, which also created problems when Hammarskjöld's interpretation differed from that of the Congolese who feared the overt interference of other African countries. As the Indian delegate noted: 'It is not for members of the Advisory Committee to approve or disapprove of any such general interpretations of authority.'[23]

While the creation of the CAC was linked to Hammarskjöld's personal view of the role of the UN as supporting the role of smaller nations, thereby allowing him to capitalise on the changing composition of the General Assembly, and carve out a more active role for the Secretariat in promoting their agenda, its structural position led to difficulties over authority in the Congo. Hammarskjöld operated in a dichotomous fashion, whereby his dynamic approach to the Charter allowed for the reinterpretation of existing norms with the simultaneous creation of innovative procedures.[24] One such procedure that arose from Hammarskjöld's efforts in the Congo, beginning with the establishment of the CAC, was to fully operationalise the use of his discretion in his relationship with the committee.[25] In creating two specific advisory committees on the Congo, he increased his leverage to steer the operation through the General Assembly and the Security Council with the support of like-minded states.[26] Hammarskjöld's policy towards the crisis, therefore, reflected his wider vision for a more activist Secretariat and a socialising space on committees specifically devoted to the Congo. These dimensions were designed to enforce each other to create policy, the viability of which was quickly tested by events on the ground, which raised precisely the questions of authority over which Indian delegates had earlier expressed concern.

Belgian intransigence

Following the first resolution on the Congo of 13 July 1960 which granted UN peacekeepers a mandate to enter the Congo, Britain and the US provided logistical and financial support for ONUC and publicly supported Hammarskjöld's initiatives during Security Council debates. Privately, they engaged Belgium in tripartite talks through July and August 1960 as the Congo and other African states repeatedly called for a strengthening of ONUC's mandate and the removal of all Belgian troops. The earlier British sympathy for the Belgian position remained consistent even when Brussels refused to withdraw Belgian troops until the situation was restored in which 'Belgian and other technicians could return and carry on their work unmolested'.[27] The British Embassy in Brussels reported that the debacle in the Congo had served as a 'moral shock' to both Belgium and the West.[28] In response the Foreign Office instructed British UN representatives to concert with their American colleagues and avoid voting for a resolution that would call for an immediate withdrawal of all Belgian troops.[29] In a conversation with Hammarskjöld, one British delegate reminded him that 'if the Africans, with the Russians behind them, resumed their harrying of the Belgians in the Security Council, we and the other friends of Belgium would be put in an exceedingly difficult position'. However, Hammarskjöld was less interested in preserving Western unity at the UN than he was in resolving the conflict. Six days later, the British UN mission noted that 'Hammarskjöld's mood has certainly hardened against the Belgians',[30] and despite their efforts to keep the Security Council resolutions more moderate, on 9 August Resolution 146 was passed, which noted that the UN had been prevented from fully implementing earlier decisions and called upon Belgium 'to immediately withdraw its troops from the province'.[31]

The Belgians responded to this hardening of attitudes at the UN by evoking the Cold War dimensions of the crisis in order to secure British and American support for their position. Wigny decried the Russian attacks on the Western position at the Security Council and pointed repeatedly to the danger of Belgian NATO bases in the Congo falling into the hands of the Soviet Union.[32] Hesitant to criticise their NATO ally openly, officials in both London and Washington were also sympathetic to Belgian arguments that they had to maintain a presence in the region to guarantee the safety of the European community there and secure the UMHK enterprise. Britain abstained from the first Security Council Resolution on 13 July, which called for the creation of a UN force to assist the Central Government to restore order and the withdrawal of all Belgian troops. Justifying their decision to the British Parliament, it was noted that 'it would be terrible if the Belgian troops withdrew and left a vacuum before the arrival of some other organised force ... Her Majesty's Government did not feel that it would be right in the present state of knowledge of the situation of the Congo to call for Belgian troops to withdraw without any qualification'.[33]

Mindful of this tacit support, instead of withdrawing its forces from the Congo, Belgium proceeded to relocate them in Tshombe's 'independent' state of Katanga. In addition to this failure to implement the Security Council Resolution, Belgian financial and political support for the breakaway regime contradicted statements from Wigny that Belgium did not officially support Tshombe. By propping up Katanga in this indirect way and encouraging other Western countries to do the same, Belgium gradually isolated its own position within the Western bloc.[34] Further hostility towards the UN and failure to implement its resolutions served to inflame relations with the Afro-Asian members and aggravated tensions with the Congolese Government. Despite assurances to the Secretary-General that all Belgian troops would be withdrawn by 29 August, there was consistent evidence to the contrary.[35] Just three days before the deadline, *Reuters* reported that Belgian troops, rather than being removed, were simply being relocated to the Ruanda-Urundi and Angolan borders. Fearing the eruption of a border war, Mr Caba, the Guinean representative on the CAC, commented: 'This is extremely dangerous, and perhaps just when we thought that the fire in the Congo was extinguished, other fires on the frontiers may break out.'[36]

The inability to persuade Belgium to adhere to UN resolutions had a damaging effect on the Secretariat and Hammarskjöld in particular. It appeared that as he sat in New York making assurances to the Congolese Government and the Afro-Asian representatives that Brussels would abide by the agreement to withdraw, the reality of troop movements in the Congo itself was very different. This complicated the discussions, bringing in allegations of collusion and partisanship between the West and the Secretary-General while, simultaneously, the Belgian actions undermined his authority. To the international public it created 'the impression of a United Nations vacillating between different aspirations, now giving its favour, now withdrawing it'.[37] The fracas caused by the Belgian actions increased Hammarskjöld's determination to strengthen the role of the African states in the civil and military missions.[38] In his report to the Security Council on 8 August detailing the difficulties of implementing the resolution on the Congo, he described Belgium's 'submission' to 'mean only the absence of active resistance and that naturally presents us with a serious problem'.[39]

ONUC had initially been well-received by Lumumba and his Government upon the entry of UN troops into the Congo in July, but as the political crisis deepened, Lumumba had quickly become frustrated with the limitations of the peacekeeping force which he believed should help him to end the secession of Katanga. Once it became clear that Hammarskjöld did not intend the peacekeeping force to be used against secession in Katanga and the neighbouring province of South Kasai, rich in diamonds, which had announced its independence under Albert Kalondji on 9 July, he set about launching his own military campaign with the Force Publique, now called Armée Nationale Congolais (ANC), to restore territorial unity across the country.[40] He appealed to Moscow for aid to support his campaign, fortifying the impression of a swing towards Communism with provocative public statements such as 'Vive l'Union Sovietique. Vive Khrushchev'.[41] The Soviet Union, aware of the logistical difficulties of granting large-scale support to the Congo, and hesitant to accelerate the Cold War, replied to his request by supplying a limited amount of materiel support: thirty Ilyushin-18 planes for troop transportation, and weapons and ammunition for the campaign against Katanga.[42] Lumumba's appeal to Moscow was both militarily and politically calamitous. The aid arrived too late to secure a victory against the well-armed and well-trained Katangan gendarmerie defending the province. Moreover, it had the effect of making Lumumba *persona non grata* in Washington, and sealed the American impression of him as a volatile and mercurial leader who should be removed from the political scene.

Ousting Lumumba

[T]read[ing] on a ground where angels fear to tread.[43]

On 5 September the Congolese President Joseph Kasavubu announced on the national radio that he had sacked Lumumba as Prime Minister, throwing the country into a constitutional crisis. The British Foreign Office reported that the situation on the ground was extremely tense and that it 'is liable within a very short time to threaten the whole basis of the United Nations operation in the Congo'.[44] London now sought to coordinate with Nkrumah to meet with the Secretary-General and discuss the possibility of strengthening the UN mandate, although it was noted that they were only prepared to consider allowing 'outside' forces to act through the UN. In an effort to preserve the unity of the Western position, the Foreign Office advised both the British Embassy in Léopoldville and the UK Mission to the UN, to coordinate closely with the US and seek common ground in their approaches to Lumumba.[45] By 1 September the British Representative Sir Harold Caccia reported that the Americans regarded Lumumba as 'a disaster' and advocated for his removal, but had not discussed their views with the Secretary-General, nor had they any plans to do so.[46] The British opinion was that a federal arrangement might be the ideal solution for the Congo and internally they debated presenting the idea to Hammarskjöld and persuading him to discuss it with the African states. Rejecting the feasibility of this idea, the UK mission reported that Hammarskjöld was largely directing UN Congo policy and the members of the CAC 'acquiesce[d] [with] his views'.[47] Against the powerful position of the Secretary-General, backed by the Afro-Asian states, the British were able to achieve little more than supporting Hammarskjöld's plans.

In the State Department, Kasavubu's attempt to dismiss Lumumba was a welcome addition to their plans to remove him altogether. 'Taking the James Bond route', as Madeline Kalb described it, from August the CIA had undertaken plans to assassinate Lumumba by dispatching an agent equipped with poison to Léopoldville.[48] There has been a long debate amongst historians about whether or not this CIA plot was carried out with the authority of the President. Recently released State Department files and the results of the United States Senate Select Committee to Study Governmental Operations with Respect to Intelligence Activities (Church Committee) into this matter in 1975 revealed that the CIA maintained a very intimate relationship with some Congolese politicians, making payments to Kasavubu, Mobutu (at that point the army Chief of Staff), Foreign Minister Justin Bomboko and others instrumental in his removal from office.[49] The Chief of the CIA station in Léopoldville, Larry Devlin, remains adamant that although he received the orders for assassination, he did not execute the plan.[50] Rather, the CIA supported Kasavubu's announcement by organising anti-Lumumba demonstrations in the capital.[51] It has also been argued that it was in fact the UN who helped Kasavubu organise his coup with the aim of ousting Lumumba.[52] Hammarskjöld's Special Representative in Léopoldville, Andrew Cordier (who was regarded by many as acting as a conduit for American policy during negotiations on the Congo), is alleged to have instructed Kasavubu along these lines in the weeks leading up to the coup.[53] Indeed a cable from Hammarskjöld giving his authorisation for Cordier's plan revealed that in his current position, the Secretary-General wanted to emphasise to the Central Government the risks of their current activities. 'Nothing is ideal', he remarked, 'but we should not sacrifice the good for the ideal'.[54] In the wake of Kasavubu's announcement, the UN decision to close the airport and the radio station – thereby preventing Lumumba from rallying support, but not Kasavubu who had access to broadcasting facilities across the river in Brazzaville – was later defended by Hammarskjöld as arising from the desire to avoid any action which would appear partisan.[55] However, this decision in particular produced exactly the opposite effect, creating a clear impression of favouritism towards Kasavubu. Although this has been interpreted as such by many historians, the allegations of UN complicity should be considered in the context of the relationship between Hammarskjöld and Lumumba, which had deteriorated rapidly between July and August 1960.

The key difference of opinion between them centred on the function of ONUC and how the mandate to restore law and order should be implemented. In Lumumba's view, the UN force should be used to militarily end the secession of Katanga but to Hammarskjöld it was 'unthinkable' that UN soldiers would be instructed to strike against Belgian forces. Relations between the two soured further during Lumumba's visit to New York in July when negotiations with the Secretary-General were dogged by a further 'series of misunderstandings and disagreements' about how the UN operation should proceed.[56] By the time their meetings were over, according to the Congolese Ambassador to the UN, Thomas Kanza, 'Lumumba had become convinced that Hammarskjöld was working mainly for Western interests'. For his part, the biographer Roger Lipsey reports that during these days of negotiation a sense of 'distance and mutual distrust increasingly prevailed, never to be overcome'.[57]

In an effort to resolve this discord and bring about a solution to the Katanga problem, Hammarskjöld personally flew to the provincial capital Elisabethville to meet with the self-declared Katangan leader, Tshombe, in August. His aim was to negotiate the peaceful entry of UN troops and the withdrawal of Belgian troops from the military bases in the province. Explaining his decision to directly engage with Tshombe to a meeting of African countries including Ethiopia, Ghana and Morocco, who were among the countries with the largest contributions of troops to ONUC, on 17 August, he described it as 'the only card really remaining in my hand'.[58] The African leaders responded positively to his efforts, but Mr Quaison-Sackey, the representative of Ghana, noted that Lumumba had objected strongly to Hammarskjöld's actions.

Early in August, Lumumba had conferred with a numerous African leaders from Tunisia, Ghana, Morocco, Ethiopia, Algeria and Ghana. The provisional revolutionary Government of Algeria in particular stoked his anti-colonial sentiments and even offered to send one of their members, Serge Michel, to serve as his press attaché. In Guinea he conferred with Sékou Touré, who urged him not to compromise, and finally he met with Nkrumah in Ghana, arguably his closest African ally, who reiterated his support for Lumumba's Government. The effect was, as Kanza describes, 'hypnotic'.[59] Upon his return to Léopoldville, Lumumba launched a tirade against the UN and in particular criticised Hammarskjöld's plans to negotiate directly with Katanga. With provocative rhetoric he announced 'the Secretary-General of UNO preferred to deal with a traitor to our country, the Belgians' puppet, Tshombe'.[60]

Hammarskjöld's response to Lumumba's increasingly irate public statements was one of annoyance. Two days after his visit to Tshombe, the gambit had proved successful and UN troops entered the province without encountering any armed resistance from Belgian troops or the Katangan gendarmerie along the way. The situation was, however, far from resolved. As Lipsey notes, Tshombe benefited from the Belgian withdrawal, as he was also now able to position his well-armed and well-trained army of European mercenaries in key locations throughout the province, entrenching his position.[61] It was at this point that Lumumba, steering events towards armed conflict, launched his own military campaign against Katanga with the ANC to forcibly disarm the Katangan army, oust Tshombe and end the secession of Katanga and South Kasai. Along the way, the ANC clashed with UN troops, exacerbating tensions and deepening the divide between the two leaders.

Lumumba continued to maintain that if Hammarskjöld did not 'hasten the speedy implementation of the Security Council's resolution, he will bear the responsibility for any possible eventualities, which may occur any day now, and which could be due to the delay in carrying out the resolution'.[62] He responded angrily to Hammarskjöld's trip to Katanga, refusing to meet the Secretary-General on his return through Léopoldville. In response, Hammarskjöld refused Lumumba's request that he delay his return to New York by one day in order to allow the Congolese UN delegation to travel with him.[63] Their exchange was published in a series of letters which caused anxiety among the African group at the UN. Such was the animosity that Hammarskjöld was asked in the CAC to outline in detail the disagreement with Lumumba and their failure to meet in Léopoldville. The strain was evident in his reply: 'quite frankly gentlemen, I saw some difficulty in a twenty-four hour journey together after an exchange of views which, on one side, at least, had been somewhat temperamental'.[64] Relations with Tshombe were barely any better. Despite acquiescing to the entry of UN troops into Katanga, he accused the UN of interfering in Congolese political affairs. As Bunche warned Hammarskjöld in a report from Elisabethville in August, 'Mr. Tshombe's appeal for "mobilisation" and the calling out of the painted-face, spear-carrying "warriors" who can arouse crowds and set off conflict, could mean that the United Nations troops would be forced into the hazardous position of using their arms in legitimate self-defence against unruly segments of the public'.[65]

The political chaos that erupted in Léopoldville following Kasavubu's announcement and rumours that the dismissal of Lumumba had been orchestrated with the help of the UN, turned Lumumba definitively against the UN efforts. The situation deteriorated further when, despite the Congolese Parliament's vote of confidence in retaining Lumumba as Prime Minister and supporting his Government, the Chief of the Army, Colonel Mobutu (later Mobutu Sese Sekou) announced a coup and established what he termed a 'College of Commissioners' to run the country and suspended both the Parliament and the Senate until the constitutional vacuum could be filled appropriately. Lumumba, still engaged in his ailing military campaign against Katanga, tried one last parting shot. On 16 September, he issued an ultimatum, denouncing the actions of the UN, which he described as 'destructive', and giving the organisation eight days to withdraw its troops after which the UN would be responsible for 'shedding the blood of its technicians and troops'.[66] In response, Hammarskjöld turned towards the African states, particularly more temperate allies like Monghi Slim of Tunisia, encouraging them to use their influence to assuage the, by now, frantic and erratic Lumumba.

Foreshadowing the later formal rupture in their unity that would occur in early 1961 when the African group became divided between the Casablanca Group (who were vehemently opposed to any manifestation of neo-colonialism in Africa and sought a Pan-African union) and the Monrovia Group (who, while also anti-colonial, believed in more moderate forms of cooperation) the larger Afro-Asian bloc now became internally divided as to the best course of action in the Congo. Some states, such as Ghana, Guinea, Mali and the United Arab Republic, were adamant that Lumumba remained the legitimate Prime Minister and continued to support his beleaguered campaign against Katanga. Others, however, such as Ethiopia, India, Indonesia, Liberia, Morocco and Tunisia, advocated a more moderate approach, placing primacy on the role of the UN, and raising doubts about the stability and political experience of Lumumba's Government.[67] What they all agreed on, however, was an effort to extort patience from him and they counselled him privately to cooperate with the UN, halt attacks on UN troops and 'mend his fences with Hammarskjöld'.[68] Following a discussion along these lines, Lumumba appeared to adopt a more conciliatory approach in the concluding speech at the Conference of Foreign Ministers of African States in Léopoldville in August, saluting the UN effort and reaffirming the trust between the Congolese Government and the UN.[69]

With the resurgence of tension between Hammarskjöld and Lumumba in September, the Afro-Asian bloc seized upon the public platform offered by the looming 15th session of the General Assembly to advocate a solution which would reinstate him as the Congolese Prime Minister. His closest ally, Nkrumah, had maintained a lengthy correspondence with Hammarskjöld since the beginning of the crisis. By the middle of September he warned the Secretary-General that the situation in the Congo placed Ghana in 'a most embarrassing and invidious situation vis-à-vis the legitimate government'. He denounced the use of Ghana's troops 'almost exclusively as [a] cat's paw' against Lumumba in preventing him from using his own radio station.[70] Following Kasaubu's dismissal of Lumumba on 5 September, UN troops had surrounded the radio station in Léopoldville in an attempt to prevent Lumumba from inciting civil unrest. However, it also had the effect of preventing him from gathering popular support to challenge Kasavubu. As a result many of the African states pointed to this UN action as evidence of complicity in his removal from office. Nkrumah warned that if the situation was not remedied, he would remove his troops from UN command and place them at Lumumba's disposal. Hammarskjöld responded defensively, maintaining that the actions of ONUC had been necessary to maintain law and order, but within a day the radio station was reopened.[71] He continued to insist that the terms of reference for ONUC were by invitation of the Congolese themselves and, in his correspondence with Congolese leaders, he rejected the accusation that he had ignored their wishes.[72]

At this point even states that had advocated a more moderate approach by the UN, such as Guinea, were disturbed by the predicament of ONUC in dealing simultaneously with the situation in Léopoldville and the secessionist regimes in Katanga and South Kasai.[73] These concerns were shared by India, one of the leaders of the Afro-Asian bloc and the provider of over a quarter of the troops to ONUC. India's material and financial support was essential to the success of the mission and Indian political support was key to maintaining the integrity of the bloc. In early September, the Indian delegation at the UN warned New Delhi that, according to reports from officials who had just attended the conference in Léopoldville, 'the situation in Congo [was] hopeless'.[74] India viewed its role at the UN as being to advocate a non-aligned position among the African states, and prevent the Cold War seeping into conflicts across the continent.[75] When the crisis had erupted, Indian officials immediately understood the symbolic importance of the Congo for other African nations. The Indian High Commission in Nairobi pointed to the racial dimensions of the conflict and its impact on the relationship between white settlers and black native populations in Kenya and Nairobi, where 'much political capital [is] being made of conditions in Congo'.[76] While India pledged technical support for the peacekeeping mission, Indian delegates at the UN quickly became irritated at Nkrumah's repeated emphasis on African rather than Afro-Asian solidarity, which Nehru sought to rectify. In his view the Congo mission needed serious revision at several levels. Speaking before the General Assembly the following month, he pushed for a stronger mandate, arguing that as the situation in the Congo emphasised the increasing responsibilities of the United Nations, the executive power of the Secretary-General should be strengthened.[77]

In an emergency session of the General Assembly from 17 to 19 September, the position of the Afro-Asian bloc and the CAC in advising the Congolese and the Secretary-General in a conciliatory capacity was formalised by Resolution 1474.[78] Indian and Ghanaian representatives now led the campaign to the main sessions of the General Assembly. In a speech on 23 September, Nkrumah criticised the failure of the UN to fully implement previous Security Council resolutions and hailed the complicity of the imperial powers in exacerbating the crisis.[79] Beyond the General Assembly he also called for the UN to act with the legitimate Government of the Congo (by which he was referring to Lumumba) and urged other African states to play their part in 'advising and counselling the United Nations … to keep the Cold War out of Africa and resist the re-introduction of colonialism in any form'.[80]

The two-thirds majority held by the Afro-Asians in the General Assembly also came into play as the push to recognise Lumumba as the Congo's legitimate leader and engineer a more proactive UN Congo policy accelerated, and was echoed through a series of lively debates on the Congo. Advocating this position in his address to the General Assembly on 3 October, Nehru called for the UN to help reconvene the elected parliament in the Congo and to send a delegation to Léopoldville to monitor the interference of foreign troops and personnel in Congolese affairs.[81] Away from the public spotlight, Nehru was adamant that unless Hammarskjöld engineered a new direction for the UN's Congo policy and took a firmer line against Belgium, he would start withdrawing his troops from ONUC.[82]

Hammarskjöld responded to this mounting pressure by moving Congo policy further into line with Afro-Asian demands. He announced a new UN policy in the Congo in October 1960 which promised a stronger line against Belgium and recognised that no solution was possible without Lumumba. Launching his annual report before the opening of the 15th session, he called for African unity on the Congo predicament.[83] This alignment towards African views was deliberate, strategic and perhaps even ideological but also certainly the result of political realities. As Slim pointed out to the Security Council, the UN was operating in the Congo within a framework of African solidarity and 'unity is essential for the Congo as well as for Africa'.[84] Caba, the representative of Guinea, went even further when, repeating comments he made in a CAC meeting, he proclaimed that 'the situation in the Congo is a dangerous threat to the specific interest of all Africans conscious of Africa as a whole … For us, Guinea is equivalent to the Congo, and the Congo is equivalent to Africa'.[85] With sentiments and statements regarding the imperative nature of the crisis for Africa echoing around New York, a push for a change in the direction of UN Congo policy now began in earnest.

The credentials debate

On a plane journey from Brussels to Brazzaville in July 1960, while discussing the crisis with Lumumba's UN representative, Kanza, Hammarskjöld remarked: 'I don't know what you think about the United States, Thomas, but it seems to me right now that America is the only ally the central Congolese government can count on.'[86] Kanza responded with scepticism. He had witnessed first-hand the hostility with which American officials had received Lumumba during his visit.[87] While it had become apparent by September that the US had no intention of supporting Lumumba, Hammarskjöld's warning that American support for the Central Government could prove formative was made clear in the campaign that American representatives at the UN waged until November, which sought recognition of Kasavubu's regime as the official Government of the Congo. The Congolese constitutional dilemma of September spilled over into the General Assembly when Kasavubu and Lumumba both sent a delegation to New York, each claiming to be the official representatives of the Congo. As both delegations lobbied for UN recognition before a vote was taken in the General Assembly on 22 November, America and Britain tried to coordinate their policies.

By September 1960, it had become clear to the State Department that 'the whole future of UN as [a] peace organization might now be at stake in Congo'.[88] Although the US contributed 50 per cent of the costs for the ONUC mission, the State Department resisted Hammarskjöld's attempts to remove the Belgians completely from the Congo and continued to support the overall position of Brussels.[89] In one of the first instances of open disagreement with the Secretary-General and the Afro-Asian bloc, the State Department opposed negotiating with Lumumba.[90] Considering the Congolese Parliament's vote of support for Lumumba on 13 September, the State Department viewed it likely that he would resume his position if Parliament was reinstated. In order to prevent this from happening, the African Bureau granted the American Ambassador in Léopoldville, Timberlake, and the CIA a wide scope to prop up Mobutu's College of Commissioners, while in New York, the American delegation waged a campaign at the UN to have Kasavubu recognised as the Congo's legitimate leader.[91]

While the Afro-Asian bloc and African leaders continued to make clear statements of support for Lumumba, American representatives engaged in a rigorous campaign of vote collection for Kasavubu, who they considered a more reliable, Western-friendly leader to install in the Congo on the basis of CIA intelligence and the advice of the Binza Group. Kasavubu himself, who normally preferred to shun the spotlight, travelled to New York at American urging to address the General Assembly and claim his right to represent the Congo.[92] At the same time, Timberlake denied Lumumba and Kanza a visa to travel to New York to do the same.[93] Such was the American activism eliciting support for

Kasavubu among other delegations in the General Assembly that one outsider remarked that he had 'never before witnessed such a display of arm-twisting'.[94] Part of the reason for the intense lobbying that the State Department now undertook with Latin American allies and former French African colonies was the recognition that Hammarskjöld regarded Lumumba as the legitimate Prime Minister. Discussions with the Secretary-General had revealed that despite the animosity of relations with Lumumba, by the middle of October, no doubt due to the pressure from the Afro-Asian states, Hammarskjöld had come to the position that no solution to the Congo was possible without him.[95] In direct contrast, US representatives were instructed to reflect the State Department's view during General Assembly and Security Council debates that there was 'no question as to the identity of the head of state of the Republic of the Congo. He is President Joseph Kasavubu'.[96]

The British remained hesitant to openly support Kasavubu's delegation, in order to maintain good relations with the other African states who loudly proclaimed their support for Lumumba. Ghana, in particular, was increasingly hostile on this issue. Responding to Nkrumah's General Assembly speech, in which he threatened to withdraw Ghanaian troops from ONUC unless the Secretary-General supported Lumumba, Macmillan appealed for calm. He urged Nkrumah not to recall his soldiers, pointing out that doing so 'would surely have the most unfortunate results, for instead of the virtually united African support for Mr. Hammarskjöld and his collaborators, both military and civilian, we should be faced with the lamentable spectacle of the disintegration of the UN force itself and the possibility of foreign support for one or other of the contending parties'. Macmillan also highlighted the emphasis on the provision of an African solution to the Congo problem and pressed the British position that it was more important to support the UN, than to choose sides in the fracas between Lumumba and Kasavubu.[97] The appeal had only a limited effect on Nkrumah, as Hammarskjöld's revised Congo policy was a direct consequence of his threat to withdraw troops. Moreover, the activism and influence of the African states now became the overriding concern for the Foreign Office and it was in this context that British Congo policy was developed.

Through the 15th session of the General Assembly, Britain was faced with a series of challenges to British African policy. From September 1960 to April 1961 the General Assembly dealt with almost twenty questions relating to colonial issues, including in British territories in Tanganyika and Cameroon and the obligations of states regarding the transmission of information on non-self-governing territories. These debates were dominated by an atmosphere of militant anti-colonialism, in which Britain could do little but continue to assuage relations through appeals on a bilateral level. Key among them was the relationship with the United Arab Republic (UAR) led by Egyptian President Gamal Abdel Nasser. Following the fallout from the Suez conflict in 1956, relations between Cairo and London were at a low ebb. On 22 September, however, the UAR approached the Foreign Office to support its candidacy for a rotating seat on the Security Council, creating an opportunity for cooperation between the two states. Engaging with the proposal, the Foreign Office turned to the US, cabling their intention to support the Egyptian candidacy. The State Department recognised that this was a 'rare British opportunity to improve relations with UAR', and subsequently agreed not to oppose the UAR for the seat.[98] By supporting the British initiative to improve relations with Cairo in this way, the US was able to leverage Britain into taking a stronger position in support of Kasavubu's delegation.

With the aim of using British contacts with African states to gather support for Kasavubu, the US now sought to elicit more active participation from the Foreign Office in the campaign to seat Kasavubu's delegation. The American position was that it was 'of the utmost importance that African opinion be exerted. Although Nkrumah is at the moment being difficult, British pressure may bring him into line again. Nigeria when independent will loyally support every effort to prevent Russian influence in Congo'.[99] In a conversation between Frank Wisner, an American UN representative, and the British delegate, H.S. Stephenson, Wisner expressed the deep concerns of the State Department over the difference of opinion between the US and the UK on the question of tactics to seat the Congolese President's delegation. Stephenson reported that 'the Americans were very upset indeed at what they termed our refusal to give full support to this operation'.[100] After striking a deal on the proposed seat for the UAR in the Security Council, British delegates at the UN now joined in the American campaign to secure a majority of votes in the General Assembly debate on the question on 22 November. The Commonwealth Relations Office (CRO) indicated that the time had come to remedy the vacuum of power in the Congo and cabled British embassies across Africa that 'it seems most desirable for practical reasons that Kasavubu's nominees who because of his position are the only group having the semblance of a legitimate claim, should be seated'. From Ottawa to Pretoria and Salisbury to Lagos, British Ambassadors were now instructed to gather support for Kasavubu among the relevant governments.[101]

The general response to the British appeal was mixed at best. In a personal message, British Foreign Secretary Alec-Douglas Home appealed to the Canadian Foreign Minister Howard Charles Green for unity among Commonwealth members, in light of the difficult British position in the General Assembly, noting that 'Once [Kasavubu is seated] it will be impossible for all of us to be attacked with the same venom by the Afro-Asians, and they will hesitate to attack one of their own colour so vehemently'.[102] However, Canada signalled its intention to abstain from the General Assembly vote. In addition, the Foreign Office miscalculated its ability to pressure Nigeria, which had just been granted independence, to act as a proxy to influence the Afro-Asian states. Despite instructions to the contrary from the Nigerian Prime Minister Abubakar Tafawa Balewa, urged on by the British Ambassador in Lagos, the Foreign Minister, Jaja Wachuku, who was representing the country at the UN, refused to follow the instructions to vote for Kasavubu's delegation.[103]

Wachuku had just been appointed head of the newly created Conciliation Commission for Congo, which had the aim of restoring Parliament as soon as possible. He rejected the directions from Lagos as he felt that it was important to remain impartial in order for the Commission's work to be successful. As a result, Nigeria refused to participate in the voting and Wachuku declared that 'he could not be a party to any vote which tended to divide the Africans'.[104] Despite British manoeuvring behind the scenes and the personal intervention of the British Consul with the Nigerian Prime

Minister in the days leading up to the vote, it was to no avail. This rebuff created resentment among Foreign Office officials and reflected the diminishing British influence among African members of the Commonwealth. In a face-saving gesture, the British Mission to the UN telegrammed the Foreign Office that despite Nigeria's actions, it was essential to maintain good relations with Wachuku and the Nigerians, who, it was pointed out, 'will be most important in other items of direct concern to us, which are about to come up in the Assembly, particularly the Cameroons and the Soviet item on colonialism'.[105]

Despite the sustained objections from the pro-Lumumba states, including Ceylon, Ghana, Guinea, India, Indonesia Mali, Morocco and the UAR, the US-led campaign eventually proved successful. After pushing the matter through the Credentials Committee, which came out in favour of seating Kasavubu on 10 November, the Ghanaian sponsored resolution of 9 November to further postpone the debate was reversed. During this period, to compensate for the apparent lack of British influence with the African group, American delegates stepped up pressure on Latin American states and the former French colonies in Africa to vote to recognise Kasavubu.[106] In the final vote on 22 November, after weeks of arm-twisting, the General Assembly voted in favour of Kasavubu by fifty-three to twenty-four with nineteen abstentions. Despite this apparent victory, the display of Anglo-American strong-arming increased resentment among the Afro-Asians and further divided the US from Hammarskjöld, who was 'appalled' by the spectacle.[107] In parallel to the controversy surrounding the credentials debate, the position of Britain and the US during the 15th session of the General Assembly was further complicated by two other issues; the Soviet troika proposal and the campaign to declare a formal end to colonialism.

The troika proposal

As early as the first week of August, Hammarskjöld had cabled his deputy, Cordier, that: 'The United Nations cannot stand for an isolated regionalism which goes against the whole of the organisation; regionalism can be accepted as a tool of, and bridge to, universalism but must be resisted by the organisation if it puts itself up against universalism'.[108] He was referring to the role of Cold War as Congo debates on the Security Council and in the General Assembly brought tensions out into the open. During one exchange between the American representative Cabot-Lodge and his Soviet counterpart Vasily V. Kuznetsov, the latter introduced a draft resolution which called for the withdrawal of Belgian troops in three days. In the course of a speech denouncing Western 'colonialism', he said that if 'the aggression' continued, more effective measures would be necessary, both by the UN and by the 'peace-loving states' that sympathised with the Congo 'a cause'.[109] Cabot-Lodge replied immediately, warning: 'With the other United Nations members we will do whatever may be necessary to prevent the intrusion of any military forces not requested by the United Nations.' This atmosphere of mounting hostility paralysed the proceedings of the Security Council. After one particularly acrimonious exchange on 17 September negotiations were suspended because the lack 'of unanimity among its members ... has prevented it from exercising its primary responsibility for the maintenance of international peace and security'.[110]

Khrushchev's decision to travel personally to New York to speak at the General Assembly indicated the extent to which Moscow viewed the crisis through a Cold War lens. During his speech he presented a proposal for radical reform of the UN, justified, he argued, by the organisation's poor handling of the conflict. He proposed that the position of Secretary-General should be abolished and replaced by three representatives from each of the voting blocs in the General Assembly – the West, the Soviet bloc and the Afro-Asian non-aligned countries.[111] The Secretary-General and Western representatives alike reacted with shock to Khrushchev's troika initiative. US Secretary of State Christian Herter termed the proposal 'a real declaration of war against the structure, the personnel and the location of the United Nations'.[112] It also demonstrated how security conflicts related to decolonisation through the infusion of Cold War politics could directly impact the UN. Such an outright attack on the UN required decisive action on colonialism to mute the Soviet proposal lest it be viewed favourably by the Afro-Asian states. It further increased American concerns about the expansion of Soviet influence among members of the Afro-Asian bloc.

Britain shared these concerns, especially after one infamous incident when the President of the General Assembly, Frederick Boland, shattered the presidential gavel while calling Khrushchev to order after he interrupted Macmillan's address by banging his shoe on the table. Responding to the troika proposal, the British UN delegation advocated a tough line to oppose the plan 'perhaps by threatening, if not withdrawal from UN by major powers, at least financial cold shoulder and tepid cooperation'.[113] The Congo debate was no exception. Many Foreign Office officials believed that in order to prevent further accusations of neo-colonialism, and maintain good relations with African states, and particularly more radical members such as the UAR, openly taking sides in the Congolese political struggle was not advisable. As one official noted, promoting Kasavubu, although he was friendly towards the West, may be interpreted by the African states as support for a 'regime which could be represented as serving Western "colonialist" purposes'.[114] The effects would be to fortify support for Lumumba among the African states, strengthening his position and ultimately diminishing British credibility.

The troika proposal, which arose in the context of the Congo debate, raised other dimensions of the problem such as the ongoing broader discussions about the nature of the UN environment and the anti-colonial crusade. British UN delegates cabled the Foreign Office that the Congo was now inextricably linked with colonial issues as it had served to unite the Africans behind the idea of keeping the Cold War out of their continent and that as a result 'the "imperialists" will have to walk very warily'.[115] Frederick Samuel Northedge has described the general nature of British policy at the United Nations as having two distinct strands; that of being hostile to fundamental changes in the structure of international politics, and also in the British preference for Hammarskjöld's brand of quiet diplomacy, where the rhetorical combat of the public speeches would be substituted for reasonable, closed-door negotiations.[116] The highly charged atmosphere in New York rendered this approach difficult as the colonial dimension of the Congo debates repeatedly raised criticisms of the colonial record of the British Government. By January 1961, two specific areas of policy development were outlined as key to improve the British position at the UN; consolidating relations with the Afro-Asian bloc, primarily through the relationship with India, and collaboration with the US. A Confidential Report recommended that the central aim should be 'achieving better Anglo-United States co-ordination of policy and tactics at the UN'.[117] It was also evident that British policymakers had a clear idea of the specific challenges to their position within the UN and the realisation that the nature of the organisation had undergone profound changes through 1960.[118] Sir Andrew Cohen, the British representative to the UN Trusteeship Council, wrote to the Foreign Office that significant ground had been lost with the UN preoccupation over the issues of colonialism. He further raised the question of whether 'there is any point at which we can hope effectively to contain UN policies in the future; what in the new circumstances, ought to be our own working interpretations of the limits of UN competence'.[119] The very question of UN proficiency in the area of colonial policy rested on the underlying assumption that Britain, with years of experience as a colonial power, would be better placed to direct policy on these issues in its own territories.[120]

Since the Anglo-American negotiations on colonialism during the Yalta conference in 1945, it had been clear that imperial practice through the creation and maintenance of the colonial system had to change. Despite the fear even then that the UN would act as an anti-colonial assembly, the British were forced to capitulate to the US on the terms of the Trusteeship system, even those the Foreign Office found most objectionable – the issue of visiting missions and the reporting on conditions within territories to the UN. Otherwise, as William Roger Louis has noted, the British were faced with the abandonment of the UN before it even came into being, something they were not willing to consider in the post-World War II atmosphere.[121] When the UN was formed, therefore, Britain had been forced to compromise on the issue of the Trusteeship Council and accept American conceptions of self-determination. This led to what Aiyaz Husain describes as 'the asymmetry between the American and British conceptions of geography when it came to postcolonial issues arising before the Security Council'.[122] In the case of both the Indo-Pakistan conflict in 1947 and the Arab Israeli war in 1948, neither London nor Washington advocated UN intervention; the US wanted to avoid any precedent for the introduction of troops which could lead to the deployment of Soviet troops elsewhere, and Britain was hesitant to become embroiled in a conflict which might destabilise India as a strategic lynchpin in the region.[123]

The main characteristic of British colonial policy at the UN became therefore passive resistance and an agreement to submit information about the status of British territories to the UN as a goodwill gesture in the hope that this would appease the anti-colonialists. Minimum cooperation with UN resolutions on colonialism in order to avoid damaging public debates and to preventing the UN from 'interfering' with colonial policy defined the British approach towards the Special Political and Decolonization Committee (the Fourth Committee) and later the Special Committee on Decolonisation (Committee of 24), established in 1961. The optics of this approach were carefully managed. Foreign Office officials cautioned that the representation of British policy on colonial matters should not be perceived as obscuring UN policy on the issue, despite the fact that the central aim was in fact to limit the effects of UN policy as far as possible to prevent embarrassment for Britain.[124] Cohen's policy became referred to as that of the 'three Fs, forthright, firm, but flexible even at the cost of some gradual eating away of our position, the object being to buy time until we are no longer greatly embarrassed by discussion of colonial matters'.[125]

Following the first recommendation to improve relations with the Afro-Asian bloc, primarily through India, London sought to position Britain as a Cold War mediator in order to allay Indian fears about the seeping of the superpower conflict into decolonisation questions.[126] The main British strategies in this regard were to council moderation on India where possible, and ensure that the Soviet propaganda in the General Assembly did not unduly influence more unpredictable Indian representatives such as Krishna Menon, the Indian Ambassador to the UN in 1960. However, the British experience with the waning extent of influence over Nigeria was replayed with India during debates on the draft resolution on the Congo. By December 1960, the continued detention of Lumumba, who had been placed into protective UN custody in October, the failure to reconvene the Congolese Parliament and the escalating hostilities between provincial leaders in Eastern Congo had again brought the question before the Security Council for a resolution to strengthen the Secretary-General's mandate. During the debates, British delegates reported to London that the Indians were 'play[ing] the Russian game by casting doubt on the sincerity of the Secretary-General'.[127] The US singled out Menon as leading the Afro-Asians to pressure Hammarskjöld to take more vigorous action in the Congo, 'producing increasing weakness on his part'.[128]

In this atmosphere, the debate on the Congo resumed in earnest with the Security Council meeting nine times between 7 and 14 December. British representatives quickly discovered that they were unable to urge moderation on any of the countries who now presented a draft resolution which called for strong action in the Congo. Together with seven of the most vociferously anti-colonial members of the Afro-Asian bloc, including Ceylon, Ghana, India, Indonesia, Mali, Morocco and UAR, Guinea presented a resolution which called for the immediate release of all political prisoners (namely Lumumba), the reconvening of the Parliament and the removal of all non-military Belgian advisers and technicians. In opposition, America and Britain presented a more moderate resolution aimed to strengthen Kasavubu's position and reaffirm Hammarskjöld's mandate for the Congo. The Soviet exercise of the veto on the question moved the debate to the General Assembly where the Afro-Asian resolution was rejected by forty-two votes to twenty-eight with seven abstentions but so too was the Anglo-American proposal by forty-three votes to twenty-two with thirty-two abstentions. Crucially this was because the French-African states, led by Cameroon, opposed strengthening the existing mandate for ONUC, preferring an African solution. The Cameroonian representative also pointed out to American UN delegates that the French African group could 'not afford to be marked as in the Western camp'.[129] Eventually the General Assembly unanimously adopted a proposal from Austria in

December which reaffirmed the existing resolutions and put the item on the agenda for the second session in March 1961.[130]

This failed Anglo-American initiative to neither direct UN Congo policy nor urge moderation upon the Afro-Asians led to increased attempts between Britain and the US to coordinate their policies, particularly as the Soviets continued their propaganda campaign with the Afro-Asians. Throughout the General Assembly debates on the Congo, the Foreign Office pressed upon the British the importance of giving the impression that 'we and not the Russians appear on the side of Africa'.[131] This connection to the anti-colonial campaign was emphasised by the Soviet Union as a means of attacking the West. Khrushchev's speeches to the General Assembly that had included calls 'for the complete and final elimination of colonial regimes'[132] were part of a twofold strategy to build relations with the Afro-Asian bloc and disparage the West at the same time. His loud demands for the independence of all colonies were perceived as threatening to British dependents in East Africa, particularly Kenya and the Central African Federation. The Sharpeville shootings and the vote in favour of a republic in October 1960 in South Africa served to shatter any remaining British illusions of maintaining significant influence in Africa, or at the UN.[133] Rather, British officials were forced to embark on a campaign to ensure that their policies were not interpreted as obstructing UN actions.[134]

The anti-colonial campaign reached its zenith on 14 December 1960 when Resolution 1541 was passed. The General Assembly called for 'immediate steps ... to transfer all powers ... [from colonial powers to their colonies] without any conditions or reservations'.[135] Such an instruction from the UN constituted a direct challenge to British colonial policy and exposed the lack of influence of British delegates in preventing the resolution from being debated. Resolution 1514 passed by a massive majority of eighty-nine votes in favour, essentially spelling the end of empire by formal means. The Colonial Office remarked ruefully that:

> if the position deteriorates further, not only in regard to the relative numerical strength of the West and of the Afro-Asian bloc, but also in regard to the spirit in which the majority approaches colonial issues ... [though] it is not the intention of H.M.G to be stampeded by the United Nations into changes of policy ... if the United Nations choose to pass resolutions demanding action by the United Kingdom contrary to H.M.G's established policy it would appear that the only way of avoiding the necessity to comply with such would be to declare them, wherever possible, to be *ultra vires*.[136]

The only option left to London by December 1960 was to deliberately obstruct UN policy under Article 2(7) of the Charter.[137] In taking such an approach, Britain diverged from the American position.

The troika proposal and the Russian attack on Hammarskjöld had now cast the US position on colonial questions into a Cold War frame and the State Department began to revise the American position on colonial issues at the UN. There were early hints from negotiations that Eisenhower's policy of automatically abstaining from voting on colonial resolutions would be scrapped under the new President John F. Kennedy from 1961. Such was the extent of the new administration's uncompromising position on the issue that a confidential telegram from the British Embassy in Washington to the Foreign Office noted, 'we should be laying waste to our powers in vain if we spent any more time in trying to persuade them that President Eisenhower's decision was right in itself or that such abstentions are in the interest of the United States, or the West, or even of ourselves'.[138] This contributed significantly to the apprehension in Whitehall over the advent of the Kennedy administration, not least because the President-elect had been signalling through his presidential campaign of summer of 1960 that he intended to revise the whole US position at the UN.[139] Before the extent of this revision of US UN policy was revealed, however, events in the Congo took a turn for the worse when it was announced that Lumumba had been assassinated.

Murder most foul

One point on which America and Britain could easily agree was the removal of Lumumba. In a conversation with Lord Home in September, Eisenhower remarked that he could think of nothing better than if 'Lumumba would fall into a river full of crocodiles'. Home responded sardonically, saying 'we have lost many of the techniques of old-fashioned diplomacy'.[140] Ambassador At Large William Averell Harriman went further, warning the State Department that 'Lumumba will continue to cause difficulties in the Congo whether he is in control of the government, in jail or released'.[141] Privately, officials confided in their French counterparts about the advantages for resolving the situation in the Congo 'if Lumumba should disappear … everything remained hopeless so long as Lumumba was on the scene'.[142] The demise of the Congolese leader turned out to be anything but an accident, albeit dramatic in a different manner. The vote to recognise Kasavubu as the legitimate leader of the Congo ultimately spelled the beginning of the end for Lumumba. Since Mobutu's College of Commissioners had been established, the Congolese leader had effectively been under house arrest, protected by Ghanaian soldiers under UN command who prevented the Congolese army from arresting him. Following the General Assembly vote in favour of Kasavubu, on 27 November Lumumba decided to make a break for the northern city of Stanleyville in Orientale province, his home base where the majority of his supporters were gathered. The reasons for his decision to leave the protection of the UN at this precise moment are unclear. Lise Namikas argues that, given the UN recognition of Kasavubu, it is possible that he no longer felt secure in UN custody.[143] The ongoing constitutional crisis and the accelerated CIA plot to assassinate him may also have influenced his plan, as would the knowledge that some of his youngest children had been successfully smuggled out of the country by the Egyptian Embassy in Léopoldville and were now out of harm's way.[144] However, more practically, his situation had become untenable. In November, Mobutu's troops had raided the homes of Lumumba's supporters, arresting the occupants and often beating them or transporting them to 'unknown locations'. These reprisals were carried out against his followers, including those within the army, but also against prominent politicians such as Remy Mwamba, the Minister for Justice, Jason Sangwa, President of the Balubakat party, and Emmanuel Nzonzi, Secretary-General of the MNC.[145]

The most recent publication on the assassination of Lumumba renders a verdict of death by a thousand blows. Emmanuel Gerard and Bruce Kuklick's *Death in the Congo* traces the 'travelling carnival of death' from Léopoldville to Elisabethville, in the process finding no clear conspiracy, rather a tale of complicity, connivance and collaboration among the American, Belgian, UN, CIA, Congolese and Katangan officials who, either through active participation or failure to act, were ultimately responsible for Lumumba's murder.[146] While the ultimate question of who was fundamentally accountable remains obscured by intrigue, cross-communication and coded messages between the various participants, Lumumba's movements in the weeks leading up to his murder on 17 January are generally agreed.[147]

Lumumba slipped out of his residence under the noses of both the UN soldiers who were guarding him and Mobutu's ANC forces who were waiting to arrest him. From Léopoldville, he started out for Stanleyville where his supporters had announced the formation of a new opposition Government under the leadership of Lumumba's former deputy, Antoine Gizenga. Lumumba had gained a small head start by instructing Kanza to issue a press statement upon his escape that he would remain in Léopoldville and await the arrival of the UN Conciliation Commission. The widely unconvincing statement did not fool the ANC or their Belgian intelligence advisors for long. As he made the perilous journey northwards by car, the forces of the Central Government and Belgian troops were soon in hot pursuit and set up roadblocks along the route in order to intercept his convoy. Lumumba's progress was further hindered by his decision to stop along the route and give speeches to villagers assuring them that he would lead the Congo to freedom. Within three days, only 1,000 kilometres from Stanleyville, Mobutu's soldiers caught up with Lumumba's party in a village called Lodi on the left bank of the Sankuru river. It is argued by both Ludo de Witte and Gerard and Kuklick that UN soldiers present at the time failed to protect Lumumba, although some Ghanaian troops, contrary to their orders, did manage to free other prisoners from his party. This, according to their arguments, points to clear UN complicity in Lumumba's murder. However, the official instructions to ONUC from New York, restated by Commander-in Chief of UN forces General Carl Van Horn, were that the UN was not responsible for Lumumba's safety and no action was to be taken by any troops who encountered him.[148] In any event Lumumba was now in the hands of Mobutu's soldiers who transported him hastily to a military camp in Thysville, outside of Léopoldville.

Up to this point, the Central Government essentially remained under the control of Mobutu and his College of Commissioners while the UN Conciliation Commission completed its work. In response to Lumumba's capture, the regime in Stanleyville continued to go from strength to strength and seized large parts of northern Katanga. Lumumba's initial escape had been received with jubilation among his supporters, Kanza noted: 'I had faith in Lumumba. Had he not been assassinated he would certainly have come back as head of the government.'[149] This jubilation served to further alarm Britain and the US who perceived that they were now faced with the very real prospect of Lumumba's return to power. Efforts intensified at the UN to install Kasavubu as soon as possible and restore the Congolese Parliament. In Léopoldville, the British Ambassador Ian Scott, who believed that Hammarskjöld's Special Representative to the Congo Rajeshwar Dayal was sympathetic to Lumumba, cabled London for more robust policy at the UN.[150]

After more than a month of being 'beaten like a dog' at Camp Hardy in Thysville, rumours emerged of a mutiny among the Congolese soldiers who threatened to free Lumumba.[151] Mobutu, Kasavubu and Bomboko went personally to the camp to negotiate with the soldiers and eventually persuaded them that setting Lumumba free would not serve their interests.[152] However, it was now clear that they needed to find a final solution to the problem; they turned towards Tshombe and asked him to receive Lumumba in Katanga. From that point his fate was officially sealed. After another round of torture, this time at the hands of drunken Katangan officials, including Tshombe himself, as observed by some of their Belgian collaborators, Lumumba and his friends, Joseph Okito and Maurice Mpolo, were executed by firing squad. In an attempt to keep the assassination secret as long as possible, the Katangan gendarmerie, buried and later exhumed the body before removing the limbs and dissolving his torso in acid, lest any burial site become a shrine for Lumumba's supporters and Congolese nationalists.

News of the murder did not break in New York until the official announcement came on 13 February.[153] However, up to that point, Lumumba's supporters amongst the Afro-Asian bloc had been active in devising a stronger policy for the UN that would restore Lumumba, or at least some of his supporters, to the legal government. The Congo was the main topic under discussion at the Casablanca conference from 3 to 6 January, following which Mali, Yugoslavia, China, the USSR, Ghana, Guinea and Egypt all sent financial and political support to Gizenga's provincial government in Stanleyville.[154] They also pushed Hammarskjöld for a new initiative, which he began undertaking with the assumption that Lumumbist elements, if not Lumumba himself, would be part of the solution to the Congo's predicament.[155] It is now clear that although Lumumba's murder was widely suspected, when the official announcement came, there was uproar and indignation in New York. The controversy and speculation about who was responsible immediately spread like wildfire through the Secretariat and the UN ground offices. Algeria, Ceylon, Ghana, Guinea, Libya, Mali, Morocco and the UAR, who had threatened to withdraw their troops from ONUC, now began to lose patience.[156] A group of Lumumba's incensed supporters even burst into a session of the Security Council on 13 February with the intention of attacking Hammarskjöld personally. Demonstrations took place on the streets of London and Moscow, protesting the policies of Britain, Belgium, the US and the UN.

Gerard and Kuklick have argued that 'the UN acted ambiguously and duplicitously' and was most certainly to blame for not protecting Lumumba at Lodi.[157] They accredited this failure to act to Hammarskjöld's unwillingness to come into conflict with the Western powers. However, Hammarskjöld's position and policy regarding Lumumba should be viewed more in light of his earlier efforts to collaborate with the Afro-Asian bloc. His failure to secure Lumumba's safety once he had been captured, despite repeated calls for humane treatment, was certainly an embarrassment to the Secretary-General. On being passed a letter from Lumumba describing his conditions during a brief visit to Léopoldville in early January, Hammarskjöld is said to have 'turned red'.[158] Certainly, as Lipsey's analysis of his personal memoirs at the time reveal, Hammarskjöld was internally distressed about Lumumba's fate, to the point of feeling guilty. However, his personal feelings aside, the repeated efforts of the ANC and the Belgian security forces to avoid all contact with the UN and its forces during the weeks of Lumumba's captivity and transfer to Elisabethville, in case they tried to rescue the Congolese leader, points to a different impression of the organisation. Even on 31 January, under pressure from the Afro-Asians, Hammarskjöld had drawn up a five-point plan for UN Congo policy, a key feature of which was the release of Lumumba.[159] Hammarskjöld responded to the threat of the withdraw of African and Asian forces by warning that such a public disassociation from the UN would have 'immeasurable' consequences for African unity and would inevitably lead to what he termed 'big power interference'.[160] Following Lumumba's internment, Dayal had organised the escape of Kanza and other remaining Lumumba supporters to New York where Hammarskjöld now granted them courtesy permits to enter discussions as representatives of the 'legal government of the Congo' in Stanleyville, which had been recognised by almost a third of UN members.[161] In addition, he announced that the UN would undertake an immediate investigation of Lumumba's assassination, which he branded 'a revolting crime against principles for which this Organisation stands and must stand'.[162]

For America and Britain the situation was ominous. Their failed attempt to get an Anglo-American draft resolution through the Security Council in December, the passing of Resolution 1514 on the ending of colonialism, which further invigorated the Afro-Asians, and the public accusations of murder and intrigue in the Congo achieved only one realisation; something had to be done. As early as 15 December representatives of both countries met with French officials in Paris in order to work out a joint strategy.[163] Now, alongside the threat from the Casablanca Group to withdraw their troops, Sudan and Ethiopia had also indicated that they were reconsidering their position on the Congo question, which had up to this point been friendly towards the West. ONUC was now also faced with the additional problem of financing as the USSR and France both refused to contribute towards the costs of the mission. Although France declined to become embroiled in the Congo issue, all three states agreed that the time had passed when the matter could be handled 'despite the UN' and now a more concerted approach towards the organisation was necessary.[164]

This revision of relations with the UN was closely linked to a broader policy change with regard to Africa and colonial issues. In January 1961, Cold War hostilities escalated when Khrushchev called for Hammarskjöld's resignation when Lumumba's assassination came to light.[165] The State Department embarked on an effort to formulate a more coherent, effective Congo policy. Kennedy sought to distance himself from Eisenhower's position and take the reins in negotiations at the Security Council in order to protect American interests in the region and bolster UN prestige. There are a variety of different views as to what extent Kennedy's revised Congo policy differed from that of his predecessor. Kent, and Gerard and Kuklick, among others, argue that the Kennedy policy with regard to Lumumba and the Congo did not deviate even slightly from Eisenhower's plans despite the enthusiasm of some members of the State Department for African independence.[166] However, this is debateable. Kanza, Kalb and Namikas, in contrast, argue that the progressives in the State Department were planning a more open policy towards Africa. Indeed, the State Department outlined the American objectives in the Congo as working in conjunction with the UN on the issue and ruled out any possibility of unilateral action: 'We believe a UN solution is still the best answer for the Congo and that the advantage of adherence to our policy of support for the UN outweighs the possible advantages inherent in a program of unilateral action in the Congo.'[167] As the new US Permanent Representative at the United Nations, Adlai E. Stevenson, put it, 'the only way to keep the Cold War out of the Congo is to keep the UN in the Congo'.[168]

The assassination of Lumumba at the end of 1960 exploded tensions between North and South as African leaders immediately accused the Western powers of being directly or indirectly responsible. It also had a divisive effect on the African group at the UN, who, after the Casablanca Conference became internally split between the Casablanca Group and the Monrovia Group. The activism of the Afro-Asian bloc served to highlight the colonial and neo-colonial dimensions of the Congo debates and brought together the role of the UN in the decolonisation process, with the effect it had on Belgian and British Congo policies and the unity of the Western bloc. African attempts to use UN forums to play the superpowers against each other met with some success as it pushed the US into taking a stronger position on anti-colonial questions from this point onwards. Although the Afro-Asian bloc would lose coherence during the next phase of the crisis in 1961–1962, they were able to capitalise on their influence through the use of structures and committees of the UN, the willingness of the Secretary-General to support their position on the Congo and the disagreement in the Anglo-American position on colonial questions to shift Congo policy towards their preferences. As the crisis accelerated through the autumn and winter of 1960–1961, the use of force against Katanga moved from being a theoretical to a practical question and, in the process, the lack of Anglo-American coordination on this issue became glaringly apparent. In an informal discussion between Eisenhower and Kennedy on the Congo situation as the latter took over the presidency, the State Department noted that 'the British have little new to offer'.[169] The disagreement about Congo policy with Britain had to be balanced against deteriorating relations with African states at the UN which produced a concerted effort at a new US Congo policy in February 1961.

Notes

1 As recorded in E. Kelen, *Hammarskjöld* (New York: Putnam, 1966), p. 186. See also Lipsey, *Hammarskjöld*, p. 401.
2 GPL, Bureau of African Affairs, BAA/RLAA/689, 'Republic of Congo'-Newspaper Clippings (Congo) 1963, 'Wire report', Reuters (10 May 1963). U Thant reported on the costs of ONUC to the General Assembly in May 1963.

3 For further details see M. Kennedy, *Ireland, the United Nations and the Congo: A Military and Diplomatic History, 1960–1* (Dublin: Four Courts Press, 2014).
4 J. Mohan, 'Ghana, Congo and the United Nations', *Journal of Modern African Studies*, 7:3 (1969), 369–406.
5 GPL, BAA/RLAA/692, 'Congo-I'- Correspondence (Congo, Ghana), Letter from Joseph Kasavubu to Kwame Nkrumah, 9 December 1959.
6 United Nations Archives, New York, New York (hereafter UNA), S-1069–0017–0001, African States Meeting, July 1960, United Nations Office for Special Political Affairs, Verbatim Record of Meeting held with Representatives of Ethiopia, Ghana, Guinea, Liberia, Libya, Morocco, Sudan, Tunisia and the United Arab Republic in the Secretary-General's Conference room on Thursday, 12 July 1960.
7 L.M. Goodrich, E. Hambro and A.P. Simons, *Charter of the United Nations: Commentary and Documents* (New York: Columbia University Press, 1969), p. 588.
8 Opening Statement in the Security Council, New York, July 13, 1960, Security Council Official Records, Fifteenth Year, 873rd meeting. A.W. Cordier, W. Foote and M. Harrelson (eds), *Public Papers of the Secretaries-General of the United Nations, Dag Hammarskjöld 1960–1961*, Vol. V (New York: Columbia University Press, 1975), p. 23.
9 Anonymous, 'Congo expressed derailed', *The Economist* (16 July 1960), p. 16.
10 873rd Meeting, Security Council Official Records, 13–14 July 1960, p. 162, www.un.org/en/sc/repertoire/59-63/Chapter%208/59-63_08-8-Situation%20in%20the%20Republic%20of%20Congo.pdf.
11 O. Bring, 'Dag Hammarskjöld and the issue of humanitarian intervention', in J. Petman and J. Klabbers (eds), *Nordic Cosmopolitanism: Essays in International Law for Martti Koskenniemi* (Leiden: Leiden University Press, 2003), p. 486.
12 Andrew Wellington Cordier Papers, Columbia University, New York, New York (hereafter AWCP), Box 220, UN Files, Public Papers of the Secretaries-General Hammarskjöld: Manuscript 1960–1961, Dag Hammarskjöld speaking at a UN Press Conference, 19 May 1960.
13 The 'Congo Club' met regularly in Hammarskjöld's office to discuss the crisis, often over dinner and late into the night. Lipsey, *Hammarskjöld*, p. 404.
14 'When the General Assembly referred to the Trust territories especially it was natural in light of the circumstances, but I have never read into its stand, given the background, any kind of priority for ex-Trust Territories in relations to other newly-independent states, and I would like to stress, and stress emphatically, that in our approach in this secretariat and in my approach in the report, there is no such priority.' UNA, S-1069–0017–0001 African States Meeting, July 1960, United Nations Office for Special Political Affairs, Verbatim Record of Meeting held with Representatives of Ethiopia, Ghana, Guinea, Liberia, Libya, Morocco, Sudan, Tunisia and the United Arab Republic in the Secretary-General's Conference room on Thursday, 12 July 1960.
15 'The Confederation of Independent African States are gravely concerned at the reports about troop movements along the frontier regions of the Congo by certain neighbouring territories … the Conference hereby collectively informs your Excellency that they are prepared to support wholeheartedly any measure which you, in consultation with the Security Council of the UN may deem necessary to assist the people of the Congo in preserving its territorial integrity after its independence.' NAD, F.N. 5(19) IN-II/60, Vol. I., 1960 Question of Congo at Security Council, Ministry of

External Relations, Cable from the Addis Ababa Conference, to Hammarskjöld, 20 June 1960.
16 UNA, S-1069-0017-0001 African States Meeting, July 1960, United Nations Office for Special Political Affairs, Verbatim Record of Meeting held with Representatives of Ethiopia, Ghana, Guinea, Liberia, Libya, Morocco, Sudan, Tunisia and the United Arab Republic in the Secretary-General's Conference room on Thursday, 12 July 1960.
17 AWCP, Box 158, Congo, African Group Meetings, Jul-Aug 1960, Hammarskjöld's statements in a Verbatim Record of Meeting held with Representatives of Ethiopia, Ghana, Guinea, Liberia, Libya, Morocco, Mali, Sudan, Tunisia and the United Arab Republic in the Secretary-General's Conference Room, Wednesday 17 August 1960.
18 For further see Connelly, *A Diplomatic Revolution*, pp. 171–213.
19 UNA, S-1069-0017-0001, United Nations Office for Special Political Affairs, African States Meeting, July 1960, Mr. Barnes, representative of Liberia, speaking in the meeting with Hammarskjöld, 12 July 1960.
20 See generally how African states at the UN tried to change the normative framework, Irwin, *Gordian Knot*, p. 52.
21 UNA, S-0849-01-00001, Records of the Congo Advisory Committee, Remarks from the Secretary-General to the first meeting of the United Nations Congo Advisory Committee, Meeting No. 1, Wednesday, 24 August 1960.
22 Firestone, *The United Nations Under U Thant*, p. vii.
23 NAD, F.5 (19) UNII, 1960, Congo in Security Council & Special Session in General Assembly, Ministry of External Relations Files, Memo on the outcome of the first meeting of the Congo Advisory Committee from the Indian Delegation in New York to Foreign, New Delhi, 26 August 1960.
24 Bring, 'Dag Hammarskjöld and the issue of humanitarian intervention', pp. 500–501.
25 UNA, S-0856-0001-05, United Nations Offices for Special Political Affairs, General Assembly Resolution 1654 (XVI) – Committee on Implementation of Declaration on Granting Independence to Colonial Peoples 1961-1969.
26 Hammarskjöld also had formal advisory groups for previous crises in Suez and Lebanon. T. Whitfield, 'Groups of friends', in D. Malone (ed.), *The UN Security Council: From the Cold War to the 21st Century* (Boulder: Lynne Rienner Publishers, 2004), p. 315.
27 NAL, FO 371/146773, African Division, Confidential memo, from A.D.M. Ross to Sir Frederick Hoyer Miller recounting a conversation with Belgian Prime Minister Pierre Wigny in which he outlined his objections to the proposed Security Council resolution, 20 July 1960.
28 NAL, FO 371/ 146643, Memo entitled: Reasons for and Effects of the Debacle in the Congo, from British Ambassador to Brussels to Foreign Office, 29 August 1960.
29 NAL, FO 371/146773, Instructions to the UK delegation to the UN, before the Security Council vote, 20 July 1960.
30 NAL, FO 371/146773, Letter recounting a conversation with Hammarskjöld before he left to negotiate with the Belgian Government. From Sir P. Dixon, UK Mission to the UN, to the Foreign Office, 26 July 1960.
31 Security Council Resolution 146, [S/4426], 9 August 1960, www.un.org/en/ga/search/view_doc.asp?symbol=S/RES/146(1960).

32 NAL, FO 371/146773, Confidential memo from A.D.M. Ross to Sir Frederick Hoyer Miller, recounts a conversation with Belgian Prime Minister Pierre Wigny in which he outlined his objections to the proposed Security Council resolution, 20 July 1960.
33 NAL, FO 371/146772, Note of reply to Parliamentary question 18 July 1960. Note from the African Department, 14 July 1960.
34 Namikas, *Battleground Africa*, p. 76.
35 UNA, S-0849-01-00001, Records of the Congo Advisory Committee, Assurances from Belgium made to, and repeated by, the Secretary-General and General Rhikye during the first and second meetings of the Congo Advisory Committee, Meeting No. 1, 24 August 1960.
36 UNA, S-0849-01-00001, Records of the Congo Advisory Committee, Comment from Mr. Caba, representative of Guinea to the Congo Advisory Committee, Meeting No. 2, 26 August 1960.
37 Editorial, *The Economist* (5 November 1960), p. 20.
38 'The strongest support we have in this great test in the instrument of the independent nations of the world – the United Nations – is the confidence and solidarity of the African Member states, acting with a common purpose, that of maintaining Africa in peace and free of all interference alien to the African world.' UNA, Dag ONUC Records, S-0845-0001-02, Dag, Miscellaneous Correspondence and Cables, 14/07/1960-02/02/1961, Telegram from the Secretary-General to Julius Nyerere, Chief Minister of Tanganyika, 7 August 1960. See also: Urquhart, *Hammarskjöld*, p. 595.
39 AWCP, Box 220, UN Files, Public Papers of the Secretaries-General Hammarskjöld: Manuscript 1960–1961, First statement in the Security Council introducing his second report on the Congo under July 14 and July 24 resolutions. UN Headquarters, New York, 8 August 1960.
40 Collins argues that Belgium also supported the secession of Kasai. C.J.L. Collins, 'The Cold War comes to Africa: Cordier and the 1960 Congo crisis', *Journal of International Affairs*, 47:1 (1993), 243–269.
41 AMAE, 1.2 Publications, Commission of Coordination of Congolese Documents, Congo Documents, Africa Files, 1616, 'Measures to implement the first phase of the dictatorship', letter from Lumumba to Mr Finant, President of the provincial government of Stanleyville, 15 September 1960.
42 Kalb, *Congo Cables*, p. 55–58.
43 AWCP, Box 158, UN Files, Subject files – Africa – Congo, African Group, Meetings, July-August 1960, Comments of Ghanaian representative at the UN Mr Quaison Sackey when raising the issue of Lumumba's comments criticising the role of the UN in Congo to Dag Hammarskjöld. Verbatim Record of Meeting held with Representative of Ethiopia, Ghana, Guinea, Liberia, Libya, Morocco, Mali, Sudan, Tunisia and the United Arab Republic in the Secretary-General's Conference room, 17 August 1960.
44 NAL, FO 371/ 146643, Foreign Office minute E.B. Boothby, 7 September 1960.
45 NAL, FO 371/ 146643, Instructions from the Foreign Office to the British Embassy in Léopoldville, 10 September 1960.
46 NAL, FO 371/ 146778, Letter from Sir Harold Caccia at the UK Mission to the UN in New York, to the Foreign Office, 1 September 1960.
47 NAL, FO 371/ 146778, Letter from the UK Mission to the UN reporting on the workings of the Congo Advisory Committee, 31 August 1960.

48 Kalb, *Congo Cables*, pp. 3–17.
49 S.R. Weissman, 'Opening the secret files on Lumumba's murder', *Washington Post* (21 July 2002). See also: L. de Witte, *The Assassination of Lumumba* (New York: Verso, 2003); E. Gerard and B. Kuklick, *Death in the Congo: Murdering Patrice Lumumba* (Cambridge, MA: Harvard University Press, 2015).
50 L. Devlin, *Chief of Station, Congo* (New York: Public Affairs, 2007), p. 95–99.
51 *Ibid.*, pp. 65–70.
52 'Evidence of U.N. complicity in the Kasavubu coup appears overwhelming.' Weissman, *American Foreign Policy in the Congo*, p. 90.
53 For more on the role of Cordier at this moment, see Gerard and Kuklick, *Death in the Congo*.
54 UNA, S-0845-0001-01, Correspondence with Bunche and Dayal, Dag-ONUC, Telegram from Hammarskjöld to Cordier.
55 NAD, F.5 (19). UNII, 1960, Congo in Security Council & Special Session General Assembly, Ministry of External Affairs, Report from the Indian Delegation in New York to Foreign, New Delhi, 11 September 1960.
56 T. Kanza, *Conflict in the Congo* (Harmondsworth: Penguin Books, 1972), p. 238. Note, Roger Lipsey, Hammarskjöld's most recent biographer, writes of Kanza and his book as trustworthy and 'without ideological baggage'. Lipsey, *Hammarskjöld*, p. 395.
57 Lipsey, *Hammarskjöld*, p. 406.
58 AWCP, Box 158, UN Files, Subject files – Africa – Congo, African Group, Meetings, July–August, 1960, Verbatim Record of Meeting held with Representative of Ethiopia, Ghana, Guinea, Liberia, Libya, Morocco, Mali, Sudan, Tunisia and the United Arab Republic in the Secretary-General's Conference room on Wednesday, 17 August 1960.
59 Kanza, *Conflict in the Congo*, p. 250.
60 *Ibid.*, pp. 254–255, quoting Lumumba.
61 Lipsey, *Hammarskjöld*, p. 415.
62 AWCP, Box 161, UN Files, Subject Files Africa – Congo Miscellaneous: K-Red, Record of conversation between Prime Minister Patrice Lumumba and Andrew W. Cordier, Executive Assistant to the Secretary-General, 1 August 1960.
63 UNA, S-0215-0001-14, Box 1, ONUC Government Records, Records of the Office for Special Political Affairs, Congo Government – press releases, Congo Government Files, Letter from Hammarskjöld to Lumumba, 16 August 1960.
64 AWCP, Box 158, UN Files, Subject Files, Africa-Congo-Civilian Operations Miscellaneous, African Group Meetings, July–Aug 1960, Verbatim record of meeting held with representatives of Ethiopia, Ghana, Guinea, Liberia, Libya, Morocco, Mali, Sudan, Tunisia and the United Arab Republic in the Secretary-General's conference room on Wednesday 17 August 1960.
65 AWCP, Box 162, UN Files, Subject Files, Africa – Congo – Miscellaneous, Congo – Reports and Correspondence, 1960–1961,Report to the Secretary-General from Ralph J. Bunche on Elisabethville, Katanga Assignment, 6 August 1960.
66 AMAE, 1616 (1616) Congo independence 'A grave and irrevocable decision taken by the Government of the Republic of the Congo' declaration of an ultimatum from Patrice Lumumba, Office of the Prime Minister, Léopoldville, 16 September 1960.
67 Kanza, *Conflict in the Congo*, p. 279.
68 Mohan, 'Ghana, Congo and the United Nations', 381.

69 Patrice Lumumba, Concluding Speech at the All-African Conference in Léopoldville, 31 August 1961, in P. Lumumba, *Patrice Lumumba: Fighter for Africa's Freedom*, trans. T. Schmidt (Moscow: Progress Publishers, 1961), pp. 26–33.
70 UNA, S-0845-0004-0011, Secretary-General's correspondence with Ghana 1960–1960, UN Department of Political Affairs, Telegram from Nkrumah to Hammarskjöld, 13 September 1960.
71 UNA, S-0845-0004-0011, Secretary-General's correspondence with Ghana 1960–1960, Telegram from Hammarskjöld to Nkrumah, 13 September 1960.
72 UNA, S-0845-0001-08, Correspondence with UN Security Council and Congolese Government, Dag – ONUC, Subject Files of the Secretary-General, Letter from Hammarskjöld to Antoine Gizenga, Acting Prime Minister, Léopoldville, 7 August 1960.
73 UNA, S-0849-01-00001, Records of the Congo Advisory Committee, Remarks of Mr Caba, representative of Guinea, United Nations Advisory Committee on the Congo, Meeting no. 4, 2 September 1960.
74 NAD, F.5 (19). UNII. 1960, Congo in Security Council & Special Session General Assembly, Ministry of External Relations, Comments of Quaison Sackey, Ghana's Permanent Representative to the UN in New York to members of the Indian Delegation, 11 September 1960.
75 For further see G. McCann, 'From diaspora to third worldism and the United Nations: India and the politics of decolonizing Africa', *Past and Present*, 218:8 (2013), 258–280.
76 NAD, CPD-14/60-AFR II, 1960, Vol. 1, Developments in Congo (formerly Belgian), Ministry of External Affairs, Telegram from Bahadur Singh, High Commission Nairobi, to Foreign New Delhi, 17 July 1960.
77 NAD, CPD-14/60-AFR II, UN Documents, PM's Speeches, etc., Ministry of External Affairs, Nehru's address to the UN General Assembly, 3 October 1960.
78 General Assembly Resolution 1474 called for a speedy solution to the internal conflict in the Congo, 'with the assistance, as appropriate, of Asian and African representatives appointed by the Advisory Committee on the Congo, in consultation with the Secretary-General'. Resolution adopted without reference to a committee, 863rd plenary meeting, 20 September 1960. www.un.org/ga/search/view_doc.asp?symbol=A/4510&Lang=E.
79 Nkrumah's speech to the General Assembly, 23 September 1960. www.nkrumah.net/un-1960/kn-at-un-1960-07.htm.
80 UNA, S-0845-0004-0011 Secretary-General's correspondence with Ghana 1960–1960, Broadcast by Nkrumah, 7 September 1960.
81 Nehru's speech to the General Assembly, 3 October 1960, in J. Nehru, *India's Foreign Policy: Selected Speeches September 1946–April 1961* (New Delhi: Government of India, 1961).
82 A. O'Malley, 'Ghana, India, and the transnational dynamics of the Congo crisis at the United Nations, 1960–61', *International History Review, Special Issue: Non-Alignment, the Third Force, or Fence-Sitting: Independent Pathways in the Cold War,* 37:3 (2015), 970–990.
83 Introduction to Annual Report of the Secretary-General to the General Assembly on the World of the Organization, 1959–1960, *General Assembly Official Records*, Fifteenth Session, Supplement no. 1A 9A/4390/Add.1, 31 August 1960. See also, O'Malley, 'Ghana, India and the Congo crisis', p. 9.

84 Statements made by Monghi Slim at the Security Council Meeting, 21 August 1960, *Security Council Official Records*, 888th meeting, 15th year, p. 25. http://repository.un.org/bitstream/handle/11176/82953/S_PV.888-EN.pdf?sequence=2&isAllowed=y.

85 AWCP, Box 158, UN Files, Subject Files, Africa-Congo-Civilian Operations Miscellaneous, Congo, Africa Group Meetings, July–Aug 1960, Verbatim record of meeting held with representatives of Ethiopia, Ghana, Guinea, Liberia, Libya, Morocco, Mali, Sudan, Tunisia and the United Arab Republic in the Secretary-General's conference room on Wednesday 17 August 1960.

86 Statement from Lumumba as recorded in Kanza, *Conflict in the Congo*, p. 241.

87 National Archives and Records Administration, Maryland, USA (hereafter NARA), State Department Central Decimal Files, Box no. 326, Congo, 330/6-160, Telegram from Department of State to American Embassy Léopoldville, 20 August 1960. Some Congolese, including Kanza, went so far as to accuse the Americans of sabotaging their visit to New York in August 1960.

88 NARA, State Department Files, UN, 310/1-460, US Delegation Records, Telegram from Karachi to Secretary of State, detailing a conversation with the Indian High Commissioner Rajeshwar Dayal on the Congo, 22 August 1960.

89 NARA, State Department Central Decimal Files, Box no. 326, Congo, 330/6-160, Telegram from American Embassy in Brussels, to Secretary of State, 9 August 1960.

90 NARA, State Department Central Decimal Files, Box no. 326, Congo, 330/6-160, Telegram from Department of State to American Embassy in Léopoldville, 10 September 1960.

91 Devlin details the financial and political support from the US to Mobutu's regime in Devlin, *Chief of Station*, pp. 79–80.

92 Kanza describes that he was 'literally rushed there by the Americans who wanted to get him accepted internationally'. Kanza, *Conflict in the Congo*, p. 304.

93 Kalb, *Congo Cables*, p. 154.

94 Weissman, *American Foreign Policy in the Congo*, p. 106.

95 Report of a conversation with Hammarskjöld as recorded in Minutes of Special Group Meeting, 27 October 1960. N. Howland, D.C. Humphrey and H.D. Schwar (eds), *FRUS, 1964–1968, Vol. XXIII, Congo, 1960–1968* (Washington, DC: Government Printing Office, 2013), p. 52.

96 NARA, State Department Central Decimal Files, Box no. 326, 330/6-160, Telegram from Department of State to USUN, 18 September 1960.

97 NAL, FO 371/146792, Minute from Macmillan to Nkrumah, 16 September 1960.

98 NARA, State Department Central Decimal File, Box 326, Telegram from American embassy in London to the State Department, 22 September 1960.

99 NARA, State Department Central Files, Congo, 755.1.00/6-160, Telegram from Harriman in London to Secretary of State, 13 September 1960.

100 NAL, FO 371/146799, Confidential telegram from Stephenson to the Foreign Office, 10 November 1960.

101 NAL, FO 371/146799, Telegram from Commonwealth Relations Office to British embassies in Ottawa, Canberra, Wellington, Pretoria, Delhi, Karachi, Colombo, Accra, Kuala Lumpur, Lagos, Salisbury, Nicosia, 15 November 1960. Ambassadors in India, Ghana and Colombo were instructed not to approach those governments given their quite different positions on the Congo.

102 NAL, FO 371/146799, Confidential telegram from the Commonwealth Relations Office to Ottawa, 17 November 1960. For more on the Canadian role in the Congo crisis see K.A. Spooner, *Canada, the Congo Crisis and UN Peacekeeping, 1960–64* (Vancouver: University of British Columbia Press, 2010).
103 NAL, FO 371/146799, Telegram from Lagos to the Commonwealth Relations Office, 17 November 1960.
104 NAL, FO 371/146799, Telegram from Patrick Dean from New York to the Foreign Office, detailing the vote on 23 November 1960.
105 NAL, FO 371/146799, Telegram from Patrick Dean in New York to the Foreign Office advising them not to give any impression to the Nigerian Prime Minister during his forthcoming visit, that Britain was in any way disgruntled with Wachuku or Nigeria, 24 November 1960.
106 Hoskyns, *The Congo Since Independence*, pp. 259–265 and Weissman, *American Foreign Policy in the Congo*, pp. 107–108.
107 Namikas, *Battleground Africa*, p. 117.
108 AWCP, Box 149, UN Files, Subject Files, Africa – Congo – Cables, III–IV, Telegram from Hammarskjöld to Cordier, 15 August 1960.
109 First Report from the Secretary-General to the Security Council on Assistance to the Republic of the Congo, New York, July 18, 1960, Security Council Official Records, Fifteenth Year, 877th Meeting. Cordier et al., *Public Papers of the Secretaries-General of the United Nations*, p. 28.
110 S/4526, Resolution 157 of the Security Council, 17 September 1960, states that: 'The Security Council, Having considered the item on its agenda as contained in document S/Agenda/906, Taking into account the lack of unanimity of its permanent members at the 906th meeting of the Security Council has prevented it from exercising its primary responsibility for the maintenance of international peace and security, Decides to call an emergency special session of the General Assembly, as provided in General Assembly resolution 377 A(V) of 3 November 1950, in order to make appropriate recommendations', in D.J. Djonovich (ed.), *United Nations Resolutions, Series II, Resolutions and Decisions of the Security Council, Series II* (New York: Oceana, 1989), p. 18.
111 Gaiduk, *Divided Together*, p. 260.
112 NARA, State Department Files, UN, 310/1–460, US Delegation Records, Letter from Theodore L. Eliot Jr., Special Assistant to the Under Secretary of State to Mr. Edward Logan, 5 October 1960.
113 NARA, State Department Files, UN, 310/1–460, US Delegation Records, Comments from Mr Moore, British delegate to the UN to James Wadsworth, American UN delegate, Telegram from USUN New York to Secretary of State, 1 October 1960.
114 NAL, FO 371/146779, Memo from E.B. Boothby, 12 September 1960.
115 NAL, FO 371/146797, Personal comments on the closing stages of the General Assembly special session on the Congo. From Mr Ewart-Biggs in New York to Mr Smith in Foreign Office, 20 September 1960.
116 F.S. Northedge, *Descent from Power: British Foreign Policy 1945–1973* (London: Allen & Unwin, 1974), p. 307.
117 NAL, FO 160953/22516, Confidential Report, 12 January 1961.
118 NAL, FO 160953/22516, Confidential Report, 10 January 1961. For more on this realisation in the Foreign Office see James, *Britain and the Congo Crisis*, pp. 73–75.

119 NAL, FO 160953/22516, Confidential Report from Sir Andrew Cohen to the Foreign Office, 10 January 1961.
120 A.N. Porter and A.J. Stockwell, *British Imperial Policy and Decolonization 1938-64, Volume 2, 1951-64* (London: St. Martin's Press, 1989), p. 64.
121 W.R. Louis, *Imperialism at Bay: The United States and the Decolonization of the British Empire 1941–1945* (Oxford: Oxford University Press, 1987), p. 529.
122 Husain, *Mapping the End of Empire*, p. 221.
123 W.R. Louis and R. Robinson, 'The imperialism of decolonization', *The Journal of Imperial and Commonwealth History*, 22:3 (1994), 462–511.
124 NAL, FO 160953/22516, Colonial Office Memorandum, 30 January 1961.
125 *Ibid.*
126 NAL, FO 160953/22516, Letter to Sir A. Clutterbuck from the Commonwealth Relations Office to 10 Downing Street discussing the analysis of British Ambassador to India Sir Paul Booth on the Indian position, 26 January 1961.
127 NAL, FO 371/146799, Telegram from Patrick Dean in New York to the Foreign Office, 22 December 1960.
128 Telegram from Wadsworth at the US Mission at the United Nations to the Secretary of State, Department of State, New York, 6 December 1960, Schwar and Shaloff, *FRUS, 1958–1960, XIV, Africa*, p. 614.
129 *Ibid.*
130 Despite close cooperation between the US and the UK to devise the resolution, the French abstention in particular hampered the possibility of gathering support among the French African states. It was noted that 'it was very disappointing that France, after all the efforts that had been made on her behalf in Algeria, chose to abstain'. NAL, FO 371/146799, Telegram from Patrick Dean in New York to the Foreign Office, 22 December 1960.
131 NAL, FO 371/146797, Confidential telegram from Foreign Office to New York, 19 September 1960.
132 NAL, FO 371/146797, From the UK Mission to the UN in New York to the Foreign Office, 27 September 1960.
133 In March 1960, sixty-seven black demonstrators were shot dead at Sharpeville and the ANC and PAC parties were banned by the South African Government. This was a particularly tense moment in South Africa where Nelson Mandela and 155 other African nationalists were on trial for treason. Lamb, *The Macmillan Years, 1957–1963*, p. 246; Porter and Stockwell, *British Imperial Policy and Decolonization*, p. 64; Darwin, *Britain and Decolonisation*, pp. 287–288.
134 NAL, FO 160953/22516, 17, Letter from Patrick Jenison, Government House, Kenya, East Africa, to Sir Hilton Poynton, 2 December 1960.
135 NAL, FO 160953/22516, 1303, As copied to the Foreign Office from the UK Delegation to the UN.
136 NAL, FO 160953/22516, 17, Letter from Patrick Jenison, Government House, Kenya, East Africa, to Sir Hilton Poynton, 2 December 1960.
137 Article 2(7) of the UN Charter states that 'Nothing contained in the present Charter shall authorize the United Nations to intervene in matters which are essentially within the domestic jurisdiction of any states or shall require the Members to submit such matter to settlement under the present Charter; but the principle shall not prejudice the application of enforcement measures under Chapter VII'. Goodrich *et al.*, *Charter of the United Nations*, p. 60.

138 NAL, FO 160953/22516, Confidential Telegram from Washington to the Foreign Office, 1 February 1960.
139 Mahoney, *JFK*, p. 4.
140 Conversation between President Eisenhower and Foreign Secretary Lord Home, 19 September 1960, Editorial note, Schwar and Shaloff, *FRUS, Africa 1958–1960*, p. 496.
141 NARA, State Department Central Files, Congo, 755.1.00/6-160, Telegram from Harriman in London to Secretary of State, 13 September 1960.
142 Comments of Mr Livingstone T. Merchant, Undersecretary with French officials. Memorandum of Conversation on the Congo, 13 September 1960, Schwar and Shaloff, *FRUS, 1958–1960*, p. 484.
143 Namikas, *Battleground Africa*, p. 118.
144 For the details see Kanza, *Conflict in the Congo*, pp. 308–309.
145 UNA, S-0845-0004-0011, Secretary-General's correspondence with Ghana, Telegram from Dayal to Hammarskjöld, 1 November 1960.
146 Gerard and Kuklick, *Death in the Congo*, p. 215.
147 See also L. De Vos, E. Gerard, J. Gerard-Libois and P. Raxhon, *Les secrets de l'affaire Lumumba* (Brussels: Editions Racine, 2005); De Witte, *The Assassination of Lumumba*.
148 De Witte, *The Assassination of Lumumba*, p. 55; Gerard and Kuklick, *Death in the Congo*, p. 181.
149 Kanza, *Conflict in the Congo*, p. 312.
150 James, *Britain and the Congo Crisis*, pp. 74–76.
151 Kanza recounts receiving a phone call from Joseph Okito, one of Lumumba's associates who had been arrested and was imprisoned with him in Thysville. He describes that Okito revealed that Lumumba was being severely beaten and he implored Kanza to 'get the UN people to do something – otherwise our prime minister will quite certainly be killed'. Kanza, *Conflict in the Congo*, pp. 317–318.
152 *Ibid.*, p. 315.
153 It was announced on Katanga Radio on Monday 13 February that Lumumba had escaped UN protective custody and been murdered along with his associates by hostile villagers. Kalb, *Congo Cables*, p. 225.
154 For further see Sergei Mazov, 'Soviet aid to the Gizenga government in the former Belgian Congo (1960–1961) as reflected in Russian archives', *Cold War History*, 7:3 (2007), 425–437.
155 It should however be noted that although Lumumba was executed by firing squad on 17 January, this news was not released by the Belgians for three weeks, therefore planning for the February Resolution continued with the assumption that Lumumba would still be part of the political architecture in the Congo. Kent, *America, the UN and Decolonization*, p. 44.
156 UNA, S-0845-0004-12, Secretary-General's correspondence with Ghana, 1961, Communiqué from the Casablanca Conference, 8 January 1961. Following the Casablanca conference in light of the situation in the Congo, Morocco, UAR, Ghana, Guinea, Mali, Algeria, Libya and Ceylon announced their intention to withdraw their troops from ONUC.
157 Gerard and Kukilck, *Death in the Congo*, p. 181.
158 De Witte, *The Assassination of Lumumba*, p. 60.

159 Telegram from the Mission to the United Nations to the Department of State, 31 January 1961. H. Schwar (ed.), *FRUS, 1961–1963, Vol. XX, Congo Crisis* (Washington, DC: Government Printing Office, 1994), p. 37.

160 He also made similar appeals to the governments of Indonesia, Morocco and the UAR. UNA, S-0845–0004–12 Secretary-General's correspondence with Ghana, 1961, Letter from Hammarskjöld to Nkrumah, 26 January 1961.

161 Kanza, *Conflict in the Congo*, p. 319.

162 AWCP, Box 220, UN Files, Public Papers of the Secretaries-General, Ham-Manuscript 1960–1961, Notes. In his first statement to the Security Council on 13 February 1961 after the announcement of Lumumba's death Hammarskjöld called for a 'full and impartial investigation'. In his second statement on 15 February 1961 he refers to the assassination as 'a revolting crime'.

163 'From the onset of the discussion of the Congolese question in the United Nations France had made it clear, both in the Security Council and in the General Assembly at its fourth emergency special session, that it felt misgivings and apprehension regarding United Nations intervention. It had therefore not supported either the resolutions adopted by the Security Council on 14 July or resolution 1471 adopted by the General Assembly at its further emergency special session on 20 September 1960. Events had proved those fears only too well founded, since the Congolese people had even, on occasion, come to consider the United Nations intervention as a threat to their newly-acquired independence.' Comments of the French representative, during a discussion on the United Nations activities in the Congo (ONUC) for the period 14 July to 31 December 1960. UNA, General Assembly, 15th session, S-1069–0015–01, Congo – Fifth Committee documents 1960, Fifth Committee, 813th Meeting, 9 December 1960.

164 Memorandum of conversation, tripartite talks between representatives of America, Britain and France, in Paris, 15 December 1960, Schwar and Shaloff, *FRUS, Africa 1958–1960*, p. 632.

165 AWCP, Box 220, UN Files, Public Papers of the Secretaries-General, Ham-Manuscript 1960–1961, Appeal in the Security Council for support of the Congo Conciliation Commission, UN Headquarters, New York, 14 January 1961. Hammarskjöld recorded this criticism as 'violent attacks on the United Nations operations in the Congo and on the Secretary-General and his integrity'.

166 Gerard and Kukilck, *Death in the Congo*, p. 191.

167 Briefing Paper prepared in the Department of State, Washington. This briefing paper, unsigned and undated, was prepared for a 19 January meeting between President Eisenhower and President-elect Kennedy, Schwar, *FRUS, Vol. XX, Congo*, p. 19.

168 As quoted in Lefever, 'The U.N. as a foreign policy instrument', p. 146.

169 Briefing Paper prepared in the Department of State, Washington. This briefing paper, unsigned and undated, was prepared for a 19 January meeting between President Eisenhower and President-elect Kennedy, Schwar, *FRUS, Vol. XX, Congo*, p. 19.

3

Fighting over Katanga

The six months between September 1960 and February 1961 fully transformed the Congo crisis from a regional Cold War conflict into a lightning rod for wider anti-colonial critiques. The hostile debates between the superpowers during the 15th session of the General Assembly had not just raised Cold War tensions but revealed the Soviet strategy of courting the attention of members of the Afro-Asian bloc by criticising the Western position on the Congo and colonial issues. The multiple ways in which the colonial dimensions of the Congo question spilled over into the wider debates about colonialism and neo-colonial actions of European states highlighted how the Congo question had morphed into a political dilemma of varying proportions. In an effort to sustain a united Western position, the US tried to persuade British officials to overcome their reservations about the UN in general and the use of force against Katanga in order to strengthen the UN force. This friction became most clearly evident in the debates about strengthening ONUC's mandate, which dominated the UN agenda in January and February 1961.

A CIA report on the situation in the Congo of 10 January 1961 concluded that 'the interests and aims of outside powers – the Bloc, the West, and the various African states – are to a large degree contradictory. These interests meet and clash in the UN; they have made a decisive UN policy impossible in the past few months'. The State Department now became intent on providing leadership and clarity to this situation, with the dual aim of consolidating its position in New York and synthesizing its relationship with Hammarskjöld, which, Herter noted, was under strain. This was also due to the fact that under increasing pressure from African and Asian states, particularly India and Ghana, to formulate UN policy with more attention towards their aims, Hammarskjöld had distanced himself from the Western powers. Commenting on developments in the Congo at a meeting of the National Security Council on 12 January, Herter noted that US interests had not been advanced by the way the UN operation in the Congo had been conducted. The newly elected President Kennedy added that one of the most serious problems facing his administration would soon be the determination of relations with the UN.[1]

From the outset, the new administration displayed a firm grasp of the changed nature of the UN under Hammarskjöld, recognising that he was making the UN 'a more meaningful, powerful instrument'.[2] The Americans now sought to harness more directly UN Congo policy as a vehicle for their own policy objectives. The State Department believed that the UN could be used more than it had been to facilitate quiet diplomacy, and the US should be the agent that would lead this initiative.[3] By the middle of January, the conflict in the General Assembly and on the Security Council with the Afro-Asians had to be balanced against Belgian warnings that the situation in the Congo was worsening daily. In a telegram from the American Embassy in Brussels, Ambassador William Burden outlined the importance of devising a coherent stance, urging:

> I am fully aware that unilateral measures outside the framework of general Western policy can serve only to destroy the position of Belgium and the West in the UN and in Africa without any countervailing advantage, but the situation is in part a result of the vacuum created by failure to formulate clear and effective US policy. If we are not able to formulate clear US policy on Congo [sic] to deal with rapidly detonating situation and sell it to our allies rather soon, different elements in Belgium will ... continue to supply their own paramilitary ad hoc solutions.[4]

The potential implications of such actions were not lost to the Kennedy administration. Secretary of State Dean Rusk instructed his staff on 25 January that 'the stakes are so large that we need to take the ceiling off our thinking as to solutions'.[5]

Pursuing a Congo policy through the UN, rather than unilaterally, was a strategic decision on the part of the State Department. The previous month, officials had ruled out any solution outside the UN framework, especially considering that the US was shouldering over half of the financial burden for ONUC. Linked to that, however, was the Cold War imperative to improve relations with the African states, both in the Casablanca Group and the Monrovia Group, as American influence with these allies had waned significantly over the Congo question. Third, there was the issue of UN prestige. As Sture Linner, Head of Civilian Operations in Congo 1960–1961, pointed out, the UN needed a success to 'blunt the Soviet vendetta against Hammarskjöld' which had started with the Troika initiative.[6] The Soviets continued to loudly criticise Hammarskjöld and the UN action in the Congo, with *Pravda* even going as far as to denounce the Secretary-General as a 'butcher' and a 'Judas' in February 1961 following the death of Lumumba.[7] Hammarskjöld's plan for the Congo included reconvening the Parliament, aiding the formation of a new and moderate government, 'neutralising' the ANC and enforcing earlier Security Council resolutions for the withdrawal of all Belgian troops and was broadly agreeable with US interests.[8] The biggest challenge was to find an effective way to cast off accusations of neo-colonialism not just over the Congo but also on other colonial questions while in the process ensuring that an 'anti-Western, anti-UN, pro-Soviet current' did not take root in Africa.[9] This required not just a new approach to the Congo but also a revised approach to the UN.

America's passive attitude towards decolonisation at the UN was seen by many, both inside and outside the US as indicative of the American approach to Africa and African-Americans, revealing that neither was a real priority.[10] Kennedy had deliberately played to the liberal and African-American voting groups by championing the cause of Africa during his presidential campaign. This had resonated with voters connected to the civil rights movement, but as Ted Sorensen argues, it also went to the heart of Kennedy's vision of America in the world. He felt that this was an area in which Republican policy had particularly failed, creating an opening for the Soviets to gain a foothold in the Cold War and damaging American international prestige.[11] Led by Stevenson, the UN increasingly became the focal point for the expression of this policy.

In order to discourage further accusations of neo-colonialism, the Kennedy administration henceforth abandoned the policy of automatically abstaining from voting on resolutions relating to colonial issues in the Security Council and the General Assembly.[12] This was particularly important in the tense atmosphere of debates on the Congo where the nature of the General Assembly was dominated by what Stevenson termed 'swirling majorities', whereby discussions tended to be highly charged due to the predominance of new members.[13] This tempestuous environment meant that it was 'increasingly difficult to mobilize a two-thirds vote for moderate and sensible proposals [and only through] much sweat and sleeplessness [was it possible] to keep action under control'.[14]

In an effort to push for more decisive action, the State Department instructed the USUN delegation to emphasise to Hammarskjöld that 'if the Congo falls under Communist domination while the UN is sharing major responsibility for the security of the country, the results in US public and Congressional opinion are likely to be extremely damaging to the UN'.[15] They presented him with a series of requests including firmer instructions to the UN command in the Congo and the 'replacement of Ambassador Dayal on the grounds that he was biased in favour of Lumumba'. This démarche provoked an angry response from Hammarskjöld who since September believed that the US and the UN were following different philosophies on the Congo. In particular he resented the accusation that his personnel were not impartial and he raised doubts about the accuracy of US intelligence reports which alleged that some officials acted in a partisan manner. As the State Department reflected, such references were reflective of his 'deep-seated distrust of US intelligence activities ... and of his belief that we are similarly involved in the Congo'.[16] This exchange took place in early January before the assassination of Lumumba and forced the State Department to adapt an even more vigorous stance with the Secretary-General, despite his now apparent hostility to being strongarmed. The American Embassy in Léopoldville warned the State Department: 'If we are determined to play the UN card, we must be prepared to ... make clear that if the necessary things are not done, we will withdraw our support of the UN effort, which means its termination.'[17] Washington now actively sought to pilot UN Congo policy with what would become Security Council Resolution 161, which 'represented a sharp break from past US policy'.[18]

The February Resolution: a pyrrhic victory?

On 1 February, Kennedy approved a revised US–Congo policy, the three principal elements of which were: a new mandate for ONUC which would increase its authority to control all military elements in the Congo; the re-establishment of a functioning government in Léopoldville; and increased efforts to block outside assistance.[19] Behind the scenes the US did not rule out the possibility of action outside the UN if the situation required it. As Rusk pointed out to Kennedy, it was 'particularly important that we identify ourselves with some constructive new initiative through the UN because if we later find ourselves faced with the necessity of making a serious effort in the Congo outside the UN framework, it would be essential to show that we had exerted ourselves to work effectively through the UN'.[20] In addition, the newly established Inter-Departmental Working Committee on the Congo noted that in the event of the failure of the UN effort 'we must consider the feasibility of other policies, including military action'.[21] As was characteristic of the crisis, however, the momentum of events soon overtook these carefully laid plans.

The announcement of Lumumba's assassination on 13 February provided the US with an opportunity to use this moment of emergency to engineer UN Congo policy more directly. However, the Afro-Asian bloc now also moved quickly in response. Overtaking the American initiative, they devised a proposal which called for the withdrawal of all foreign military and personnel from the Congo and granted UN troops the right to use force to prevent civil war. Ceylon and the UAR presented the plan to the Security Council on 17 February. Their recommendations drew on the findings of the Conciliation Commission in the Congo, mandated by the General Assembly the previous October. The Commission was composed of a selection of African countries from both the Casablanca and Monrovia groups, alongside the major Asian contributors to ONUC: India and Pakistan.[22] After six weeks of negotiations with Congolese politicians and using its good offices to secure agreements, the Commission had recommended to Hammarskjöld and the CAC that urgent UN action was needed to help create a federal structure for the Congo in order to avoid civil war.[23] Their agreement on the actions mandated in the draft resolution reflected the predominance of the Afro-Asian bloc in determining the course of action for the UN and the means by which a solution could be devised: strengthening ONUC by allowing the use of force. The response in the State Department was 'bitter disagreement'.[24]

Debating the merits of the draft resolution, there was internal division in the State Department between the Africanist group (including Bowles and Williams) who advocated that the US should support the Afro-Asian resolution with certain amendments and the Timberlake group (including Rusk and Ball) who opposed it. The result was a compromise on the original American position and Stevenson was instructed to present two amendments to the resolution: a statement of support for Hammarskjöld and recognition of the Kasavubu Government. However, despite a hard weekend of lobbying before the Security Council met on 17 February, Stevenson failed to persuade the Afro-Asians to adopt the amendments and so the US was left in the position of having to accede to a resolution that it had spearheaded the initiative for, but which was drastically different from what had been intended.

In its final form, the Afro-Asian resolution was presented to the Security Council by Liberia, and passed on 21 February by nine votes to zero, with both France and the USSR abstaining.[25] In an ambivalent decree the resolution authorised forces to '[take] all appropriate measures to prevent the occurrence of civil war in the Congo, including arrangements for ceasefires, the halting of all military operations, the prevention of clashes, and *the use of force, if necessary,* in the last resort'.[26] This military order was in response to the escalating problems in Katanga, where UN troops were coming under increasing attack from Tshombe's mercenary army. This had produced frustration and confusion both among the peacekeepers on the ground, who often lacked efficient communications equipment, and their military commanders in Léopoldville and New York as the interpretations of the existing mandate seemed to vary widely between different national contingents. This lack of clarity in the existing mandate, from the perspective of many African states, was a direct result of the situation in which the mandate had initially been created in the summer of 1960 and represented more a compromise between the powers on the Security Council, rather than a positive scheme to assist the Congo.[27] The strengthening of the mandate, particularly in allowing the peacekeepers to use force, was militarily and politically strategic, designed to produce a more effective peacekeeping mission, but also to assuage political tensions which had erupted after Lumumba's assassination. The application of the new mandate as it has been described by former UN diplomat Conor Cruise-O'Brien, 'would be nothing short of revolutionary'.[28]

Stalling the debate: the British position

As early as 4 February, the US had noted that during deliberations, despite the deteriorating situation, the British remained strongly opposed to the use of force against Katanga. The British viewpoint on the amended US–Congo policy was less than enthusiastic. Although they agreed to support the effort, the Foreign Office was keen to avoid further UN adventurism and was wary of becoming isolated within the UN on the question of the use of force. However, the Head of the African Department, Basil Boothby, warned the Foreign Office ahead of the Security Council meeting that there was little option but to cede to the American request to strengthen ONUC's mandate. 'In order to avoid a deadlock in which we might alienate the sympathies of the moderate Africans and make them withdraw their support from the UN effort', he noted, 'we could, in the last resort, accept the amendments the Americans proposed as a minimum'.[29] The British Cabinet noted that although there had been little choice but to vote for the resolution, the British UN delegation had succeeded in entering a clarification that the resolution could not be used to empower the UN to use force to impose a political settlement.[30] In this way, the Foreign Office sought as a minimum to influence how the resolution would be implemented. The following month, policy planners drafted a position paper for British initiatives at the UN, and formed a set of proposals for the direction of Western policy towards the Congo. Though officials understood the importance of outwardly maintaining support for the resolution, they were not prepared to let the Afro-Asians assert further control over the direction and implementation of policy.[31] Rather, they sought a moratorium on the issue to prevent further deterioration in the British UN position and the relationship with the US.

While the Foreign Office and the Commonwealth Office (CO) were busy strategising about how to limit the effect of the resolution, the State Department was growing increasingly concerned about the direction of British colonial policy. During the week following the passing of the resolution, Kennedy dispatched Undersecretary of State for Political Affairs, Averell Harriman, on a visit to London, Bonn and Rome in order to drum up support among the relevant heads of state for the new Congo plan.[32] Over dinner in Admiralty House, Macmillan emphasised the great work that Britain was doing in unwinding the empire and decried the activities of Williams in Africa. During a high-profile visit to East Africa in early 1961 the American Assistant-Secretary of State for African Affairs had made several statements about the British failure to adequately advance its colonies towards independence. Macmillan defended British colonial policy and plans for decolonisation in Africa, stating: 'It was deeply wounding to Britain when the United States Government or Americans individually accused the United Kingdom of being an evil reactionary influence and pilloried her in the United Nations.' He implored Harriman to communicate to Kennedy that all Britain wanted was to be allowed to finish the job of dismantling the empire, unhindered by outside influences. 'If American sniping at British policy went on', he said, 'bitter feelings would be aroused in the United Kingdom which would do real damage to Anglo-American relations.'[33]

As Hammarskjöld and ONUC sought to implement the resolution, these Anglo-American differences rose to the surface. British officials were under the impression that the Americans were 'overly sensitive to Afro-Asian opinion', which had the effect of granting too much legitimacy to ONUC.[34] A senior British Foreign Office official reported in April 1961 that 'the use of force by the United Nations is not going to produce an answer in the Congo. The Congolese are learning to be quite skilful at non-violent non-cooperation which is liable to develop (as in India in the old days) into occasional violence'.[35] In an attempt to limit the implementation of the resolution against Katanga, and crucially, in order to prevent a public schism with the Americans, Britain secured a guarantee from the US for a moratorium on the Congo at the UN. Conceding that the crisis was proving detrimental to Western unity, the State Department recommended President Kennedy to agree to a limiting of the debate on the Congo.[36] In avoiding the public debates, the US agreed to 'work in the United Nations corridors in order to head off or defeat radical resolutions which may be presented and to encourage a moderate outcome'.[37]

This decision to introduce a moratorium on the Congo was a direct response to the general feeling of 'advancing steadily into a bog with no way out'.[38] As the British Permanent Representative to the UN, Sir Patrick Dean, warned, 'we keep on saying that we are there to give the United Nations full support ... at the same time we are not ready in fact to back the Secretary-General up to the extent which he thinks necessary to accomplish his purpose'. He continued, 'we are drifting into an increasingly difficult position ... although we avowedly support the UN effort we really do not want it to succeed too well ... The time really has come when we ought to think out carefully what our objective is and if possible reach agreement about it with the Americans'.[39] The debate on the Congo was damaging to British interests, to their relationship with other countries and to the UN as a whole. The moratorium did little to effect any change in the atmosphere at the UN or solve the crisis; by May 1961 the organisation still faced the same questions over the reintegration of Katanga and the US continued to urge Britain to pressure Tshombe into negotiations. The American consent to a 'moratorium' reflected that considerations of Anglo-American relations played a role in policymaking at the UN where Western dominance was under threat.[40] In this instance, the public nature of debate at the Security Council and the General Assembly undermined Anglo-American efforts to coordinate Congo policy. It also set the tone for the dynamic between them on the issue: the struggle to limit ONUC and the increasing difference of opinion over how resolutions should be implemented.

The February Resolution also destroyed Western consensus on the Congo and forced a wedge between members of the Western bloc. Many European states including Belgium and France shared the British view that the resolution went too far.[41] Belgium, having been opposed to the new American plan for the Congo from the outset, was particularly hostile to paragraphs calling for the removal of all Belgian military and political advisors from the Congo.[42] UN troops in Katanga were considered 'an ever-present threat to Belgian interests' and the whole UN operation was regarded as damaging to Belgian economic interests in the Congo.[43] Smeared with Lumumba's blood, the struggling Belgian Government, led by Eyskens, threatened to withdraw from NATO. This was another serious below to Western unity exacerbated by a disparaging anti-UN press campaign in Britain and Belgium which criticised the increasing assertiveness of the organisation, further damaging UN prestige.[44]

In the week following the adoption of the resolution, relations between the UN and the Central Government also deteriorated. Kasavubu's regime was resistant to the resolution, which they viewed as a violation of Congolese sovereignty. In Stanleyville, pro-Communist forces led by Lumumba's former Deputy Gizenga gained ground, reigniting fears of a Communist takeover of Léopoldville, or at the very least a full-blown civil war between the two factions.[45] The clashing of Sudanese soldiers under UN command with the ANC at the port of Banana in March further stoked discord between the UN and the Congolese. The Minister of the Interior, Albert Delvaux, demanded that his Government be allowed to decide which countries should be part of ONUC.[46] Their opposition to the February Resolution and shared criticism of the UN did, however, serve to bring Kasavubu and Tshombe closer together. On 5 March, following a lengthy meeting in Tananarive, they agreed on a federal structure for the Congo that would allow the provinces of Katanga and Kasai certain freedoms in return for a directing a greater proportion of their revenues to the Léopoldville Government.[47] Despite the promise of these terms, the agreement was contrary to the nation-state

Lumumba had espoused and so risked being rejected by his supporters in Parliament. Moreover, the idea that the Congo should evolve as anything other than a unified, fully integrated state was anathema to the Secretary-General and the State Department.

Drifting apart: relations with Hammarskjöld

Hammarskjöld acknowledged that the February Resolution added to the duties of ONUC, widening the scope and application of the existing mandate.[48] He was adamant that it be executed with full force, viewing the mandate as enhancing the moral value of the mission.[49] Yet despite this further empowerment of ONUC to deal with the conflicting factions they encountered, in effect, implementation of the resolution increased pressures on Hammarskjöld, particularly with regard to two key issues: reconvening the Congolese national Parliament and balancing relations with members of the Afro-Asian bloc who supplied the majority of the troops for ONUC, against the opposition of European states to the direction of the mission. As the largest supplier of troops, Indian representatives warned Hammarskjöld that although they would increase their troop commitment, Indian soldiers were not to be used for the suppression of any popular movements, but could be used against Belgian military and mercenary forces.[50] Ghana similarly agreed to supply more troops but Nkrumah declared the situation so serious that he planned to travel to New York personally to discuss with the Secretary-General how to 'Africanise' ONUC in order to 'eliminate the Cold War from the Congo'. He also signalled his intention to communicate his views to the press in order to drum up public support for his plan.[51]

Harnessing public opinion was a direct and successful response to the British effort to stall the Congo debate which Toure and Nkrumah denounced as a wicked manoeuvre.[52] Following the resolution, in March 1961, along with India's commitment of three battalions, Liberia sent one company, Malaya 800 and Tunisia 600 officers and men to bolster ONUC.[53] Hammarskjöld's reliance on African and Asian troops in order to implement the resolution led him to respond to their objectives, resisting American efforts to direct the operation and contributing towards dismantling the image of the UN as a tool of Western policy. However, this effort to consolidate the reinforced UN Congo policy with the Afro-Asians soon brought him into conflict with the State Department.

The first issue of contention which arose between Hammarskjöld and the Americans was the proposed removal of Dayal as his Special Representative in the Congo. As early as 5 November 1960, Albert Kalonji, the leader of South Kasai, accused Dayal of partisan behaviour in allowing Guinean and UAR forces to distribute weapons, ammunition and uniforms to Lumumba rebels, 'for the purpose of generalizing the chaos'.[54] The US, Belgium and Britain similarly regarded him as an adversary responsible for clashes between Congolese soldiers and UN troops.[55] Timberlake cabled the State Department in December outlining the differences he had with Dayal who considered the Belgian activities in 'advising' Mobutu as being part of a US effort to undermine the UN mission.[56] This condemnation of US policy turned officials firmly against Dayal and they now tried to find a way to remove him from the Congo. During a discussion at the White House on 3 March, it was agreed that Rusk would urge Nehru to recall him and Stevenson would take up the issue with Hammarskjöld. What the State Department had underestimated, however, was the relationship between the Secretary-General and the Indian diplomat. As Richard J. Mahoney has described it: 'There was a monkish quality to both men-in manner, aloof and ascetic; in mind, privately consumed with spiritual questions and publicly engaged in their defence'.[57] Hammarskjöld saw his alter-ego in Dayal and supported him publicly against a Western-led press campaign that had denounced the Indian as 'arrogant' and '[ignorant of] how to get along with Africans'.[58] Dayal had held out against these attacks and Hammarskjöld refuted the charges against him. He set about devising a strategy that would pave the way towards reconvening the Parliament, and in the process improve the relationship between Dayal and Kasavubu as a way of deterring US efforts to get rid of him.[59]

First, the Secretary-General resisted direct pressure from the US, telling Stevenson bluntly that 'over the table' attacks on him by the Russians were no worse than the 'under the table' attacks on Dayal by the West.[60] He was adamant that any effort to remove the Indian might be construed as the UN bowing to American pressure, damaging the perception of neutrality which was important in safeguarding the activities of UN peacekeepers. Further, he was critically dependent on the supply of Indian troops for ONUC and had no wish to sour relations with Nehru, who refused to recall Dayal for at least another three months.[61] Dayal himself soon ended the standoff. In light of the controversy surrounding his position he offered to step down in order to 'safeguard the office of the Secretary-General'.[62] Hammarskjöld capitalised on this change of personnel to advance the second stage of implementing the resolution. He seized the opportunity to improve relations with Kasavubu, pushing him more forcefully towards a restoration of Parliament. Through a series of messages, Hammarskjöld sought an accommodation, pointing out that the Congo was still financially reliant on UN support. After the clashes between UN troops and Congolese forces in Banana, Hammarskjöld issued Kasavubu with an 'urgent appeal to exercise your great influence as Chief of State so that a solution may be found very quickly to the immediate problems, without the complications involved in the attitude hitherto taken by the Congolese spokesmen – complications which, I greatly fear, would have very widespread and dangerous consequences'.[63]

These consequences are more explicitly outlined in a later telegram in which Hammarskjöld threatens to suspend or withdraw UN financial aid to the Congo, a worrying predicament given the state of Congolese finances.[64] In April 1961, the UN received a report from the Governor of the National Bank of the Congo on the economic situation and the action required to tackle it. It was grim reading. Albert Ndele revealed that in the first nine months since independence, the state had accumulated a budget deficit of 4,500 million francs. He appealed for more UN aid, stating: 'Serious though the situation is, it should not be regarded as desperate; but a real effort is required if it is to be prevented from becoming so'.[65] This realisation that cooperation with ONUC and financial aid were tied together quickly led Kasavubu to adopt a more conciliatory tone as efforts were made to reconstitute the national

Parliament through the summer of 1961. Dayal's departure, which Kasavubu had long desired, alongside Hammarskjöld's careful bargaining with economic aid, succeeded in improving relations with the Central Government. This in turn fortified his ability to use his personal agency and quiet diplomacy to shape Congo policy and resist American influence.

In order to consolidate the position of the UN further, Hammarskjöld initiated the third phase of his plan, which was to further crystallise the support of the Afro-Asian bloc. He turned back to the CAC, in order to reflect his preference for Afro-Asian rather than an Anglo-American interpretation of the resolution.[66] The CAC advocated the establishment of a second Conciliation Commission for the Congo, composed of seven members who would help the Congolese leaders achieve reconciliation.[67] This was in conjunction with an Investigation Commission to examine the circumstances of Lumumba's death, to directly address one of the biggest concerns of the group.[68] The Commissions were formally announced on 15 April alongside a General Assembly Declaration that called again on Belgium to withdraw all military and political personnel.[69] In the face of this productive and cooperative relationship, American and British policy achieved very little.

While Dayal's departure from the Congo had been well received in the State Department, during this period the Kennedy administration seemed similarly occupied with removing Timberlake. A leftover from the Eisenhower administration, he was largely considered by the new administration to be too heavily influenced by the Congolese.[70] He advocated a hard-line approach towards the neutralists, which was in contrast to the Africanist group at the State Department who believed that courting African leaders such as Nkrumah was the best way to outflank the Russians in Africa. While Kennedy sorted out his house, the Americans lost the vigour with which they had approached the Congo question at the UN in January. Although the State Department did work the diplomatic channels with Nehru and other allies such as Prime Minister Ikeda of Japan in order to mobilise support for the Secretary-General, this was primarily a Cold War strategy. In communications with Nehru, the Americans emphasised that the USSR was 'continuing to exploit every possibility to attempt to denigrate the Secretary-General and the UN operation in the Congo'.[71] The American focus on emphasising the Cold War dimensions of the conflict in communications with the Afro-Asian bloc reflected that their main aim was still the prevention of the spread of Soviet influence, rather than a clear emphasis on the creation of a coherent policy towards the implementation of the resolution. They actually abstained from voting on the 15 April resolution urging Belgium to withdraw its troops, believing that there was little chance of persuading Belgium to cooperate.[72]

Through the summer of 1961, the US continued to be indecisive, even when the Congolese Parliament was eventually reconvened with half of the ministries held by former Lumumba supporters. What efforts the State Department did make to assure the election of Cyrille Adoula, the new Western-friendly Congolese premier, were primarily through its embassies in Léopoldville and Elisabethville, and through the

CIA, rather than through the UN. What dominated the US agenda in terms of UN relations was not the Congo question but tensions with the USSR and their proposed restructuring of the Secretariat. The result of this increasing Cold War perspective of the Americans at the UN, despite their earlier declarations to reinvigorate USUN policy, had the effect of destroying consensus between Hammarskjöld and the State Department on the Congo.

In the months following the February resolution there was a sense of jubilation at the Secretariat. In a memo to Rusk, Harlan Cleveland in New York noted the Secretary-General's satisfaction with what he termed a 'major water-shed in his career'. In response to the implementation of the February Resolution, the USSR had revised its position on the Congo, backing down from its earlier calls for the removal of the UN and replacing Hammarskjöld with a troika power structure.[73] Hammarskjöld considered that the Soviets had learned that it was 'difficult to deal with the situation where the Afro-Asian group and the UN executive are together on an issue'.[74] As Cleveland summarised it to Rusk: 'in spite of all the talk about the devastating effects of the Soviet attack on the Secretary-General, that estimable executive clearly won the 1960–61 round in what will doubtless be a continuing fight'.[75]

While this Cold War 'victory' was welcomed in Washington, there was a growing concern about the ways in which Hammarskjöld could use his office when he had the support of the Afro-Asians, which undercut the US position. Close cooperation with the Afro-Asians had demonstrated that the UN Charter was a flexible instrument, 'capable of development along lines not originally foreseen, and that one of the most significant of these is the expanding role of the Secretary-General'.[76] Over the summer, there was a concerted effort among American policymakers towards the 'prevention of further slippage of the Secretary-General towards the position of the Soviets or the Afro-Asians'.[77] From this point onwards, the UN was increasingly assertive in the Congo until U Thant took over the position of Secretary-General in September 1961. Weissman has described that 'by institutionalizing neutral opinion, the United Nations could exercise some constraint on the actions of the big powers'.[78] Hammarskjöld had implemented the resolution in such a way as to realise his vision for the UN as a forum for decolonised powers and smaller nations. Any attempt to court African and Asian leaders had thus far resulted only in encouraging them to consolidate their position with the Secretary-General. Realising that Western consensus on the Congo caused the US to be tarred by association with European former colonial powers, the US now pursued a parallel strategy, toughening again its stance towards colonial issues at the UN. Outlining the broad views of the administration and its thinking behind American policy on colonial questions, Stevenson pointed out that Western imperialism in its classical form was dead and an expansive interpretation of the objections of the Afro-Asians to the mere notion of colonialism was fundamental as they pursued their own agenda with regard to colonial matters.[79] By performing more anti-colonial sentiments, the State Department now sought to change its image in the eyes of African and Asian leaders. This, however, had serious consequences for the Anglo-American relationship.

'Pushing at an open door': Anglo-American relations and anti-colonial struggle in 1961

By March 1961, the colonial dimensions of the Congo question increasingly served the broader agenda of the anti-colonialists across Africa, as the Commonwealth states themselves openly disagreed about how the UN operation should proceed. Efforts to devise a common position on the issue of seating Kasavubu's delegation in the General Assembly had exposed to the Foreign Office not just the limits of British influence in constructing a united approach, but also the damage the Congo problem posed for the unity of the Commonwealth as a whole. British officials now sought again to engineer an agreement between the Commonwealth states on how to implement the resolution, in order to bolster its UN position while recognising that there 'is likely to be a good deal of disagreement and disillusionment over what can be done in practice'.[80] By securing a base of support among members of the Commonwealth, Britain attempted to undercut the impact of colonial debates both on the British position at the UN and British plans for decolonisation. As part of this approach the Foreign Office advised the Prime Minister that newly decolonised states should be excluded from these discussions at the Commonwealth Prime Ministers' Conference in March 1961.[81] This was a bid to prevent anti-colonial sentiment from pervading internal discussions. Hoping to agree a common position, Britain sought to obstruct the General Assembly's Special Committee on Decolonization (henceforth: the Committee of 24).[82] Formed on 22 December 1961 with the aim of speedily implementing Resolution 1451, the Committee of 24 presented a series of resolutions to the General Assembly regarding the reporting of the political status of remaining colonies which directly affected British policies in those territories.

Alongside the effort to draw the Commonwealth members into agreement on the Congo question and on colonial issues, the Foreign Office also strove to work as closely as possible with the State Department and overcome differences surrounding use of force. Efforts were intensified when the Colonial Secretary, Ian McLeod, pointed out that officials in the State Department now tended to make decisions based on their own information, 'being careful not to consult with, for example, the UK before they decided, lest they be influenced or contaminated'.[83] Realising that cooperation at the UN posed the potential for real conflict, British officials now tried to work more closely with their American counterparts to offset the damaging effects of the Committee of 24.[84] The aim was to combine British and American initiatives to present a united front to other delegations in order to maintain the Western position.[85]

However, as Britain had experienced in trying to influence Nigeria and India over the Congo question in November, there was growing realisation in the Foreign Office that British influence among former colonies was waning. British representatives at the UN experienced déjà vu in discussions with the Afro-Asians on the Committee of 24 and the Special Political and Decolonization Committee (henceforth the Fourth Committee) which was set up to deal with a range of issues arising from decolonisation. In both spaces, delegates contended with similar questions of when Britain would grant independence to remaining territories, what preparations were being made and why this was not taking place more quickly. Commonwealth Secretary Duncan Sandys remarked to Macmillan that he was 'tired of resolutions on Colonialism, why should we not sponsor resolutions on freedom?'[86] With regard to granting independence to dependent territories he said that British policy was 'pushing at an open door'. The problem in the British view was that UN involvement in colonial matters constituted interference in its domestic affairs. A confidential memo to the Prime Minister noted that Britain would have to 'work hard' at the UN in order to justify its objections to resolutions on colonialism as peace and success in remaining dependent territories may be prejudiced by provocative speeches and resolutions. 'In particular, we are absolutely opposed to the establishment of deadlines for independent states; this applies whether the resolution is general or specific.'[87] This position, however, clashed with the Kennedy administration's shift away from abstaining on colonial resolutions, in order to demonstrate that the US still defended the right of nations to independence and freedom.[88] The perception that Britain, and by extension the US, was a target for criticism because of British colonial policy put colonial issues at the centre of the agenda for Anglo-American talks in March 1961.

The looming General Assembly debate on the implementation of Resolution 1514 in British colonies was among the primary concerns for the State Department during the talks. American officials pressed their British counterparts to set specific dates for the independence of non-self-governing territories. The British naturally objected, arguing that the Congo itself was one example of how setting a specific date for independence before the domestic government had been settled was disastrous.[89] Though they recognised that the Kennedy administration would no longer automatically abstain from resolutions on colonialism, British representatives requested that the US consult with them in cases where there may be a divergence in views before stating their position publicly.[90] In a discussion with the Permanent Under-Secretary of State for Foreign Affairs Sir Harold Caccia Rusk pointed out that, despite British objections about infringement on their policies, the over-arching danger was that a division between the West and what he termed 'new nationalism' would encourage the spread of Communist influence, and therefore the US could not be publicly or privately associated with any form of neo-colonialism. As Caccia ruefully noted later, 'It was clearly not possible at these talks to secure from the Americans an undertaking in principle to back us or secure a blank cheque for support in the United Nations'.[91]

Efforts to cooperate on colonial questions were a double-edged sword for the US, especially as Kennedy rolled out his policy of engaging more closely with Africa by widely publicising personal meetings with African leaders at the White House.[92] Although UN cooperation and the creation of clandestine Anglo-American working groups aimed to harmonise positions on colonial questions and develop better Anglo-American relations in the area, the consultation process also made the representation and execution of policies at the UN more difficult when agreement could not be reached. The State Department attempted to balance this cooperation against consistent criticism from African leaders of America's alliances with European colonial powers. In a telling remark in July 1961, the Foreign Minister of Mali, Jean-Marie Kone, put it bluntly to Kennedy, quoting an African proverb: 'The friend of my enemy is my adversary.'[93] This growing condemnation also served to increase US determination to vote alone on colonial issues. British Congo policy, and the issue of the independence of Portuguese colonies, combined both of these challenges for American foreign policy in Africa in 1961.

The outbreak of violence in Angola in February between the forces of the Portuguese administration and black Angolan freedom fighters forced the issue, revealing the tension between American policy in Africa and British colonial policy. For the first time, the US broke with Britain and voted for a Security Council resolution on 9 June, calling for Portugal to end colonialism.[94] This was highly significant. The US publicly supported Angolan independence, much to the annoyance of Portugal, Britain and France, who abstained. The resolution also drew on General Assembly Resolution 1514 and directly condemned the repressive measures of the Portuguese authorities in Angola. It employed the language and terminology of the Committee of 24 in pointing to Portugal's responsibilities regarding non-self-governing territories. It was interpreted by the European former colonial powers therefore as an example of UN interference and a clear condemnation of their colonial policies by the US. The Foreign Office noted that although they had managed to persuade the Americans to abstain from voting for Resolution 1514, the American vote against Portugal basically amounted to a vote for the same principles. The British Embassy in Washington was instructed to inform its State Department colleagues of the Foreign Office view that 'resolutions of this sort present a real practical problem for us in a way which they do not for the Americans … it is quite wrong to vote for them merely in order to curry favour with some of the Afro-Asians and other so called neutral delegations'.[95] Although the risk of losing a NATO base in the Azores, essential for re-fuelling and airlifting troops on flights to the Middle East, stopped the US from voting in favour of any more resolutions condemning Portuguese colonial policy, the die had been cast. America had voted for African nationalism at the UN, formally breaking with the British position on colonial issues.

'Sacred drama' at the General Assembly[96]

While the public nature of debates on colonial questions were one dimension of the UN's impact on Anglo-American relations, the role of the organisation as a space for socialisation and an incubator for ideas also came to the fore during the 16th session of the General Assembly in September 1961. Hammarskjöld's determination that the UN act as an 'agent for the liquidation of colonialism', and the insistence of the Afro-Asian bloc and non-aligned leaders that Resolution 1514 be implemented in a timely manner, put colonial issues on top of the agenda.[97] Up to the closing of the session in June 1962, thirty-four separate resolutions were passed (without including those on the Congo) relating to colonial conflicts in Algeria, Angola, Rwanda, South-West Africa and Tanganyika, and the status of non-self-governing territories in other areas. The momentum behind the anti-colonial campaign, in addition to the support of the Secretariat and their majority in the General Assembly, led the Afro-Asians to direct the debate towards the issues they deemed pertinent. In the drafting process for the tabling and passing of resolutions, they were, to a significant extent, able to formulate and finalise recommendations on their own terms (as they had done with earlier resolutions on the Congo), which for the most part did not require the support of either the West or the Soviet bloc.

The importance of the ability of the Afro-Asian bloc to bring its influence to bear on the more powerful nations within the General Assembly is significant because, through these debates, traditional European colonialism became officially illegitimate. The Fourth Committee and the Committee of 24 served as important socialising spaces where African and Asian representatives directly challenged the former colonial powers and presented the outcomes of their debates as resolutions on colonialism which were aimed at exposing the futility of European colonial policies. The American decision to distance itself from European allies on colonial questions in voting for such resolutions had the effect of legitimising African and Asian perceptions of how and when decolonisation should take place. It also served to challenge the policies of European colonial powers to the extent that their colonial policies and plans for postcolonial relations which sustained colonial networks of power became rapidly delegitimised. Such were the effects of this altered normative environment that despite earlier pronouncements to the contrary, in September 1961 Britain was forced to announce that in future, information on the political and constitutional progress of British self-governing territories would be submitted to the UN.[98]

The informal restructuring of the UN also had a significant impact on the organisation's potential to develop agency in this area. Not only were member-states and Secretariat officials empowered to operationalise the concept of self-determination but the UN was largely able to constrain the Western powers on colonial issues, with the exception of Portuguese conduct in Angola and the question of apartheid in South Africa. The strongly worded resolutions on colonial problems across Africa and Asia passed in the 16th session was devastating for European colonial policies and signalled the end of empire by formal means. Empowered by the energy of the previous year, the Afro-Asian bloc, alongside the Latin American group, led an assault on the position of the Western powers on a range of different colonial questions, from the ongoing anti-colonial struggle in Algeria and Angola, to the continued intransigence of South Africa, the struggle of South-West Africa and the wider racial dimensions which these issues increasingly brought into focus. In a speech before the General Assembly, the Brazilian delegate went as far as to suggest that the Portuguese and South Africans should 'clear out if they could so easily flout the Universal Declaration of Human Rights'. Meanwhile, the newly elected President of the General Assembly, Monghi Slim, declared that 'peace will be consistently threatened if the hideous spectre of racism is not banished forever', angering South Africans with his provocation.[99]

Such proclamations and the committee work of the Afro-Asian bloc on colonial issues emphasised the moral authority of the UN, enhancing the agency of the Secretariat and the changing the way the organisation was perceived. Indeed, many African and Asian delegations believed that the power and authority of the UN was being tested by the process and therefore connected the success of the decolonisation campaign directly with the prestige of the UN as a whole. In addition, they judged that remaining colonial powers such as Portugal and the apartheid regime in South Africa continued to survive because the Great Powers supported them and hence they sought to, and succeeded in, splitting Western unity on colonial questions.[100] The Congo crisis, with clear colonial dimensions, resonated with these wider debates and the dynamics of the anti-colonial campaign. It reflected that within the UN the colonial dimensions had in fact an even wider resonance than the Cold War arguments for the development of UN Congo policy. The shift in both British and American UN policies on colonial issues revealed how 'the UN developed from being viewed by many as the arm of US intervention abroad to being an altogether different organization'.[101]

'A dialogue with the deaf'[102]

This backdrop of differing positions on colonial matters, the shifting normative environment and differing views on the role of the UN led to what Stevenson referred to as a 'dialogue with the deaf' in Anglo-American relations during the spring of 1961. Escalating tensions in the Congo exacerbated matters. Since March, and despite Kasavubu's more temperate attitude, ONUC had experienced increasing resistance from various elements within the state, with sporadic confrontations breaking out in various areas. Hammarskjöld became convinced that the Central Government wanted to hinder the work of the UN by closing various airports and preventing the free passage of UN troops. Despite the by now publicly different positions on colonial issues, the US sought an accommodation with Britain in order to consolidate the Western position in support of the UN to discourage separatist elements within the Congo from gaining ground.

On 4 April, Home visited Washington and discussed views on the situation with Rusk. He maintained that the British had been using their influence to urge moderation on the Congolese through their representatives in Léopoldville and Elisabethville in order to downplay media reports of a rift in relations with Tshombe, although he re-stated their objection to the use of force against Katanga. Rusk was adamant that the two countries should remain on an even keel with regard to developments in the Congo.[103] Part of the reason for this was what he termed the 'glassy stare' the US had received from France in response to a request for financial and moral support. Home willingly concurred, referring to the French policy as being to 'do nothing, pay nothing, say nothing'.[104] In order to reconstitute the Western position, therefore, even without French support, it was agreed that Stevenson and Dean would jointly approach Hammarskjöld to work out the next steps for the UN in the Congo.

This Anglo-American effort to regain a commanding influence at the UN was certainly central to the agenda of Macmillan's first official visit to Washington with Kennedy as President in April 1961. In parallel with the renewed attempt to formulate a joint position on the Congo, the Prime Minister again pushed that the Foreign Office should be left to its own devices when it came to colonial questions and the winding down of the empire, or as he put it, 'the development into the Commonwealth'.[105] He questioned the value of continued attempts to court the favour of the Afro-Asian bloc, asking: 'did it always pay to vote with the[m]?'[106] Dean went further, stating that the Afro-Asian group were 'subject to hysteria', whereby a vote against their resolutions was a vote against all of Africa; a position which was encouraged by the Soviets.

Despite British efforts to sow seeds of doubt among the Americans about the reliability of the Afro-Asians in order to gain more room for manoeuvre, Stevenson remained adamant that favourable relations were essential to the formulation of acceptable Congo policies. He noted that it was 'not always fatal if the US and the UK did not always vote identically', and that that from this point onwards, efforts to formulate a joint Anglo-American position on the Congo would not necessitate voting together on resolutions or on other colonial matters. Rather, he signalled the intention of the US delegation to present itself as 'an honest broker' which would always take a position in favour of self-determination, especially when dealing with sensitive colonial questions. Thereby, the US hoped to 'exercise restraint on the extremists'.[107] Overall, while both sides committed to closer cooperation at the UN, the American support for self-determination and the British resistance towards any interference with its own colonial agenda led to stalemate on formulating a joint position on the Congo. The only thing that they could agree on was that any rift that occurred between them in light of these contrasting positions, should, at least, be kept private.

Despite Macmillan's assurances in Washington for closer cooperation at the UN, the vitriolic attacks on the Western colonial powers by the Committee of 24 soon dominated the focus of British UN delegates. Britain was represented on the Committee by Sir Hugh Foot, who was resolute about the British position. Evoking Churchill's rhetoric, he stated: 'We shall fight on resolutions. We shall fight in the corridors. We shall fight in the Committees. We shall never abstain.'[108] The pressure on the British Government mounted when the USSR conducted an investigation into what it termed 'British perpetration of neo-colonialism', issuing a report alleging that Britain continued to deliberately foster a dependence on London among its African colonies, through the creation of 'federations'. The purpose of such, according to the Soviets, was for Britain to delay the process of granting independence to these colonies.[109]

In the context of this escalating Soviet campaign to influence the Afro-Asian bloc and alongside the East–West conflict, the issue of China's representation at the UN further highlighted the extent of disagreement between American and Britain on UN issues. The question that arose was whether or not the Peiping Government of Communist China would be recognised and granted a seat, despite the fact that Taiwan was already a member. Kennedy was adamant that the US would never acquiesce to their admission. He referred to his last meeting with Eisenhower on 19 January in which the latter stated that he 'would feel it necessary to return to political life if the Chinese communists were admitted to the United Nations'.[110] The State Department was of the view that such an action, or the passing of any resolution granting admission, would have a two-fold negative effect for the US. Not only would it unleash a wave of distrust within the UN, but it would also bolster the overall position and credibility of Communists worldwide. Domestically it was also perceived that for the new administration to be defeated on a resolution regarding Chinese admission to the

UN would cause 'incalculable problems' for the US.[111] However, the Foreign Office considered that Britain was already bound by its recognition of Communist China and therefore, according to Home, 'would have to vote for [them] in any credible vote'.[112] The discussion of how to solve this problem produced a number of different resolutions including the most drastic suggestion of amending the UN Charter or an enlargement of the Security Council.[113] Home believed that the Americans understood the British position but outwardly disagreed with it.[114] For its part, the State Department specifically instructed the US delegation to the UN to refrain from any negotiation with the British representatives regarding the Chinese issue.[115] In a testament to the growing disparity between them a progress report several days after the discussion revealed that the two had essentially agreed to disagree. This impasse was similarly reflected by ineffective efforts to influence Hammarskjöld on the Congo issue again over the summer of 1961.

Ganging up on Hammarskjöld

On 1 May, a memo for President Kennedy on Soviet tactics at the UN revealed the growing concerns of the State Department about the balance of power within the organisation.[116] Despite the fact that the position of the Secretary-General had been fortified by positive votes in the General Assembly, officials were still sceptical about a possible resurgence from the Soviets and believed that Hammarskjöld was being too optimistic in his belief that Khrushchev would back down over the Congo issue.[117] They now looked to Britain to step up pressure on Tshombe to negotiate with Kasavubu and tried to consolidate the Anglo-American position by improving relations with Hammarskjöld on the Congo.

Following the visit of the Secretary-General to Britain in May 1961, the Foreign Office cabled the State Department with the view that he was rather too sanguine about the extent to which he could rely on the uncommitted countries in their support against tri-partism.[118] They shared concerns about the 'wearing effects of the Soviet propaganda strategy within the UN' and pointed out that although the direct danger to Hammarskjöld's position had been removed by the overwhelming vote supporting his position on the Congo in April, the USSR had succeeded in raising valid questions about the responsibilities of the Secretariat. Along those lines Hammarskjöld had begun a reorganisation of the Secretariat in order to reflect the altered political composition of the UN. This essentially consisted of changing the number of Under-Secretaries from four to five in order to allow for more representation from Afro-Asian and Eastern European member-states, with a geographical distribution of power. Hammarskjöld's plan aimed to vest more authority in his direct subordinates, ensuring that two Under-Secretaries would represent each of the seven geographical areas. But insisting upon equal representation for each of the groups would mean, from the American perspective, that it would be impossible to avoid having a Soviet Under-Secretary, which was something they were not willing to accept.[119] Not only was this considered by State Department officials as basically handing the USSR a position of influence within the UN, it would also reduce their own weight with the Secretary-General.

Reflecting his earlier resilience towards American pressure, Hammarskjöld held his ground again against these objections from the US. He stated that he 'saw no reason why the US should be disturbed by his plans for reorganisation, nor how, having in mind the altered composition of the UN, [the US] could be considered as entitled to more than one position at Under-Secretary level'.[120] In response the US tried to play hardball in the usual way, indicating that the American Congress may find it difficult to understand why they should continue to authorise such large contributions to finance UN operations when the US had essentially suffered a reduction in its formal position within the organisation. Hoping to circumvent Hammarskjöld's plan for the reorganisation of the secretariat, it was even suggested that if a British representative were to hold one of the Under-Secretary positions alongside an American in another, the whole plan might seem more agreeable.[121] In a policy planning meeting at the State Department, Cleveland talked in general terms about the broad perceptions and functions of the UN, revealing that the Americans recognised that the nature of the UN was changing and the days when they controlled the institution were gone. US policy planners believed that the forces of nationalism, which were changing the nature and structure of the UN, could be harnessed in order to suit US interests.[122]

The broader context of decolonisation was crucial in this reconsideration of the UN, with the State Department repeatedly pressing upon the American delegation that providing firm leadership to the Afro-Asians was the best strategy to improve their UN position.[123] Harnessing British colonial networks and Commonwealth influence with members of the Afro-Asian bloc also produced a strategy to strengthen the Anglo-American position in order to gain ground with the African states in particular. From the American perspective it was important to exercise more control over the Secretariat to prevent the Soviets from climbing the UN ladder. Indeed Western solidarity both in the face of Afro-Asian deliberations and against the Soviets was increasingly important towards the end of 1961 as the USSR had indicated that though Hammarskjöld may have won the first round over the troika proposal, the State Department anticipated that Soviet delegates would 'hammer at the door' during the forthcoming 16th session of the General Assembly.[124]

For their part, the British expressed pessimism about adding more responsibilities to the Secretariat with any form of restructuring, pointing out that due to dilution of power and the constant Soviet attacks, it was becoming increasingly difficult to 'get the job done'.[125] British contributions to ONUC also caused domestic problems. The death of British soldiers who had been serving with the Ghanaian contingent in the Congo and questions over others who were missing raised the issue about the extent to which Britain should be involved in the conflict. There were also concerns about support for Tshombe. On 3 May, the House of Commons debated the detention of Tshombe in Léopoldville and the general situation in Katanga.[126] Edward Heath, the Lord Privy Seal, stressed that despite the accusations that had been cast over the impartiality of UN officials, Britain was bound by obligations under the February Resolution and, therefore, could not encourage British subjects to help what was termed 'this friendly African nationalist community'.[127] This cordial description of Katanga is telling of the Conservative attitude towards the secessionist province, which would prove a significant problem when the UN launched its first military action against Tshombe in August. The brooding belligerence of the backbenches of the Conservative Party over Katanga went hand in hand with what the Department of State noted about the 'shop-worn and defensive' condition of the party.[128] Despite Macmillan's best efforts to retain the 'Macwonder'[129] image, the effect of his length of time in office and the undertones of division over the question of Katanga were about to come to the fore.

For a variety of reasons, therefore, the situation led the Foreign Office to try to pressure Hammarskjöld not to take any action against Katanga. The British delegation in New York were instructed to make very clear to him that any attempt to end the secession of Katanga by force would 'raise a lot of political trouble here and jeopardize the support we so much want to give to the United Nations'.[130] In the weeks that followed, Hammarskjöld's 'attitude' became an increasing problem for the British as the violence in Katanga escalated, leading to growing concerns for the welfare of British citizens. With the sense that they were not being kept fully informed about developments, some of Katanga's more staunch defenders pushed the delegation in New York to 'draw out' Hammarskjöld on his plans.[131] Hammarskjöld refused to yield. Instead, he assumed an even more activist position on the Congo, preparing plans for ONUC military action against Katanga and choosing a controversial Irish diplomat as his Special Representative in Elisabethville.

Burnt bridges: relations between Léopoldville and Elisabethville

On 27 July 1961, while the diplomatic manoeuvres between America and Britain were ongoing at the UN over the reorganisation of the Secretariat, in the Congo, relations between Katanga and the Central Government had reached deadlock. The Secretary-General's new Special Representative, Conor Cruise O'Brien, reported that 'we must consider that bridges between Katanga and rest of Congo are burnt'.[132] The relationship between the two had deteriorated following Tshombe's arrest and detention by Congolese authorities investigating the assassination of Lumumba.[133] The Katangese leadership had as a result become increasingly hostile towards any interference in their affairs, including 'help' from Belgium. In July the Katangan Minister for Foreign Affairs, Evariste Kimba, announced a break in diplomatic relations with the former colonial power, pointing out that the Belgians continued to pursue a policy contrary to the interests of Katanga and, therefore, the breakaway province could do without 'their assistance and their advisors'.[134]

Since April certain achievements had been made towards the restoration of the Congolese Parliament and the attempt to honour Loi Fondamentale, which had been rendered unconstitutional by the breakdown of the Central Government the previous summer. In a letter to the Secretary-General, the now Deputy Prime Minister Antoine Gizenga expressed the hope that it would be possible to bring the disparate factions together in Kamina in order to allow all members of Parliament to attend without posing any problems for their security.[135] However, representatives of Katanga complicated efforts to find a peaceful solution to the constitutional crisis by arguing that as all the Western powers were essentially aligned against them, the UN could no longer resolve the crisis and what was needed was an African solution.[136] In his 27 July press conference, Kimba stated that 'this rebel province is the last refuge of Belgian colonialism with the complicity of the US and the UN'. He argued that the US and the UN either could not, or did not want to, find a regional solution to the crisis but that Congolese unity was being demanded by the Security Council and enforced by armed UN contingents, who were essentially there to end the secession of Katanga. Alleging that the main concern of the UN was to ward off Soviet attacks on the Secretariat he proclaimed that in the face of such ambitions, 'the misery and ruin of the Congolese people counts for very little'.[137]

Public statements of this nature from Katanga did not engender its cause among African and Asian leaders, despite calls for an Africansiation of the crisis. Moreover, they proved damaging to the Secretary-General and to the wider perception of the Congo operation. Hammarskjöld remained adamant that the restoration of the Congolese Parliament was crucial in dealing with the problem of Katanga as one way or another the Central Government had to authorise all actions taken against the breakaway province. In the hope of restoring the Parliament to full effectiveness, he guaranteed the safe passage of delegates to Kamina in July.[138] By facilitating the restoration of the Parliament he sought to gain more support for the UN operation as well as a legal basis to proceed. Fearing that the secession would be ended by force, Katanga resisted all efforts to cooperate with Léopoldville, refusing to send representatives to the talks at Kamina. Regardless of urgings from Western Governments and from the UN, when the Central Government was formally convened at Louvanium University in July, Tshombe's Conakat deputies were noticeably absent.[139] Their non-attendance threatened the carefully arranged balance of power between the Lumumbist group from Stanleyville, led by Gizenga, and the Binza group from Léopoldville. Cyrille Adoula was selected as Prime Minister in order to bring these two groups together. For the Lumumba supporters he was agreeable because he had not been implicated in the assassination. For the Binza group, his opposition towards a federal arrangement and preference for ending the secession of Katanga rendered him a suitable choice. The UN Belgium, Britain and the US also welcomed his election as it represented the formation of a stable coalition government with which to carve out a solution for Katanga.[140] However, Adoula's immediate push for the full implementation of the February Resolution contradicted the aims of some Western powers, most notably Belgium and Britain.

Just as the constitutional crisis of the Central Government was resolved, relations with Tshombe began to seriously deteriorate and the situation began to spin out of control. Following a series of fruitless negotiations in which he had tried to persuade Tshombe to cooperate with the newly formed Central Government, O'Brien was quoted in the international press as saying 'If Tshombe does not go to Léopoldville and if Adoula appeals for military help to reduce the secessionist state of Katanga the international organisation will put its forces at the disposal of the Adoula government'.[141]

Further statements attributed similar remarks to O'Brien, with one alleging that UN troops would be used to 'liquidate the Katangan secession'.[142] O'Brien himself makes no mention of having made such remarks in his own account of events but he was certainly under pressure from the Secretariat to propel Tshombe into some form of an agreement with the Central Government.[143] Whether or not these statements were accurate, or whether this was propaganda from the increasingly volatile Katangan press, they caused panic, both in Elizabethville and in New York.

In Katanga, Tshombe reacted very strongly, railing against the UN and the international community, declaring 'such an intervention was unprecedented in UN history and constituted a complete violation of the UN charter'.[144] Similarly, in New York, these statements caused alarm and Linner, the head of ONUC in Léopoldville, urgently telegrammed the Secretary-General in order to clarify immediately that the UN in no way intended to disarm the Katangan gendarmerie, or fight the regime. He warned that: 'There is no change in our basic principles that we cannot serve as a military arm under the Central Government, and its specific purposes, beyond what is our clear mandate under the resolutions.'[145] The ambiguity that existed between the wording of resolutions and how exactly they were to be implemented in practice was designed to be strategic in giving the Secretary-General and his representatives more scope to interpret them.[146] However, among his officials in the Congo, the interpretation and implementation of the February Resolution accelerated events on the ground. In this instance, the difference between ONUC not formally acting as a military agent of the Central Government and yet fulfilling the mandate provided by the last resolution was a distinction that proved crucial to the next phase of action by the UN.

With the reconstitution of the Central Government, power was now vested through the legitimate Parliament. Asserting his authority over all of the territory of the Congo, including Katanga, at the urging of Hammarskjöld, Adoula issued a decree calling for the removal of all non-Congolese forces serving in the province. The statement offered the first official view of the Congolese Government on Katanga since the constitutional crisis of September 1960 and also ruled out the creation of any federal structures on a permanent basis within the Congolese state. Failure to recognise that Katanga had any credible sovereignty was one of the factors which led to Operation Rumpunch, the first in a series of concerted efforts between the Central Government and the UN to fully implement all General Assembly and Security Council resolutions on the removal of foreign forces from the Congo, in the process allowing UN troops to use force in self-defence.

When Adoula issued the call for the removal of all non-Congolese personnel from Katanga, it was a strong indication of the intention to end the secession of Katanga by whatever means available but it also constituted a threat to European interests in the region. Tshombe's regime included many mercenaries but also Belgian and British advisors who were there to protect Western interests. The physical and moral support of the UN in the removal of these officials led to conflict with the Secretary-General. To the CRO, the prospect of armed conflict raised concerns about the permeable nature of the border between Katanga and the CAF and the crossing of hundreds of refugees into Northern Rhodesia.[147] However, the State Department reacted in a very different way, declaring support for the UN operation, and turning a deaf ear to British protests.[148] Months of talks and cooperation between the two allies to devise a joint Anglo-American position on the Congo had come to nothing. Now, military action would set Congo policy in London and Washington on different trajectories, from which they would never again be realigned.

Operation Rumpunch

> If [suppression] is sought with threats, canons, machine guns and Indian, Irish, Swedish and other soldiers we are ready to die and history will say if we are right.[149]
> (Moise Tshombe, 26 August 1961)

On the 24 August, the Central Government passed Ordinance No. 70, which legalised of the use of force by the Congolese army against foreign elements within Katanga.[150] Four days later ONUC troops in Katanga executed Operation Rumpunch, a surprise manoeuvre in which 338 mercenaries and 443 advisors were captured and expelled, to the shock of Britain, Belgium and the US.[151] The purpose of the mission was to give the initiative to the Central Government to disarm the Katangan army, oust Tshombe and essentially end the secession.[152] The move confirmed Belgian fears about the aims of ONUC. In response, Brussels swiftly issued a declaration to fully cooperate with the resolution and repatriate all of its remaining personnel in Katanga. The result was immediate; the remaining 104 personnel were not interned and the UN suspended the operation.[153] By halting the removal of foreign elements, however, the mercenaries gained the opportunity to regroup and join forces with the Katangan gendarmerie so that by the next bout of action, ONUC had lost the element of surprise.

On 29 August, O'Brien wrote a letter to his wife stating rather prematurely, 'we're very happy here and probably dangerously cocky and euphoric about our *coup* on Monday'.[154] O'Brien's reference to a *coup* was indicative of the problems inherent in the next round of UN action – the follow-up Operation Morthor. It also reflected that O'Brien considered removing Tshombe from power and ending the secession as the objectives of the UN mission. Up to two days before the military action took place, Tshombe had been resolute in telling O'Brien that he had the fullest support of the peoples of Katanga, declaring that the UN was no longer an organisation for peace, but one in the service of governments, such as that of Adoula, whose aim was the suppression of the Katangan secession. In a speech on 26 August his deputy, Godefroid Munongo, even went as far as to accuse the UN of being an organisation in 'the service of great powers to crush the weak'.[155] With an almost hysterical edge, he declared that no communication had been received from Adoula about the military action and, if it took place, it would represent a case of the UN interfering in what did not concern them, under which conditions he would no longer be a free man and was ready to die for his people. Other reports of Munogo's statement declare that he even called for O'Brien's death in a speech outside the post office in Elisabethville.[156] Such opposition from the Katangan regime towards the UN points to the importance of the element of surprise in executing the operation peacefully but also warned of the resilience of the Katangan officials and the violence which was to come. After O'Brien's next meeting with Munongo, on the evening of 28 August he recorded: 'He came over and shook my hand. "Vous m'avez eu" ... He did not add, or have to add, "... this time."'[157]

The American and British reactions to Operation Rumpunch openly revealed their different approaches to the Congo. The Americans had a preference for a diplomatic solution but they realised that Katanga's leaders 'still hold many economic cards'.[158] Given the economic superiority of the province, the Central Government needed to integrate Katanga to ensure its own survival. With this reasoning, the use of force by the UN against Katanga was now a point of open contention with the British. Stevenson telegrammed the State Department on 6 September that Hammarskjöld had called for a joint meeting with the British and the Americans, indicating that 'he believes the next week or so [will be] very critical and he desires our understanding and cooperation'.[159] However, the very next day, the Foreign Office instructed Dean to request a private meeting with the Secretary-General to discuss the Katanga problem, 'without your United States colleague whose interests are so different'.[160]

The willingness of the US to openly break with Britain on this point in September can also be explained by the domestic response to Operation Rumpunch. In the Senate, a prominent member of the Foreign Relations Committee, Thomas Dodd, a New England Democrat, used his anti-Communist platform to garner support for Tshombe.[161] Dodd would later develop an even more substantial and formal position of support for Katanga by granting his backing to the American Committee for Aid to the Katangan Freedom Fighters officially launched on 14 December 1961. The self-proclaimed aim of the organisation was to 'mobilise maximum support for the Katangan fight for self-determination against the United Nations military aggression and to protest the illegal United Nations operation against Katanga and United States support of this operation'.[162] Though it would shortly face financial difficulties, the Committee had in the region of 3,000 members and soon also garnered the support of Senators Everett M. Dirksen, Barry Goldwater, Thruston B. Morton and Richard Nixon. Running a high-profile campaign against the UN in publications such as the *New York Times* and in one instance sending its own observer to Katanga, the group quickly provoked a wide public debate on American foreign policy in the Congo.

This caused headaches for the State Department and the African Bureau in particular who defended their support of Adoula and the Central Government. Undersecretary of State for Political Affairs George C. McGhee and Soapy Williams gave several rousing speeches to the US Senate Committee on Foreign Relations which, on Dodd's urging, had launched an investigation into events in the Congo. Dodd argued that given the weight of the Communists (i.e. Lumumba supporters) with the Adoula Government, 'unless we do something to reverse the course of UN policy, the outcome is virtually a mathematical certainty'.[163] By 'doing something', he advocated the withdrawal of US financial support to the UN.[164] Strengthening Tshombe's defiance in the process, Dodd cooperated with Michael Struelens, a Belgian agent of the Katanga Information Service, in assuring Tshombe that US support would soon turn in his favour.[165] Such an idea was unthinkable to Stevenson, Ball, Williams and Cleveland, who believed that the only course of action was to take a firm hand against Tshombe, in the framework of UN policy. As support for the UN operation gradually became unpopular in the US, the role played by European allies in colluding with Tshombe's regime exacerbated the situation.

On 11 September, Edmund Gullion, the new US Ambassador in Léopoldville, informed Washington that Linner had 'no illusions' about the fact that the French were supporting Tshombe. In addition, although the British chargé d'affaires remained adamant that British official policy was not to support the Katangan leader, he reported that 'activities in the British Consul in Elizabethville led Tshombe to conclude that he has British support'.[166] One such activity was the reading aloud to Tshombe of a particularly ferocious speech from Roy Welensky, which included a commitment on his part to 'do what is necessary and legally possible' to defend Katanga. Hoskyns maintains that this statement from the British Vice-Consul in the presence of the British Consul in Elisabethville, Denzil Dunnett, to Tshombe, was tantamount to a declaration of support from the British Government and was certainly interpreted as such by Tshombe and others. Such an impression was fortified by statements from British representatives in New York who argued that the UN had no mandate to use force to remove 'essential foreign civilians'.[167]

The British publicly denounced Operation Rumpunch at every turn. Macmillan had been concerned by the choice of Adoula and Gizenga, who had been Lumumba's second in command, as his deputy.[168] Neither did he expect Hammarskjöld to support the Ordinance calling for the military enforcement of the resolutions. He also underestimated the extent of the impact the military action had on his own position. As Simon Ball notes, 'initially Macmillan was insouciant, remarking that MP's might froth over their club claret but they were not going to risk their seats and their emoluments over a very large country a long way away of which they knew very little'.[169] However the UN action was criticised, particularly by Welensky's supporters, urged on by the indignant proclamations of the Rhodesian leader. In the wake of the operation Welensky issued a strongly worded statement denouncing the UN action. He accused Hammarskjöld of 'wanting to do something spectacular, dramatic before the opening of the next session of the General Assembly', and pledged his outright support for Tshombe.[170] Welensky had the backing of some right-wing Tory backbenchers, who, perhaps after frothing over their claret, did persuade Macmillan to take a stronger position over events in Katanga. In response the Prime Minister dispatched Lord Lansdowne, an Under-Secretary of State at the Foreign Office, to Elisabethville to mediate between the UN and Tshombe and also report an accurate picture of relations with O'Brien.

Since the secession of the Katanga had begun, Welensky had not only turned a blind eye to the stream of British and Belgian mercenaries from his territory into Katanga, but also provided material and political support to the regime. Following Operation Rumpunch, despite Macmillan's instructions to the contrary, he deployed well-equipped troops to Ndola, a town just inside the border with Katanga, where Hammarskjöld's plane would shortly crash. It has been claimed that he did so with the support of Lord Alport in Salisbury in the anticipation of the second round of the UN operation.[171] British condemnation of the UN action was also perceived by Tshombe as tantamount to support for his regime to the extent that the 1 September edition of the Katangan newspaper, *L'Echo du Katanga*, carried the headline 'The British Consul conveys his Government's sympathy to the Katangese cause'.[172] Overall these activities strengthened the allegations of collusion between the British Government and the Katangan authorities. Hammarskjöld was particularly critical of Dunnett, arguing that the UN had 'not received much help from the British locally'.[173] These allegations were confirmed when Tshombe was discovered taking refuge in Dunnett's residence during the next round of action by the UN.

These developments in the Congo also had an effect on British colonial policy. On 1 September negotiations took place at the State Department between Foot and Cleveland regarding the new British agreement to provide political and constitutional information on their remaining colonies to the UN.[174] This agreement, however, was termed 'the only area of manoeuvrability' on British colonial policy at the UN in response to Resolution 1514.[175] The supply of information on remaining colonies was predicated on US support and it was stipulated that the UN could not use the information to make recommendations for specific territories. Cleveland quickly welcomed this changed position from Britain and pushed that self-determination be the eventual goal for all these countries, which Foot resisted on the basis that such urgings from the General Assembly constituted an unacceptable interference in British affairs. This preference to limit the impact of the UN on British colonial policy was the same approach that Britain had to Katanga, where they also sought to limit UN action. These differing views of the role of the organisation in resolving the crisis and in managing decolonisation served to hinder the development of a coherent Anglo-American policy in the Congo and drove a further wedge between the Foreign Office and the Secretary-General. It also pointed to the glaringly different perceptions of the UN that now existed between London and Washington.

Operation Morthor

Despite the frantic scrambling of the British behind the scenes to try to negotiate privately with the Secretary-General, discussions on the follow-up mission continued unabated between O'Brien in Elisabethville, Mahmoud Khiari, the head of UN civilian operations in Léopoldville, Linner and Hammarskjöld. It is generally agreed that the plan drawn up by Linner and O'Brien was approved by Hammarskjöld but that he left open the right moment to execute the operation.[176] Others, including Susan Williams in her recent book, maintain that Hammarskjöld never gave his approval for the mission to begin and was shocked by the news that it had started when his plane landed in Léopoldville on the evening of 13 September.[177] However, the cable he sent to Linner on 8 September can be interpreted as granting authorisation for this mission. Hammarskjöld states: 'I trust your judgment entirely. We shall inform the Belgians right away. Thus you can go ahead as you plan and we shall get explanations in due time.'[178] On the night of Sunday 12 September, it was decided among the UN ground commanders that Morthor would commence at 4 a.m. on Monday 13 September. This was not arbitrary timing. Since Rumpunch had taken place, Munongo had launched a vitriolic anti-UN propaganda campaign with stirring effect. Even by 9 September, O'Brien reported to the Secretary-General that the violent campaign had been combined with inter-tribal incitement and demonstrations openly being led by Lucas Samalenghe, the Katangan Minister for Information, with the support of an extremist youth organisation named Jenakat, which he referred to as being equivalent to a 'Hitler Youth organisation'.[179]

Two additional factors played a role in the decision of when and how to proceed. The first was the growing fear that the Katangan gendarmerie were increasingly considered as being on the verge of turning against the European population and as they committed further racial massacres against their tribal colleagues.[180] The Baluba tribe was politically split between the Kasai Baluba (who were traditionally pro-Lumumba) and the Katanga Baluba who supported the Conakat party and were therefore favoured by the Belgians.[181] Conakat only held a narrow majority in the Katangan Parliament, which was secured only by the casting vote of Kalonji, now a member of the Central Government. From this tenuous arrangement, inciting inter-tribal rivalry was provocative and effective in the extreme. Katangan forces perpetrated an ethnic cleansing campaign against the Kasai Baluba since the beginning of the conflict, sacking villages and burning huts.[182] This was now extended. The extent of the fighting was such that by 12 September there were 45,000 Kasai Baluba refugees in UN refugee camps in the province. The extension of the violence to persecute the European population was now perceived as a real possibility. Britain, Belgium and France warned Hammarskjöld that any bloodshed among the European population would ultimately be down to UN actions.

Despite this mounting humanitarian catastrophe, the eyes of the world were still focused on the political situation and the fate of the European population. One anecdote highlights the racial focus of the Western press. O'Brien describes the reaction of a photographer who was uninterested in taking pictures of the back of a man who had been flogged: 'Wheals, he said, don't show on a black back.'[183] In the midst of these tensions and internal strife, Tshombe refused Hammarskjöld's invitation to talks in Léopoldville. Between the political stalemate with Tshombe, the ethnic tensions in Katanga and the ongoing sporadic violence, the situation was set to explode. When Hammarskjöld's emissary Khiary left Elisabethville on the evening of 12 September, his parting words, according to O'Brien, were 'Surtout pas de demi-mesures'.[184]

The relative success of Operation Rumpunch was greatly overshadowed by Operation Morthor. Though it was recognised and expected that this time the UN did not have the element of surprise, the level of armed opposition from the Katangan gendarmerie and the associated mercenary army was drastically underestimated by intelligence sources. Once the operation was launched on 13 September, the arrest warrants for all members of Tshombe's Government, apart from the leader himself, were issued, but within twenty minutes, gunfire broke out when UN forces attempted to seize the main post office. When a UN escort was dispatched to Tshombe's presidential palace to bring him to the UNHQ in Elisabethville, where he had agreed an hour earlier on the phone to issue a statement on Radio Katanga announcing the end of the secession and calling for an end to fighting, he had disappeared.[185] To make matters worse, not a single UN soldier was found in the vicinity. It subsequently emerged that Tshombe found refuge from the bloody street fighting in Dunnett's residence.[186] Not only were UN forces unable to arrest most members of his Government as planned, the fighting continued for the next eight days.[187] Telegrams from Elisabethville reported combat and sniper fire at main areas like the post office, the radio station and the Red Cross hospital.[188] This was not limited to skirmishes and battles between UN forces, the Katangan gendarmerie and foreign mercenaries, but also included Europeans. Far from standing by helplessly, those who had remained in Elisabethville up to this point were mainly in the service of Tshombe's regime in one form or another and were therefore opposed to what they viewed as the UN attempt to quash the secession. Press reports and statements issued to the world recorded the impressions of these European witnesses and painted an appalling picture of events. In one inflammatory report a journalist was quoted as saying that '[what] the UN forces [had done] was worse than anything the Nazis did'.[189] As Young describes, with this depiction of the operation, in addition to the abject failure to satisfy most of its objectives with the mission, 'the UN suffered a humiliating reverse'.[190]

It was not just the prolonged fighting and the mutiny of the civilian European population which rendered the mission a failure. On the evening of 13 September O'Brien issued a statement that the secession of Katanga was now at an end. In his own words he was adamant that 'the UN action had been designed solely towards that end'.[191] This is the most contested point in the events which transpired in Katanga in September 1961 as it cast a shadow of ambiguity over the main objectives of operation. Statements and resolutions prior and subsequent to Operation Morthor do not indicate that the secession of Katanga was ever the primary objective of the UN. The official argument is that in the early hours of 13 September, UN forces took security precautions similar to those applied on 28 August, deemed necessary to prevent inflammatory broadcasts or other threats to the maintenance of law and order while the UN resumed its task of apprehending and evacuating foreign military and paramilitary personnel.[192] Dismissing this defence, America and Britain reacted with revulsion to Operation Morthor, demanding that Hammarskjöld explain UN actions.

Within one day of the launching of the operation, on 14 September, the British Ambassador in Léopoldville, Ian Scott, presented Hammarskjöld with a démarche from Home which warned that the British Government would withdraw all support from ONUC unless 'Hammarskjöld could provide an acceptable explanation for what had happened in Katanga; or Hammarskjöld could provide an assurance that the fighting would be swiftly ended'.[193] To Britain, the decision to furnish O'Brien with arrest warrants for Tshombe and his associates was a clear indication of the intention to end the regime in Katanga. Internally there was bitter disagreement over what MacLeod termed 'how we got ourselves into this position unless we had motive which did not appear on the surface'.[194] On learning of his location on the first day of the fighting, the UN quickly telegraphed Dunnett, through the British Ambassador in Léopoldville, asking him to 'do everything possible to arrange a meeting between him and O'Brien in order to bring about a ceasefire', with no success.[195] The result was the further worsening of relations between the Foreign Office and Hammarskjöld, who resented the British intransigence.[196] Adoula also expressed anger at what he termed the 'UK action against the UN'. In a meeting with Gullion, he was regretful of the turn of events in Katanga, stating that neither he nor the UN had ever wanted a war in Katanga but that Munongo and Tshombe had 'prepared the combustible to which the least spark set fire'. Moreover, however, Adoula believed that the British were now anti-UN, and for what he termed 'impure reasons'.[197] The problem also spread to British allies who increasingly believed that Britain was in collusion with Tshombe, an impression that was enhanced when he sought refuge at the home of the British Consul.[198] For example, by the end of September, relations with India had deteriorated due to what was termed Nehru's 'bitter suspicions of the motive of British policy in the Congo'.[199]

The State Department was also left reeling from events in Katanga. Kennedy was reportedly 'extremely upset' that Hammarskjöld had used increased political and financial support from the US against Katanga without consulting Washington.[200] The State Department was concerned about the actions of the European population, with Gullion noting that the UN was now 'helpless to prevent participation by Europeans in what has become a "war of liberation" against the UN'.[201] He also reported coming under pressure from the Belgian and the British Consulates to denounce the 'atrocities of the UN monstrosity'.[202] Despite the pressure from Brussels and London, however, the State Department line on Morthor was clear: although the UN had committed an inexcusable blunder, the US supported the UN in the Congo.[203] Part of the reason why the US did not condemn the action in Katanga may also have had to do with Hammarskjöld's insistence that he had *not known* that the operation was to take place when it did, and at that point was already on his way to Léopoldville to negotiate with the Central Government on the next steps.[204]

Operation Morthor revealed that the extent of British opposition to the use of force to end the secession was a willingness to break with the US and the UN on this question. Until 16 September, frantic telegrams flew between London, Washington and Léopoldville as British and American officials both urged Hammarskjöld to formulate a peaceful resolution to the fighting. At the same time, in contrast to the assurances of Foreign Office cooperation with the UN, Dunnett continued to obstruct the UN actions, even after the arrival of Lord Lansdowne, the British special emissary. The duplicitous British approach to Katanga had now been fully revealed through UN actions. The disagreement between the Foreign Office and the State Department over how UN resolutions should be implemented against Katanga was out in the open. As the crisis deepened through the final months of 1961, Anglo-American cooperation on the Congo achieved less and less. The essentially different perceptions of what the UN was and how it should manage decolonisation and the conflicts associated with it, kept London and Washington divided.

Notes

1 Herter also remarked at this meeting, in response to a question from the President, that both the Secretary-General of the UN and Dayal, the UN representative in the Congo, were responsible for this situation. 474th Meeting National Security Council, 12 January 1961, Schwar, *FRUS, XX, Congo*, p. 14.
2 T. Sorensen, *Kennedy* (New York: Harper Perennial, 2009), p. 520. See generally, J.P. Lash, 'Dag Hammarskjöld's conception of his office', *International Organization*, 16:3 (1962), 542–556.
3 UNA, S-209-0018-17, ONUC Records on Foreign Countries, Correspondence with the United States, Press Statement from the US Mission to the UN, Statement by Adlai Stevenson, 7 March 1961.
4 Telegram from the Embassy in Belgium to the Department of State. Brussels, 23 January 1961, Schwar, *FRUS, XX, Congo*, p. 22.
5 Comment from Secretary of State Dean Rusk at a staff meeting, 25 January 1961, Schwar, *FRUS, XX, Congo*, p. 24.
6 As quoted in E. Lefever, *Crisis in the Congo: A United Nations Force in Action* (Washington, DC: Brookings Institution, 1965), p. 210.
7 Kalb, *Congo Cables*, p. 234.
8 Telegram from the Mission to the United Nations to the Department of State, 31 January 1961, Schwar, *FRUS, XX, Congo*, p. 37.
9 Memorandum by the Deputy Representative-Designate to the United Nations Security Council (Yost), 17 February 1961, Schwar, *FRUS, XX, Congo*, p. 69.
10 Odd Arne Westad contends; 'many African and Asian diplomats at the UN drew parallels between what they saw as the US's federal government's weak response to the American civil rights struggle and its inability to condemn colonial violence abroad'. Westad, *The Global Cold War*, p. 136.
11 T.J. Noer, 'New frontiers and old priorities in Africa', in T.G. Paterson (ed.), *Kennedy's Quest for Victory: American Foreign Policy, 1961–1963* (New York: Oxford University Press, 1989), p. 256.
12 NAL, PREM 11/5183, Records of the Office of the Prime Minister, Telegram from British Ambassador to the United States, Harold Caccia, in Washington to the Foreign Office, 1 February 1961.
13 Telegram from the US Mission to the UN, to the Department of State. New York, 6 February 1961, Schwar, *FRUS, XX, Congo*, p. 57.
14 Seeley G. Mudd Manuscript Library (hereafter, MMLP), Princeton Ambassador Adlai E. Stevenson Papers, Adlai Stevenson papers, Folder 1, Box 351, Series 5, Memorandum for the President, 27 April 1961.
15 Woodrow Wilson Centre, Cold War International History Project, Congo crisis (hereafter, WWC), NSF Congo, Analytical Chronology, Secret, 72, p. 73. www.wilsoncenter.org/sites/default/files/Congo1960-61_1.pdf.
16 *Ibid.*
17 Paper prepared in the Embassy in the Congo, Léopoldville, undated, Howland *et al.*, *FRUS, 1964–1968, Vol. XXIII, Congo, 1960–1968*, p. 88.
18 Mahoney, *JFK*, p. 65.
19 As detailed in Memorandum from Secretary of State Rusk to President Kennedy, Washington, 1 February, Schwar, *FRUS, XX, Congo*, pp. 45–46. The principle elements

Fighting over Katanga 103

    were also outlined in a telegram from the Department of State to the embassy in India, dated 2 February, Schwar, *FRUS, XX, Congo*, p. 48.
20 Memorandum of conversation, Washington, 4 February, Schwar, *FRUS, XX, Congo*, p. 51.
21 WWC, Box 8, Bureau of African Affairs, Central Africa, State Department Files, Secret memorandum for the record, Working Committee on the Congo, 7 February 1961. www.wilsoncenter.org/sites/default/files/Congo1960-61_1.pdf.
22 Members of the Conciliation Commission included representatives from: Ethiopia, Ghana, India, Liberia, Malaya, Morocco, Nigeria, Pakistan, Senegal, Sudan and Tunisia.
23 UNA, S-0845-001-6-00001 Correspondence Advisory Committee and Conciliation Commission, Dag – ONUC, Message from the Chairman of the United Nations Conciliation Commission in the Congo to the Secretary-General.
24 Weissman, *American Foreign Policy in the Congo*, p. 142.
25 Statement by Hammarskjöld in the Security Council After Adoption of [what is entitled] Afro-Asian Resolution, New York 21 February 1961, Security Council Official Records, Sixteenth year, 942nd meeting as published in Cordier *et al.*, *Public Papers of the Secretaries-General of the United Nations*, p. 359. The resolution was passed with just two abstentions from France and the USSR.
26 Paragraph A1 of Security Council Resolution 161 [S/4741], 21 February 1960, Appendix 1, https://documents-dds-ny.un.org/doc/RESOLUTION/GEN/NR0/171/68/IMG/NR017168.pdf?OpenElement. Emphasis added.
27 PRAAD, RG 17/2/25, 1961, Misc. – Congo crisis, Special Collection Bureau of African Affairs (SC/BAA) RG 17, Letter from Nkrumah to Kennedy, 22 February 1961.
28 O'Brien, *To Katanga and Back*, p. 40.
29 NAL, FO 371/155103, E.B. Boothby, Foreign Office Minute, Discussion with Rusk, Stevenson and Sir P. Dean on tactics in Security Council, 20 February 1961.
30 NAL, FO 371/155103, Notes for Cabinet from Africa Department on Congo, 21 February 1961.
31 NAL, PREM 11/3214, Policy paper entitled 'Future of the Congo in the case of the failure of the United Nations effort', for the Commonwealth Prime Ministers' Conference, March 1961.
32 NAL, PREM 11/4590, Letter to Macmillan from Kennedy, 23 February 1961.
33 NAL, PREM 11/4590, Record of a conversation at dinner in Admiralty House, Monday February 27, 1961.
34 John F. Kennedy Presidential Library and Museum, Boston (hereafter JFKL), National Security Files, Box 174, UK Subjects, Macmillan Briefing Book, 4/4/1961–4/9/1961, Confidential position paper on the Congo for the President in lieu of Macmillan visit, 4–9 April 1961, 31 March 1961.
35 NAL, FO 371/155075, Confidential telegram from Léopoldville to the Foreign Office, 5 April 1961.
36 JFKL, National Security Files, Box 174, UK Subjects, Macmillan Briefing Book, 4/4/1961–4/9/1961, Confidential position paper on the Congo for the President in lieu of Macmillan visit, 4–9 April 1961, 31 March 1961.
37 *Ibid.*
38 NAL, FO 371/155075, Confidential letter on the Congo from P. Dean to Sir Frederick Hoyer Miller at the Foreign Office, 29 March 1961.

39 NAL, FO 371/ 155104, Confidential telegram from Patrick Dean in New York to the Foreign Office, 13 March 1961. Dean even went so far as to say that in the current atmosphere, the debate would be to the benefit of the Russians.

40 JFKL, National Security Files, Box 174, UK Subjects, Macmillan Briefing Book, 4/4/1961–4/9/1961, Confidential position paper on the Congo for the President in lieu of Macmillan visit, 4–9 April 1961, 31 March 1961. 'They would in fact prefer a moratorium on United Nations discussion of the Congo.'

41 Belgian Paul-Henry Spaak, who would become Belgian Foreign Minister in April 1961, served as Secretary-General of NATO during this time. As Kent recounts, he was keen to complain about the apparent American neglect of NATO allies and quick to raise the spectre of NATO disunity. Kent, *America, the UN and Decolonisation*, pp. 46–47.

42 Weissman, *American Foreign Policy in the Congo*, p. 140.

43 D.N. Gibbs, 'Dag Hammarskjöld, the United Nations, and the Congo crisis of 1960-1: a reinterpretation', *The Journal of Modern African Studies*, 31:1 (1993), 168–174.

44 Telegram from the Department of State to the Embassy in Belgium, Washington, 1 March 1961, Schwar, *FRUS, XX, Congo*, p. 87.

45 Hoskyns, *The Congo Since Independence*, pp. 323–324. See also Weissman, *American Foreign Policy in the Congo*, p. 141; Kalb, *Congo Cables*, p. 237.

46 UNA, S-0845-0001-06, Dag-ONUC, Statements of A. Delvaux, Minister of the Interior in press conference on 7 March 1961.

47 For a detailed and colourful description of the Tananarive conference, see Kalb, *Congo Cables*, pp. 244–246. Also Young, *Politics in the Congo*, pp. 332–337.

48 Statement by Hammarskjöld in the Security Council After Adoption of Afro-Asian Resolution, New York, 21 February, 1961, Security Council Official Records, Sixteenth year, 942nd meeting, Cordier et al., *Public Papers of the Secretaries-General of the United Nations*, p. 359.

49 *Ibid.*

50 UNA, S-0845-0004-16, Secretary-General's Correspondence with India 1960–1961, Subject Files of the Secretary-General Dag Hammarskjöld, Letter from Indian Ambassador Jha to Hammarskjöld, 3 March 1961.

51 UNA, S-0845-0004-12 Secretary-General's correspondence with Ghana, 1961, Subject Files of the Secretary-General Dag Hammarskjöld, Telegram from Nkrumah to Hammarskjöld, 18 February 1961.

52 PRAAD, Special Collection Bureau of African Affairs (SC/BAA) RG 17, RG 17/2/25, 1961, Misc. – Congo crisis, Telegram from Kwame Nkrumah to Sekou Toure thanking him for the warning about the efforts ongoing at the UN to delay decisions on the Congo in the Security Council, 21 February 1961.

53 UNA, S-0215-0001-18, ONUC-Congo Government Records, Records of the Office for Special Political Affairs, President Kasavubu, Cables 01/02/1961–31/10/1961, Letter from the Secretary-General to President Kasavubu, March 1961.

54 NARA, State Department Files, UN, 310/1–460, US Delegation records, Message from Albert Kalondji to Hammarskjöld refusing Dayal smooth passage back in to the Congo as recorded in telegram from American Embassy in Brazzaville to Secretary of State, 5 November 1960.

55 Mahoney, *JFK*, p. 82. See also James, *Britain and the Congo Crisis*.

56 'He said, frankly more by implication than direct accusation, that US policy was in league with the Belgians.' Telegram from Timberlake, US Ambassador to the Congo to the Department of State, 14 December 1960, Schwar and Shaloff, *FRUS, 1958–1960, XIV, Africa*, p. 628.
57 Mahoney, *JFK*, p. 82.
58 O'Brien, *To Katanga and Back*, p. 64. For more on Dayal's role see R. Dayal, *Mission for Hammarskjöld* (Princeton: Princeton University Press, 1974).
59 Kalb, *Congo Cables*, p. 247.
60 Mahoney, *JFK*, p. 82.
61 UNA, S-0845-0004-16 Secretary-General's correspondence with India, 1961, Subject Files of the Secretary-General Dag Hammarskjöld, Telegram from Narasimhan in Delhi to Hammarskjöld in New York recounting discussions with Nehru and Menon on Congo, 28 February 1961.
62 O'Brien, *To Katanga and Back*, p. 64. See also Urquhart, *Hammarskjöld*, pp. 517–519. It should be pointed out that O'Brien's version of events differs from Kalb and Mahoney who maintain that Hammarskjöld recalled Dayal to New York temporarily and simply never sent him back. See Mahoney, *JFK*, p. 84; Kalb, *Congo Cables*, p. 248.
63 UNA, S-0215-0001-18, ONUC-Congo Government Records, Records of the Office for Special Political Affairs, President Kasavubu, Cables 01/02/1961–31/10/1961, Letter from the Secretary-General to President Kasavubu, 10 March 1961.
64 UNA, S-0215-0001-18, ONUC-Congo Government Records, Records of the Office for Special Political Affairs, President Kasavubu, Cables 01/02/1961–31/10/1961, Letter from the Secretary-General to President Kasavubu, undated.
65 UNA, S-0845-0001-07, Dag-ONUC, Correspondence with UN Advisory Committee and Congolese Government, 03/03/1961–11/08/1961, Statement from Albert Ndele, Governor of the National Bank of the Congo, on 'The Financial and Economic Situation in the Congo (excluding Katanga) and the action required' to the 50th Meeting of the Congo Advisory Committee, 27 May 1961.
66 O'Brien, *To Katanga and Back*, p. 62.
67 General Assembly Resolution 1600 (XV), 958th Plenary meeting, 15 April 1961, https://documents-dds-ny.un.org/doc/RESOLUTION/GEN/NR0/198/15/IMG/NR019815.pdf?OpenElement.
68 UNA, S-0845-0001-07 Correspondence with UN Advisory Committee and Congolese Government, 03/03/1961–11/08/1961, 37th Meeting of Congo Advisory Committee, Memo, 'Terms of reference for investigation under paragraph A-4 of Security Council Resolution S/4741 of February 21 1961'.
69 General Assembly Resolution 1599 (XV), 958th Plenary Meeting, 15 April 1961, https://documents-dds-ny.un.org/doc/RESOLUTION/GEN/NR0/198/15/IMG/NR019815.pdf?OpenElement.
70 See Kalb, *Congo Cables*, pp. 242–263.
71 NARA, State Department, UN Files, 310/1–561, Telegram to the American Embassy in New Delhi, from the State Department. 26 March 1961.
72 Weissman, *American Foreign Policy in the Congo*, p. 144.
73 NARA, State Department, UN Files, 310/ 1–561, Secret memo of a conversation with Hammarskjöld, from Harlan Cleveland to Dean Rusk, 10 April 1961.
74 *Ibid*.

75 Memo from the Assistant Secretary of State for International Organization Affairs Harlan Cleveland to Secretary of State Dean Rusk, Washington, May 2, 1961, P. Claussen, E.M. Duncan and J.A. Soukup (eds), *Foreign Relations of the United States, 1961–1963, Volume XXV, Organization of Foreign Policy; Information Policy; United Nations; Scientific Matters* (Washington, DC: Government Printing Office, 2001), p. 334.

76 NARA, State Department, UN Files, 310/1–561, Letter from Harlan Cleveland to Helen Stewart, 25 April 1961.

77 NARA, State Department, UN Files, 310/1–561, Telegram from USUN to the Department of State, 1 June 1961.

78 Weissman, *American Foreign Policy in the Congo*, p. 144.

79 MMLP, Stevenson Papers, Box 341, Folder 1, Series 5, Memo, 'Stray thoughts on Colonialism'.

80 NAL, PREM 11/3214, Policy paper entitled 'Future of the Congo in the case of the failure of the United Nations effort', for the Commonwealth Prime Ministers' Conference, March 1961.

81 *Ibid.*

82 GPL, BAA/RLAA/496, '16th Session of the United Nations General Assembly, 1961': Newspaper Clippings (United Nations), Bureau of African Affairs. The Special Committee on Decolonization was known, until 1962, as the Committee of 17, when the addition of more members, transformed into the Committee of 24. In 1963 it was also merged with the Committee on Information from Non-Self-Governing Territories.

83 NAL, PREM 11/4590, Minute from Macleod to the Prime Minister, 27 February 1961.

84 NAL, PREM 11/4590, Letter to Macmillan from Kennedy.

85 NARA, State Department Files Congo, 321/1–560, Confidential telegram from US delegation in New York to the State Department, March 14, 1961.

86 NAL, PREM 11/5183, Note for the record, extract of conversation between Duncan Sandy's and Macmillan, 10 Downing Street, 23 March 1961.

87 NAL, PREM 11/5183, Secret note from the UK delegation to the UN to the Prime Minister, March 1961.

88 NAL, PREM 11/5183, Telegram from British Ambassador to the United States, Harold Caccia, in Washington to the Foreign Office, 1 February 1961.

89 NAL, PREM 11/5183, Secret note from the UK delegation to the UN to the Prime Minister, March 1961.

90 NAL, PREM 11/5183, Telegram regarding the progress of Anglo-American talks, from Caccia to Foreign Office, 7 February 1961.

91 NAL, PREM 11/5183, Telegram from Caccia to the Foreign Office, 15 March 1961.

92 See Rakove, *Kennedy, Johnson and the Non-Aligned World*; Muehlenbeck, *Betting on the Africans*.

93 Noer, 'New frontiers and old priorities in Africa', p. 253. The Angolan rebellion broke out on 4 February 1961 when the emerging nationalist movement clashed with the Portuguese military in Luanda, killing thirty-three people. From then, until the independence of its final colony, Mozambique, in 1974, the African colonies of Portugal were increasingly beset with violence from guerrilla groups backing nationalist campaigns. The British province of Rhodesia was a particular supporter of the Portuguese resistance efforts and Britain tended to abstain from UN resolutions

calling for Portugal to grant independence to these territories. In contrast, the US was a firm supporter of the nationalist movements, which was reflected in its positive votes for such resolutions at the UN. See further: Z. Laidi, *The Superpowers and Africa: The Constraints of a Rivalry: 1960-1990* (Chicago: University of Chicago Press, 1990); N. MacQueen, *The Decolonization of Portuguese Africa: Metropolitan Revolution and the Dissolution of Empire* (London: Longman, 1997); Mahoney, *JFK*; E. Schmidt, *Foreign Intervention in Africa: From the Cold War to the War on Terror* (Cambridge: Cambridge University Press, 2013); G. Wright, *The Destruction of a Nation: United States' Policy Towards Angola Since 1945* (London: Pluto, 1997).

94 Security Council Resolution [S/4835] 956th Meeting, 9 June 1961, www.un.org/en/ga/search/view_doc.asp?symbol=S/RES/163(1961).
95 NAL, FO UN/15116, Telegram from J.G. Tshourdin, Foreign Office, to D.A. Greenhill, British Embassy, Washingtonm DC, 6 December 1961.
96 O'Brien referred to this as a 'sacred drama', whereby the floor of the General Assembly became the central battleground for rhetorical combat between the opposing factions. See generally, C. Cruise O'Brien and F. Topolski, *The United Nations: Sacred Drama* (London: Hutchinson, 1968).
97 University College Dublin Archives, Dublin (hereafter UCDA), Frank Aiken Papers, Microfilm Reel P104/6256, Speech by Frank Aiken for general debate at the General Assembly, 15 October 1960.
98 General Assembly Official Records, 16th Session, 1017th Plenary Meeting, 27 September 1961, Goodrich *et al.*, *Charter of the United Nations*, p. 455.
99 PRAAD, BAA/RLAA/496, '16th Session of the United Nations General Assembly, 1961': Newspaper Clippings (United Nations), Bureau of African Affairs, 'Neutralists' power stood prominent in discussion of Dag's office', *Ghanaian Times* (5 October 1961).
100 PRAAD, BAA/RLAA/496, '16th Session of the United Nations General Assembly, 1961': Newspaper Clippings (United Nations), Bureau of African Affairs. In the Trusteeship Committee, Guinea calls for the NATO powers to stop supporting Portugal, 'Wire report', *Reuters* (8 November 1961).
101 Westad, *The Global Cold War*, p. 135.
102 MMLP, Adlai Stevenson papers, Box 341, Folder 1, Series 5, Memo, 'Stray thoughts on Colonialism'.
103 Memorandum of Conversation between Dean Rusk, Lord Home and other officials, Washington, 4 April 1961, Schwar, *FRUS, XX, Congo*, p. 117.
104 *Ibid.*, p. 118.
105 JFKL, National Security Files, Box 175, Folder 2, Memorandum of Conversation at the White House during Macmillan's visit to Washington, 5 April 1961.
106 *Ibid.*
107 *Ibid.*
108 W.R. Louis, 'Public enemy number one: the British empire in the dock at the United Nations, 1957-71', in M. Lynn (ed.), *The British Empire in the 1950's: Retreat or Revival?* (Basingstoke: Palgrave Macmillan, 2005), p. 198.
109 NAL, FO 160953/22516, Editorial, *The Times* (24 November 1961).
110 JFKL, National Security Files, Box 175, Folder 2, Memorandum of Conversation on Chinese Representation at the UN, 5 April 1961.

111 *Ibid.*
112 Kenneth Young develops the Foreign Office point of view a little further on this one, though perhaps in a polemic fashion in his book about Home, when he credits the Foreign Secretary with the remarks: 'Britain thought that the Chinese would be a cursed nuisance in the place – worse than the Russians – it was better to have them in since at least it was possible to see what they were doing.' K. Young, *Sir Alec Douglas-Home* (London: Fairleigh Dickinson University Press, 1971), p. 127.
113 JFKL, National Security Files, Box 175, Folder 2, Memorandum of Conversation on Chinese Representation at the UN, 5 April 1961.
114 Young, *Sir Alec Douglas-Home*, p. 127.
115 JFKL, National Security Files, Box 172, Folder 1, Memo for Ralph A. Dungan, The White House, 1 May 1961. Progress report on actions agreed upon during discussions with the President and Prime Minister Macmillan on April 5–8, 1961.
116 NARA, State Department, UN Files, 310/1–561, Memorandum for the President on 'The Soviet campaign in favour of Tripartism'.
117 NARA, State Department, UN Files, 310/1–561, Telegram from Thompson to Department of State in which he describes the Secretary-General as 'over-optimistic' about the apparent reversal of the Soviet position, 13 April 1961.
118 NARA, State Department, UN Files, 310/1–561, Memorandum of conversation between Cleveland and various officials at the British Foreign Office, 7 June 1961.
119 NARA, State Department, UN Files, 310/1–561, Telegram from the Department of State, to the US delegation at the UN, rejecting the revised proposals for the reorganisation of the Secretariat, 25 June 1961.
120 NARA, State Department, UN Files, 310/1–561, Telegram from the US delegation in New York, to Secretary of State, detailing the Hammarskjöld's reaction when American objections were put to him, 27 June 1961.
121 NARA, State Department, UN Files, 310/1–561, Telegram from the Department of State to USUN delegation, 25 June 1961.
122 NARA, State Department, UN Files, 310/1–561, Record of policy planning meeting concerning the United Nations at the Department of State, 1 June 1961.
123 NARA, State Department, UN Files, 310/1–561, Record of policy planning meeting concerning the United Nations at the Department of State, 1 June 1961.
124 NARA, State Department, UN Files, 310/1–561, Telegram from the US delegation to the UN in New York, to the Secretary of State, 16 August 1961.
125 NARA, State Department, UN Files, 310/1–561, Memorandum of conversation between Cleveland and various officials at the British Foreign Office, 7 June 1961.
126 NAL, FO 371/155004, House of Commons, Parliamentary question, 3 May 1961. Mr Richard Marsh also raised a second question: 'To ask the Lord Privy Seal what information he has received from the United Nations in Léopoldville concerning the death of two British officers serving with the Ghanaian contingent of the United Nations forces in the Congo.' The reply states that the two soldiers were under the care of the UN who would supply all relevant information to the British Government. There was also a second question: 'Is not Tshombe's survival vital to British interests?' The response for this maintained the official British position: 'We have all along made it clear that we wish to see maintained the conditions of stability which have been established in the southern part of Katanga province. However, we believe this should be achieved within the framework of some general settlement which will allow the Katanga to play its proper role in the Congo as a whole.'

127 NAL, FO 371/155004, House of Commons, Parliamentary question, 3 May 1961. The member proposing the questions was Mr Biggs-Davison, a member of the Conservative Party and also a member of the Conservative Monday Club which had considerable support for Tshombe and Katanga.
128 NARA, State Department, Central Decimal Files, 741.00/7–1561, Telegram from the American Embassy in London to the Secretary of State, 17 July 1961.
129 NARA, State Department, Central Decimal Files, 741.00/7–1561, Telegram from the American Embassy in London to the Secretary of State, 17 July 1961.
130 NAL, FO 371/155004, Telegram from the Foreign Office to the United Kingdom delegation to the UN in New York, 6 May 1961.
131 NAL, FO 371/155004, Memo from Mr Ewart Biggs at the Foreign Office to Campbell, member of the UK delegation to the UN in New York, 25 May 1961.
132 UNA, S-0845-0003-01, Dag, ONUC files, Telegram from the United Nations Headquarters in Léopoldville, to Secretary-General in New York, 27 July 1961.
133 GPL, BAA/RLAA/691, 'Republic of Congo': Newspaper Clippings (Congo), Jan 1963, Bureau of African Affairs, 'Mandat d'arrêt', arrest warrant issued for Moise Tshombe, Godefroid Munongo, Evariste Kimba, Jean Kibwe and Lutaka Wa Dikowbe, 9 September 1961, for 'asassinats, arrestations arbitraries and tortures corporells' signed by 'A de Loop, Central Government'.
134 UNA, S-0845-0003-01, Dag, ONUC files, Extract from Brazzaville radio report on press conference given by Katangan Minister for Foreign Affairs, sent to UN New York, 27 July 1961. It should be pointed out however that this was merely a manoeuvre to save face from the Katangan Government. In reality the extent of their reliance on Belgium and the level of involvement of Belgian 'advisors' in the Elisabethville regime was very high.
135 UNA, S-0845-0003-01, Dag, ONUC files, Letter from Antoine Gizenga to the Secretary-General, 7 June 1961.
136 UNA, S-0845-0003-01, Dag, ONUC files, Cable, 27 July 1961. In response to a question from a journalist as to whether or not Katanga needed UN aid, Kimba declared, 'We have no time anymore for the UN, we must find an African solution'.
137 UNA, S-0845-0003-01, Dag, ONUC files, Extract from Brazzaville radio report on press conference given by Katangan Minister for Foreign Affairs, sent to UN New York, 27 July 1961.
138 UNA, S-0845-0003-01, Dag, ONUC files, Press release from the Secretary-General guaranteeing safe passage for senator and delegates to parliament, 13 July 1961.
139 Young, *Politics in the Congo*, p. 337. However, this contrasts with O'Brien's account in which he is adamant that Tshombe did send some representatives to Léopoldville, but refused to attend himself. In any case, it is probable that Tshombe did send some delegates to Léopoldville for the restoration of the Parliament, but that crucially, they were not part of the coalitions formed. Therefore, their absence, as referred to above, merely indicates that they were not part of the new coalition Government in any formal sense, but may well have been there to represent Katanga. O'Brien. *To Katanga and Back*, p. 203.
140 Young, *Politics in the Congo*, p. 340.
141 UNA, S-0845-0003-01, Dag, ONUC files, Telegram from Linner to the Secretary-General, detailing some of the statement in a broadcast from Radio Katanga, that day at noon, 25 August 1961.

142 *Ibid.*
143 For instance, Kalb argues that O'Brien was convinced that Tshombe 'could not be persuaded to dismantle his independent state and re-join the Congo'. Kalb, *Congo Cables*, p. 289.
144 UNA, S-0845-0003-01, Dag, ONUC files, Telegram from Linner in Léopoldville to the Secretary-General in New York, 26 August 1961.
145 *Ibid.*
146 It is reported to have been joked among UN officials at this time that the motto of the Secretary-General ought to have been 'Per Ambigua ad Astra', given that the greater the ambiguity in the resolutions, the more scope the Hammarskjöld actually had interpreting and implementing them. O'Brien, *To Katanga and Back*, p. 47.
147 James, *Britain and the Congo Crisis*, p. 137.
148 There is some deliberation over this with Kalb in particular arguing that behind closed doors the Americans were expressing some concern over the passage of events. However, Weissman points out correctly that American policy was contributory with UN policy. Either way it is clear that publicly, though Washington may have been taken by surprise, it was an opportunity for them to move in concert with UN action, a move which decisively divided them from their European allies, particularly Britain. Weissman, *American Foreign Policy in the Congo*, p. 158; Kalb, *Congo Cables*, p. 290.
149 UNA, S-0845-0003-01, Dag, ONUC files, Telegram from the Linner in Léopoldville to the Secretary-General in New York detailing a discussion between Tshombe, Munongo and O'Brien, 26 August 1961.
150 Ordinance No. 70 called for the expulsion 'from the territory of the Republic of the Congo all the non-Congolese officers and mercenaries etc.'. O'Brien, *To Katanga and Back*, p. 212.
151 The exact number of mercenaries captured and expelled is from Young, *Politics in the Congo*, p. 340. Also A.W. Rovine, *The First Fifty Years: The Secretary-General in World Politics 1920–1970* (Leiden: Slijthoff, 1970), p. 323.
152 Haskin, *The Tragic State of the Congo*, p. 32.
153 Rovine, *The First Fifty Years*, p. 323.
154 As quoted in O'Brien, *To Katanga and Back*, p. 219.
155 UNA, S-0845-0003-01, Dag, ONUC files, Telegram from the Linner in Léopoldville to the Secretary-General in New York detailing a discussion between Tshombe, Munongo and O'Brien, 26 August 1961.
156 Williams, *Who Killed Hammarskjöld?* p. 46.
157 O'Brien, *To Katanga and Back*, p. 218.
158 Telegram from the Department of State to the American Embassy in the Congo, 1 September 1961, Schwar, *FRUS, XX, Congo*, p. 201.
159 Telegram from Adlai Stevenson, at the Mission to the United Nations to the Department of State, New York, 6 September 1961, Schwar, *FRUS, XX, Congo*, p. 204.
160 NAL, FO 371/155092, Telegram from the Foreign Office to New York, 7 September 1961, 3.
161 Weissman, *American Foreign Policy in the Congo*, p. 159. See also Williams, *Who Killed Hammarskjöld?* p. 148.
162 Kansas University Library, Kansas City (hereafter, KUL), Wilcox Collection for Political Movements, American Committee for Aid to Katanga Freedom Fighters,

RH WL Eph 198, Title: Ephemeral Materials, 1961 (OC0LC) 17949950, Control No: ocm18265195, Letter to 'Sponsors, Contributors and Friends' from Max Yergan, Chairman of the American Committee for Aid to Katangan Freedom Fighters, outlines aims of the organisation and lists these American Senators as supporting the cause. 29 December 1961.

163 Weissman, *American Foreign Policy in the Congo*, p. 159.
164 Williams, *Who Killed Hammarskjöld?* p. 148.
165 Helmreich, *United States Relations with Belgium and the Congo*, p. 235.
166 Telegram from the American Embassy in the Congo to the Department of State, Léopoldville, 11 September 1961, Schwar, *FRUS, XX, Congo*, p. 207.
167 Hoskyns, *The Congo Since Independence*, p. 411.
168 As Horne points out, '[Macmillan] regarded Kennedy's man, Adoula, with apprehension as a potential Kerensky to whom Gizenga would play Lenin'. Horne, *Macmillan*, p. 400.
169 Ball, *The Guardsmen*, p. 363.
170 UNA, S-0845-0003-01. Dag, ONUC files, Transcript of a press statement from Roy Welensky, as telegrammed from Linner in Léopoldville to the Secretary-General in New York, 31 August 1961.
171 Williams, *Who Killed Hammarskjöld?* p. 52.
172 Headline in *L'echo du Katanga*, Friday 1 September 1961. As quoted in O'Brien, *To Katanga and Back*, pp. 228–229.
173 Telegram from Rusk at the Department of State to the American Embassy in the Congo. Washington, 15 September 1961, Schwar, *FRUS, XX, Congo*, p. 216.
174 NARA, State Department Central Decimal Files, 741.00/7–1561, Memorandum of Conversation between Sir Hugh Foot, UK Ambassador to the UN and Assistant Secretary of State Harlan Cleveland, 1 September 1961.
175 Memorandum of Conversation between Sir Hugh Foot, UK Ambassador to the UN and Assistant Secretary of State Harlan Cleveland, 1 September 1961, 741.00/7–1561, State Department files, Britain, NARA.
176 That Hammarskjöld approved of the proposed arrest of all the leaders of the Katangan regime except Tshombe and the temporary disarming of the gendarmerie and the seizure of the radio station is confirmed by most accounts of events. See generally O'Brien, *To Katanga and Back*; James, *Britain and the Congo Crisis*, p. 103; Rovine, *The First Fifty Years*, p. 323. However the recent work of Williams, *Who Killed Hammarskjöld?* maintains that the Secretary-General was not informed of the events which were to take place and only learned that Morthor had been launched when his plane touched down in Léopoldville on 13 September 1961 (pp. 55–57). What is most likely is Weissman's view of events – the median position that Hammarskjöld was aware of the details of the operation, but had not approved the timeframe. Weissman, *American Foreign Policy in the Congo*, p. 157.
177 Williams, *Who Killed Hammarskjöld?* p. 57.
178 UNA, S-0845-003-07, Dag, ONUC Files, Telex of communication between Hammarskjöld and Linner, 8 September 1961.
179 UNA, S-0845-0003-01, Dag, ONUC files, Report from O'Brien in Elisabethville, via Khiary, to the Secretary-General in New York, 9 September 1961. 'The Hitler Youth' refers to a demonstration by the JENAKAT, which was the Katangan National Youth organisation.

180 O'Brien, *To Katanga and Back*, p. 225.
181 The extent of this favouritism is evident from Pierre Davister's definition of Conakat as 'an African party which the Europeans had intellectually sponsored at baptism, and whose strings they clearly pulled in the wings'. Davister, *Katanga: Enjeu du Monde*, p. 79.
182 Author's interview with Sergeant Magnus Lemmel, who worked in Air Operations, UN Headquarters, Elisabethville, 1960, in which he described tribal violence involving the Balubas as early as 1960.
183 O'Brien, *To Katanga and Back*, p. 241.
184 *Ibid.*, p. 246.
185 *Ibid.*, p. 249. See also Kalb, *Congo Cables*, p. 292.
186 Williams, *Who Killed Hammarskjöld?*; Kalb, *Congo Cables*, p. 292.
187 Rovine, *The First Fifty Years*, p. 323.
188 UNA, S-0845-0003-01, Dag, ONUC files, Telegram from Linner in Léopoldville to Narasimhan in New York, 15 September 1961.
189 Though he does not reveal the name of this journalist, nor where or whether this statement was published, it is dubious whether O'Brien fabricated this remark considering how it reflects on the UN and in particular on his command of the operation. O'Brien, *To Katanga and Back*, p. 260. Williams also attributed similar remarks to Roy Welensky who apparently stated: 'The United Nations troops have done things that were only equalled by the Nazis and some of the other gentlemen from behind the Iron Curtain.' Williams, *Who Killed Hammarskjöld?* p. 53. She attributes these remarks to a private letter from Welensky dated 21 December 1961.
190 Young, *Politics in the Congo*, p. 340.
191 O'Brien, *To Katanga and Back*, p. 266.
192 UNA, S-0845-0003-01, Dag, ONUC files, Telegram from Hammarskjöld to Narasimhan quoting the report of the Officer-In-Charge in Elisabethville, 14 September 1960. NAL, FO 371/155092, Telegram from Riches, British Embassy. Léopoldville to the Foreign Office, 14 September 1961.
193 As quoted in A.L. Gavshon, *The Mysterious Death of Dag Hammarskjöld* (New York: Walker Publishing, 1962), p. 130. NAL, FO 371/155092, Telegram from Riches, British Embassy. Léopoldville to the Foreign Office, 14 September 1961.
194 NAL, PREM 11/3175, Iain MacLeod, as quoted in a telegram from Walker to the Commonwealth Relations Office, 18 September 1961.
195 UNA, [UK] S-0735-0004-01, Cooperation and Liaison-Britain, Registry Files Political and Security Matters, Mission Files United Nations Operation in the Congo, Telegram from Riches, British Ambassador in Léopoldville, via UN channels to Denzel Dunnett, British Consul, Elisabethville, 14 September 1961.
196 Telegram from the Rusk, Department of State to the American Embassy in Léopoldville, 15 September 1961, Schwar, *FRUS, XX, Congo*, p. 216.
197 Telegram from Gullion, American Embassy Léopoldville to Department of State, 18 September 1961, Schwar, *FRUS, XX, Congo*, p. 231.
198 NAL, PREM 11/3175, Telegram from Walker, the British Ambassador in Delhi, to the Commonwealth Relations Office, 18 September 1961.
199 NAL, PREM 11/3175, Report from P. Petrie, Office of the High Commissioner for the United Kingdom, Delhi, to the Commonwealth Relations Office, 29 September 1961.

200 Kalb, *Congo Cables*, p. 296. Also Mahoney, *J.F.K.*, p. 100.
201 Telegram from Gullion in Elisabethville to the Department of State, 14 September 1961, Schwar, *FRUS, XX, Congo*, p. 212.
202 *Ibid.*, p. 213.
203 Conversation between Gullion and Hammarskjöld in Léopoldville, as communicated to the Department of State, 15 September 1961, Schwar, *FRUS, XX, Congo*, p. 215.
204 Telegram from Gullion, American Embassy in Léopoldville, to the Department of State, 17 September 1961, Schwar, *FRUS, XX, Congo*, p. 226.

4

'After Dag – what?'[1]

Asked if I have the courage
To go on to the end,
I answer Yes without
A second thought.

(Dag Hammarskjöld,
Markings, April 1961)[2]

The Afro-Asian bloc responded in a largely positive manner to Operation Morthor as it represented a significant step towards restoring territorial integrity to the Congo. Nkrumah viewed the action as firm representation of the UN's intention to end the secession and despite clashes with the Katangan gendarmerie and mercenary forces in the following weeks, he called for further military action against Katanga to definitively restore territorial integrity to the Congo.[3] Other states, such as Liberia, heralded the work of Hammarskjöld and the Secretariat in implementing the February Resolution and criticised countries who continued to obstruct the work of the organisation.[4] They stated their continued support for the Secretary-General's actions in the face of the criticism he received from Britain and the US' and publicly and privately they denounced the role of Britain and Belgium in obstructing the UN operation.

By the end of September 1961, Britain was increasingly isolated over the Katanga issue. Allegations of collusion and collaboration with Tshombe's regime were levelled at the Foreign Office by members of the Afro-Asian bloc, the USSR and the British press. The *Daily Mirror* even branded Macmillan a 'Traitor', and accusing him of having betrayed the UN.[5] Home refuted these accusations defending the British position in support of the UN by arguing that in Katanga ONUC had exceeded its mandate.[6] Despite public British denials of support for Katanga, the activities of Dunnett and the British Consulate in Elisabethville created a different impression.[7] Dunnett continued to offer support to Tshombe, turning a blind eye to the aid and materiel pouring in from Rhodesia and counselling him through negotiations with the UN. As a result, Tshombe concluded that he had support from the British Government, and requested its formal intervention to guarantee his safe passage to Léopoldville.[8] This artifice was exacerbated by British policy in New York. Protesting the use of force against Katanga, British representatives threatened to withdraw all support for the UN operation if the Secretary-General failed to reign in ONUC.[9] They also increased efforts to cooperate with the State Department, with the aim of persuading their American colleagues that the secession should not be ended by force.[10]

Operation Morthor had come as a sharp shock to the State Department and the disastrous results only added insult to injury. Although publicly the Americans continued to support for the UN operation, privately Rusk warned Hammarskjöld that 'American support would evaporate' if the UN used further military action.[11] The determination that now spread through the State Department to reassert American authority over the Secretary-General and UN Congo policy was strengthened by Hammarskjöld's death and the escalation of events in Vietnam.[12] In a concerted effort to reassert American influence over the direction of the UN operation, the State Department now advocated a hard-line approach towards ending the secession. This required policymakers in Washington to directly confront the tension between supporting the position of European allies Belgium and Britain by not supporting the use of force against Katanga or moving closer to the positions of the Afro-Asian states and empowering the UN to strike against Tshombe's neo-colonial regime. Mirroring the more forthright position that the US adopted towards colonial issues, the American policy on the Congo now moved towards a more assertive and open stance against Katanga, pitting American officials against their British counterparts. The State Department increased pressure on the Foreign Office to use the Elisabethville Consulate to press Tshombe into negotiating with the Central Government.[13] The lack of coherence between British UN policy in New York and the actions of British officials in Elisabethville resisting the UN had been noted, strengthening suspicions of duplicitous British actions.[14] In order to offset these allegations, in response, Britain agreed to use Lord Lansdowne as a special emissary to push Tshombe into dialogue with the Adoula Government.[15] Aware of these various British connections to Tshombe, the State Department sought to utilise them as a conduit for American influence, while at the same time muting British objections to the further use of force by the UN.

On 17 September Hammarskjöld arranged to travel to Ndola in Northern Rhodesia to meet with Tshombe in order to negotiate a ceasefire between the Katangese gendermarie and UN troops. It has been argued that Hammarskjöld himself undertook the initiative to 'meet with Tshombe outside the bitter cauldron of the Congo and to persuade him to call a ceasefire'.[16] Indeed, given the atmosphere of hostility which existed between the Secretary-General and the State Department following its threat to withdraw support to ONUC, and the Foreign Office given its continued indirect support of Tshombe, it is unlikely that either state compelled him to travel. His earliest biographer and former colleague Brian Urquhart records his reaction to the démarche he had received from the State Department over Morthor as vitriolic and quite out of character for the soft-spoken Swedish diplomat. He recalls Hammarskjöld's reaction as saying: 'It's better for the UN to lose the support of the US because it is faithful to law and principles, than to survive as an agent whose activities are geared to political purposes never avowed or laid down by the major organs of the UN.'[17]

The unease between Hammarskjöld and the West provides fuel for claims that his plane crash on 18 September on his way to Ndola was no accident. Four days previously, the State Department was already discussing choices for his successor with Britain, debating the merits of whether the Indian delegate Chakravarthi V. Narasimhan or the Tunisian President Monghi Slim would be a better candidate for Secretary-General. Hammarskjöld had been re-elected as Secretary-General in 1958 for another five-year term until 1963. Yet, on 14 September Stevenson had cabled the State Department: 'West and Soviet Bloc could probably agree only candidate from Asia or Africa (unless Hammarskjöld continued) and Slim about as "Pro-West" Afro-Asian as we could expect get agreement on.'[18] Hammarskjöld had been re-elected as Secretary-General in 1958 for another five-year term until 1963. The discussion of his replacement seems rather premature, and certainly suspicious in the circumstances, but it was part of a broader debate at the UN through September and October 1961 as delegates seriously considered the imposition of new Under-Secretaries, which would see either geographical regions or power blocs represented equally. This was the product of the Soviet 'troika' proposal in September 1960 which had stimulated a long discussion of restructuring the UN. As part of the process of selecting Hammarskjöld's successor, which reached deadlock by the end of October, negotiations were undertaken around the question of appointing advisors as envisaged in Khrushchev's original proposal. Stevenson later cabled the State Department following deliberations with Chile, Britain, France, Ireland, Norway and Venezuela that the 'general feeling as that we would probably have to accept advisors ultimately.'[19] While the US appeared willing to compromise on the restructuring of the Secretariat, it held to its preferences on Hammarskjöld's successor, the Burmese delegate U Thant, a pro-West, Afro-Asian who replaced him as Acting Secretary-General in October 1961. Indeed, the debate surrounding Thant's nomination was revealing of Western fears about the power of neutralist countries at the UN, and the public embracing of Thant by the Afro-Asians pointed to his perceived ability to further strengthen the Office of the Secretary-General with the support of the Afro-Asian bloc.[20]

Hammarskjöld's decision to travel personally to Ndola was in keeping with his interpretation of the role of the Secretary-General and the interventionist nature of the office, but it was also strategic. He had been severely criticised for his actions during Morthor by many of the countries upon whom he was relying for political and material support for ONUC. By negotiating a ceasefire, he asserted his influence over the crisis in an attempt to silence his critics. In addition, this action lessened the burden of blame on his subordinates on the ground in Léopoldville and Elizabethville, such as Linner and O'Brien, who had been roundly condemned by the international press. It has been further argued by Peter B. Heller, among others, that Hammarskjöld may have had reservations about O'Brien's performance, adding another reason for his decision to travel to Northern Rhodesia.[21] The stakes were high for the Secretary-General personally but also for the authority and integrity of the UN as a whole.

Hammarskjöld's plane travelled to Ndola in the early morning of 18 September but it never arrived. The following day the wreckage was eventually discovered by the Rhodesian authorities, but the exact details and reasons why the plan went down, killing Hammarskjöld, and eventually resulting in the death of all on board, remain unclear. In 2012 Williams released a book in which she tracked down African charcoal workers who reportedly witnessed a flash of light in the sky before the plane crashed, fuelling suspicions that it had been attacked. Newspaper reports from the public enquiry into the crash, held in January 1962, also record the evidence of witnesses who remember being awoken by the sounds of a crash and the low flying of aircraft over their property.[22] The official report of the investigation into the crash records one survivor, Sergeant Harold Julian, Hammarskjöld's bodyguard, as living for several days after being rescued with burn injuries and a broken ankle.[23] His testimony also supports accounts of explosions before the plane crashed but this was discounted by the official enquiry despite his repetition to investigators and his doctor and nurses that 'It blew up … Then there was the crash … There were lots of little explosions all around'.[24] A recent panel investigation dismissed reports alleging that bullet holes were found in the bodies and the fuselage; that Hammarskjöld had a small black hole in his forehead when found; and that his body was moved after the plane crashed.[25] As a result of the continued speculation, a UN commission led by Tanzanian prosecutor Mohamed Chande Othman concluded on 6 July 2015 that a new investigation should be undertaken into the event. At the centre of the new investigation are documents relating to the crash, in particular, the transcript of the plane's last radio communication, believed to be in the archives of the US, Britain and South Africa.

The 2015 panel noted that Paul Abram, a former US military official who was working at a National Security Agency listening post on the night of the 17 September, 'remembered hearing that the plane had been shot down by ground fire'.[26] It was also revealed that the National Security Agency bugged the cryptographic machine Hammarskjöld used. A telegram from the US Embassy in Salisbury to the Secretary of State on 18 September records that according to information they received from the Foreign Office, Hammarskjöld's plane 'started landing pattern at Ndola airport which had given it instructions to land, but at last moment revved up motors and flew off in unknown direction'.[27] This report, as corroborated by the panel's review, provides evidence to dismiss the argument that pilot fatigue or pilot error was responsible for the crash. Rather, all the signals point to an interference of some sort. Goesta Ellhammar, the manager of the Swedish Transair Company, the operators of Hammarskjöld's plane, told the press on 25 September 1961 that 'nobody within the UN believes [the] crash [was] caused by accident'.[28] Indeed suspicions that the plane had been shot down were spurred by the fact that the British Rhodesian authorities did not launch a search until four hours after daybreak despite reports of a flash of light in the sky just after midnight the previous day. Emmerson, an American diplomat who was granted access to the crash site shortly after the plane came down, reported to the State Department: 'We cannot understand why a radio operator who was in voice contact with DC-6 apparently did nothing, when aircraft failed to land, until following morning'.[29] In addition, it took fifteen hours to locate the crash site which was just eight miles from the landing strip in Ndola. Emerson further noted the displeasure 'about the delay and manner in which search efforts were conducted'.[30]

Alongside the flurry of telegrams from the US Embassy in Salisbury, the American Ambassador in Léopoldville, Edmund Gullion, also communicated the loss of Hammarskjöld's plane. Even before the wreckage was discovered he speculated that 'There is possibility he was shot down'. During the 1962 public enquiry Major Joseph Delin, a jet pilot from the Katanga Air Force, denied that his Fouga jet, the only armed fighter in Katanga, was in the air on the night of the crash. He admitted, however, trying, on other occasions, to force down planes similar to Hammarskjöld's, by firing bullets at them in the air.[31] In July 2016, in response to a request from Secretary-General Ban Ki-moon, the US refused to declassify top-secret National Security Council records relating to the incident, and Britain similarly has declined to release files, citing security concerns.[32] While the forthcoming investigation into this mystery will hopefully return a definitive answer, continued suspicion surrounding the role of America and Britain, alongside the premature discussions about his replacement and the bugging of his equipment by the National Security Agency, bears out the impression that, by the time of his death, there was at the very least a distinct lack of trust, if not open hostility between Hammarskjöld, America and Britain.

Indeed, the Congo operation had proceeded at times without the direct influence of the US and in fact contrary to what Britain would have preferred. The Operation reflected precisely Hammarskjöld's interpretation of his office and his willingness to use overt action when quiet diplomacy failed.[33] This approach turned the events that transpired over Katanga from being a mere diplomatic fracas into a military dispute. Hammarskjöld's personal influence clashed with American and British efforts to control the UN Congo operation. For Britain, Hammarskjöld's actions threatened the order which may otherwise have existed in Katanga and the Foreign Office was keen to rein in his powers, viewing him as altogether too dominant.[34] The State Department had trouble retaining control of UN Congo policy, as stressed continually by Stevenson, and the actions of ONUC in Katanga yet again displayed the growing tendency of the organisation under Hammarskjöld to act in accordance with the Afro-Asians.[35] Both countries agreed therefore that their approaches to the UN needed to be revised, but whereas Britain sought to mute the influence of the organisation, the US sought to reinforce it. Without an active Secretary-General to intervene now, the State Department set about developing a stronger Congo policy. The Foreign Office concentrated on getting rid of O'Brien, who, in the eyes of British policymakers, embodied 'an organisation which seemed to be getting too big for its boots'.[36]

The man in Katanga

> HMG will do their best to see that this [moving O'Brien back to the Secretariat] happens.[37]

A meeting of the British Cabinet on 19 September firmly placed the blame for the disastrous results of Operation Morthor at the foot of the Special Representative of the Secretary-General in Elisabethville, O'Brien. Many Cabinet members believed that he had exceeded his authority in implementing the UN mandate and in using military force unnecessarily. In addition, O'Brien (and others) had misjudged the reaction of the Katangan Government, which had led to a prolonged military conflict.[38] The Foreign Office was adamant that O'Brien be removed from the Congo and that he issue a public retraction of his statements which alleged that Operation Morthor had been executed at the behest of the Central Government and that the secession had been ended.[39] Home, who was particularly opposed to O'Brien, began the process by pointing out to Bunche that O'Brien had lost the confidence of Tshombe and was therefore rendered useless as a representative of the UN in Katanga.[40] In his book, To Katanga and Back, O'Brien defends his actions and maintains that the Foreign Office tried to make him a scapegoat since Hammarskjöld's death created a vacuum of responsibility for events in Katanga. By the middle of October, it was suggested by sources close to him that O'Brien 'might be wise to apply for a transfer from Katanga'.[41] O'Brien disregarded this suggestion.

However, Britain maintained pressure towards this objective. When it was discovered in November that O'Brien was receiving quiet visits from Maire MacEntee, a member of the Irish Foreign Service, the Foreign Office found a way to discredit him. Alleging that his marital infidelity was unacceptable in his position, the Foreign Office pressed the acting Secretary-General, U Thant, to take the opportunity to remove him. Thant eventually demanded that O'Brien be recalled by the Irish Government as an alternative to him being officially dismissed by the UN.[42] O'Brien subsequently engaged in a bitter and disparaging campaign against the British Government, accusing them of being fundamentally opposed to the implementation of the February Resolution and of ousting him from his position in Elizabethville. His statements inflamed allegations of British collusion with Tshombe and the failure of Operation Morthor. In order to offset this impression the Foreign Office attempted, at the urging of the State Department, to push Tshombe into a summit meeting with Adoula with a view to restoring law and order in Katanga. Efforts to again bolster the authority of the Central Government were spearheaded by the US as the President appointed George Ball as his 'Commander in Chief for Congo Affairs' in order to formulate a more coherent approach.[43] However, despite American pressure on Tshombe through Britain, the Katangan leader used Belgian support to avoid being pushed into negotiations with Adoula through October and November. With the failure of diplomatic efforts, the question of a final military push by the UN to end the secession once and for all solidified the split between American and British policies in December 1961.

Following Hammarskjöld's death the State Department revised US Congo policy with the aim of strengthening Adoula's Central Government, by advancing the campaign against Katanga. Ball composed a three-point plan for US policy that the President approved without revision. This envisaged a UN military build-up in Katanga, increased material and financial support of the Central Government and the eradication of all sources of foreign support for Tshombe. In order to avoid aggravating relations with the Afro-Asian bloc, and to prevent further allegations of collusion, Ball proposed that pressure on Tshombe to negotiate should be increased with the help of Britain and Belgium.[44] At the UN, American representatives held secret talks with the representatives of the UAR, Ceylon and Liberia in an effort to coordinate policies. The US supported the Afro-Asian proposal to strengthen ONUC's mandate with a Security Council resolution and sought to extend this to action against Katanga and Gizenga's regime in Stanleyville.[45] As Cleveland pointed out to Williams, 'This is a chance now to impress upon [Tshombe] to listen to us. Ball said the shots are being called'.[46]

From September to December the US tried to influence the separatist leader by all means available, including through his relationship with the UN, to enter into talks with Adoula.[47] British resistance towards ending the secession and subsequent failure to get Tshombe to the negotiation table exacerbated tensions with the US. By 3 November, Kennedy, who was becoming increasingly impatient, demanded to know what the British were doing to this effect. Williams could do little but assure him that the 'British were sending someone with a rather strong message' to turn the screws on Tshombe.[48] However, Tshombe proved impervious to Dunnett and Lansdowne's efforts to bring him to the negotiation table with Adoula, which directly served the British policy of passive resistance to the American approach. Indeed, he was emboldened in this resistance by speeches such as that of Dean in the Security Council in which he rejected the American proposal to allow the Secretary-General to remove or prevent the use of military aircraft, arguing that this would worsen the situation.[49] In the meantime, a tenuous ceasefire in Katanga allowed Tshombe to prepare his mercenary army and pilots for the next round of military action against UN forces.

Hammarskjöld's death also accelerated American efforts to restructure the UN and led to a concerted effort of the Afro-Asian bloc to work to ensure that in response to his sudden departure, the activist nature of his office would be continued by his successor. Ghana, Liberia and India led the debate in the General Assembly about how UN reform should take place, emphasising that while they were against the Soviet troika proposal, the Congo experience had revealed the shortcomings of the existing UN power structure.[50] In discussions on the restructuring of the Secretariat, they pursued the objective of a larger role for the African states in particular, who accounted for a quarter of the organisation's members. India pressed the need to continue support for the UN mission in the Congo, arguing that the whole future effectiveness of the UN relied on its success.[51]

On the CAC, the contributing countries to ONUC also called for stronger action against the mercenaries remaining in Katanga and Tshombe himself. In the first meeting after Hammarskjöld's death, the Nigerian delegate, Mr Ngileruma, requested to know the situation regarding reports that UN stations were coming under fire from a 'wandering aircraft'. Bunche described the story of 'this lonely jet bandit plane [as] one of the most incredible pages in military history'. He outlined that two jet planes, one piloted by a Rhodesian and the other by a Belgian, were dominating the skies over Katanga, bombing UN targets and severely hindering the UN operation which had no aircraft at its disposal.[52] This incredible situation persisted through October and November as Tshombe continued his defiance and the mercenary forces gathered strength. By November, Krishna Menon demanded that the Secretary-General take a more assertive position with regard to the mission, and challenged Thant directly in the CAC, stating: 'We should like to know what degree of harmony, I would say what degree of liaison, what degree of inter-working access there is between the 38th floor and the field of the Congo because there must be somebody responsible.'[53]

The pressure to unify Katanga with the Congo was growing on all sides and the central point of contention between the State Department and the Foreign Office was again the use of force by the UN. Ball confirmed that in September the UN had entered a 'general state of demoralisation with a lot of politicking going on'.[54] By the middle of October, Stevenson advised the State Department that the 'mood at the UN [is] now bad'.[55] The atmosphere was intensified by the increasingly loud calls from the Afro-Asian bloc for a Security Council meeting to discuss a revision of the UN's mandate in the Congo to deal with the secession definitively.[56] Thant supported the convening of a meeting as requested by Ceylon, UAR and Liberia, the three non-permanent Afro-Asian members on the Security Council. American officials were aware that revision of the UN mandate would raise differences with their British colleagues given their position on the use of force. In the weeks leading up to the Security Council meeting, the State Department instructed Stevenson and the American delegation that although there was a potential for 'serious differences' with Britain, France and Belgium, the British position could not be allowed to prejudice the American objectives of strengthening Adoula's Government through whatever means possible.[57]

The US now sought to engineer a solution along the lines of Balls' three-point plan, which would formally bring an end to the secession. A secret memorandum leaked from the UN revealed an aggressive plan to deal with the mounting tension between the Central Government and Tshombe. It proposed that Ceylon present a resolution to the Security Council, which would instruct ONUC to take control of key mining facilities and suspend all flights over Katanga. In order to avoid the situation in which Britain would apply its veto, the plan recommended moving the debate to the General Assembly 'where it will be adopted with no serious difficulty'.[58] Since the beginning of October, militia groups, some of whom had strong Communist leanings, began to mass on the border between the Congo and Northern Rhodesia in preparation for a military strike against the Katangan army's aircraft facilities. If they did not support the proposed military initiative, the US feared that Soviet backing for the operation would give the USSR the upper hand in the conflict. As Ball pointed out, 'the people in New York at the UN are very keen to have us give support to the announcement they are proposing to take action against aircraft to carry out the terms of the mandate, this involves shooting down planes or killing them on the ground'.[59] However Kennedy was hesitant about issuing any outright statement of support, even if it would have the effect of thwarting Soviet influence, as it may be interpreted as a justification for the UN to break the official ceasefire, which may lead to civil war. He was concerned that the US should not appear to have authorised the action in order to avoid any obligation to provide further military support, but yet he understood that firm action was required. Eventually, he relented, instructing Ball: 'We are with them [the UN] all the way, let them go ahead and do it.'[60]

The Cold War lens of the State Department now became fully focused on US Congo policy. Violence in Vietnam, with the rise of the Viet Cong and the failure of the Alliance for Progress in Latin America, created more emphasis for efficient policy regarding the Cold War in the Developing World.[61] As Cleveland put it to Ball, 'the urgency is simply to make sure we do something before the Soviets'.[62] The Security Council debates which now resumed on the Congo increased tensions with the Soviet Union, which supported some of the more hard-line African states such as the UAR and Ghana. Simultaneous deliberations over the restructuring of the Secretariat reached a stalemate with Soviet representatives continuing to press for five advisors plus the Secretary-General, a structure the US refused to consider.[63] Efforts to moderate and stall the Security Council debate were connected to other areas of Anglo-American cooperation and in the process again revealed to the US the growing distance between Britain and many members of the Afro-Asian bloc. The issue of the election of a member of the Commonwealth to a 'non-permanent' seat on the Security Council was one such example.

Ghana was the candidate for election to the Commonwealth seat but American perceptions of Nkrumah's pro-Soviet behaviour in his Congo policy led them to support the selection of Nigeria instead and American representatives urged Britain to do likewise. However, Britain was resistant towards removing Ghana as a candidate, especially as Nkrumah had the support of many other Commonwealth nations and the Foreign Office needed to preserve, if not improve, these relationships. A memo from Stevenson to the State Department noted that relations between London and Accra 'were in a severe state of crisis' due to Nkrumah's decision to send soldiers to Communist countries for training.[64] Without being able to use British contacts to influence the voting process, Ghana secured the seat, against the wishes of the State Department.

British intransigence over the Congo, and much diminished influence with Afro-Asian countries and within the Commonwealth, closed down avenues of Anglo-American cooperation and increased the determination of the State Department to generate a Congo policy more in line with the Afro-Asians. The US willingness to support a final move by the UN against Katanga reflected a shift towards the Afro-Asian position, a decision that was solidified by their shared impressions of continued British collusion with Katanga. As the American Embassy in New Delhi reported to the State Department, there was bitter feeling in India about the role of Britain in the Congo.[65] The damage British Congo policy caused for Afro-Asian relations, combined with the Cold War imperative and the perceived need for stronger leadership at the UN, led American and Britain into open conflict over the 'bombs for the UN' question in December 1961.

Bombs for the UN

On 1 November, Permanent Under-Secretary at the Foreign Office Sir Frederick Hoyer Millar telegraphed the State Department with the reflections of the British Government on the development of policy in the Congo. The memo included a long discussion of the mandate granted to the UN and how it was to be weighed against the circumstances of potential civil war. It concluded that: 'The Resolution does not authorise the use of force against Tshombe to subdue Katanga as a political measure. It does justify the use of force against him if that is necessary to prevent a civil war. Exactly at what point the use of force would be justified is a matter for appreciation.'[66] Recognising that American Congo policy was on a divergent course to that of Britain, the memo pressed the urgent need for further consultation with the US on this matter. Although Britain may have been keen to coordinate strategies with the State Department, British refusal to budge on the question of using force against Katanga continued to undermine efforts to formulate a joint Anglo-American position. As the State Department led the campaign to end the secession through November and December British delegates again became increasingly marginalised from the development of UN policy. Exacerbating the problem further, Welensky continued to protest UN actions in Katanga while supplying political and materiel resources to Tshombe through back channels from Rhodesia. These actions were criticised by the UN, leading Thant to appeal to Britain about the 'deliberately mischievous' activity of Rhodesian forces on the border of Katanga and the movement of vehicles into the province from the Federation.[67] This issue of the supply of military resources to the UN was precisely what brought the debate on UN Congo policy to a head in December.

A crucial factor in the failure of Operation Morthor had been the fact that the UN was severely materially disadvantaged due to a lack of aircraft with which to respond to the air attacks from Katanga. It was agreed in Washington that the supply of aircraft to ONUC would be a central part of the implementation of the Security Council Resolution of 24 November 1961.[68] After some wrangling, the Afro-Asian draft was adopted as the final resolution. It authorised the Secretary-General to 'take vigorous action, including the use of the requisite measure of force, if necessary, for the immediate apprehension, detention pending legal action and/or deportation of all foreign military and paramilitary personnel and political advisers not under the United Nations Command, and mercenaries', thereby reinforcing Thant's authority to fully implement the February Resolution.[69] The most significant number of aircraft at the disposal of the UN for this operation was six Canberra jets, in the possession of India, but manufactured in Britain. Therefore, Britain was requested to supply the bombs. This proved highly controversial for Macmillan's Government and was immediately criticised by the Katanga lobby within the Conservative Party.[70] Cabinet ministers acknowledged on 14 December that Tshombe and his regime were beneficial for both British interests in the region and British African policy, with one member arguing that 'It would not be in our interests nor would it help our multi-racial policies in Africa if Mr Tshombe were overthrown'.[71] By this point British efforts to induce Tshombe to negotiate with Adoula had stalled completely as the Katangan leader refused to leave the province for fear of being arrested or ousted from power. Efforts to introduce a mediator had also failed, with Nigeria turning down a British request to take the lead. This lack of progress can also be explained by the widespread sympathy among the British Cabinet for Tshombe's position and the resistance towards both Congolese and UN efforts to remove him by force.

Indeed, as his biographer Alistair Horne aptly describes it, 'although in spirit Macmillan was with Katanga, he continued to pay lip-service to the United Nations'.[72] In such a position, the Prime Minister took the decision on 7 December to supply twenty-four 1,000-pound bombs for use against Tshombe's mercenary pilots. In an exchange of letters between Thant and Dean, Britain specified the terms and conditions under which these bombs were donated, outlining that they were only to be used in self-defence and against airstrips.[73] This was in accordance with an agreement that Home would increase negotiations with the US to urge Adoula to cooperate with Tshombe, thereby hopefully avoiding the situation in which the bombs would ever be required for use.[74] However, earlier fears about the damage supplying the bombs would do for the British position was confirmed in the immediate uproar among the backbenchers of the Conservative Party, particularly those such as Lord Salisbury who was a forthright supporter of the Katangan regime. As Macmillan himself later reflected: 'we were in for a row'.[75]

After much debate, on 24 November, the Security Council passed a resolution reinforcing ONUC's mandate and crucially 'completely rejected the claim that Katanga was a sovereign nation'.[76] In response, the British Government internally reflected apprehension that the Secretary-General would go too far in the use of force against Katanga.[77] American UN representatives engaged their British counterparts in consultation before the vote was passed in an effort to create cohesion between them but to no avail.[78] The vote passed with the US voting in favour and Britain abstaining alongside France, which, as Dean warned, created a poor impression among the Afro-Asian states whose support Britain needed for further resolutions regarding British colonial policies.[79] America's positive vote in favour was also significant in reflecting its support for the use of force by the UN against Katanga, despite British objections. Kennedy fortified this more active approach by also approving a plan to retrain and rearm the ANC, and granted the CIA in Léopoldville the power to buy off or neutralise Adoula's opponents to shore up the position of the Central Government through the UN.[80] With Ball leading Congo policy formation, the US had now made its position in the Congo clear; and it was directly opposed to British objectives.

This more cohesive and activist US Congo strategy was a direct result of a reconfiguration of Kennedy's foreign policy advisory team. His 'point man on Congo', Ball, assured National Security Advisor, McGeorge Bundy, that he was consulting with the State Department on this 'just about every day until we get our real policy'.[81] A task force operation was set up between the State Department, the Department of Defence and the CIA in order to formulate a coherent US policy which supported the UN military action against Katanga, but without the direct involvement of American military. The intention was to create the illusion of distance in order to maintain friendly relations with the Afro-Asian bloc to dispel any allegations of collusion between the US and the UN. Part of the reasoning behind the US support for the final push from the UN was the assumption that if Adoula did not receive assistance through the UN, he would expect some form of bilateral aid.[82] This would have required the US to play a direct role in the Congo, which was to be avoided given existing military commitments in Vietnam and Laos. Additionally, there remained a fear that if the US did not support Adoula, he would turn to Moscow for help, thereby offering the Soviets a foothold in the Central Government. What was now evident in American Congo policy was that while the preservation of relations with Belgium and Britain had proven an important component up to this point, the US was beginning to embark on a Congo policy and an approach to Africa more generally that did not have the preservation of relations with European allies as its dominant component. On 5 December, Kennedy finally gave the go-ahead to support the building of a hydroelectric dam on the Volta River in Ghana, even though Nkrumah supported O'Brien's claims about British behaviour in the Congo and widely condemned British collusion with Tshombe. This irked the British Government, leading Macmillan to urge Kennedy not to support the project.[83] However the Prime Minister's refusal to agree to affirmative action against Katanga was matched by Kennedy's refusal to back down from the Volta project, resulting in no compromise on either issue.[84]

Despite agreeing to supply the bombs in principle, Britain stalled the actual transfer of material when contradicting statements from UN officials caused confusion about what ONUC would do in Katanga, and how exactly the bombs would be used. Contrary to assurances given by Thant to Dean on 8 December that the bombs would only be used in self-defence, Linner gave a controversial interview to a Swedish newspaper the following day in which he stated that the long-term aim of the United Nations was to force a political solution on Katanga by smashing the present political leadership and their military strength. 'He also maintained that United Nations officials in the Congo had carte blanche for the conduct of military operations there.'[85] Things really began to fall apart when Ethiopian soldiers in the service of the UN killed three Red Cross workers in a military blunder.[86] These inconsistencies between statements from the UN in New York and the actual events in Katanga created further controversy around the supply of bombs in London.[87] Dean was asked to secure a repudiation of Linner's statements but the reply from Thant was less than reassuring. He denied that a free hand had been given to forces on the ground and repeated the claim that the bombs would only be used in self-defence.[88] Despite this promise, the Foreign Office remained adamant that it was not the duty of the UN to impose a political solution on Katanga. British officials became increasing frustrated, arguing with the Secretary-General that ONUC was exceeding its original mandate and acting in a partisan manner.[89] Tensions became progressively more frayed with Thant, who, in an unusual move, publicly released the correspondence with Britain in an effort to pressure the Government into acceding to the UN request.[90]

Effectively the British were caught in a no-win position. The decision to supply the bombs, with or without attaching conditions for their use, opened the Government up to attack from the Katanga lobbyists within the Conservative Party. However, to withdraw the statement which promised the bombs would make it appear that the Government had changed its mind, and likely stir up allegations of succumbing to pressure from these supporters of Katangan independence and increase the impression of collusion with Tshombe's regime. In addition, Dean cabled Home from the UN that 'our reputation here will suffer severely' if Britain revoked the promise to supply the bombs.[91] Caught between the UN and the Conservatives, the decision of the Cabinet was to compromise and hope that Thant's guarantee that the bombs would only be used in self-defence would bear out. In addition, British representatives in Katanga continued to urge Tshombe to negotiate an agreement with the Central Government to end the secession.[92]

The British stance over the bombs for the UN affair confirmed the fears of the State Department about London's hostile attitude towards ONUC in Katanga.[93] American delegates came under intense pressure from the Afro-Asians who denounced the atrocities committed. Armed with the resolution of 24 November, they advocated further use of force to definitively end the secession. They were particularly incensed by Tshombe's declarations in response to the Security Council resolution that he would defend Katanga by force and was prepared to fight to the death.[94] The Indonesian representative, Mr Wirjopranoto, on the CAC now pushed Thant again, calling for cooperation and coordination and strong action to implement the resolution.[95] Kennedy remained insistent that there could be no ceasefire until Tshombe agreed to negotiate.[96] However, he also did not want a major fallout with Macmillan over the Congo just weeks before the two were to meet in Bermuda to discuss the resumption of atmospheric nuclear tests on the British territory of Christmas Island. Domestically, the conflict also squeezed Kennedy's support base in the Senate when the well-financed Katanga lobby in Washington, led by Dodd and the Senate minority leader, Everett McKinley Dirksen, announced on 13 December the formation of the American Committee for Aid to Katanga Freedom Fighters.[97] Such was the tense atmosphere in the White House that Ball warned Cleveland, 'what is bothering the President is that people have been getting to him'.[98]

For the Foreign Office, in addition to the realisation that London and Washington were poles apart on the Katanga question, Macmillan's Government now faced a direct challenge from the backbenches. The Conservative Party was split between those who believed that the supply of bombs was not enough to bring about a whole solution to the crisis, and the Katanga lobbyists, urged on by the indignant Welensky, who supported the secession. Tory sympathies for significant business interests in Katanga, support for the CAF and resistance towards the total dissolution of the British Empire all came together around the Congo question at this moment. As Macmillan noted in his diary, 'the trouble in the Party is that in addition to the small group of people who really hate me … the anxiety about [the] United Nations performance in the Congo had spread to the whole *centre* of the Party'.[99] The challenge to Macmillan's leadership came in the form of a House of Commons debate on foreign affairs on 14 December, which included a motion signed by eighty Tory MPs that condemned the Government's actions over the affair.[100] The level of personal anxiety Macmillan was feeling about this was well expressed in his 15 December letter to the Queen in which he observed, 'The 1000lb bomb however became the detonator of a kiloton row, which threatened yesterday to become almost a megaton row in the House of Commons'.[101] The Labour Party, the Liberals and the broadly speaking 'left-leaning wing' of the Conservative Party supported the UN action in opposition to the right-wing and centre Tories, who believed the Government had reneged on its promise not to let Katanga be crushed by the UN.[102] Facing the Commons debate on 14 December, Macmillan began to panic that his Government would fall over the issue.

Since the source of Macmillan's problems lay at the UN, he now looked for a possibility to negotiate a solution in New York. If the question of further use of force by ONUC against Katanga could be avoided by arranging a ceasefire, the UN action could be contained and the impasse in which Macmillan found himself both with the US and his own party could be resolved. The Foreign Office instructed the British delegation to negotiate with American representatives and members of the Afro-Asian bloc to find a diplomatic solution with a more moderate Security Council resolution. Cabling the Foreign Office on 11 December, Dean warned that it would be impossible to summon a Security Council meeting unless an agreement could be reached with the Americans, who 'take a different view about the present situation in the Congo and are clearly prepared to go further in support of the United Nations and the use of force in Katanga than we would deem desirable'.[103] Furthermore, he warned that even if an agreement was reached with the US, securing seven votes on the Security Council would be virtually impossible, while in the process, Britain would be heavily attacked by the Afro-Asians who would try 'to make us the scapegoat for the United Nations lack of success'.[104] The failed efforts of the British UN delegation and the Foreign Office to halt further UN action led Macmillan to then seek a solution through his personal relationship with Kennedy.

Desperate to garner votes within his party for the Commons debate, he telephoned the President on 13 December to enlist his support to restrain UN action in the Congo. He insisted that Britain believed that the UN was exceeding its mandate with the indications that it would quash the secession by force and its response to the escalating violence in Katanga.[105] The British Ambassador to the US, David Ormsby Gore, who was a close personal friend of Kennedy, was instructed to use his influence to press the British case with the President.[106] Over dinner at the White House that evening, Ormsby-Gore persuaded Kennedy that Britain would be able to induce Tshombe to negotiate with the Central Government and that, therefore, there was no need for a further UN military action against Katanga. While this negotiation was in process, Rusk reported from a NATO Foreign Ministers' meeting in Paris that the Congo question was dominating the agenda. Home had warned Rusk that the British Government would completely withdraw support if the fighting continued.[107] Mindful of the stability of the Anglo-American relationship and the wider impact a prolonged disagreement would have on NATO, Kennedy instructed Ball to contact Stevenson and press the Secretary-General to restrain ONUC. On 13 December, just in time for the House of Commons debate, Thant issued a press release withdrawing the request for bombs, due to the 'considerable anxiety expressed in the United Kingdom'.[108] As a result, Macmillan emerged with a majority of ninety-four votes in support of the Government's Congo policy, but in private he raged against the 'follies from ignorance and inexperience' committed by the UN.[109] In reality, however, this episode was reflective of the lack of British influence within the UN and its inability to unilaterally restrain the organisation from executing Congo policy in line with Afro-Asian objectives.

The Kitona Accords

Following significant diplomatic haranguing from both the British and the Americans, Tshombe finally agreed to negotiate with Adoula on 15 December.[110] Through

Dunnett in the British Consulate in Elisabethville, Tshombe agreed to go to talks in Ndola if the UN called off its air attacks on Katanga.[111] Gullion was instructed to meet Tshombe and travel with him to talks with Adoula, which would guarantee his presence but also allowed the Ambassador time to extend American authority over him.[112] The US was now drawn into the conflict in a more direct way, and exerted a series of efforts towards negotiating a settlement between the Central Government and the breakaway province, in order to offset the necessity of further military action by the UN. Guillon 'pulled out all the stops' with Adoula and Kasavubu in order to secure an agreement.[113] On 21 December the two leaders reached a settlement within the terms of which Tshombe agreed to announce the end of the secession. The Kitona Accords were decidedly weak from the moment of their inception. Tshombe immediately raised questions over the legal validity of his signature without further ratification from the Katangese Parliament. A month later the Katangese regime adopted the Accords only 'as a potential basis of discussion'.[114] The US engaged in significant arm-twisting with both the Central Government and Tshombe to secure the ceasefire. The speed at which Tshombe seemed to have veered from his original position and announced the end of the secession created further doubts about whether or not he did so of his own free will.[115] Belgium, also seeking to avoid military action against Katanga, had a hand in forcing Tshombe to an agreement by warning him that otherwise Thant would return to the Security Council for what would likely be tougher resolutions against the breakaway province.[116] That Tshombe's hand was forced in the signing of the agreement became evident the moment he arrived back in Elisabethville, where, under the protection of the Katangan gendarmerie, he rolled back his consent by insisting that he had only acquiesced under duress.[117] Efforts to enforce the Accords through the spring and summer of 1962 also achieved little. Officials became increasingly frustrated with Katangese representatives who refused to abide by the terms of the agreement. The inability of the UN to implement it was further damaging for the Central Government in Léopoldville as opposition parties weakened Adoula's position by exploiting his failure to end the secession.[118]

American support for the UN and unity with Thant rendered fruitless efforts to coordinate Congo policy with Britain during the Bermuda talks at the end of December 1961. The British Cabinet had earlier agreed to investigate the possibility of allowing the US to hold nuclear tests on Christmas Island. Although nuclear cooperation was one of the keystones of the Anglo-American relationship, Kennedy's request to hold tests on the island had been viewed with unease. Macmillan himself expressed concern that the effects of such atmospheric tests were not fully known and that such an exercise was likely to give rise to further negative world opinion.[119] From the US perspective, the State Department was adamant that the British would not use the Christmas Island issue as a 'wedge for widening our bilateral atomic relationship, because basically we hope that British atomic activity will increasingly be Europeanised'.[120] The negotiations pivoted around Soviet provocations over Berlin, producing an agreement to begin testing to maintain the effectiveness of the nuclear deterrent.[121] Despite his personal reservations, Macmillan was keen to use the negotiations to strengthen the Anglo-American relationship after the Congo debacle, stressing to Kennedy that on nuclear cooperation 'whether testing occurred on Christmas Island or not, we were in it together and Britain would have to back up the United States'.[122]

Despite the tacit agreement regarding nuclear cooperation, discussions of Congo policy and the UN at Bermuda reflected the impasse between London and Washington. British feeling that the organisation was a 'damned nuisance' continued to divide Anglo-American opinion even after the Kitona Accords.[123] The British agreement to continue to pressure Tshombe towards a diplomatic solution was quite different from the economic imperative the State Department now wished to impose on the Katangese regime. They suggested that Katanga's tax revenues be diverted to Léopoldville, and that the UN would assume control over the major infrastructure in the region. The British completely opposed these ideas given that they would again strengthen the role of the UN. Instead, representatives argued for the complete withdrawal of UN forces from Katanga, reiterating that the secession should not be ended by force. In contrast, State Department officials remained adamant that through whatever means necessary Katanga should become part of the whole Congo territory.[124]

The differences between America and Britain at Bermuda went beyond the means by which the UN should deal with Katanga but reflected a deeper divergence of views about the organisation as a whole. Similar to earlier beliefs about Hammarskjöld, Macmillan was openly critical of UN policy, believing U Thant to be altogether too much influenced by the Afro-Asians.[125] This was a view shared by Home, who, in a discussion on the future of the UN, expressed the view that nationalism had taken over, thereby casting a shadow on the whole future usefulness of the organisation.[126] Rusk, in contrast, stressed that as long as the Soviets were making use of the UN as a means to wage the Cold War, the organisation would not be abandoned by the US. Instead he proposed a reorganisation of the Secretariat in order to safeguard emerging nations from falling under the influence of the USSR. The only agreement that could be reached on the Congo was a general commitment to foster peace between Adoula and Tshombe and avoid any further armed conflict in the region.[127]

The Bermuda talks did little to improve relations over the Congo question, with Britain staunchly opposed to the UN action while, in contrast, America wanted to strengthen the means by which the organisation could execute its mandate to end the secession. So different were positions that the State Department now began a series of bilateral talks with Britain on the Congo in order to avoid 'future serious policy splits'.[128] British representatives, including Dean and Ormsby-Gore, argued that only economic measures could encourage Tshombe to cooperate with the UN and that threats and shows of force against him would achieve little. In contrast, the US, represented by Stevenson and Cleveland, believed that the threat of further military force against him was a useful means by which to leverage Tshombe into an agreement. The Americans also argued that Britain underestimated the nationalist pressures on the Adoula Government to resolve the situation and reintegrate Katanga. They warned that if the situation erupted into violence again, these differences would continue to divide London and Washington. The disagreements about the fundamental elements of Congo policy increasingly had the effect of revealing the difference in views of the UN between the two countries. Tory MPs had used the House of Commons debates as a platform to exercise their long-held grievances about the UN since Suez whereas American officials, desperate to reassert American control over the mission and denude the Afro-Asian influence with the Secretary-General, sought to enforce the mandate against Katanga. As *The Economist* reflected, the situation led to a period of acrimony for the 'special relationship' in the coming months.[129]

The American efforts with Adoula, Kasavubu and Tshombe signalled the beginning of a long-term strategy of trapping Tshombe into an agreement, with the ultimate goal of extracting the UN from its operation in Katanga, 'a face-saving formula allowing ONUC to retire militarily'.[130] From this point onwards, the US was gradually drawn more directly into the conflict through an increased support for the UN mission and Adoula's Government, which was carefully managed with 'bribery, blackmail and threats'.[131] The imperative to preserve the prestige of the UN and considerations of what the role of the organisation could be in solving future crises emerged directly as a result of the Congo experience. In the view of the State Department, the fighting in Katanga had raised questions about the 'United Nations' capabilities and intentions'.[132] Despite the problems with the UN operation, it was still 'far preferable to having big power troops fighting in the heart of Africa'. The shifting of the US Congo policy towards that of the UN reflected both efforts to reassert American authority over the direction of policy and how Cold War anxieties underpinned these efforts. The active role of the organisation, which had proven so problematic, had shifted perceptions in the State Department of what the organisation could achieve and the extent to which the Afro-Asian bloc influenced the development of policies. By aligning Congo policy closer with its approach, the US sought to maintain relations with African and Asian leaders, while simultaneously, this required Washington to distance itself from British Congo policy and their own traditional position on colonial issues.

Fundamentally opposite impressions of the UN were now clear in the Foreign Office. During the US–UK talks in January 1962, the State Department branded as 'premature' the British belief that 'there should be no more UN operations such as that in Congo'.[133] The use of force by the UN against Katanga and the anti-colonial tenor of General Assembly debates had created a serious political challenge for Macmillan's Government. The Congo issue forced an open split between the 'left' and 'right' wing of the Conservative Party as it echoed through a variety of dimensions of foreign policy: British colonial policies; plans for decolonisation; the protection of economic interests; and ultimately the question of how to manage the conversion of the empire into the Commonwealth. Through 1961 the events in the Congo had displayed the inability of Britain to influence substantially either US or UN policy on the Congo or on decolonisation. Even among members of the Commonwealth or among former colonies the British influence was found to be limited, a dynamic that would be replayed before the Congo crisis was finally resolved. The steady unravelling of Anglo-American consensus on the Congo translated into definitively different positions which, through 1962, spilled over into other areas of the relationship, namely decolonisation, as the crisis rumbled on.

Notes

1 NARA, State Department Central Files, Congo, 310/9–961, Letter from Arthur Larson, Duke University School of Law to Assistant Secretary of State for UN Affairs, 19 September 1961. There was at this time an ongoing project at Duke University considering the problems relating to the future of the UN. One section was entitled 'After Dag—what?'
2 D. Hammarskjöld, *Markings* (New York: Vintage, 2006), p. 206.
3 AWCP, Box 103, UN Files, UN Administration, Secretariat, 4, General Assembly Debates, Nkrumah's position as detailed by his representative to the General Assembly Mr Adjei in October 1961.
4 AWCP, Box 103, UN Files, UN Administration, Secretariat, 4, General Assembly Debates, Comments of the Liberian representative Mr Grimes, to the General Assembly, October 1961.
5 *Daily Mirror* headline as quoted in H. Macmillan, *Pointing the Way 1959–1961* (Basingstoke, Macmillan, 1972), p. 457.
6 UNA, [UK] S-0735–0004–01, Cooperation and Liaison-Britain, Registry Files Political and Security Matters, Mission Files United Nations Operation in the Congo, Statement by the British Foreign Secretary Lord Home in London 22 September 1961, As recorded by the Press Commission of the United Nations. Bulletin Britannique, No. 6, 22 September 1961.
7 UNA, [UK] S-0735–0004–01, Cooperation and Liaison-Britain, Registry Files Political and Security Matters, Mission Files United Nations Operation in the Congo, Edward Heath, the Lord Privy Seal, speaking in Kent on 22 September 1961, As recorded by the Press Commission of the United Nations, Novelles de Grande-Bretagne, No. 40, 25 September 1961.
8 UNA, [UK] S-0735–0004–01, Cooperation and Liaison-Britain, Registry Files Political and Security Matters, Mission Files United Nations Operation in the Congo, Letter from Riches, British Ambassador in Léopoldville to Sture Linner, Officer-in-Charge United Nations Operation in the Congo, Léopoldville, 30 September 1961.
9 Williams, *Who Killed Hammarskjöld?* p. 61. See also Kalb, *Congo Cables*.
10 NAL, CAB 128/35, Meeting of the Cabinet, Admiralty House, 28 September 1961.
11 Urquhart, *Hammarskjöld*, p. 575. Mahoney, *JFK*, p. 100.
12 The failure of Operation Morthor, coupled with the death of Hammarskjöld on the same day that a provincial governor in Vietnam was beheaded by the Viet Cong, all combined to reflect to the administration that it 'could no longer afford to "preserve options"'. Mahoney, *JFK*, p. 107.
13 As recorded in a telegram from the Department of State to the American Embassy in Belgium, 8:51 p.m., 26 September 1961, Schwar, *FRUS, XX, Congo*, p. 240.
14 NARA, State Department Central Decimal Files, Memo from Rusk to the State Department, 1 October 1961.
15 As recorded in a telegram from the Department of State to the American Embassy in Belgium, 8:51 p.m., 26 September 1961, Schwar, *FRUS, XX, Congo*, p. 240.
16 Williams, *Who Killed Hammarskjöld?* p. 60. NAL, CAB 128/35, Meeting of the Cabinet, Admiralty House, 19 September 1961. The discussion among British Cabinet members reveals that it was actually Hammarskjöld's initiative to seek a meeting with Tshombe, and their emissary, Lansdowne, had aided him in this endeavour.

17 Urquhart, *Hammarskjöld*, p. 575.
18 NARA, State Department Central Files, Congo, 310/9–961, Confidential telegram from Stevenson to the Secretary of State, 14 September 1961.
19 NARA, State Department Files, UN, 310/9–2961, Sept–Nov 1961, Telegram from Stevenson to Secretary of States, 23 October 1961.
20 GLP, BAA/RLAA/496, '16th Session of the United Nations General Assembly, 1961': Newspaper Clippings (United Nations), Bureau of African Affairs, 'Neutralists' power stood prominent in discussion of Dag's office', *Ghanaian Times* (5 October 1961).
21 Heller, *The United Nations Under Dag Hammarskjöld*, p. 138.
22 GPL, BAA/RLAA/688, 'Republic of Congo': Newspaper Clippings (Congo), Bureau of African Affairs, 'Katanga jet man at Ndola crash inquiry', *Daily Telegraph* (17 January 1962). 'Mr. David Bermant, of Ndola said that on the night of the crash he was woken by a plan flying very low over his house. The engines appeared to be working "very hard" and there was tremendous vibration.'
23 UNA, S-0845–0002–02, U Thant Secretary-General Files, Official report of the commission investigating the death of Hammarskjöld.
24 GPL, BAA/RLAA/508, 'Report of the Commission of Investigation into the Conditions and Circumstances resulting in the tragic death of Mr. Dag Hammarskjöld and of the members of the party accompanying him'. Appendix I, Examination of the Eye-Witnesses Statements, pp. 10–11.
25 Williams, *Who Killed Hammarskjöld?* pp. 3–15.
26 S. Sengupta, 'U.N. chief calls for new inquiry into 1961 plane crash that killed Dag Hammarskjöld', *New York Times* (6 July 2015), www.nytimes.com/2015/07/07/world/americas/un-chief-calls-for-new-inquiry-into-1961-plane-crash-that-killed-dag-Hammarskjöld.html.
27 NARA, State Department Central Files, Congo, 310/9–961, Telegram from Salisbury to Secretary of State, 18 September 1961.
28 NARA, State Department Central Files, Congo, 310/9–961, Telegram quoting this statement from the US Embassy in Copenhagen to the Secretary of State, 25 September 1961.
29 NARA, State Department Central Files, Congo, 310/9–961, Telegram from Emmerson, American Embassy in Salisbury to the Secretary of State recording the findings of his investigation into the crash, 22 September 1961.
30 GPL, Office of the Advisor to the Prime Minister on African Affairs, BAA/RLAA/397, 'Death of Dag Hammarskjöld, 1961', 'Wire Report', *Reuters* (27 February 1962).
31 GPL, BAA/RLAA/688, 'Republic of Congo': Newspaper Clippings (Congo), Bureau of African Affairs, 'Katanga jet man at Ndola crash inquiry', *Daily Telegraph* (17 January 1962).
32 AFP at the United Nations, 'UN says evidence justifies further inquiry into 1961 Hammarskjöld crash', *Guardian* (7 July 2015), www.theguardian.com/world/2015/jul/06/un-further-inquiry-dag-Hammarskjöld-crash.
33 Bring, 'Dag Hammarskjöld and the issue of humanitarian intervention', p. 501.
34 NAL, FO, 330.1/161, Telegram from UK Delegation to the UN, 12 May 1961.
35 MMLP, Adlai Stevenson Papers, Box 351, Folder 3, Presidential Memos 1960–1963, Telegram to the State Department, 14 June 1961.
36 James, *Britain and the Congo Crisis*, p. 111.

37 UCDA, Papers of Conor Cruise O'Brien, Microfilm P82/72, Letter from O'Brien to Frank Aiken, 8 November 1961.
38 NAL, CAB 128/35, Meeting of the Cabinet, Admiralty House, 19 September 1961.
39 UNA, S-0735-0004-01, Cooperation and Liaison-Britain, Registry Files Political and Security Matters, Mission Files United Nations Operation in the Congo. The demand for a record of a retraction of these remarks was issued in a letter from Riches, British Ambassador in Léopoldville, to Sture Linner, Officer-in-charge, United Nations Operation in the Congo, Léopoldville, 13 October 1961.
40 James, *Britain and the Congo Crisis*, p. 121.
41 O'Brien, *To Katanga and Back*, p. 301.
42 NAL, CAB 128/35, Meeting of the Cabinet, Admiralty House, 5 December 1961. When this issue was raised in the meeting Home rebutted such allegations.
43 Mahoney, *JFK*, p. 105.
44 MMLP, George W. Ball Papers, Box 150, Series 5, Telecons, Telephone records, conversation between Ball, Cleveland and Williams, 23 September 1961.
45 GPL, BAA/RLAA/496, '16th Session of the United Nations General Assembly, 1961': Newspaper Clippings (United Nations), Bureau of African Affairs, 'Wire report United Nations', *Reuters* (20 November 1961).
46 MMLP, George W. Ball Papers, Box 150, Series 5, Telecons, conversation between Rostow and Ball about presenting Tshombe with a plan of action in the President's response to a letter from him, 23 September 1961.
47 As part of this strategy, the State Department tried to turn the domestic situation to its advantage too, appealing to Senator Thomas J. Dodd, who had previously publicly railed against US policy in the Congo, to use his influence to urge Tshombe to talks. Weissman, *American Foreign Policy in the Congo*, p. 161.
48 MMLP, George W. Ball Papers, Box 150, Series 5, Telecons, conversation between Williams and Ball, in which the former recounts his conversation with the President, 3 November 1961.
49 GPL, BAA/RLAA/496, '16th Session of the United Nations General Assembly, 1961': Newspaper Clippings (United Nations), Bureau of African Affairs, 'Wire report, United Nations', *Reuters* (22 November 1961).
50 AWCP, Box 103, UN Files, UN Administration, Secretariat, 4, Krishna Menon, India's UN Ambassador, speech to the General Assembly on the General Assembly Debate concerning the reorganisation of the Secretariat, October 1961.
51 AWCP, Box 103, UN Files, UN Administration, Secretariat, 4, Nehru's comments to the General Assembly concerning the reorganisation of the Secretariat in October 1961.
52 AWCP, Box 174, UN Files, Subject Files, Africa – Congo-Advisory Committee, Bunche's comments during the first meeting of the Congo Advisory Committee after Hammarskjöld's death, 21 September 1961. Bunche records that one of Hammarskjöld's last acts had been to send a message to Spaak with the name of the Belgian pilot in order to stop the activities of this lone plane. These two aircraft are also likely those referred to in later accounts of Hammarskjöld's death when the question of the Katangan pilot arises. In addition, Adoula told the US Ambassador Edmund Guillon that he believed that the Secretary-General 'had been shot down'. Telegram from Guillon, American Embassy in the Congo, to the Department of State, 18 September 1961, Schwar, *FRUS, XX, Congo*, p. 230.

53 AWCP, Box 174, UN Files, Subject Files, Africa- Congo-Advisory Committee, Krishna Menon speaking in a meeting of the Congo Advisory Committee, 17 November 1961.
54 MMLP, George W. Ball Papers, Box 150, Series 5, Telecons, Telephone records, Kitchen and Ball, 26 September 1961.
55 NARA, State Department Central Files, Congo, 310/9–961, Confidential telegram from New York to the Secretary of State, 26 October 1961.
56 NARA, State Department, Central Files, Congo, 330/11–1561, Telegram from New York to the Secretary of State, 8 November 1961.
57 NARA, State Department, Central Files, Congo, 330/11–1561, Telegram from the Department of State to USUN, New York, 11 November 1961.
58 KUL, Wilcox Collection for Political Movements, American Committee for Aid to Katanga Freedom Fighters, RH WL Eph 198, Title: Ephemeral Materials, 1961 (OC0LC) 17949950, Control No: ocm18265195, Secret Memorandum of the plan developed by the UN Secretariat for dealing with Katanga, 1 October 1961.
59 MMLP, George W. Ball Papers, Box 150, Series 5, Telecons, President Kennedy and Ball, 31 October 1961.
60 *Ibid.*
61 For a brief overview see M.T. Guilderhus, *The Second Century: US-Latin American Relations since 1889* (Lanham: Rowman & Littlefield, 2000); G.M. Joseph and D. Spenser (eds), *In from the Cold: Latin America's New Encounter with the Cold War* (Durham, NC: Duke University Press, 2008); S.G. Rabe, 'Controlling revolutions: Latin America, the Alliance for Progress and Cold War anti-communism', and L.J. Bassett and S.E. Pelz, 'The failed search for victory: Vietnam and the politics of war', in T.G. Paterson (ed.), *Kennedy's Quest for Victory: American Foreign Policy, 1961–1963* (New York: Oxford University Press, 1989); D.J. Ryan and V. Pungong (eds), *The United States and Decolonization: Power and Freedom* (Basingstoke: Palgrave Macmillan, 2000); B. Sewell, 'A perfect (free market) world: economics, the Eisenhower administration and the Soviet economic offensive in Latin America', *Diplomatic History*, 32:5 (2008), 841–869.
62 MMLP, George W. Ball Papers, Box 150, Series 5, Telecons, President Kennedy and Ball, 31 October 1961.
63 NARA, State Department Files, UN, 330/9–2961, Instructions from Rusk, State Department to Stevenson, USUN New York, 27 October 1961.
64 NARA, State Department, Central Files, Congo, 330/11–1561, Telegram from New York to the Secretary of State, 1 September 1961.
65 NARA, State Department Central Files, Congo, 310/9–961, Telegram from American Embassy in New Delhi to the Secretary of State, 21 September 1961.
66 NAL, FO 371/155100, Memo from Millar to the Secretary of State detailing the legal analysis of the UN's position according to Vallet, and the reflections of the Lord Privy Seal when the policy was discussed, 1 November 1961.
67 UNA, S-209–0018–12 United Kingdom, ONUC Records on Foreign Countries, Records of the Office for Special Political Affairs, Letter from U Thant, to Sir Patrick Dean, UK Permanent Representative at the United Nations, 30 November 1961.
68 MMLP, George W. Ball Papers, Box 150, Series 5, Telecons, Ball and Vance agree that the UN requires the supply of aircraft, 12 November 1961.

69 S/5002, Security Council Resolution, 24 November 1961, http://repository.un.org/bitstream/handle/11176/82329/S_5002-EN.pdf?sequence=2&isAllowed=y.
70 NAL, CAB 128/35, Meeting of the Cabinet at Admiralty House, 14 November 1961.
71 *Ibid.*
72 Horne, *Macmillan*, p. 401.
73 UNA, S-209-0018-12 United Kingdom, ONUC Records on Foreign Countries, Records of the Office for Special Political Affairs, Exchange of letter between Acting Secretary-General U Thant and British Permanent Representative to the United Nations Sir Patrick Dean, 7-8 December 1961.
74 NAL, CAB 128/35, Meeting of the Cabinet at Admiralty House, 7 November 1961.
75 Macmillan, *Pointing the Way*, p. 449.
76 S/5002, Security Council Resolution 24 November 1961, http://repository.un.org/bitstream/handle/11176/82329/S_5002-EN.pdf?sequence=2&isAllowed=y.
77 NAL, CAB 128/35, Meeting of the Cabinet, Admiralty House, 30 November 1961.
78 MMLP, George W. Ball Papers, Box 150, Series 5, Telecons, Ball and Wallner discussion consultation with the British at the UN before their position is officially announced, 11 November 1961.
79 NAL, CAB 128/35, Meeting of the Cabinet, Admiralty House, 1 December 1961.
80 Mahoney, *JFK*, pp. 113-114.
81 MMLP, George W. Ball Papers, Box 150, Series 5, Telecons, Ball and Bundy, 8 November 1961.
82 MMLP, George W. Ball Papers, Box 150, Series 5, Telecons, Ball and Vance, November 1961.
83 MMLP, George W. Ball Papers, Box 150, Series 5, Telecons, Ball and Bundy, 8 November 1961. See also T.J. Noer, 'The new frontier and African neutralism, Kennedy, Nkrumah and the Volta River Project', *Diplomatic History*, 8:1 (1984), 61-80.
84 Mahoney, *JFK*, p. 114.
85 NAL, CAB 128/35, Meeting of the Cabinet at Admiralty House, 11 December 1961.
86 Mahoney, *JFK*, p. 116. Hoskyns, *The Congo Since Independence*, pp. 450-455.
87 NAL, CAB 128/35, Meeting of the Cabinet at Admiralty House, 11 December 1961.
88 James, *Britain and the Congo Crisis*, p. 111.
89 UNA, S-209-0018-12 United Kingdom, ONUC Records on Foreign Countries, Records of the Office for Special Political Affairs, Aide-Memoir from the British Government to the Acting Secretary-General, 13 December 1961.
90 GPL, BAA/RLAA/496, '16th Session of the United Nations General Assembly, 1961': Newspaper Clippings (United Nations), Bureau of African Affairs, 'Wire report', *Reuters* (15 December 1961).
91 NAL, PREM11/3168, Telegram from UK Delegation to the UN, 12 December 1961.
92 UNA, S-209-0018-12 United Kingdom, ONUC Records on Foreign Countries, Records of the Office for Special Political Affairs, Aide-Memoir from the British Government to the Acting Secretary-General, 13 December 1961.
93 Mahoney, *JFK*, p. 117.
94 AWCP, Box 174, UN Files, Subject files – Africa – Congo Advisory Committee, Comment from Thant in meeting of the Congo Advisory Committee, referring to telegrams from Tshombe on 25 November in which he made statements of this nature, 28 November 1961.

95 AWCP, Box 174, UN Files, Subject files – Africa – Congo Advisory Committee, Statement from Mr Wirjopranoto in a meeting of the Congo Advisory Committee, 28 November 1961.
96 Namikas, *Battleground Africa*, pp. 154–156. See also Kalb, *Congo Cables*, pp. 316–318.
97 KUL, Wilcox Collection for Political Movements, American Committee for Aid to Katanga Freedom Fighters, RH WL Eph 198, Title: Ephemeral Materials, 1961 (OC0LC) 17949950, Control No: ocm18265195. This Committee formed in 1961, condemning the UN attacks on the 'peace-loving and Western friendly Katangese'. By the end of 1962 they had over 3,000 supporters. For more details see also Weissman, *American Foreign Policy in the Congo*, pp. 168–171.
98 MMLP, George W. Ball Papers, Box 150, Series 5, Telecons, Ball and Cleveland, 31 October 1961.
99 Macmillan, *Pointing the Way*, p. 451.
100 GPL, BAA/RLAA/688, 'Republic of Congo' – Newspaper clippings (Congo) January 1962, Bureau of African Affairs, 'Katanga, running from parliament's storm', *The Economist* (16 December 1961).
101 Ashton, *Kennedy, Macmillan and the Cold War*, p. 126.
102 JFKL, Box 128, President's Office Files, Folder 2 United Nations, Telegram from Thomas Finletter, US Ambassador to France to the Secretary of State on the status of US and UK talks on the UN, 14 July 1962.
103 NAL, FO 371/155107, Telegram from Dean to the Foreign Office, 11 December 1961.
104 Ibid.
105 James, *Britain and the Congo Crisis*, p. 150.
106 Kalb argues that Ormsby-Gore would play a major role in Kennedy's Congo policy, 'balancing the activist views of the New Frontiersmen … with the traditional British advice: go slow, avoid the use of force'. Kalb, *Congo Cables*, p. 307.
107 Ibid., p. 316.
108 UNA, S-209-0018-12 United Kingdom, ONUC Records on Foreign Countries, Records of the Office for Special Political Affairs, United Nations Press Service, Press release from U Thant, 13 December 1961.
109 Macmillan, *Pointing the Way*, p. 455.
110 UNA, S-209-0018-17, United States, Records on Foreign Countries, Records of the Office for Special Political Affairs, Statement from the State Department to the United States Mission to the United Nations, 15 December 1961. It should however be noted that given the amount of diplomatic pressure which was exerted behind the scenes, this 'request' from Tshombe is likely to have been merely the formality to force him into talks with Adoula.
111 NARA, State Department Files, UN, 310/9-2961, Telegram from the American embassy in Salisbury to the Secretary of States, 18 December 1961.
112 Telegram from the Consulate in Elisabethville to the Department of State, 15 December 1961, Schwar, *FRUS, XX, Congo*, p. 381.
113 Telegram from Embassy in the Congo to the Department of State, Léopoldville, 15 December 1961, Schwar, *FRUS, XX, Congo*, p. 320.
114 Library of Congress Archives, Washington, DC (hereafter LOC), W. Averell Harriman Papers, Box 448, Subject Files, Congo, Special Files: Public Service, Kennedy/Administrations, 1958–1971, Folder 5, Subject File Congo (1), Research Memorandum to the Secretary of State from Roger Hilsman, Subject: Congo chronology, January–September 1962: Negotiations, 13 February 1963.

115 Ashton, *Kennedy, Macmillan and the Cold War*, p. 119.
116 Weissman, *American Foreign Policy in the Congo*, p. 187.
117 Kalb, *Congo Cables*, p. 322.
118 LOC, W. Averell Harriman Papers, Box 448, Subject Files, Congo, Special Files: Public Service, Kennedy/Administrations, 1958–1971, Folder 5, Subject File Congo (1), Research Memorandum to the Secretary of State from Roger Hilsman, Subject: Congo chronology, January–September 1962: Negotiations, 13 February 1963.
119 NAL, CAB 128/35, Cabinet Records, Meeting of the Cabinet at Admiralty House, 16 November 1961. This view was also recognised by the Americans as outlined in JFKL, National Security Files Box 235, Folder 1, Draft paper for the Bermuda briefing book.
120 JFKL, National Security Files, Box 235, Folder 1, Memorandum for the President from McGeorge Bundy, 19 December 1961.
121 For further see J.R. Walker, *British Nuclear Weapons and the Test Ban 1954–1973, Britain, the United States, Weapons Policies and Nuclear Testing: Tensions and Contradictions* (Surrey: Ashgate, 2010), p. 203.
122 JFKL, National Security Files, Box 235, Folder 2, Bermuda, Top Secret, Memorandum of Conversation pertaining to Nuclear Matters, 22 December 1961.
123 Ashton, *Kennedy, Macmillan and the Cold War*, p. 119.
124 JFKL, National Security Files, Box 235, Folder 1, Bermuda, Telegram to the State Department on the highlights of Kennedy's talks with Macmillan at Bermuda, 23 December 1961.
125 Horne, *Macmillan*, p. 404.
126 JFKL, National Security Files, Box 235, Folder 2, Bermuda, Top Secret, Memorandum of Conversation pertaining to Nuclear Matters, 22 December 1961.
127 JFKL, National Security Files, Box 235, Folder 2, Bermuda, Brief note on the Congo.
128 Telegram from the State Department to the Embassy in the Congo, 17 January 1962, Schwar, *FRUS, XX, Congo*, p. 364.
129 GPL, BAA/RLAA/688, 'Republic of Congo' – Newspaper Clippings (Congo) January 1962, Bureau of African Affairs, 'What the UN wants', *The Economist* (16 December 1961).
130 UNA, S-0292-015-04, Chef du Cabinet Files, Memo from Philip Dean, Director of the United Nations Information Centre, Washington, to Narashiman, Under-Secretary for General Assembly Affairs, entitled, 'Declared and Underlying United States thinking on World Problems', 12 September 1962.
131 W. Mountz, 'The Congo crisis: a re-examination (1960–1965)', *The Journal of the Middle East and Africa*, 5:2 (2014), 151–165.
132 NARA, State Department, Central Decimal Files, Congo, 330/11-1561, Confidential Memorandum for the President, 11 November 1961.
133 Telegram from the State Department to the Embassy in the Congo, 17 January 1962, Schwar, *FRUS, XX, Congo*, p. 364.

5
'A nice little stew'[1]

Through 1962, the fracas caused by the disagreement between the Foreign Office and the State Department over the direction of the Congo operation increased as efforts mounted to devise a lasting solution to the crisis. In January, American and British officials renewed attempts to construct a cohesive policy on Katanga, with a series of bilateral talks aimed at creating a joint position on the Congo during UN debates. The failure of Tshombe to abide by the terms of the Kitona Accords and the growing challenge to Adoula's Government from pro-Lumumba supporters led by Gizenga, kept the conflict stewing through 1962. Although he had been appointed as Adoula's deputy in the agreement of August 1961, Gizenga now refused to leave the Lumumbist stronghold in Stanleyville, where he issued statements denouncing the legitimacy of the Central Government.

Gizenga renewed the operation of the opposition Government in Stanleyville, with the help of Lumumba's former Minister for Education Pierre Mulele and aid from the Soviet Union and some members of the Casablanca Group, including Ghana, Guinea and Mali.[2] In an attempt to force his hand and simultaneously undercut the Stanleyville regime the Congolese Chamber of Deputies voted in January that he return to Léopoldville. After mounting an armed resistance to ANC soldiers who attempted to arrest him for refusing to cooperate, he was imprisoned until July 1964.[3] His detention was a source of frustration for the African states that supported him and the Afro-Asian Peoples' Solidarity Organisation quickly organised a public campaign for his release, alleging that he had been poisoned with arsenic by the Adoula clique in collaboration with the US.[4] Representatives from Algeria, Cuba and Sudan later pleaded the case for his release at the UN, without success, as officials maintained that this was a matter under the jurisdiction of the Central Government.

The insurgency in Stanleyville destabilised the Central Government and combined with the unresolved question of Katanga, the Congo crisis remained on the international agenda. In the Security Council, Soviet activism and a splintering of the previous unity between members of the Afro-Asian bloc increased as various solutions were debated. Moreover, deliberations reflected the escalating Cold War tensions between the superpowers and the growing division between the Afro-Asian states who were increasingly critical of what they perceived as the heavy-handed influence of the US in the Congo. In the meantime, Tshombe reneged on his agreements at Kitona and continued to resist UN policies by moving aircraft and troops to strategic locations around the region, ordering the gendarmerie to deny passage to UN troops located at military bases in Kolwezi and Jadotville and encouraging the re-entry of mercenaries from Northern Rhodesia.[5]

The situation was exacerbated by the Indian invasion of Kashmir in February, and the subsequent Sino-Indian war, which diverted Nehru's attention away from the Congo. The escalation of civil wars in Guatemala and Laos from January to November and the expansion of Viet Cong insurgency in the south of Vietnam also drew the attention of the State Department towards other problems. The arguments over the Congo, therefore, reflected the wider trough of Cold War hostilities even more than at previous points in the crisis. This led UN officials to cooperate more closely with the State Department to formulate a definitive solution to the crisis as the organisation was besieged by demands for aid, intervention or mediation from a multitude of other countries including Algeria, Angola, Kenya, Palestine, Pakistan, Southern Rhodesia and South Africa, among others. The spillover effect of the Congo into colonial questions in other countries now accelerated challenges to British decolonisation plans across Africa.

The outbreak of violence in the Congo again was only one of a multitude of African problems the Foreign Office faced in 1962. In Bermuda in January, Macmillan had ruminated on the ways in which the struggle against Communism in the Congo intersected with colonial issues affecting the development of the UN.[6] What he had once described as 'the rising tide of African nationalism' now became a tidal wave against British policy throughout the continent. While the nationalism he had referred to tended to be fragmented, ideas about self-determination, the violation of human rights by the apartheid regime in South Africa, and the crackdown on rebel activities in the brutal police-state in Nyasaland, opened the British Government up to a renewed wave of criticism. The Mau Mau massacres at the Hola detention camp in Kenya in 1959 re-emerged in the public imagination when Kenya brought a resolution demanding independence before the General Assembly in December.[7] Failure to implement the General Assembly Declaration 1514, on the granting of independence to colonial countries and peoples in other British territories such as Basutoland (Lesotho), Bechuanaland (Botswana) and Swaziland, further weakened Britain's position at the UN. The right-wing Tory group which had led the charge against Macmillan's Government in December 1961 continued to act as a pressure point on British colonial policy. What was viewed by many Conservatives as acquiescence among British colonial administrations towards black leaders and their demands for independence led to great bitterness in the party.[8] This was echoed through resistance to the transfer of power and further anxiety about the behaviour of the UN in the Congo. 'The United Nations', remarked one official, 'came into being to promote peace and fair dealing: instead it has turned out to be a Godless, anti-British racket, and a tool for enriching still further the greedy international financiers who are bent on getting everything into their own hands'.[9]

In the context of the wider challenges to British colonial policies in Africa, relations with the US on the Congo question remained at a stalemate. Bilateral talks on the Congo during Macmillan's visit to Washington in April 1962 served to underline Anglo-American disagreement. Imploring the President not to let these tensions undermine the whole Anglo-American partnership, Macmillan pressed that 'if the Congo talks fail it looks as if the United States and Britain will find it difficult not to be in open disagreement'.[10] British officials continued to maintain that a federal arrangement, whereby Tshombe would retain a considerable level of autonomy in Katanga, was the only solution to the crisis. This was in contrast to the American position, which was to push for further UN action to end the secession definitively in order to unite the country under the Adoula leadership of the Central Government in Léopoldville. Macmillan remained adamant that Britain would not support another UN action against Tshombe, arguing 'we are prepared to use our influence with Tshombe but we could not accept another United Nations military operation against him'.[11] The Foreign Office believed that not only would any military action be unsuccessful but the resulting bloodshed in the province would be unjustified and, in British eyes, unacceptable. The British attitude also hardened against the imposition of economic sanctions against Katanga, as it would be detrimental to British copper exports.[12] Officials in the State Department, anxious that time to find a solution was running out, were determined to reintegrate Katanga, beginning with restructuring the economic relationship between Elisabethville and Léopoldville. Before the beginning of a series of tripartite talks between America, Britain and Belgium, Kennedy instructed the British Ambassador in London, David Bruce, that 'failure to achieve a viable solution will most certainly result in catastrophe for the commercial enterprises in the Congo'.[13]

The centrality of the economic prowess of Katanga to the economy of the country as a whole was recognised by the Central Government in Léopoldville and by the State Department as an important hinge around which to pivot the whole reintegration process. The UMHK mining group now became the focus of efforts to dismantle Tshombe's regime. Up to 1962, the company had continued to operate business as usual, refusing to abide by UN resolutions regarding the removal of Belgian technicians and mercenaries. As one Liberian delegate put it at the Security Council in June, 'it was reasonable to ask why Union Minière had hitherto been immune to the enforcement of United Nations policies'.[14] From the beginning of the crisis, UMHK had retained significant economic and political clout within Katanga, with many employees intimately involved in Tshombe in a variety of guises, some even serving as 'political advisors'. The wealth and influence of the company, and its connections with both the Belgian and British Governments, granted its officials considerable ability to monitor and heavily influence political developments in Katanga, thereby resisting the implementation of UN resolutions. A Security Council report for the year from July 1961 to July 1962 noted that it was increasingly clear that not only did UMHK provide a means with which authorities could defy the instructions of the UN, but by supplying political advisors, financial resources and mercenaries to Katanga, the company itself remained impervious to UN resolutions.[15]

Upon secession in July 1960, Tshombe had requested the continued cooperation of Belgian technicians in order to maintain peace and stability. UMHK played a significant role in this objective, threatening to dismiss anyone who abandoned their job for reasons of security fears.[16] Throughout the first two years of the secession the group continued to prop up Tshombe's regime, while simultaneously managing to avoid transferring the shares and profits of the company to Léopoldville. In the face of this stranglehold UMHK had over Katanga's social, economic and political infrastructure, company officials denied that any direct support was given to the regime, although they remained in favour of secession.[17] The influential position of these officials with the Katangan regime had already led the British Government and the State Department officials to turn to them to urge Tshombe into talks with the Central Government in 1961. In response the company had maintained that it was 'not their policy to exert pressure on political matters' but Gibbs argues that second-level executives blocked any coalition with Léopoldville, and avoided bringing any pressure to bear on Tshombe.[18]

The State Department now presented a plan to initiate economic sanctions against Katanga in order to destabilise the link between Tshombe's regime and UMHK. This became the focus of UN policy as a first step towards the transfer of revenue from Katanga to the Central Government. Rolling this initiative into what he called the 'Plan for National Reconciliation' in August, Thant highlighted the role of the company in continuing to prop up Tshombe's regime by failing to pay the taxes and fees to the Central Government, and instead directing the funds straight to the Katangan Government.[19] There was little sympathy for the UMHK in the State Department where some, including McGhee, considered the company to be 'a greedy, narrow-minded group, interested only in holding on to this copper concession for the greatest possible profit'.[20] UN officials who worked in Elisabethville outlined the means by which the company also provided political support. O'Brien had earlier argued that UMHK officials often pressured Tshombe towards one objective or another, which served the interests of the Belgians. Referring specifically to two individuals who were generally perceived to be pulling the strings behind Tshombe, Prince de Linge, the front man of the group, and an advisor, Mr Walker, he had previously tried to exert pressure on Tshombe through UMHK. He noted in 1961: 'it is apparent that to frighten these gentlemen in a reasonable degree can have quite a satisfactory effect on the ruling authorities here'.[21] This was a view shared by Thant, who turned his attention towards coercing UMHK to pay taxes to the cash-poor Central Government, which would simultaneously destabilise Tshombe's regime.[22] The company was estimated to have paid $52 million in taxes and dividends to Katanga in 1961, a percentage of which was supposed to go to the Central Government, given its 18.4 per cent interest in the company, inherited from Belgium upon independence.[23]

The pertinence of UMHK to a solution in Katanga was also evident to the Foreign Office and the State Department. But during the Prime Minister's 1962 visit to Washington, DC in talks on the Congo Macmillan was pessimistic about how the influence of the company could be harnessed successfully.[24] In response, Ball commented that 'the Union Minière hopes for a white enclave in Katanga ... We should make it clear that this [i]s not possible. It would only invite chaos'.[25] By reorienting the company towards the Central Government, the American perspective was that UMHK could be instrumental in producing an end to the secession. In order to utilise the company towards this objective, they proposed the imposition of economic sanctions against Katanga, which would affect the company's operation and profits. Since they had previously believed that the British 'officially see eye-to-eye with us on the overall Congo picture', American officials were taken aback by the sharp rebuffing of the idea by the Foreign Office.[26] Kennedy elicited only a begrudging commitment from Macmillan to give the issue priority.[27]

To renew attempts to cooperate, tripartite talks with Belgium were organised for the following month in order to keep up the diplomatic pressure on Tshombe. Macmillan agreed to discuss the issue of sanctions during the talks as the US sought to use Belgian and British links to Tshombe's Government to negotiate the end of the secession on economic grounds.[28] Ultimately, however, British officials believed that Tshombe would not buckle under a sanctions regime. As they later pointed out to the State Department, 'he would rather go back to eating nuts than capitulate to the United Nations or Adoula'.[29] By the end of the summer, after months of fruitless negotiations Macmillan reflected that there were serious differences with the Americans on this question.[30]

British resistance towards imposing a sanctions regime on Katanga was directly linked to the insistence that the UN would not resort to using force again as both schemes constituted, in the view of British officials, an over-extension of the UN role in resolving the Katanga problem. Following American insistence that the Secretary-General was 'very anxious to reduce the UN presence in the Congo', Macmillan met with Thant during his visit to the US.[31] The Prime Minister repeatedly encouraged Thant to convert the overall UN mission into a programme of economic development for the Congo, without the problematic peacekeeping element. He pushed for an agreement that would be palatable to both Adoula and Tshombe and would allow for the withdrawal of UN forces.[32] In August, Home pressed Thant further to include this as the main focus of the Plan for National Reconciliation. During Thant's visit to London in September, Home worked to convince him that 'Her Majesty's Government saw no possibility of bringing about a satisfactory settlement of the Katanga problem by force. We should seek to convince him that to proceed by negotiation was the only possible way'.[33] Thant, however, showed little enthusiasm for turning the Congo mission into a development programme, leaving the British in a position of isolation over Katanga once again when the Foreign Office publicly announced British opposition towards the imposition of sanctions on the grounds that it would lead to further violence.

The continued non-compliance of UMHK officials with the UN reflected their contempt for the organisation and exacerbated relations with Tshombe. Over the summer Belgium and Britain failed to pressure the company to comply with UN resolutions. The refusal of the Foreign Office to consider economic tariffs or boycotts of Katangan produce reflected the British Government's concern with preserving the position of the company. As Mahoney has described with apt simplicity, the reality was that the Tories liked Tshombe. He represented a Western-friendly ally in a mineral-rich corner of the Congo, who was politically aligned with Welensky, and who protected British interests in the region. He adds: 'the fact that a score or so of Macmillan's backbenchers had a piece of Leopold's nest egg heightened the attraction.'[34] Towards the end of 1962, questions began to be raised about the direct links between the Conservative Party and the

UMHK group. A *Daily Express* article entitled 'Vendetta' questioned whether Home himself had shares in Union Minière.[35]

The allegations regarding the personal financial interests of British officials in Katanga's commercial enterprises, and the links between companies and British Government officials, amplified negative perceptions of British policy towards Katanga and magnified the impression of collusion with Tshombe's regime. Members of the Afro-Asian bloc continued to denounce the role of UMHK as part of the 'massive and divisive foreign influences [which] continue [sic] to impede the work of the organisation'.[36] The British delegation at the UN advised briefing the American press more fully on the British reasons for opposing sanctions in order to improve the public view of the British position. British UN delegates recommended negotiating privately with the Irish and Canadian representatives on the CAC in order to rebut suggestions of further military action, however they warned the Foreign Office that India, the most important contributor to ONUC, was 'likely to be unhelpful in any case'.[37]

The allegations of collusion between the British Government and Katanta's commercial partners were not without merit. UMHK, Unilever and other corporations active in Katanga had become increasingly critical of the UN as the organisation accelerated its campaign against Tshombe. In a letter to Home, A.H. Smith, a high-level representative of the Unilever group, warned that 'relations between Her Majesty's Government and the Central Government of the Congo may not be allowed to deteriorate to the point at which our Congo companies are exposed to serious consequences'.[38] In response, the British Foreign Secretary acknowledged that economic sanctions would severely impact upon British firms operating in the Congo as their activities were subject to the approval of the Central Government. He assured Smith: 'I agree that sanctions would be most undesirable, not only for your company but also for our commercial interests in general. The Government's policy will continue to take account of this major factor.'[39] By December, the manifold manifestation of the influence of Union Minière and other commercial groups on British Congo policy was made even more evident when Home outlined the three main reasons why the Foreign Office opposed sanctions. Arguing that the implementation of sanctions or military action by the UN would mean that ONUC would have to exceed its mandate, he pointed out that the status of the organisation and the prestige of the Secretary-General would be badly damaged if sanctions failed. Even if Tshombe were defeated, he maintained, it would mean that the UN would have to remain in the Congo for years to come, which raised the very real prospect that the organisation would face bankruptcy. In this case, Home pointed out, 'It is almost sure that the Union Minière would be destroyed in the process and could probably never be rebuilt.'[40]

A Plan for National Reconciliation

Despite British objections to economic sanctions, in August Thant presented a plan to unite the Congo and end the secession of Katanga definitively. There was a shared realisation between the UN and the State Department that the situation was becoming an increasing financial and political burden and what was needed was either further commitment of resources, or a withdrawal of troops altogether. Speaking in Helsinki in July, the Secretary-General expressed impatience with the lack of progress in achieving a settlement, referring to the Katangese as 'a bunch of clowns'.[41] He believed that the solution to the crisis was to secure tax revenue from UMHK for the Central Government, not just Katanga. Formulated with the close cooperation of the State Department, the plan proposed splitting Katangese revenue evenly with the Central Government and integrating the Katangan gendarmerie with the ANC. Alongside its political support for the plan, the US offered further economic and materiel bilateral aid to Léopoldville, in order to strengthen Adoula's hand against Tshombe's resistance. The weakness of Adoula's Government, the possibility of the withdrawal of Indian troops within the next ten months (given the looming Indo-Pakistan war), the precarious financial position of the UN, and fears about the volatility of Tshombe, all propelled Washington's efforts to drum up support for Thant's plan before the opening of the 17th session of the General Assembly in September 1962.[42]

The plan was extensively debated with the African group and the Afro-Asian bloc in New York as members negotiated a procedure to implement it. The representative of the UAR warned the Secretary-General that if he turned to the Security Council for a fresh mandate, the whole plan might be vetoed by one of the permanent members, which would be very damaging to his Office. Balanced against this however was the fear that unless substantial progress was made in the Congo, and the racial violence stemmed, countries which had donated troops would start withdrawing them, constituting a 'shattering failure' for the UN and for nations which had supported the Congo operation.[43] A meeting of the CAC on 24 July decided that rather than taking the issue back to the Security Council, the Secretary-General was to be granted 'greater latitude in assisting the [Central Government] in reintegrating Katanga [and] a reinterpretation of the 21 February resolution'.[44]

The State Department also sought to engineer a stronger hand in implementing the plan with British and Belgian colleagues, noting: 'relations with [the] UN are best maintained from Washington and New York, we must obviously retain overall US control here, as well as 3-power Madison on progress of mediation'.[45] However, despite efforts to maintain 'the intimacy and dynamism of the US-UK relationship', the State Department soon detected that the British position had the effect of paralysing negotiations.[46] During the discussions, British representatives continued to object to the imposition of sanctions and the use of force while simultaneously agreeing that some action was needed. Stevenson appealed to the President to try to convince the British to change their stance in negotiations and restated the American position that 'the problem of the Katangan secession must be solved and [we] will back strong efforts in that direction'.[47] McGeorge Bundy wrote to British Cabinet Secretary Philip de Zulueta to urge him to press the Prime Minister, pointing out: 'I have had the feeling that our difference of view as to how we should act if there should be a showdown may be preventing us from taking a common action that would forestall such a showdown.'[48]

The fate of the UN operation as a whole was now very much at stake and for this reason, the Secretary-General sought to prevent the issue going back to the Security Council where the Soviets would doubtlessly seize the opportunity to launch another attack on the organisation, and to avoid a British veto. Among the representatives, and particularly the Irish and the Indians who had donated a considerable number of troops to the operation, it was believed to be 'essential that Belgium, Britain, France and others cooperate effectively in necessary action to bring Tshombe to heel. If they did not do so [a] S[security] C[council] meeting would shortly become necessary to decide the fate of the UN operation'.[49] Thant's action plan against Tshombe therefore quickly swung into full force with Washington's support.[50] As the UN accelerated its implementation, questions were raised over whether or not a new mandate for ONUC should be brought before the Security Council. This had been the British fear since May when Macmillan had cautioned Kennedy that 'If there were to be a United Nations operation about which we were in disagreement, I fear bad effects not only in the United Nations and in Africa but in Anglo-American relations'.[51] Given the British insistence on opposing military action against Katanga, if the question now came before the Security Council, Britain would be forced to veto, which would be very damaging to relations with the US and with the Afro-Asian bloc who, the British Mission to the UN warned, would perceive a veto as an action deliberately engineered to prevent Tshombe being threatened with effective combat.[52] Dean further cautioned the Foreign Office that if Britain vetoed such a resolution the British position would be 'greatly harmed'. In any event it would then be moved to the General Assembly, which was likely to endorse the majority view and support sanctions and intervention.[53]

For many of Katanga's European business and economic partners, Thant's plan of economic sanctions and the State Department proposal to boycott Katangan produce represented a form of 'dollar imperialism'.[54] The plan proposed a new federal constitution for the Congo, an even sharing of foreign exchange and tax revenues and reunification of currencies. Crucially, there was also the provision for the imposition of penalties and sanctions if companies operating in Katanga refused to cooperate.[55] This American-led economic crusade against Katanga through 1962 drew criticism from European allies, including Britain, Belgium, France and Germany, who viewed the proposal as interference with European affairs. Belgium in particular undertook a vicious press campaign criticising US policy in the Congo, highlighting American economic interests as a means of discrediting Washington's aims. German Chancellor Konrad Adenauer even went as far as to claim 'the US wanted to reduce Europe's role on the dark continent'.[56] There was in fact some truth in this claim, since at the time, America imported 75 per cent of its cobalt from Katanga and a small percentage of the uranium for its nuclear programme.[57]

The dispute with the European states eventually defeated the question of sanctions and boycotts, undercutting the plan as a whole. Following Belgium's insistence that cobalt be added to the boycott list, Kennedy retreated from the proposal by announcing that 'American participation in the boycott would no longer be the automatic result of Tshombe's refusal to accept the [Thant plan]'.[58] The British rejection of sanctions against Katanga was supported by other European powers, particularly Belgium and France, who thus far had refused to play any role at all in the Congo.[59] In addition, Kennedy was said to be 'furious' when he learned that Home had reassured Tshombe that Britain would 'never' support sanctions against him.[60]

The Anglo-American disagreement over Katanga had spread from questions of use of force to the issue of economic sanctions and in the process shattered Western unity in the Security Council. To make matters worse, it hindered the implementation of UN initiatives by paralysing the debate and allowing pro-Katanga supporters to continue to resist UN efforts on the ground, leading to sporadic violent clashes. Not only was the overall success or failure of the operation hinged on the next round of action against Katanga, but the reputation and integrity of the organisation itself also hung in the balance.

The UN was increasingly hamstrung by the problem of how to proceed during the latter half of 1962, as the question of financing the operation exacerbated the polarity between the superpowers. Khrushchev, entrenched in his views about the poisonous collaboration between the US and the UN in the Congo, ruled out any possibility of Soviet financing for ONUC during the Secretary-General's meeting with him in Moscow in September.[61] The controversy around the issue was heightened when International Court of Justice (ICJ) issued an opinion stating that the costs of the Congo operation, must, under Article 17(2) of the UN Charter, be borne by all member-states.[62] The Soviet Union was not the only member-state to withhold financial contributions. Following the Suez crisis in 1956, other members of the Soviet bloc refused to honour their financial obligations under the Charter to pay for UN peacekeeping. Even amongst the countries that continued the meet their financial obligations to the UN, there was growing concern about the long-term effects of sustaining ONUC and the civilian mission in the Congo. The Canadian Prime Minister John Diefenbaker pointed out that 'for more than two years, limited resources of the organisation have been so heavily committed that its future effectiveness … may be mortgaged for some time to come'.[63]

Thant was keen to avoid serious fallout over the issue of how to pay for ONUC, and postponed the introduction of a draft resolution to the 17th session of the General Assembly, urging all members to honour the commitment to pay under the Charter. The Secretary-General believed that if a successful solution could be found for the Congo relatively quickly, those member-states refusing to contribute would then alter their positions and take up their share of the financial burden.[64] However, he was also realistic about the prospect of bringing about a peaceful resolution, pointing out to Stevenson privately that a period of 'real difficulty' lay ahead for the Congo, and that unless the strain on current resources was relieved, a speedy UN disengagement from the country may be the only feasible option.[65]

This period of 'real difficulty' was to happen sooner than anybody had anticipated. Thant put his Congo plan into action almost immediately following his visit to the White House on 13 September. What he advocated was an end to the secession of Katanga, and the uniting of the country under the rule of Adoula and the Central Government in Léopoldville. To do so, he had the support of both the Americans and the Afro-Asians. Mohammed Ali, the Pakistani Minister for External Affairs, noted in a press conference that: 'If the Katanga leaders were to implement faithfully the Secretary-General's plan of reunification, the United Nations would emerge from its long and bitter ordeal in the Congo greatly strengthened and would vindicate the faith of all small states in the world in its efficacy.'[66]

Thant's whistle-stop tour of European states to drum up support for the plan also produced a consensus of broad support among members for a speedy resolution to the crisis by the forced reintegration of Katanga. Ali's statement reflected the urgency among members of the Afro-Asian bloc who privately informed Thant that unless the situation in the Congo improved rapidly, the General Assembly would not authorise further financing for ONUC. For their part Adoula and Tshombe accepted the plan under duress as, although it aimed to stabilise the Central Government, there was little 'Congolese involvement or input'.[67] Efforts to have the plan ratified by the National Parliament in Léopoldville were hampered by the skirmishes and political unrest in the provinces of Kasai and Kivu. Moscow also denounced the plan as a Western conspiracy to prevent the reintegration of the Congo.[68] As tensions frayed, Thant struggled to roll out his plan precisely at the moment the Cold War reached its height when a Soviet ballistic missile facility was discovered to be under construction in Cuba. Diverting the attention of the State Department and the Kremlin towards Cuba, the missile crisis also served to strengthen determination on all sides to prevent the Congo becoming a full-blown superpower battle, thereby paving the way towards the final military push by ONUC against Katanga in December.

Changed perceptions of the UN

Over a thirteen-day period from 16 to 28 October, the US and the USSR engaged in a diplomatic cat-and-mouse game as Soviet ships carrying nuclear weapons approached their intended base in Cuba. The imposition of a naval quarantine zone around the island to prevent the ships landing on 23 October, alongside the intervention of Thant as a mediator between Washington and Moscow, prevented the outbreak of nuclear war. However, this brush with nuclear disaster had an important impact on the Congo in two capacities; it contributed to changing the impression of the UN amongst officials in the State Department while also strengthening their resolve to prevent a superpower military confrontation in the Congo. The events that led to the missile crisis also contributed to doubts about US policy in the Congo and the Third World more generally.[69] The Cuban leader, Fidel Castro, publicly encouraged revolution and insurgency throughout Africa. Already in 1961 he had sent weapons to the Algerian rebels in Casablanca, and seemed set to provide similar aid to anti-American factions in the Congo.[70] Havana's role as a base for the exportation of Communism, and the provision of aid and training to African nationalists by revolutionary guerrilla leaders, raised questions about the success of Washington's Alliance for Progress in Latin America. The scheme for democracy and development throughout the region had been intended to provide a means through which to control the spread of insurgency and rebellion.[71] However, the crisis, which evolved in Cuba in addition to a military coup in Peru and continuing conflict in Vietnam, pointed to deeper difficulties between the administration's approach to the Third World and the incompatibility of their policies with local realities.[72]

In parallel to this ideological challenge, the Cuban crisis was important in shaping perceptions of the UN and its utility. A memorandum for the President, prepared by Rusk, highlighted how the role played by Thant as a mediator in particular had 'underlin[ed] the utility of the United Nations as an instrument of disengagement and as an effective instrument for international meditation'.[73] Building on Hammarskjöld's pioneering of a third -party role for the UN as an organ of arbitration and his personal negotiations with the Chinese Government in 1955 to release fifteen American pilots, Thant had adopted a similar role, acting as a go-between in the early days of the crisis and later as an arbiter between Moscow and Washington.[74] From the perspective of the State Department, he 'provided a face-saving element, especially for the Soviets and the Cubans, and helped keep diplomatic exchanges relatively temperate'.[75] Public discussions of the Cuban problem in the General Assembly from 7 October also provided a filter for debate and an opportunity to discuss a variety of solutions. By facilitating dialogue between the superpowers and other nations, the UN established a mechanism through which the debate was be monitored and mediated. In policing the settlement by inspecting weapons sites in Cuba, the organisation also became more strategically important to US Cold War policy. The State Department believed that in this role, the UN was able to exert an influence over the normally intransigent Khrushchev, noting his 'unprecedented agreement to the idea of UN inspection and verification of notion of arms removal *on the spot*.'[76]

The expansion in the prestige and functionality of the UN from the American point of view had been taking place since the Congo crisis had begun as international customs became more representative and institutionalised. An internal memo on UN developments in August 1962 revealed the recognition among USUN officials that the organisation provided a means by which to resolve disputes and approach Cold War questions through a variety of different, active roles, in the process easing the burden on the US to stage-manage various international crises.[77] One of the mechanisms that the UN employed in an active capacity, which allowed the organisation to transcend bloc politics and Cold War divisions, was the use of rapporteurs during negotiations to avoid inflaming tensions during public debates. The USUN delegation noted their enthusiasm for the practice of using specially appointed representatives or rapporteurs to circumvent public debate and promote quiet negotiations behind closed doors on a range of issues. Cleveland argued that:

> The greater complexity of the UN General Assembly's parliamentary system and the desire of its steadily expanding membership to air publicly, deeply felt grievances, have made similar developments in the Assembly more difficult … There is an urgent need, however, to supplement the Secretary-General's activity and to get more items out of public debate in the Assembly and into some form of quiet negotiation by especially appointed representatives or rapporteurs.[78]

The State Department increasingly held the view that with the evolution and expansion of the organisation, the value of public debate had been much reduced, both in solving disputes in the General Assembly and in the Security Council. The problem was most acute within the enlarging General Assembly when the Afro-Asian bloc used their majority and coherence on colonial issues to propel the anti-colonial campaign and induce normative changes in the way the European powers developed and executed colonial policies. As they had done with Britain, the African and Asian members, with the help of Latin American states, activated the channels and mechanisms of the UN to increase pressure to adhere to these new normative practices and standards with regard to colonialism and imperial rule. Oftentimes, however, bitter colonial disputes, coupled with Cold War hostilities, reduced the efficiency of General Assembly debate and hindered the creation of effective and consolidated solutions. By 1962, the problem had also spread to the Security Council, which was paralysed on Cold War questions that had plagued its efficiency since 1945 but also had to moderate issues regarding decolonisation and the implementation of resolutions on the political status of remaining colonies. There, such debates exacerbated tensions between the superpowers but also between non-permanent members and former European colonial powers, especially Britain and France. In order to circumvent the acrimony between the opposing blocs, the use of rapporteurs, special representatives and conciliation commissions allowed the Secretariat to function more efficiently, effectively and relatively independently. Although the officials could not operationalise any of the decisions reached without tabling resolutions in the General Assembly, or the Security Council, their ability to act outside the direct prescription of the P5 was increased. As the Indian Deputy Secretary for External Affairs privately pointed out to the American officials in 1961, within 'the enlarged UN, the US no longer has an assured majority on anything'. New member-states, he argued, 'were not going to be restrained in pressing their demands, however irresponsible or unrealistic they might be'.[79]

The actions of newly independent nations on the Committee of 24 in implementing General Assembly Resolution 1514 from 1961 onwards increased the impression among British Foreign Office officials of the UN as an unwieldy and unpredictable organisation that had been converted into 'an organ of the anti-colonial movement, a kind of Holy Alliance in reverse'.[80] The embittered rhetoric from imperial internationalists, such as one of the leading British scholars of International Relations in the 1960s, Martin Wight, about the dismantling of the world of empires overseen by a quixotic UN, had also found sympathisers in the Colonial Office and the CRO. In a series of Anglo-American talks in 1961, Caccia outlined the British objections to UN interference in the political affairs of non-self-governing territories to Rusk. Reporting back to the Foreign Office, he pointed out that 'while we welcomed the United Nation's participation in economic and social development we were most anxious to resist political interference during the next few years while we grappled with our last remaining colonial problems'. In response, Rusk remained adamant that the UN should be strengthened in the area of colonial policy.[81]

Despite the continued British resistance, the Committee of 24 proceeded with its objective of establishing a deadline for the independence of all non-self-governing territories. In response to the pressure created by the Committee and the continual criticism of British colonial policy, in 1962 the Foreign Office conducted an internal review on the situation regarding relations with former and remaining African colonies.

The final report was grim reading. As de Zulueta summarised it for Macmillan: 'this Report shows that we are still too set in our old view of Africa as divided into a series of appendages of the European Powers ... Our objectives remain very vague and our methods old-fashioned and prim.'[82] The three main recommendations of the report were to reiterate the British position on colonial policy at the UN, to create a Commonwealth Advisory Group to oversee newly independent territories, and to pay East African Governments the cost of retaining British officers in their security forces to prevent the breakdown of law and order. These proposals arose from the broader context at the UN in which the British objective was to split the Afro-Asian alliance by encouraging Asian investment in European companies in Africa.[83] Moreover, the British sought to isolate African problems from 'more general world complications' and to try to counter-attack more effectively by promoting a campaign for the general acceptance of better standards of human rights.[84]

As British prestige at the UN withered and negative views of the organisation spread through the Foreign Office, the opposite took place in Washington. By the end of 1962, the State Department considered the overall position of the United Nations and U Thant to have improved by the 'extension of the role of the Secretary-General in connection with ... the Cuban crisis ... served to place the organisation on a sounder operational basis and strengthen its executive capacity'.[85] In its three-fold capacity as a forum for negotiation, as a mediator between the two parties and as a monitor of the settlement, the functionality and power of the UN expanded. However it had also raised questions in Washington over the direction of American plans for Third World policy in general and had shown how the superpower dispute could easily become part of a localised conflict. The Congo remained at the centre of these seeming disparate problems. As Washington sought to expand its role in the conflict and steer the UN mission more directly, Britain privately questioned whether or not it was in its interests to keep the UN in the Congo at all.[86] It viewed the Afro-Asian focus on the Congo as a gateway to the ultimate Afro-Asian objective of dismantling colonial regimes in Angola and South Africa. Together with the imperative of continuing 'to exploit the mineral wealth of southern Africa', the Foreign Office now turned its focus to undermining the UN in Africa rather than empowering the organisation. As de Zulueta pointed out to the Prime Minister, 'our main weapon is bound to be finance, and here it would be essential to try to carry the United States with us. Our object should be to prevent finance or logistic support being available for any United Nations operations in southern Africa ... It may also be in our interests that the Congo should remain an area of confusion and expense for the United Nations for as long as possible'.[87]

During Macmillan's visit to Washington in April, Kennedy had stressed the need for Britain to reconsider coordinating colonial policies more closely with the US, pointing out that when the General Assembly resumed on 7 June, the question of independence for Southern Rhodesia was the first item on the agenda.[88] Before the debate, Home proposed that British withdraw completely from the Fourth Committee, as it was noted that: 'However much we argue that these resolutions [on colonialism] are void, even the wildest of them are bound to have some impact on world opinion. Moderate resolutions are to that extent better than extreme ones and we should do what we can – it may not be much – to secure them.' Michael Cary from the Colonial Office instead picked up an earlier suggestion that British representatives at the UN should take the initiative during General Assembly debates to re-establish Britain's reputation as an international power by enlisting the support of all Commonwealth Governments.[89] The idea for a declaration on British colonial policy at the UN was investigated over the summer by the Official Overseas Coordinating Committee in the Foreign Office. Ultimately, it was concluded that it would be both 'inexpedient' and 'disruptive' to issue any declaration along these lines, either at the UN or the forthcoming Commonwealth Prime Ministers' Conference.[90] Rather, the Committee's report argued that it would in fact be difficult to secure a vote for such a statement among the Commonwealth members, and it would be better to concentrate on drumming up support for entry into the European Economic Community (EEC). As Home viewed it, 'If such a declaration as this was on the agenda it would only serve to team up Ghana and India and Ceylon and cause trouble with Welensky'.[91] Instead of risking the exposure of the lack of unity among Commonwealth members on Britain's colonial policies, therefore, the British delegation at the UN had little choice but to remain largely silent during discussions of colonial questions on the Fourth Committee and the Committee of 24.

As these reconfigurations of the British position at the UN on colonial issues took place, the Foreign Office was simultaneously preparing Britain's first application to join the EEC, as part of which fostering good relations with France became an important focus. Despite staying out of the debates on the Congo and vetoing all related resolutions in the Security Council and the General Assembly, France was insulted at being excluded from the tripartite talks with Belgium in May. Alan James has argued that French President Charles De Gaulle believed that essentially Britain and France were in agreement over what should happen in the Congo, the only difference being that the British 'had let the Americans interfere'.[92] The perceived meddling of the Americans with British policy in a range of areas was particularly damaging for the Anglo-French relationship and contributed to exacerbating tensions between the Quai d'Orsay and the Foreign Office.[93] With the British application to the EEC, Macmillan could reorient the position of the Foreign Office towards Paris, while maintaining British economic and political clout in the face of 'the unreliability of the Anglo-American alliance'.[94] The Congo posed a particular problem for the relationship with France, not just in producing accusations of neo-colonialism in British and French policies in the region, but more directly by threatening the security of trade routes and British and French commercial interests in East Africa. Through the summer of 1962, Thant also criticised what he viewed as British obstruction of the UN mission when British customs officials hampered the delivery of supplies to ONUC through Tanganyika and Uganda. Efforts to accede to his request to cooperate by opening up transport routes were balanced against the desire to protect British and French interests, lest the situation irritate relations with Paris further. Macmillan responded to Thant's requests tacitly, promising more cooperation but lamenting the fact that 'some of the extremists seemed to have got control of the United Nations committees'.[95]

The continued British refusal to consider the imposition of sanctions against Tshombe's regime up to December 1962 was maintained as the Foreign Office continued to argue for the introduction of a federal constitution that would grant power to a provincial Government in Elisabethville under Tshombe. At the same time, costs for ONUC continued to spiral and by July were an estimated $10 million per month. In order to ease the financial burden on the UN, Thant proposed that member-states buy UN bonds in order to secure the financing of the mission up to the end of 1962. During his visit to London, he encouraged the British Government to purchase bonds in order to guarantee the success of the operation. Considering the request, the Foreign Office noted that British purchase of UN bonds needed to take account of the necessity to leverage the Secretary-General towards the British position in case the UN acted 'objectionably in the Congo'.[96] A confidential memo to the Prime Minister advised the purchase of £12 million of UN bonds in order to strengthen the British position at the UN and urge moderation on Adoula in his escalating military campaign against Tshombe. The decision to purchase the bonds reflected an awareness not just of the limited British position with regard to the Congo question but also the impending likelihood of another military action against Katanga.

Operation UNOKAT: the end of the secession

If we don't have a Congo policy, we don't have an African policy.[97]

For both America and Britain, Thant's mounting determination to implement his Plan for National Reconciliation in the Congo, and the increasing likelihood of military action as part of the process, led to a renewed effort to coordinate policies towards the Congo and Africa generally. In early December the State Department and the Foreign Office held another series of talks on the general direction of policy across the continent. Although officials did not discuss the Congo directly, they considered the ways the crisis impacted the political situation in neighbouring Northern Rhodesia and Nyasaland. The State Department agreed to cooperate with Britain to maintain what was referred to as the 'good' position of the West in East Africa, and signalled its intention to devote more focus to developing a strategic approach to South Africa, which was increasingly destabilised by racial tensions.[98] On the question of the future of the CAF, Deputy Assistant Secretary of State for International Organization Affairs Woodruff Wallner urged British officials that 'the United Kingdom should exercise a stronger moral influence in the federation to ensure the success of the multi-racial society in its territories'. Defending the British position however, Mr W.S. Bates argued that nothing should be done to weaken the position of Sir Edgar Whitehead's Government (in Southern Rhodesia) and that sooner or later some conciliatory gesture would be made towards the UN.[99]

Of concern to both groups was the shifting constellation of the African Group at the UN and the reconciliation between the Casablanca and Monrovia factions. While American officials reflected their enthusiasm for 'an all-embracing African organisation' British representatives revealed their fears that this might solidify anti-Western voting at the UN. The evolution of the Afro-Asian bloc was also discussed. Officials recorded that India's failure to make a success of non-alignment and African dominance in the Afro-Asian group on the Congo question had exposed some fissures in the unity of the group. This was central to African pressure for representation in the Security Council and in particular their claims to take over what was traditionally the Commonwealth seat, an idea that was in direct opposition to British interests.[100]

The talks ultimately failed to devise a combined strategy towards the Afro-Asians or Southern Africa. In the following months American officials criticised British policy in Africa, especially with regard to former colonies and remaining territories under the control of the Foreign Office. Following a tour of the former French colonies in West Africa, Frederick P. Bartlett, Director of the Office of African and Malagasy Union Affairs in the State Department, declared loudly to several officials at the British Embassy in Paris that Britain had not done enough to guarantee the economic and technical advancement of its former colonies, in comparison with the efforts made by the French in the same regard. The Foreign Office received the comments with growing concern, having already been made aware that further correspondence was circulating between the State Department and American embassies concerning the American 'growing irritation' with British policy in Africa, and in the Congo in particular.[101] Officials in the Foreign Office viewed this criticism as further evidence of the ways in which the Congo question spilled over into other areas of British foreign policy, especially colonial issues. Privately, officials could do little but fume that the officials in the African Bureau of the State Department were becoming too specialised, producing diplomats who couldn't see the wood for the trees.[102]

In December, American delegates sought to prevent the question of further action being brought before the Security Council to avoid an open dispute. In addition to Anglo-American tensions, the internal battle in the State Department between the 'European' and 'African' camps also underscored the need for decisive action against Katanga.[103] The Europeanists, particularly Ball, were keen to find an expedient solution to the problem whether or not that was through the UN, but the 'Africanist' group, led by Williams and Deputy Assistant Secretary of State for African Affairs, Wayne Fredericks, consistently opposed any efforts to act outside the organisation. There was also the question of cooperation with Britain at the UN where Thomas Finletter, the US Ambassador to NATO, described British leadership as 'desultory' and argued that it had damaged the Western position on a variety of issues.[104] The sense of inevitability about the UN using force against Katanga, again coupled with further intrusions on British colonial policy, led to what the State Department referred to as 'unease' in Britain about the UN.[105] This 'lack of drive, energy and focus' in UK policy at the UN frustrated American officials and contributed to the eventual decision to back strong UN action against Katanga later that month.

British officials attempted to repeat the initiative of the previous year by enlisting American support for a démarche to Thant, requesting him to extend his deadline of 15 November for Tshombe's acceptance of the National Reconciliation Plan. However, their counterparts in the State Department believed that Thant should not be forced to back down from his position and supporting the British attempt to reverse his position 'would become known to Tshombe and would lead him to think US and UK [are] backing away from Plan'.[106] The Foreign Office realised the extent of American exasperation with the British position on the Congo when the State Department refused to support its initiative and Kennedy later rejected a personal appeal from Macmillan to hold back the UN from further military action as he had done the previous year.[107] Thant had noted as early as October that in the event of a military strike to end the secession, 'The United States will judge itself bound, as in the past, by UN decisions, and will supply the necessary transport aircraft and, later on, helicopters'.[108] It came therefore as little surprise when Operation UNOKAT took place from 28 December to 3 January. UN military forces quickly moved against the Katangese and quashed Tshombe's regime. The UN action resulted in a serious cooling of relations between London and Washington. As Ashton has argued, American unwillingness to use their influence with the Secretary-General to stall military action was propounded by their rejection of British reservations, through their support, politically and militarily of Operation UNOKAT, the last UN effort to end the secession militarily.[109]

In November 1961, the General Assembly had passed Resolution 169, which called for ONUC to act decisively to prevent civil war and halt the increasing human rights atrocities in Katanga. Reviewing the situation the following month, Cleveland pointed out to President Kennedy that the US could no longer afford to bluff Tshombe with the threat of military action and since 'United States and UN policy have for all practical purposes been indistinguishable, the Organization's failure in the Congo would be a major failure of this Administration's policy and would seriously undermine the peacekeeping role of the United Nations'.[110] To avoid the failure of the next UN military initiative against Tshombe, Cleveland urged the President to place US air force units at the disposal of ONUC. Thant and members of the CAC responded positively to the idea and Kennedy dispatched Lieutenant General Louis W. Truman to Katanga to review the situation. Before any decision could be taken, clashes erupted between UN troops and Katangan gendarmerie on Christmas Day, and in response Thant authorised UN soldiers to seize strategic positions in Elisabethville and close down the gendarmerie.[111] An Indian Gurkha unit quickly moved to control Elisabethville and the question of supply of US forces became redundant when UN troops grounded Katangan aircraft by seizing the Katanga air force base at Kolwezi, which had proved so important to Katangan forces in Operation Morthor.

With no opportunity to use the Anglo-American relationship to influence UN Congo policy, Britain responded immediately by turning to Commonwealth members, especially those who contributed to ONUC. As the fighting continued between UN forces and Tshombe's gendarmerie and mercenary army in December, Home attempted again to get the Canadians on side, calling on the Canadian Secretary of State for External Affairs, Howard Green, to use his influence at the UN to urge moderation on the Secretary-General.[112] Green agreed to instruct the Canadian representatives in New York to advocate moderation in the resolution of the crisis. However, the military campaign proved impossible to halt as no ceasefire could be agreed and on 3 January ONUC forces entered Jadotville and Tshombe's regime was finally dismantled.

British attempts to again halt the implementation of UN Congo policy through Commonwealth allies had had little to no effect.

In Britain there was public outcry over the UN's use of force. One House of Commons member asked: 'Must Britain, the home of freedom, stand by silent while United Nations murders freedom in Katanga?'[113] Even Macmillan's wife, Lady Dorothy Macmillan, received a telegram from a group of Rhodesian women condemning the 'deplorable, barbaric behaviour of certain contingents serving under United Nations Congo command'.[114] The Foreign Office hurriedly issued a statement on 29 December criticising as 'futile' the UN military actions, much to the irritation of officials in Washington.[115] Thant strongly defended ONUC's strike against Katanga, claiming that the force was operating within existing resolutions and acting in self-defence against attacks from Tshombe's mercenary army. Macmillan rejected this defence but he acknowledged that Britain was caught in a no-win position. Financial commitments to support ONUC through 1962–1963 had already been made, and crucially, almost all other Security Council members, including the US, supported the military action. For their part, African states meeting at the Pan-African Freedom Movement of East and Central Africa (PAFMECA) conference in Léopoldville denounced Macmillan's attempts to undermine the UN action and British manoeuvres to further entrench foreign interests in Katanga.[116]

As Tshombe retreated to the Rhodesian border, he threatened to resort to a scorched earth policy by blowing up mining facilities at Jadotville and Kolwezi, and in the chaos, the fighting significantly damaged the social and economic infrastructure of Katanga. There were reports of UN attacks on UMHK facilities such as hospitals and seminaries and widespread looting and violence among the population, culminating in the murder of two Belgian women by Ethiopian soldiers.[117] The damage to mining facilities was also condemned by the chairman of the Unilever group, Smith, who urged Home to arrange a ceasefire urgently after UMHK suspended all activities on 7 January.[118] Backed into a corner and without being able to resort to cooperation with the US to restrain the UN, Home had to concede that ultimately the UN action produced a resolution of the Katanga question and that profitable lessons for the future of the UN could be learned from the Katanga experience.[119] In this instance, Anglo-American cooperation had failed entirely. Although it would receive a boost in the areas of nuclear and defence strategy at the Nassau conference in January 1963, the impasse over the Congo remained and had a sustained impact on Britain's approach to the UN from that point onwards. As Finletter summarised it: 'Pathology of UK Congo policy ... will continue for a time to infect all UK Government thinking on UN matters.'[120]

The tension over the Congo and colonial questions in the Anglo-American relationship was brought to a head at the Nassau meeting between America and Britain in December 1962 with the controversy around the Skybolt issue. Nuclear cooperation, one of the keystones of the relationship, had, by December 1962, been dramatically affected by the American decision to discontinue production of the Skybolt nuclear system, which had been intended to form the basis of the British nuclear defence capacity. Relations had deteriorated rapidly in the previous months since US Defence Secretary Robert McNamara began to have doubts about the effectiveness of the system after a series of failures during testing. The British, however, believed that the Americans 'owed' them the replacement, Polaris, when production of the Skybolt missile was finally cancelled. The row over the supply of Skybolt had been simmering through the autumn of 1962 and, as Donette Murray has described, 'everything hung in the balance'.[121]

The deal struck at Nassau to deliver the Polaris weapons system to the British has been described as one of the most impressive achievements of the Anglo-American relationship at the time.[122] Macmillan presented the request for Skybolt in the terms of the close and intimate nature of the Anglo-American relationship, which, he argued, transcended all formats and emphasised the indivisible common purpose of the two nations.[123] The State Department afterwards protested that Kennedy's agreement to supply the weapons was the result of his being seduced by the romance of the 'special relationship'. Indeed, despite the agreement, in the post-Nassau settlement between the two countries, very little had changed in the general American position. Even by the following month, the State Department held to the belief that the British 'feeling' and policy would ease, and accordingly move closer to American nuclear aims, which firmly revolved around creating a strong multilateral force in Europe, rather than providing Britain with an independent nuclear force.[124]

In the wake of the Nassau agreement, there was also continued distance between London and Washington on the Congo. In discussions at Nassau, the tone was remarkably sharp in contrast to the parallel talks on other questions. Home pushed for the UN role to be completely converted from a military presence to a source of technical and economic aid and re-emphasised the British objection to the UN involvement in the political governance of any country. He rejected the US suggestion of putting further military pressure on Tshombe to hand over the revenues of UMHK to the Central Government, insisting that any military action would essentially amount to US intervention, and is quoted as saying: 'Personally speaking, he was all for the United States taking over a new African colony: "Best idea I have heard in years."'[125] American officials, for their part, held to the position that the UN role should be strengthened militarily in order to thwart any possibility of Tshombe reneging on his agreement.[126]

In the immediate aftermath of Operation UNOKAT, there was widespread criticism in Britain of the ways in which the UN handled the operation and particularly the question of responsibility for occupation of Jadotville and Kolwezi, the most important mining towns in Katanga and the centre of UMHK installations.[127] Similar to the earlier military operations in Katanga, there was a sense that decisions taken by UN officials in New York were often not communicated clearly to UN commanders on the ground. In the case of the strike against Jadotville, the Ethiopian commander-in-charge in Léopoldville, Kebede Guebre, was accused of acting of his own accord. Denouncing his actions as irresponsible, in an effort to gather evidence of the bungling of UN officials the Foreign Office instructed the British Embassy in Addis Ababa: 'We are not concerned in this row … nor do we of course wish to become involved … but you should … report any Ethiopian reactions which you hear.'[128]

By the end of January, Tshombe had been accepted as provincial President in Katanga but Thant's attitude towards him had stiffened considerably. A press release from the UN Office of Public Information in Léopoldville outlined that: 'The Secretary-General is definitely not seeking a resumption of negotiations over the Katanga problem. He is not trying to bring Mr. Adoula and Mr, Tshombe together again and sees no need for further discussions except at a technical level.'[129] At the basis of this resilient UN approach was Thant's desire to complete the military operation and withdraw the troops as soon as possible. This, at least, was something the British could agree with. In a conversation with Thant, Lord President of the Council Quentin Hogg Hailsham explained the reasons behind the British reservations about the methods and tactics of the UN troops in Katanga and pressed the Secretary-General on the 'justness of British colonial policy' in CAF.[130] In response, Thant indicated his desire to have the UN troops removed as quickly as possible from the Congo although he admitted that a considerable civilian effort would be required for longer. He also pointed out that several African states had indicated a willingness to provide aid to stabilise and help develop the Congolese economy, noting that 'this would be the first occasion on which African states would have taken part in a venture of this sort'.[131]

Home's remarks at Nassau, and the fears among the British UN delegation about the debate on the Committee of 24 and in the General Assembly over Southern Rhodesia were an early indication of the next challenge to colonial policy in 1964. The reaction of British officials, who denied that Southern Rhodesia was a non-self-governing territory according to UN standards, and their attempt to limit the extent to which the UN could compel a shift in colonial policy to lift the ban on African parties in Southern Rhodesia, was indicative of the British policy of ignoring or resisting the Committee on uncomfortable questions. The realisation of the potential influence of the UN in these areas, as well as the actual political damage to British policy caused by UN military action in Katanga, enhanced negative perceptions of the UN in Britain by the end of 1962. The *Daily Telegraph* declared that the UN was 'no longer an agency of nations ... but a power of peculiar morality ... writing its own mandate in the form of secret military plans'.[132] Such press coverage, and the Foreign Office statement on 29 December attacking the UN and the Secretary-General, created resentment among UN officials such as Bunche and Thant who reiterated their defence of UN actions through January, but also among American officials who had quite a different view of events.

Fundamentally different impressions of the UN now prevailed in Washington. The experience in the Congo, and even more so in Cuba, had served to revitalise the image of the organisation in the minds of policymakers at the State Department who perceived that although the UN could limit US room for manoeuvre on certain questions, as had happened in the Congo, through activism and its role as a mediator, it provided a useful mechanism of conflict resolution. The ending of the secession by the UN in January 1963 was, in particular, received with enthusiasm among American officials. Kennedy was so relieved that he wrote personally to U Thant congratulating him on 'an ultimate and satisfactory conclusion to one of the most complex and costly peacekeeping missions of the United Nations'.[133] After Operation UNOKAT, the military contingent of ONUC was gradually reduced but the Congo remained on the agenda of the

State Department up to 1964 when the Stanleyville hostage crisis posed another challenge to US Congo policy. What had become clear already by the beginning of 1963 was that the different views of the UN in London and Washington belied opposing opinions on what the role of the organisation should be in managing decolonisation.

As these contrasting visions of the role the UN should play in decolonisation became evident in the way London and Washington approached the Congo question, the effects of the ending of the secession also had an impact on the ways in which America and Britain would henceforth seek to coordinate policies in Africa. In the aftermath of Operation UNOKAT the UN representative in Léopoldville, Robert Gardiner, had urged the Congolese Central Government to play 'practical politics' and not jeopardise the UN mission by a fallout with Britain: 'because of the special relationship between the UK and the US, any incident with UK would necessarily effect relationship with US whose assistance was essential to UN operation'.[134] However, the perception of the 'special' nature of the relationship was increasingly unrepresentative of the reality of Anglo-American relations on African issues. Although the fear of a British veto of Thant's plan had been avoided in November, the conflict surrounding British colonial policy in Southern Rhodesia and South Africa continued to threaten Anglo-American relations at the UN. The activities of the Committee of 24 kept the pressure on the Foreign Office to accelerate plans for decolonisation while at the same time poor relations between London and Léopoldville resulted in the stagnation of British Congo policy. The State Department, in contrast, continued to emphasise the anti-colonial nature of its policies in Africa and at the UN, and played a progressively more active role influencing political developments in the Congo. The final episode of the conflict in 1964 surrounding the Stanleyville hostages would seal the differences in their approaches to the Congo and towards Africa, definitively undercutting the image of a 'special' Anglo-American relationship on colonial issues and decolonisation questions at the UN.

Notes

1 NARA, State Department Files, Congo, 330/6–162, Telegram from the United States delegation to the UN in New York to the Department of State, quoting comments from Irish representative O'Sullivan on the next steps to be taken in the Congo, 23 July 1962. This is a direct quote from him, regarding Soviet activity and their behaviour towards the Congo issue in conjunction with the forthcoming re-election of the Secretary-General.
2 Mazov, 'Soviet aid to the Gizenga government', p. 429.
3 Muehlenbeck, *Czechoslovakia in Africa*, p. 84.
4 GPL, BAA/RLAA/687, 'Republic of Congo': Newspaper Clippings (Congo) March 1962, Bureau of African Affairs, 'Organisation for Afro-Asian solidarity denounces U.S. plot against Gizenga's life', *Hsinhua* (12 March 1962).

'A nice little stew' 159

5 GPL, BAA/RLAA/687, 'Republic of Congo': Newspaper Clippings (Congo) March 1962, Bureau of African Affairs, 'Wire report on Tshombe's opposition to the UN', *Reuters* (23 February 1962).
6 NAL, PREM 11/4052, Personal telegram from Macmillan to Kennedy, 5 January 1962.
7 Eleven Mau Mau rebels died after being beaten by prison guards in the Hola detention camp in Kenya in 1959. It was alleged in the Commons that the Kenyan authorities and the Colonial Office were aware of what was taking place. Lamb, *The Macmillan Years*, p. 223.
8 D. Reynolds, *Britannia Overruled: British Policy and World Power in the Twentieth Century*, second edition (London: Routledge, 2000), p. 110.
9 NAL, FO 371/167212, Anonymous letter to the Foreign Office, 19 December 1962.
10 NAL, PREM 11/4052, Records of the Office of the Prime Minister, 25 May 1962.
11 *Ibid.*
12 NAL, PREM 11/3629, Record of confidential discussion between Macmillan and Sir D. Wright, 10 August 1962.
13 Eyes Only Telegram from the Department of State to the American Embassy in the UK, 14 May 1962, Schwar, *FRUS, XX, Congo*, p. 450.
14 NARA, State Department Files, 330/8-162, Congo, Comment from the representative of Liberia, Draft Report of the Security Council to the General Assembly, July 1961–July 1962.
15 NARA, State Department Files, Congo, 330/8-162, Comment from the representative of Liberia, Draft Report of the Security Council to the General Assembly, July 1961–July 1962. Even by November 1961, the representative of Liberia queried, 'it would be interesting to know what steps Belgium was taking to implement the Council resolution of 21 February, particularly with respect to mercenaries and the activities of Union Miniére'.
16 Hoskyns, *The Congo Since Independence*, p. 145.
17 *Ibid.*, p. 284.
18 Gibbs, *The Political Economy of Third World Intervention*, p. 134.
19 UNA, S-0888-008-06, U Thant Secretary-General Files, Report of the Secretary-General to the Security Council on the implementation of resolutions relating to ONUC, 4 February 1963.
20 McGhee, Yale-UN Oral History, p. 11.
21 UCDA, Conor Cruise O'Brien Papers, Microfilm P82/89, Remarks from O'Brien, the Special Representative of the Secretary-General in the Congo, in a personal letter regarding the situation in Elisabethville with regard to Union Miniére, 13 July 1961.
22 NARA, State Department, Central Files, Congo, 310/6-562, U Thant comment during a press conference in Oslo, 13 July 1961. By former practice, U Thant is referring to the fact that Union Miniére must pay taxes not only to the Katangan Government but also to the Central Government, as it had up to Congolese independence.
23 GPL, BAA/RLAA/688, 'Republic of Congo': Newspaper Clippings (Congo), Bureau of African Affairs, 'Congo, lull', *The Economist* (23 December 1961).
24 NARA, State Department, Central Decimal Files, 755a.00/6-160, Memorandum of Conversation, 28 April 1962. He remarked during his talks with Kennedy on the Congo that he 'did not see what Union Miniére could do'.

25 NARA, State Department, Central Decimal Files, 755a.00/6-160, Comment from George Ball during a discussion about the Congo at the White House, Memorandum of conversation, 28 April 1962.
26 JFKL, National Security Files, Box 235A, Folder 3, Briefing paper outlining British positions, Correspondence with Macmillan.
27 NARA, State Department, Central Decimal Files, 755a.00/6-160, Summary of Discussion, Subject-Congo, 28 April 1962.
28 JFKL, National Security Files, Box 175, File 3, Telegram from Stevenson in New York to Dean Rusk and the President, recounting dinner conversation with Macmillan and the British Representative at the UN, Patrick Dean, 27 April 1962.
29 NAL, PREM 11/3629, Secret memo from the Foreign Office to Rusk, 10 August 1962.
30 NAL, PREM 11/3629, Note from Macmillan to Philip de Zulueta, 9 August 1962.
31 NARA, State Department, Central Files, 755a.00/6-160, Memorandum of conversation, 28 April 1962.
32 NAL, PREM 11/4048, Record of Conversation between U Thant and Harold Macmillan in the Secretary-General's Office at the UN, 26 April 1962.
33 NAL, CAB 129/110, Memorandum from the Foreign Secretary for the Cabinet, 20 August 1962.
34 Mahoney, *JFK*, p. 129.
35 NAL, FO 371/167212, Letter to Lord Home and the Political Editor of the *Daily Express* from Hugh E.E. Baker, 4 January 1963.
36 NARA, State Department Files, 330/8-162, Congo, Comment from the representative of Liberia, Draft Report of the Security Council to the General Assembly, July 1961-July 1962.
37 NAL, PREM 11/3629, Confidential Telegram from the UK Mission to the UN, to the Foreign Office, 9 August 1962.
38 NAL, FO 371/167212, Letter to Lord Home, from A.H. Smith of the Unilever group, 9 January 1963.
39 NAL, FO 371/167212, Letter from the British Secretary of State, in response to the letter to Lord Home, to A.H. Smith of the Unilever group, Africa House, 19 January 1961.
40 NAL, CAB 129/111, Memorandum from the Foreign Secretary for the Cabinet, 7 December 1962.
41 NARA, State Department Files, 330/6-162, Congo, Telegram from the United States Embassy in Helsinki to the Department of State, 20 July 1962.
42 UNA, S-0735-0004, ONUC Registry Files, Political and Security Matters, Mission Files, United Nations Operation in the Congo, Telegram to Léopoldville, from UNHQ New York, December 1962.
43 NARA, State Department Files, Congo, 330/6-162, Telegram from the United States delegation to the UN in New York to the State Department, detailing a conversation about the Congo one member of the delegation had over lunch with Riad, a member of the delegation from the United Arab Republic, 25 July 1962.
44 UNA, S-0849-0001-01, Records of the Congo Advisory Committee, 24 July 1962.
45 JFKL, National Security Files, Box 175, File 3, Secret memo from State Department to US Mission to the UN in New York (among other recipient embassies), 2 May 1962.
46 JFKL, National Security Files, Box 235A, Folder 3, Correspondence with Macmillan, Secret position paper on the objectives and scope of American foreign policy.

47 JFKL, National Security Files, Box 175, File 3, Eyes Only Telegram from Stevenson in New York to the Secretary of State in Washington, 31 May 1962.
48 JFKL, National Security Files, Box 172, File 3, Letter of a personal nature from McGeorge Bundy to Philip de Zulueta, 23 May 1962, Correspondence with Macmillan.
49 NARA, State Department Files, Congo, 330/6-162, Telegram from the United States delegation to the UN in New York to the State Department, detailing a conversation about the Congo one member of the delegation had over lunch with Riad, a member of the delegation from the United Arab Republic, 25 July 1962.
50 NARA, State Department, Central Files, Britain, 755a.00/6-160, Memorandum of conversation noting Washington's support for the plan and the British objections to it, 28 April 1962.
51 NAL, PREM 11/4052, Secret telegram from Macmillan to Kennedy, 25 May 1962.
52 NAL, PREM 11/3629, Telegram from the UK Mission to the UN to the Foreign Office, 8 August 1962.
53 James, *Britain and the Congo Crisis*, p. 177.
54 'Dollar Imperialism' was a term used by the London Metal Bulletin, 15 December 1961, when denouncing American pushing for heavy economic sanctions against Katanga. From Gibbs, *The Political Economy of Third World Intervention*, p. 138.
55 McGhee, Yale-UN Oral History, p. 8.
56 As quoted in Gibbs, *The Political Economy of Third World Intervention*, p. 138.
57 Kalb, *Congo Cables*, p. 349. Also, L. Arnold and M. Gowing, *Independence and Deterrence, Britain and Atomic Energy, 1945-1952, Volume 1 Policy-Making* (Basingstoke: Palgrave Macmillan, 1974).
58 Kalb, *Congo Cables*, p. 349.
59 It should be noted that all of these countries actually gave their support in the UN for the plan, but simultaneously sought to discredit it in the press outside the UN. France was the exception, refusing to participate in any aspect of the Congo question. Mahoney, *JFK*, p. 141. Kalb, *Congo Cables*, p. 349. Gibbs, *The Political Economy of Third World Intervention*, pp. 203-204.
60 Mahoney, *JFK*, p. 141.
61 NARA, State Department files, Congo, 310/4-302, Telegram from United States Mission to the UN in New York, to the State Department, 8.42 p.m., 5 September 1962.
62 Article 17(2) of the United Nations Charter states: 'The expenses of the Organization shall be borne by the Members as apportioned by the General Assembly.' B. Simma, H. Mosler, A. Randelzhoffer, C. Tomuschat and R. Wolfrum, *The Charter of the United Nations: A Commentary*, second edition, Vol. 1 (Oxford: Oxford University Press, 2002) p. 293.
63 NARA, State Department files, Congo, 310/4-302, Extract of a speech from Prime Minister Diefenbaker, telegrammed from the United States Embassy in Ottawa to the Department of State, 3.05 p.m., 4 September 1962.
64 NARA, State Department files, Congo, 310/4-302, Extract from a Memorandum of Conversation between U Thant and the Austrian Foreign Minister Kreisky, during the Secretary-General's visit to Austria, 3 September 1962.
65 NARA, State Department files, Congo, 310/4-302, Conversation between Stevenson and U Thant telegrammed to the Department of State, 8 p.m., 12 September 1962.
66 NARA, State Department files, Congo, 310/4-302, Statement from Mohammed Ali, the Pakistani Minister for External Affairs on U Thant's plan for the Congo.

Telegram from the US embassy in Karachi to the Department of State, 12 September 1962.
67 Namikas, *Battleground Africa*, p. 164.
68 Kalb, *Congo Cables*, p. 352.
69 Mahoney, *JFK*, p. 143.
70 The Cuban revolutionary Che Guevara did go to the Congo in 1964 but in fact achieved only a limited success in stirring up revolution against the American backed regime. The same was the case in Congo (Brazzaville) where he withdrew even by 1965. P. Gleijeses, 'Cuba and the Cold War, 1959–1980', in M.P. Leffler and O.A. Westad (eds), *The Cambridge History of the Cold War, Volume 2* (Cambridge: Cambridge University Press, 2012), pp. 331–332.
71 M.E. Latham, 'Ideology, social science, and destiny: modernization and the Kennedy-era alliance for progress', *Diplomatic History*, 22:2 (1998), 204.
72 M.E. Latham, 'The Cold War in the Third World, 1963–1975', in M.P. Leffler and O.A. Westad (eds), *The Cambridge History of the Cold War, Volume 2* (Cambridge: Cambridge University Press, 2012), p. 280.
73 NARA, State Department, Central Files, 310/9-162, Confidential memo entitled, 'Analysis of the Principal Actions of the 17th General Assembly', from Dean Rusk to President Kennedy, 24 December 1962.
74 For a fuller account of the role of the UN in the Cuban Missile crisis see A.W. Dorn and R. Pauk, 'Unsung mediator: U Thant and the Cuban missile crisis', *Diplomatic History*, 33:2 (2009), 261–290.
75 NARA, State Department, Central Files, 310/9-162, Confidential telegram on 'UN Developments' from the Department of State to a selection of American embassies around the world, 2 November 1962.
76 *Ibid.*
77 NARA, State Department Files, Congo 330/8-162, Memo on developments in the United Nations. See also C. De Visscher, *Theory and Reality in Public International Law* (Princeton: Princeton University Press, 1957).
78 NARA, State Department Files, Congo, 330/8-162, Report on the 'Increased use of Rapporteurs by the United Nations', from Harlan Cleveland in New York to the Secretary of State, 3 August 1962.
79 NARA, State Department Files, UN, 310/9-2961, Memorandum of Conversation on the Collective UN Secretary-General between Mr Ramesh Bhandari, Deputy Secretary, Ministry of External Affairs and John Eaves Jr., Seond Secretary, Embassy, Ministry of External Affairs, Delhi, 9 November 1961.
80 Wight, 'The United Nations', undated lecture. See I. Hall, 'The revolt against the west: decolonisation and its repercussions in British international thought, 1945–75', *The International History Review*, 33:1 (2011), 49; M. Wight, 'The power struggle in the United Nations', *Proceedings of the Institute of World Affairs*, 33rd session (Los Angeles: University of South California, 1956), p. 248.
81 NAL, PREM 11/5183, Secret Telegram from Harold Caccia in Washington to the Foreign Office, 15 March 1961.
82 NAL, PREM 11/4978, Confidential note from Philip de Zuleta to Harold Macmillan summarising the contents of the Report of the Africa Official Committee, 24 June 1962.

83 NAL, PREM 11/4978, Secret memo from Philip de Zulueta to the Prime Minister, 19 January 1962. This had already been attempted with some success in a trade deal for iron ore from Swaziland with the Japanese.
84 NAL, PREM 11/4978, Note from Harold Macmillan to Philip de Zulueta following a discussion with the Commonwealth and Colonial Secretaries on the problem of British policy in Southern and Eastern Africa, 31 January 1962.
85 NARA, State Department, Central Files, 310/9-162, Confidential telegram on 'UN Developments' from the Department of State to a selection of American embassies around the world, 2 November 1962.
86 NAL, PREM 11/4978, Draft minute on Africa from Philip de Zulueta to the Prime Minister, 31 January 1962.
87 NAL, PREM 11/4978, Secret memo from Philip de Zulueta to the Prime Minister, 19 January 1962.
88 NAL, PREM 11/4564, Record of a meeting in the White House, 28 April 1962.
89 NAL, PREM 11/4564, Secret note from Michael Cary, Colonial Office, to the Prime Minister, 6 June 1962.
90 NAL, PREM 11/4564, Extract from brief sent by Sir Norman Brook, 21 August 1962.
91 NAL, PREM 11/4564, Memo from Home to the Prime Minister, 20 August 1962.
92 James, *Britain and the Congo Crisis*, p. 246.
93 For more on the end of the French empire and Anglo-French relations, see Thomas, *Fight or Flight*.
94 Ashton, *Kennedy, Macmillan and the Cold War*, p. 127.
95 NAL, PREM 11/4564, Record of a conversation between the Prime Minister and U Thant at Admiralty House, 5 July 1962.
96 NAL, PREM 11/4565, Confidential telegram from New York to the Foreign Office, 9 October 1962.
97 Deputy Assistant Secretary of State for African Affairs Wayne Fredericks to Secretary of State Dean Rusk, as quoted in Mahoney, *JFK*, p. 145.
98 NAL, FO 371/167140, Draft Record of Anglo-American talks on Africa, held at the Foreign Office, 5-6 December 1962.
99 NAL, FO 371/167140, Discussion on 'The Federation', Draft Record of the Anglo-American Talks on Africa, 5-6 December 1962.
100 NAL, FO 371/167140, Discussion on 'Possibility of an African Seat on the Security Council', Draft Record of the Anglo-American Talks on Africa, 5-6 December 1962.
101 NAL, FO 371/167140, Letter from P.E. Ramsbotham, British Embassy in Paris, to G.E. Millard, Foreign Office, London, 21 January 1963.
102 NAL, FO 371/167140, Letter from Roger du Bomlay, British Embassy, Washington, DC to the Foreign Office, 8 February 1963.
103 Mahoney, *JFK*, p. 145.
104 JFKL, President's Office Files, Box 128, Folder 2 United Nations, Telegram from Thomas Finletter, US ambassador to NATO to the Secretary of State on the status of US and UK talks on the UN, 14 July 1962.
105 *Ibid*.
106 NARA, State Department Files Congo, 330/11-262, Telegram from the State Department to the American embassy in London, 12 November 1962.
107 Ashton, *Kennedy, Macmillan and the Cold War*, pp. 120-122.

108 KUL, Wilcox Collection for Political Movements, American Committee for Aid to Katanga Freedom Fighters, RH WL Eph 198, Title: Ephemeral Materials, 1961 (OC0LC) 17949950, Control No: ocm18265195, Secret Memorandum of the plan developed by the UN Secretariat for dealing with Katanga, 1 October 1962.
109 Ashton, *Kennedy, Macmillan and the Cold War*, p. 126.
110 Memorandum for President Kennedy, New Policy on the Congo, 13 December 1962. Schwar, *FRUS, XX, Congo*, p. 730.
111 Namikas, *Battleground Africa*, p. 173.
112 Spooner, *Canada, the Congo Crisis*, p. 198.
113 NAL, FO 371/167212, Telegram from Paul Williams MP to Prime Minister Harold Macmillan, 29 December 1962.
114 NAL, FO 371/167212, Telegram to Dorothy Macmillan from 'Rhodesian Women' Salisbury, Rhodesia, 10 January 1963.
115 GPL, BAA/RLAA/691, 'Republic of Congo': Newspaper Clippings (Congo), Jan 1963, Bureau of African Affairs, 'Sharpening contradiction between new and old colonialists in Congo', *Hsinhun* News Agency (2 January 1963).
116 NAL, FO 371/167212, Telegram from Mbiyu Koinange, Secretary-General PAFMECA to Prime Minister Harold Macmillan, December 1962.
117 NAL, FO 371/167212, Letter from the Foreign Office explaining the situation, 12 March 1963. Two Belgian women, Madame Dister and Madame Derriks, were killed by Ethiopian soldiers serving under UN command near Jadotville in December 1962. An official UN enquiry into the events later concluded that there had been a situation of confusion between the women and the soldiers.
118 NAL, FO 371/167212, Letter from A.H. Smith to Lord Home, 9 January 1963.
119 NAL, FO 371/167212, Letter from Lord Home to Lord Chalmer, The National Union of Conservative and Unionist Association, 4 July 1963.
120 JFKL, President's Office Files, Box 128, Folder 2 United Nations, Telegram from Thomas Finletter, US Ambassador to France to the Secretary of State on the status of US and UK talks on the UN, 14 July 1962.
121 D. Murray, *Kennedy, Macmillan and Nuclear Weapons* (Basingstoke: Palgrave Macmillan, 1999), p. 81.
122 Dumbrell, *A Special Relationship*, pp. 49–75.
123 JFKL, President's Office Files, Box 127A, Folder 1, Telephone conversation, Macmillan speaking to Kennedy, 19 January 1963, Transcript of Kennedy-Macmillan phone calls 1963, Macmillan referring to the Skybolt issue.
124 JFKL, National Security Files, Box 230, Folder 3, Post Nassau Strategy paper, drafted by Walt Rostow, State Department, 2 January 1963.
125 'Memorandum of conversation, Nassau, Subject: Congo', 19 December 1962, Schwar, *FRUS, XX, Congo*, p. 763.
126 GPL, BAA/RLAA/691, 'Republic of Congo': Newspaper Clippings (Congo) 1963, Bureau of African Affairs, 'British reservations on US official statement', *The Times* (4 January 1963).
127 GPL, BAA/RLAA/691, 'Republic of Congo': Newspaper Clippings (Congo), Jan 1963, Bureau of African Affairs, 'Wire report', *Reuters* (30 December 1962).
128 NAL, FO 371/167311, Confidential memo from the Foreign Office to Addis Ababa, 5 January 1963.

129 NAL, FO 371/167311, Statement of ONUC spokesman in Léopoldville, UN Office of Public Information, 3 January 1963.
130 NAL, FO 371/167311, Confidential telegram from New York to the Foreign Office recording a conversation between Hailsham and Thant, 25 January 1963.
131 *Ibid.*
132 GPL, BAA/RLAA/691, 'Republic of Congo': Newspaper Clippings (Congo), Jan 1963, Bureau of African Affairs, *Daily Telegraph* as quoted in 'Wire report', *Reuters* (3 January 1963).
133 JFKL, President's Office Files, Folder 1, Box 128, General United Nations 1961–1963, Personal letter from Kennedy to U Thant, 29 January 1963.
134 UNA, S-0370-0045-09, Records of the Office for Special Political Affairs, Office of the Under-Secretary for Special Political Affairs, Security Council Code Cables, Telegram from Gardiner in Léopoldville to the Secretary-General, detailing discussions held with Adoula and Central Government, 11 January 1963.

6

The Stanleyville hostages and the withdrawal of the UN, 1964

The secession of Katanga officially ended on 18 January 1963 when, alongside an arrangement that UMHK would contribute a larger part of its profits from Katanga to the Central Government, Tshombe signed an agreement with the UN, handing over control of his last remaining strongholds in the province.[1] Due to the quickly escalating conflict in Elisabethville in December 1962, the US had been forced to follow through on the agreement with U Thant to supply air force support to ONUC. From January 1963, officials concerted to increasingly use the UN mission as a cover for US policy in the Congo. In response, the Afro-Asian bloc and the members of the CAC, particularly Morocco and Tunisia, objected to further American intrusion into the UN mission. Urged by the Congolese representative not to accept proposals that the US would participate in the retraining of the ANC under a UN umbrella, the CAC failed to reach an agreement on allowing military aid from countries that had not contributed directly to ONUC.[2] Dean cabled the Foreign Office following a discussion with Bunche that 'It is clear that the United Nations from U Thant downwards are by now rather resentful at United States efforts both on the civil and military sides of the Congo problem to take the United Nations cover and machinery too much for granted in the execution of United States policy'.[3]

The Foreign Office was now concerned with how the UN mission would henceforth develop, and in particular how quickly ONUC could be withdrawn. Relations with the US had soured further in the wake of Operation UNOKAT. The Congolese Government believed that Britain continued to collude with Tshombe, as the new British Consul in Elisabethville, Derek Dodson, had brought him back to Katanga after the UN operation and extracted a promise from him to cooperate with the Central Government. The new British Ambassador in Léopoldville, Derek Riches, warned the Foreign Office that Britain should cease intervening in Elisabethville. He pointed out that most of the Congolese, and Tshombe himself, perceived that he had British support and that this damaged the relationship with the Congolese Government. He advised that Dodson should be instructed to refrain from offering any more political advice to Tshombe, and that the Foreign Office should stop 'the foreign consul … concerning himself so intimately with internal affairs'.[4] Riches' predictions proved accurate the following day when the Congolese Government called for the removal of Dodson, whose 'attitude and activities' in support of Tshombe's regime were perceived as amounting to a public political stance that infringed upon the sovereignty and basic interests of the Congo. Officials in Léopoldville demanded that the Foreign Office 'cease once and for all its interference in the internal affairs' of the Congo.[5] Such was the uproar at Dodson's behaviour that a mob of 500 students stormed the British Embassy in Léopoldville on 15 January, chanting 'The British always spilled black blood. Down with the British. Hang Tshombe, the British stooge'.[6]

The Congolese demand for the withdrawal of Dodson and the attack on the British Embassy provoked the ire of the Foreign Office and the Prime Minister. Macmillan went as far as to draft a message to Kennedy on how to deal with what he termed the insulting attitude of the Congolese Government towards Britain and 'this divergence in our views'. He declared that if the Congolese Government persisted in its demand for the removal of Dodson, Britain would withdraw support for the UN operation, which 'would be unfortunate for both the United Nations and … for Anglo-American relations'.[7] Although Macmillan did not send the message, the text conveys the British exasperation with the Congo situation and the sense that continued problems with the UN and the Congolese Government were increasingly detrimental to the Anglo-American relationship. In a progress report to the House of Lords, Home defended what he termed the conciliatory actions of the British and Belgian officials in Elisabethville, without whom 'ruin might have overtaken Katanga'.[8] For his part, Dodson was hastily reassigned to another posting the following month.[9]

Exacerbating this sense of frustration was the negative perception of British Congo policy among the Commonwealth nations. The 6th PAFMECA Conference was held in Léopoldville from 28 to 30 December 1962, primarily to discuss the situation in the Congo. The representatives, who hailed from African states both inside and outside the Commonwealth, openly criticised Britain for 'maintaining a policy of ensuring the success of the groups behind Tshombe'. Noting the dissatisfaction among members of the Commonwealth, the conference participants agreed to take measures to challenge the activities of British, Belgian, French and Portuguese companies operating within their countries. In an open statement to the British Government, delegates warned that British 'policy in the Congo is the surest way for them to lose the confidence anywhere else in Africa'.[10] In contrast despite earlier protests at the UN, they praised the shift in American policy towards taking a more hard-line approach against Tshombe and UMHK. Following the PAFMECA meeting the Ugandan Prime Minister Milton Obote denounced the British Government's policy towards Katanga. He informed the British Secretary of State that 'most of the delegates and delegations [at PAFMECA] felt that the position of the British Government in respect of the Congo was directly leading not only to misunderstandings but also to a loss of confidence by African states in Britain'. He argued that if the British Government persisted with its interference in Katanga, it would negatively impact upon relations with 'even the Commonwealth countries in East and Central Africa'.[11]

The negative influence of British Congo policy on relations with the Commonwealth on colonial issues and on the British UN position in general was increasingly clear through 1963. In a report on the relationship with the Commonwealth nations at the UN in January, Dean cautioned the Foreign Office that on the issues of Southern Rhodesia and British Guiana, there was dwindling support from Commonwealth members who 'suspect that our policy is not what we state it to be'. He warned that 'the rise in influence of extremists endangers our policy of orderly and peaceful decolonisation at a pace set by the needs of each individual territory'. He advised making a further effort to improve coordination with the Commonwealth countries at the UN, in order to give the group a meaningful political role: 'we cannot in my judgement afford another year in which the Commonwealth concept is to be shown to be so empty of political content, and in which our own wishes are so blatantly and successfully disregarded.'[12] Unless the views of Commonwealth members were taken into consideration on questions of British colonial policy, Dean argued that such was the extent of disillusionment among them that further negotiation and any attempt to retain a Commonwealth seat on the Security Council would be pointless.

Within this context, Thant also announced what he termed a radical change in the emphasis and direction of UN Congo policy to address the state-building requirements of the Congo, which essentially involved phasing out the military component. In an unprecedented move he announced that the UN would publish a pamphlet of questions and answers on its Congo operation 'in a bid to counter hostile opinion over the quelling of Katangese secessionism'. He declared the mission to be the most misunderstood action in the world body's history and outlined the difficulties the UN had encountered in trying to implement its mandate for the Congo with memberstates including Britain, France, Russia and Belgium.[13] The Foreign Office responded to this assault on British Congo and colonial policy by attempting to stall the momentum of UN policy and undermining the Committee of 24. British officials condemned the negative impact of the decrees and debate provoked by the Committee on British decolonisation plans, which they believed constituted direct interference with British internal affairs. Over the summer of 1963, an internal report investigated the possibility of bringing a case before the ICJ to declare the activities of the Committee of 24 illegal. It was argued that the Committee overstepped its authority and violated Article 2(7) of the Charter that prohibits the UN from interfering with the internal affairs of a country unless there is a threat to international peace and security. By July, however, even the British Attorney-General Sir John Hobson advised the British Government that prospects of successfully arguing this before the ICJ 'were not very bright' and Home subsequently concluded that there was no point in pursuing the matter.[14]

Colonial policies also continued to be a source of tension between the Foreign Office and the State Department. British opposition to the imposition of direct rule in British Guiana, combined with escalating tensions in Southern Rhodesia and the negative perception of British Congo policy, served to undermine Anglo-American relations on colonial issues even further. The 1961 election in British Guiana had produced a majority Government under the People's Progressive Party, a group with links to Communist organisations. The US regarded the establishment of a Communist country in Latin America as a direct threat to its sphere of interest, and although British Guiana was self-governing from 1961 onwards, urged the Foreign Office to re-impose British rule and delay full independence until a more Western-friendly arrangement could be established. American officials pressed the point during Kennedy's visit to London in June 1963 when the President argued that considering strategic interests, the perceived threat of the establishment of a Communist regime required the Colonial Office to resume a more active role in government. The British Secretary of State for the Colonies Lord Edwin Duncan-Sandys and Home were, however, hesitant to resume responsibility in British Guiana given the economic burden it would place on Britain, but more importantly because of the damage this would do to Britain's position at the UN and the problems it would cause for dealing with Southern Rhodesia.[15] While the independence struggle of British Guiana rolled on until 1966, its impact on the Anglo-American relationship in 1963 was significant.

A series of article in *The Times* and the *Sunday Mirror* in May 1963 argued that the Anglo-American relations were at the time characterised by 'Dislike, Distrust and Enmity', and that Macmillan had been publicly snubbed by Kennedy.[16] The piece, written by Richard Crossman MP, alleged that the dispute between London and Washington related to Britain's quest for an independent nuclear deterrent as, despite the deal made at Nassau, the State Department had not extended any material provisions. The controversy had originated with an article in *The Times* on 14 May entitled 'US Cool about Meeting Mr. Macmillan', in which the Washington correspondent reported that he had been summoned to the White House personally and been 'given a hand-out so deliberately offensive to the British Premier that it could only have been issued on the President's express instructions'. The author went on to argue that Macmillan's repeated requests that the President meet with him during his planned visit to Europe in June 1963 were embarrassing to the President and part of Macmillan's campaign for re-election in autumn 1963.

The internal furore these press reports caused in the White House and the Prime Minister's Office produced a flurry of apologetic correspondence between officials. But the press continued their attack on the Anglo-American relationship with the *London Daily Express* alleging that following the discussion at Birch Grove (on British Guiana among other issues) the President had been 'dismayed and disappointed by Mr. Macmillan's lack of grip on international affairs'.[17] Defending the President, Bundy wrote to de Zulueta, assuring him that Kennedy had found the discussions 'most useful'. De Zulueta replied that although 'it was difficult to avoid the conclusion that some Press comment reflected something more than the state of the writer's liver … the time to get alarmed about Anglo-American relations is when they look good but really aren't'.[18] Although the Birch Grove talks reflected efforts between London and Washington to formulate a cohesive position on British Guiana, nuclear testing and the issue of apartheid in South Africa at the UN, the inflammatory nature of the press coverage indicated the querulous tenor of relations, particularly on colonial issues. At the UN, American representatives consistently urged their British colleagues to cooperate with the resolutions of the Committee of 24 in order to 'keep temperature[s] down'.[19]

The State Department was at this point concerned about the effect of the withdrawal of UN forces on the stability of the Congo. The question was a pressing one for the US, as it sought to convert its support for the Congolese Government into limited economic aid and assistance, preferably under a UN umbrella. In communications with Mobutu, the General insisted that he could maintain law and order without the UN if he had bilateral military aid from the US to strengthen the ANC. In response, the State Department agreed to continue the supply of materiel aid to the ANC in the form of trucks, communications equipment, etc. The objective with the aid programme the US rolled out to the Congo was to allow the country to become as self-sufficient as possible within a short period (the estimate was two years), given its considerable economic resources and raw materials but also to maintain US influence among Congolese leadership.[20] At the same time, however, the State Department was hesitant about becoming drawn into a position of providing long-term life support for the Congo and sought to coordinate aid programmes with the UN and other states, including Belgium, who, in the view of American officials such as Williams, should take primary responsibility in rehabilitating the Congolese state.[21]

US Congo policy was at this point guided by a report produced by Cleveland following his visit to Léopoldville in early 1963, which was designed to reduce the American presence and recommended multilateral cooperation between all states contributing to the Congo.[22] This, Cleveland argued, was the preferred course of action for Adoula, as it would allow him 'to maintain the posture of non-alignment while seeking the advantages of aid from the West'.[23] He pointed out that it would be 'unnecessary and unwise' to go back to the Security Council or the General Assembly to strengthen the UN mandate, as this would allow for interference from the Soviet bloc.[24] Following his recommendations, the State Department set about coordinating aid to the Congo from Belgium, Britain, the EEC and Germany under a UN umbrella, although it was noted that both the UN and Belgium were reluctant to assume responsibility for what was essentially becoming an economic state-building exercise.[25]

Thant had indicated as early as December 1962 that the US should look to the Belgians to 'assist in ways appropriate to their own resources'.[26] In May 1963, he announced that the UN force would be withdrawn by the end of the year and he refused to add to the considerable duties of the peacekeeping and civil missions that remained a serious burden on UN finances. Formulating an exit strategy for the UN, while not destabilising the Adoula Government, remained an important focus of both US and British Congo policies through 1963 as the deadline for the removal of UN troops loomed closer. The State Department, concerned by the timeline for withdrawal, developed policy towards this end in two main directions; by retraining the Congolese army to police the more problematic areas of the country in order to prevent another secession or civil war; and by establishing what were referred to as 'nation building' programmes for the socio-economic development of the state. These dual aims of US Congo policy after the ending of the secession were however contingent upon a renewed role for the Europeans, especially the Belgians in the providing economic support.

The relationship between Brussels and the Congo now came full circle. By agreeing to send officers, technicians and political advisors to Léopoldville, Belgium, with the support of the US and the UN, asserted its influence in the Congo again. Washington similarly urged the Foreign Office to continue bilateral aid to the Congolese Government. As Harriman asked Home, considering the British Government's close relationship with neighbouring countries, surely they shared the American view that the UN job in the Congo must be completed? He advocated cooperation with Belgium and encouraging the Organisation of African Unity to send a force to guarantee peace in the Congo – something the British were opposed to.[27] The British view was essentially that 'the sooner the United Nations troops were out the better'.[28] Recognising that the UN was in dire financial straits, the British Government committed a further £4.5 million to sustain the Congo operation until the end of 1963. The sense of frustration at American demands for increasing financing for the Congo operation had been growing since 1961, when de Zulueta had privately asked: 'If the US think the UN need all this, should they not pay?'[29] In order to offset tensions, the Foreign Office instructed the British Mission to the UN to cooperate with American efforts to do everything possible to urge other UN members, in particular France and the Soviet Union, to abide by the ICJ judgement and honour their commitments to the UN by providing their financial contribution.[30] In creating a UN umbrella as a means of coordinating aid to the Congo, and allowing for the withdrawal of UN troops, the US sought to encourage other states to resume payment of contributions to the UN, to improve the finances of the organisation and to reduce their own burden. Unwittingly, however, this plan provided the incentive and the means by which Western countries and interest groups re-established operations in the Congo, in a complete reversal of earlier policy. In the process, coordinating financing for the Congo also led to a renewed effort to bring American and British policies into line as governments changed on both sides of the Atlantic.

Trying to find common ground

Macmillan's tenure as Prime Minister came to a sudden end in October 1963 when surgery forced him to abdicate the leadership of the Conservative Party. Home assumed the Prime Minister's post, while in Washington, the assassination of President Kennedy on 22 November led Lyndon B. Johnson to become President. As Namikas has described it, Johnson 'was not prepared to deal with foreign policy crises, especially in the Congo'.[31] Part of the problem was that the ending of the secession had created the false impression among the public that the crisis had been resolved.[32] Together with the scaling up of US commitments in Vietnam in response to the assassination of the President of South Vietnam Ngo Dinh Diem, Congo policy stalled. The State Department continued to urge European and African states to take a more active role in the Congo, both bilaterally and under the aegis of the UN.

Thant's announcement that UN forces would be withdrawn from the Congo by the end of 1963 led to a surge among African states to coordinate plans to keep the country stable. The Nigerian Minister of Foreign Affairs Jaja Wachuku and Ghanaian Foreign Minister Kojo Botsio assured American officials at the UN that they would support

Adoula's request to the Secretary-General that some UN presence would remain in the Congo from 1 January 1964. Many Latin American states, led by Peru, similarly instructed their delegations to support the retention of troops in the Congo until June 1964.[33] Skirmishes between Congolese troops and the Angolan army along the border, the breakdown of relations between Léopoldville and Congo-Brazzaville and the outbreak of ethnic violence in Eastern Congo reflected the tenuous nature of Congolese unity through 1963.[34] The Binza Group at this point started to turn against Adoula in light of his inability to quash rebellions in South Kasai against forces loyal to Kalonji and against the Baluba in North Katanga.[35] By the end of the year, growing opposition to Adoula's leadership among Léopoldville politicians and the discovery of 'Communist' training camps led by Mulele in the jungle, served as ominous auspices for events in 1964, when a rival, Communist-led Government was re-established in Stanleyville.[36]

Following the dismantling of Gizenga's opposition regime in Stanleyville in 1962, the exiled Lumumbists had found refuge in neighbouring Congo-Brazzaville. Led by Christophe Gbenye they now began to agitate for a new, more representative Government in Léopoldville, arguing that Adoula was being completely controlled by the US.[37] In response to this growing threat from the political exiles, the US sought to stabilise the Adoula Government by reintroducing Tshombe as Prime Minister. The decision to bring the former Katangan leader into the national Government was extensively discussed and coordinated with the British and the Belgians who used their own networks to advance the idea among Congolese politicians.[38] When other African leaders criticised this move, Brussels, London and Washington insisted that bringing Tshombe in was an effort to consolidate the Central Government, rather than a means by which to protect their interests, but these two motivations were not mutually exclusive. Following the creation of a new constitution in June, with the powers of his office severely reduced, Adoula was sidelined and Mobutu and other members of the Binza Group, including Kalonji, welcomed Tshombe back.[39] Rather than stabilising the Central Government, however, his re-emergence in Congolese politics had the opposite effect, spurring rebel insurgency across the country. Many Congolese politicians, including Lumumba's supporters and other African leaders, believed that Tshombe remained a Belgian stooge and a neo-colonialist. The Ugandan Minister for Foreign Affairs expressed the suspicion widespread among many African leaders, including members of the OAU, about Tshombe's 'almost spectacular overnight return'. Odaka pointed out to an American Embassy official in Kampala that it was almost inconceivable that his return was not engineered by Belgian or other unnamed forces who wished to use Tshombe as a 'confusion factor' to prevent the formulation of a lasting solution for the Congo.[40] Protesting his selection as Prime Minister, they opted instead to support a rebellion by Gbenye, Gaston Soumialot and 'General' Nicholas Olenga.

In September 1963 the rebels Gbenye and Soumialot created a provisional Government, the Conseil National de Liberation (CNL), which was composed of an array of exiled Lumumbists, Gizengists, leftists and an assortment of exiled Congolese in Brazzaville and Burundi. Rebel leaders drew the ire of the US almost immediately by accepting the support of Chinese Communists as they organised and actively encouraged various rebellions across the country.[41] By July 1964, as UN troops were quietly withdrawn from Congo, associated groups gained control at least one-third of the territory. A British correspondent for the *Daily Telegraph* interviewed Soumialot in Albertville in early August 1964. The correspondent, Ian Colvin, communicated to Millard, the British Chief of West and Central African Department in the Foreign Office, that Soumialot's political orientation was based on resentment of the inefficiency, corruption and inaction of the Léopoldville Government towards improving the lives of ordinary Congolese citizens. 'Soumialot claims to be Lumumbist with ultimate aim to bring the entire Congo under a Lumumbist regime. Soumialot further claimed that one objective of his campaign in Eastern Congo was to relieve pressure on Mulele in Kwilu.'[42]

Since August of the previous year, Mulele had led a separate rebellion from the Kwilu province in Eastern Congo and his followers, known as the 'Jeunesse' because of their young age profile, quickly became feared for their brutal warfare.[43] With a fundamentalist philosophy, Mulele preached to the Jeunesse that their power came from the land on which they were fighting and that they would soon be vanquished when the ANC forces ran out of foreign-manufactured bullets. Using poison-tipped arrows against the Congolese army, they successfully engaged Government forces in a campaign of guerrilla warfare across the province.[44] His idealistic followers were fuelled by frustration with the Adoula Government and by deep suspicions of the US in particular, whom they feared would send military forces to crush their rebellion at any moment. Their resistance movement inspired another group called the Simba rebels, a rag-tag group of freedom fighters rather than a disciplined army, who loosely associated themselves with the former regime of Gizenga.[45] Similar to the Jeunesse, it was reported that the Simbas believed in black magic and witchcraft, promoted human sacrifice for their cause and threatened to consume the flesh of their enemies.[46] Such was the atmosphere of suspicion and fear surrounding them, that many Congolese soldiers were terrified of the Simbas and often dropped their weapons and fled from the rebels during confrontations. Both groups openly accepted support from Communist China and, later, other regimes in North Africa, including Algeria, Morocco and Egypt.

Alongside warnings from Belgian technicians that the Kwilu uprising was 'something entirely different from normal tribal outbursts', three factors prompted an accelerated American response to the gradual breakdown of Congolese unity.[47] The rebels' acceptance of aid from the Soviet Union and China was an obvious concern to the State Department, as too was the growing popularity of the rebel groups among the Congolese people generally opposed to Tshombe who was widely viewed as a direct manifestation of foreign influence. It was the increasing attacks on Western missionaries, however, and the inept response of the ANC in defeating the rebels that led the US to help retrain the Congolese army in guerrilla warfare techniques.[48] It was also at this point that both Britain and the US sanctioned the use of mercenaries as a short-term way of crushing the resistance. As Piero Gleijeses describes, Washington was keen to stay in the background when it came to the implementation of policy in the Congo, turning to the British and the Belgians to supply the mercenaries with provisions that would be delivered to the Congo by American means.[49]

The State Department dispatched Harriman to Brussels as early as 6 August with the instructions to 'vigorously' urge the Europeans to move immediately to prevent the total collapse of the Congo.[50] With the promise of American military support, the State Department now pushed Belgium and Britain to strengthen the ANC in order to secure the Central Government and vital European interests in central Africa. Johnson gave his formal commitment to create a mercenary officered gendarmerie force with a 'tentative force level of four thousand gendarmes and two hundred white officers'.[51] Within two days of Harriman's arrival to negotiate with the Belgians, a joint agreement was reached to instruct Colonel Frederick Van De Walle to act as a military advisor to help Tshombe organise the white mercenaries and to work in conjunction with the ANC to stamp out rebellion throughout the country. Though the Belgians had baulked at first, their intricate involvement in the affairs of Congo, both economically and politically, and the pre-existing network of mercenaries that had operated in Katanga as part of Tshombe's regime there, allowed them to quickly re-invigorate old structures and reintroduce white mercenaries. Crucially this was in direct contravention to the efforts by the UN between 1960 and 1963 to remove mercenaries from Katanga and represented the State Department strategy of using covert methods to execute its Congo policy.

The US adopted a two-pronged approach designed to materially strengthen the inept ANC while also encouraging Tshombe to appeal to the OAU for reinforcements against the rebels. It refused to send parachute regiments to Léopoldville but agreed to supply four C-130 transport planes and three helicopters with a platoon of US airborne infantry.[52] The American Embassy in Léopoldville was instructed to organise Tshombe to write to Nigeria, Liberia, Senegal, Malagasy and Ethiopia asking them not to harbour the rebels and instead to supply troops for the ANC. The appeal for troop supplies from other African countries was part of the State Department's efforts to Africanise the Congo problem and strengthen the OAU. As Harriman pointed out to Bundy, however, 'Tshombe's unpopularity with the African leaders may still cause difficulties'.[53] After further American strong-arming, Tshombe also asked Thant to instruct Burundi and Brazzaville not to offer the rebels a base and instructions were sent to the US delegation to the UN to support the initiative. Rusk advised the American delegation however that it was 'not a good idea to have the Secretary-General consult [the] Congo Advisory Committee'. Rather, they were to advocate a private line of enquiry by Thant's Special Representative in order to 'sound out' the possibility of bilateral assistance to Congo.[54]

The State Department further instructed its ambassadors across Africa to seek meetings with African leaders in order to drum up support for Tshombe. However, alongside the criticism from both large and small African states, however, even some American officials criticised the decision to support him. The former Ambassador to the Congo, Edmund Guillon, sent a sharply worded letter to Rusk in August, criticising the State Department's policy. Arguing that by supporting Tshombe the rebels gained legitimacy and a cause, he pointed out that it also 'put flesh on the bones of Communist bogey-men'. Similar critiques were echoed by leaders of many African states, including Somalia and Tanzania. The Somali Government expressed reservations about the reintroduction of Tshombe, pointing out that since he had previously led an armed resistance to the Congo state, he was an inappropriate leader for the Congo.[55] Nyerere denounced Tshombe's return along similar lines, asking, 'who had arranged this defiance of Africa?' He pointed out that Tshombe evoked revulsion among 'committed Africans' who opposed him and 'all that he represented as pawn of colonial, financial and racist interests who regard Africa as their property and Africans as less than human'. He denounced the American decision to support him, alleging that such an alliance was 'creating major openings for Communists in Africa that the US had previously sought to avoid.'[56] Instead, he advocated a stronger role for the OAU and a round of free elections in the Congo. Touré echoed Nyerere's call for an OAU solution, which he stressed 'would be far preferable from [the] viewpoint [of] US interests than present Tshombe formula which, even if it succeeded in establishing temporary Tshombe dictatorship, would be disastrous in [the] long run for both US and for Africa'.[57]

In the face of this African criticism, the US turned towards Britain and Belgium to use their networks of influence in Africa to drum up support for Tshombe and American policy. As Namikas has argued, 'no-one in the Johnson administration wanted to talk about direct U.S. intervention in the Congo'.[58] The American crusade in Vietnam was accelerating again, despite domestic criticism from the conservative Republican Party presidential candidate, Barry Goldwater, who denounced Johnson's foreign policy as failing to protect freedom around the globe. In addition, Johnson was faced with a series of race riots through the summer of 1964, as members of the Ku Klux Klan attacked civil rights activists in retaliation for the signing of the Civil Rights Act in July.[59] Confronted with the potential of a military conflict in the Congo, the State Department stepped up pressure on Britain and Belgium to take the lead, in the process securing American interests in Africa.

After an appeal from the American Embassy in Lusaka, '[to] activate HMG more' in support of the American position,[60] Harriman again pushed the British instead to use the Commonwealth connection to encourage African nations to take a 'more sensible' line on the Congo. In response, Harold Wilson, who became Prime Minister after a narrow election victory in October, agreed to try to use British influence through colonial and Commonwealth networks to rally support among African nations for US policy in the Congo.[61] Harriman also appealed to the Belgian Foreign Minister Paul-Henri Spaak to send further military aid, advisors and supplies to shore up the Congolese Government forces. Belgium responded by dispatching further instructions to Van de Walle, who immediately began reorganising the ANC and the mercenary army alongside a British mercenary leader, Mike Hoare. With the use of mercenaries as proxy actors to protect Anglo-American interests and strengthen the ANC, Brussels, London and Washington worked to promote US Congo policy while simultaneously trying to preserve the British network of relations with other African states such as Nigeria, Kenya and the Federation of Rhodesia and Nyasaland. However, the re-emergence of Tshombe, the re-invigoration of these networks and the atrocities committed by white mercenaries against the rebels produced a storm of protest against British and American Congo policy when the Stanleyville hostage crisis came to a head in November 1964.

Operation Dragon Rouge

The outbreak of rebel insurgencies in eastern areas of the Congo soon led to the collapse of the Adoula Government, already buckling under the socio-economic pressure of reunification with Katanga. Mulele's revolt Kwliu soon spread across north-eastern Congo as different groups seized upon his initiative before the CNL and the Simbas declared that they had control of the former Lumumba stronghold of Stanleyville on 5 August. The Simba rebels proceeded to round up several hundred white hostages, including some American Consulate officials and British and Belgian citizens, and held them in the Victoria Hotel in the centre of the city. According to official UN reports, thousands of Congolese, including Government officials, police officers and schoolteachers believed to have been 'Westernised', were brutally murdered.[62] The violence and the pro-Communist attitude of the parties involved led to renewed efforts in Washington and London to urge the Congolese Government to take affirmative action to crush the rebellion. Rusk cabled the American Embassy in Léopoldville instructing them to immediately talk to Kasavubu and Tshombe and 'with all the muscle you can put into it, you should press upon them the necessity of maintaining government control where it now exists'.[63] The taking of hostages also introduced a new dimension to the dilemma, and discussions began about if, and how, a rescue mission could take place, with the compliance, if not the assistance, of the Tshombe Government.

As already noted, the increasing Western influence over the Congolese Government and the support for Tshombe's mercenary army was met with widespread criticism from other Congolese and African politicians.[64] Inevitably, this also had the effect of increasing the popularity of the rebel movements and adding legitimacy to their cause. By September, alongside the fall of Stanleyville where a significant European population was now held hostage, the CNL regime was also being supported by some African states, including the former British colony Tanzania where Nyerere's Government did nothing to block the supply lines to the rebels across Lake Tanganyika.[65] Even among the Western nations the situation was viewed as bleak. One official described Tshombe's re-emergence as equivalent to his 'jumping on and now leading a bandwagon built of despair, disillusionment, friction and opportunism'.[66] When Wilson himself later questioned how Tshombe had gotten back into power he was met with the response that the situation had been 'forced on the people [of the Congo] by bribery and other means of subversion'.[67]

When the rebels seized the hostages, therefore, it was clear that although they were taken as leverage against the advancing ANC forces led by the mercenaries, it was also an act of retaliation against the European population in Stanleyville in response to British and American support for Tshombe. A telegram sent from the rebels who controlled the former US Consulate in Stanleyville on 20 November 1964 alleged that 'US responsibility [for] interference Congolese internal affairs well established … material and other aid furnished Tshombe provoke very serious consequences … all American citizens are in danger'.[68] The telegram went on to urge the Americans to negotiate with the rebels in order to preserve the lives of the hostages. The situation escalated rapidly when intelligence sources revealed that, aware of the advancing ANC forces led by Van de Walle and Hoare, the Simba rebels selected several Americans, including a young missionary doctor called Paul Carson and American Consulate official David Grinwis (who was in fact the chief of the CIA station in Stanleyville), for ritualistic sacrifice.

In response to the immediate danger to the hostages by November, the American Ambassador in Léopoldville, Godley, pushed US officials for stronger action. The State Department through the US Ambassador to Kenya, William Attwood, had quietly entered negotiations for the release of the hostages with the OAU who formed an Ad Hoc committee to talk terms with the rebels, represented by Lumumba's former deputy Kanza. By November, the rebels remained defiant, explaining to Jomo Kenyatta and Guinean diplomat Diallo Telli who led the Ad Hoc Commission, that there could be no negotiation on the hostages until Tshombe halted the advance of the ANC and mercenary forces to Stanleyville and the US withdrew all aid to the Tshombe Government. Godley now vigorously argued to the State Department that if any attempt was made to force Tshombe into this position, it would lead to a significant loss of US prestige in Africa and around the world and would strengthen the arguments of the rebels and other African states that the US was interfering directly in the Congo. Godley believed that the rebels were attempting to buy time with the negotiations to strengthen their forces and that Kanza and Telli were also using them as a way to allow the rebels to consolidate their positions. He argued that 'any negotiations with rebels at this time are against our interests if price involves a slow down on military advance on Stan[leyville]. We can't afford to play this game, for American prestige in Africa as well as fate our own people are at stake'.[69]

Over the following days, Godley kept up the pressure on the State Department from Léopoldville. He followed his tirade against the rebels on 21 November with an urgent message that Stanleyville had deteriorated into a situation of panic. Intercepted messages from the city alleged rebel threats to burn alive or eat foreigners if the ANC advance was not halted. This sense of panic was convenient to Godley's objective of forcing Washington's hand to order the deployment of Dragon Rouge, a rescue plan which had been under negotiation with Belgium since early November. He warned that the situation of escalating danger in Stanleyville was one in which the rebels were 'more likely to kill hostages or at least take them into bush'. He reminded Washington that 'if we don't act and hostages are massacred we will be in terrible trouble. We are also convinced that, having gone as far as we have, respect for the West in Africa would suffer disastrously if we allow massacre in Stan[leyville]'.[70] Godley's views highlight the wider scepticism that Washington had about the usefulness of the negotiations and parallel discussions about a rescue operation with the British and the Belgians reflect a half-hearted effort to use the negotiations effectively and a determination to intervene militarily.

Given the mounting pressure to act decisively, Ball contacted the American Embassy in Brussels with precise instructions for the operation. He emphasised that the Dragon Rouge force, comprised of Belgian paratroopers, was to be withdrawn immediately after the hostages, and Congolese who faced reprisals, had been rescued. 'Intervention by DR', he directed, 'can only be undertaken for an operation solely humanitarian in character'.[71] Spaak remained pessimistic about the possibility of separating the military retaking of Stanleyville by Van De Walle from the humanitarian dimensions of the mission but, in an effort to save the hostages, agreed to proceed with the drop at dawn on 24 November.[72] What was still needed, however, was the permission of the Congolese Government to enter its territory to carry out the operation.

Kasavubu had earlier rejected American pressure to appeal for African forces to join the ANC as there was a widespread feeling in Léopoldville that other African states were gathering on the borders in order to launch an intervention for a share of Congo's resources. Politically, it was also likely that after the withdrawal of UN forces, the presence of non-Congolese African troops would appear to undermine the authority of the Government. Tshombe had only appealed to African states for help after heavy prompting from Williams because he believed this was the only way to secure continuing American aid.[73] Without help from other African states, however, Tshombe and Kasavubu had been left with little option but to resort to the use of mercenaries, which was now going to prove instrumental in re-taking Stanleyville. Finally, on 21 November, Tshombe gave authorisation for the rescue forces to land in Stanleyville to accomplish the humanitarian purpose of evacuating the hostages.[74] Although Kasavubu and Mobutu both rejected American suggestions that they change the wording to 'invited' rather than 'authorised', American officials did not quibble over the wording of the agreement, which would later prove crucial when the issue of Congolese acquiescence was debated at the UN. Similar to Tshombe's attitude towards asking African countries for reinforcements, Kasavubu had initially rejected the idea and 'only with great reluctance acquiesced to authorizing the humanitarian effort', a sceptical position that was shared by virtually all of the Congolese press and many others.[75]

As plans for the rescue operation coalesced, Attwood's negotiations with Telli and Kenyatta were simultaneously faltering. Through October, the US had continued to pay lip service to the OAU conciliation efforts, assuring Nkrumah that 'in supporting and encouraging OAU efforts to assist the Government of the Congo to resolve its problems … we do not wish to interfere in any way'.[76] Unable to locate Kanza for a final round of talks on 21 November, however, negotiations for the release of the hostages broke down. Telli insisted that as OAU Secretary-General he was only there to assist Kenyatta as Chairman of the Ad Hoc Commission and could not take part in any discussions as 'assistant' to Kanza. He shortly excused himself on urgent business. Privately, Attwood recounted that Telli followed him to his car where he said that it was necessary for him to disassociate himself from any connection with the rebels.[77] The dissolution of the final round of negotiations with the OAU also reflected the wider atmosphere of derision among African leaders on the question of a rescue mission. The previous week the movement of Belgian paratroopers to Ascension Island, in preparation for an intervention, had been leaked to the press, causing a wave of criticism. Kenyatta himself issued a statement criticising American and Belgian assistance to Tshombe.[78] African delegates also held an impromptu press conference at the UN where they condemned the movement of Belgian troops. Marof of Guinea roundly denounced the preparations, alleging: 'This sets us back four years. Americans,

Belgians and British have been involved in this ever since Lumumba. Why can't they let Africans in Congo get together.'[79] Similarly, Quaison Sackey of Ghana warned that any intervention would precipitate a massacre. This criticism served to undermine the negotiation efforts further and many American officials, including Godley, believed that the OAU could not deliver a viable solution.

Efforts to coordinate a strategic response for the rescue were further hampered by disagreements between the State Department and the Foreign Office about who was responsible for leaking details of the rescue mission which had the effect of further endangering the hostages. An irate Harriman told Rusk: 'Haven't concerted with the British ... the leak came out of London.'[80] It had been agreed that Britain would participate in the rescue operation but only if the Americans committed the materiel aid. British officials were anxious that supporting the intervention militarily would be perceived by other African nations as another endorsement of Tshombe's Government, which would further damage relations with Commonwealth members and neighbouring countries.[81] In addition, it was felt that an intervention would pose a risk to the security of British bases in Africa.[82] After much deliberation the Foreign Office had agreed to participate by allowing the rescue planes to land at the British base in Ascension Island, and await the instructions to finally move into Stanleyville.

On 24 November, Operation Dragon Rouge was launched. Three hundred and fifty Belgian paratroopers were flown into Stanleyville airport in ten American C-130 planes, from where they proceeded to the Victoria Hotel, where most of the hostages were being held. The Stanleyville rescue operation was limited in success. As soon as the Belgian paratroopers landed confusion took over and the rebels started killing hostages, murdering sixty before the city was under the control of the intervening forces.[83] Among those killed was the missionary doctor Paul Carson who was inadvertently killed in a gunfire battle between the rebels and Belgian troops.[84] The paratroopers managed to rescue the remaining hostages and airlifted out 1,800 European and a further 400 Congolese people. In the following days, the mercenary-led ANC arrived in Stanleyville and proceeded to seize the city, in the process slaughtering between at least 10,000 and 20,000 Congolese in retribution for their perceived collaboration with the rebel regime. With savage brutality, ANC and mercenary forces murdered anyone who was considered a collaborator of the Simbas. Accurate numbers do not exist for the amount of Congolese killed because, as Ludo de Witte has recently described it, 'no one bothered to count their bodies'.[85] This outcome, with its clear racial undertones, had disastrous consequences and longer political repercussions. Both London and Washington immediately issued statements to a host of African leaders through all their African channels announcing that the operation had been strictly humanitarian in nature and was in no way an attempt to impose a political solution on the Congo.[86] But for many, especially the most outspoken African statesmen the exercise was an aggressive act by three imperialist states.

However carefully the operation had been stage-managed, the landing of Belgian paratroopers in Stanleyville, flown in American planes from a British base and with British support, was reminiscent of the first Belgian intervention which had sparked the initial crisis in 1960. The justification of the protection of foreign citizens also echoed earlier rhetoric. Unsurprisingly, therefore, the rescue was immediately denounced by African leaders and the USSR as an effort to protect neo-colonial interests and no amount of humanitarian arguments could convince leaders such as President Ben Bella of Algeria, who declared that the 'pretext of hostages would deceive no-one'.[87] This reflected the perception of American and British policy in the Congo and Africa as neo-colonialist and further revealed that Western powers would violate Congolese sovereignty when their interests were threatened. Focusing on this violation of international law and the disregard for norms governing the use of force, the African states now sought a formal condemnation of Western policy in the Congo at the UN. As officials in Léopoldville enjoyed a 'glorious' lunch with the American Consulate officers rescued from Stanleyville, African states at the UN prepared to raze US Congo policy.[88]

Fallout in New York, December 1964

The condemnation of the rescue operation was a wide-ranging as it was violent. Across Africa anti-US demonstrations took place in Nairobi, Khartoum and Cairo. In the Egyptian capital several groups converged into a mob which attacked the American Embassy and compound, burning the library of the United States Information Service and the marines' quarters to the ground. Demonstrations also took place Prague and Sofia and criticism mounted from a variety of groups, including the African Liberation Committee, the All African Trade Union Federation, the Afro-Asian Peoples' Solidarity Organization and the OAU. Adverse reactions also emanated from officials in Algeria, Congo-Brazzaville, Ghana, Guinea, Kenya, Liberia, Mauritania, Somalia, Sudan, Tanzania and Tunisia. Privately, American officials reflected that even countries which were sympathetic to the humanitarian arguments, such as Nigeria, Sierra Leone, Argentina, Ecuador and Santo Domingo, such was the strength of the African critique that more conciliatory countries were unwilling to publicly support the operation. Others, including India, were annoyed at the lack of advance notice about when the rescue mission would take place, particularly in light of their contribution to ONUC.[89]

African delegations at the UN began to organise their protest immediately. The African group issued a statement expressing their abhorrence at the intervention and alleging that Britain, Belgium and the US were responsible for the consequential loss of life. With the support of Thant, who was critical of the fact that the UN had also not been notified in advance of the mission, a committee was formed to study the situation and determine specific instructions for a Security Council meeting.[90] The OAU soon joined the chorus too when Kenyatta publicly urged the US not to continue to supply Tshombe with arms and equipment. He vowed that as far as Kenya, and many other African states were concerned, since Tshombe's selection as Prime Minister had never been ratified, it was not legitimate, and as long as the US continued to support him, other African states would continue to support the rebels in Stanleyville.[91]

This support was more than just political. Completely rejecting the humanitarian characterisation of the mission and denouncing it as a 'premeditated act of aggression against territory of Congo, having far-reaching repercussions on independence of Congo and other African nations, in complete disregard of OAU charter', Algiers authorised a shipment of arms to the rebels to support their campaign against the ANC. The Algerian chargé d'affaires pointed out to American Embassy officials in Algiers that the 'US-Belgian action had perhaps dealt mortal blow to OAU since it [is] clear now that great powers could always take matters into its own hands in Africa if it saw fit'.[92] Washington could do little to fend off this attack from all sides except pressure moderate regimes such as Nigeria and the Governments of those countries whose hostages had been rescued to speak out to limit this damage to the Western position.

The stakes of this debate were considerable. In retaliation for the intervention, rebel groups in other provinces exercised vicious retribution on so-called 'intellectuals' – Congolese who had more than six years of education – alongside plantation workers, foreign advisors from Malay and Indonesia, and the remaining European populations.[93] Operation Dragon Rouge was initially planned alongside another mission code-named Operation Dragon Noir, which was a similar airdrop plan to rescue other Europeans held hostage at Bunia, Niangara, Paulis and Watsa in the Orientale province in Eastern Congo. Despite the criticism of the Stanleyville operation, the first leg of the mission in Paulis went ahead on 25 November with the understanding that it was to last no longer than twenty-four hours and the force should 'not under any circumstances delay its departure from Paulis to permit ANC to reoccupy city'.[94] This time the Belgian paratroopers encountered sustained resistance; one was killed and five were wounded. Although 200 foreign refugees, including an American woman and her three children, were evacuated, sixteen hostages and one American missionary were killed in 'extremely brutal circumstances'. Facing the prospect of similar reprisals in Bunia, Niagara and Watsa where hundreds more European hostages were being held, Belgian, British and American military advisors realised that they would need support from the ANC in order to safely remove the remaining hostages, estimated to be around 1,000 men, women and children. They devised a plan which recommended launching three ANC columns to attack Watsa from different directions, but which again required the agreement of Mobutu.[95] Notably, all ANC columns were to contain mercenary spearheads and, as distinct from the Stanleyville airlift, this operation was designed in direct cooperation with the ANC suppression of the rebels, leaving no doubt as to the intentions behind the intervention. Following the storm of protest at the UN, however, these plans were later abandoned, leaving the remaining hostages to their own fate.

Together with the African group, the Afro-Asian bloc organised a committee to press fervently for a formal Security Council condemnation of Belgium, Britain and the US. Unable to prevent the question coming before the Security Council, the US and Britain worked behind the scenes drafting a resolution designed to protect or improve their position, which called for recognition of Article 3 of the Geneva Convention and urged the immediate release of all hostages and for respect for the rights of all persons involved in the conflict.[96] British and American representatives negotiated the resolution with the Ivory Coast and Morocco in the hope of persuading moderate African opinion to carry the vote on their resolution. The Ivory Coast agreed to sponsor the resolution in order to prevent the Congo issue from becoming a litmus test separating 'African' (revolutionary) from 'neo-colonialist' (moderate) Governments, but remained adamant that the use of mercenaries was a 'gross political mistake'.[97] Having secured limited lines of cooperation at the UN, the State Department further instructed the Embassy in Léopoldville that it was essential that Tshombe did not reject or violate any Security Council resolution, because if he were to do so he would give enemies of Congo a basis for continuing assistance to rebels.[98] By this point it was increasingly evident to American and British officials both at the UN and across Africa, that the rebels had the moral support of a significant portion of African and Asian states.

Despite the careful orchestration of the American reaction to this public critique, and the repeated insistence by Brussels, London and Washington that the intervention was a humanitarian mission, internally, the racial dimensions of the operation also began to play out in American politics. On 30 November Charles O.P. Howard, editor-in-chief of the Howard News syndicate, sent a telegram to President Johnson reflecting the bitter resentment among African-Americans that 'one penny of their tax money' would be spent entertaining Tshombe, 'the man who stands accused of the murder of the first Prime Minister of the Congo and the man at whose direction thousands of Congolese have been brutally murdered by United States paid "white mercenaries"'. Pointing to the self-determination record of the US he called for the reversal of American Congo policy.[99] Similar criticism emanated from the International Committee in Defence of Africa, an advocacy group for African-Americans who viewed American action of saving white hostages while leaving thousands of black Congolese to be slaughtered as reflective of attitudes towards racial issues at home.

Publicly, however, at the White House and the UN, the Johnson administration insisted that the mission had only been used to rescue hostages and was not part of a wider strategy to crush the Simba rebellion. The State Department also tried to deflect criticism from the Afro-Asians by encouraging Britain to defend the operation more forcefully, pointing to the dangers the situation posed for the Cold War.[100] The British shared the American view and in UN negotiations with Commonwealth members such as Canada, British representatives were at pains to stress that if the Africans themselves had been more constructive, foreign intervention may have been avoided.[101] In an effort to secure the support of Commonwealth members for a more moderate resolution, they pressed that the coherence of the Commonwealth was also at stake in the Security Council debate. For their part, British policymakers were keen to avoid further public condemnation, which was damaging to relations with African states and their remaining plans for decolonisation.[102]

By 2 December the storm continued unabated. Sixteen African countries signed a letter requesting a Security Council meeting and it was recognised in London and Washington that the African states were determined to position the issue as a broader critique of Western policies in Africa. The British representatives at the UN spelled this out clearly, reporting to Whitehall that 'the impression here is that the Africans have no clear objectives other than to condemn [the] Belgian, United States and United Kingdom "intervention"'.[103] The new British Foreign Secretary Gordon Walker further relayed that the 'present situation in the UN was very bad'.[104] Even

Thant rebuffed suggestions from American and British representatives that he send a Special Representative to Stanleyville in order to cast a UN veil over the operation.[105] He ruled out any further UN involvement in internal Congolese politics as he did not believe that 'any further action by the United Nations at this stage could be effective'.[106]

The intervention also had the effect of souring relations with the USSR even further. Pointing to the Russian supply of arms to the Stanleyville rebels, the US argued that the rebellion itself destabilised Congo and threatened to turn the civil war into a Cold War conflict. On 7 December, the Soviet Minister of Foreign Affairs Andrei Gromyko condemned the neo-colonialist intervention which hardened Russian attitudes towards the resumption of financial contributions to the UN. Moscow had suspended payments in 1961 in protest against UN policy in Congo following the assassination of Lumumba. In a meeting with Walker, Gromyko attributed the failure of the USSR to deliver its contribution to the UN to the politics of the operation in Congo. He declared that: 'In no circumstances would the Soviet Government pay expenses incurred as a result of colonial policies; if they did they might be asked to pay for the Belgian paratroopers who had gone into the Congo.' Walker continued to deny that the intervention had been an effort to impose a military solution on the Congo and attempted to play on the Sino-Soviet split by pointing out that it was the Chinese who were 'causing the most trouble of all'. However, it was clear that the mission damaged the stability of the UN, setting back negotiations with Moscow on financial contributions and inflaming Cold War tensions.[107]

The debate about the Stanleyville intervention raged over seventeen meetings. On 15 December, the new British Ambassador to the UN Hugh Foot continued to hold to the joint Anglo-American position, delivering a strongly worded speech defending the action in Stanleyville, and echoing State Department sentiments that the resolution of the Congo's difficulties had to come from within the Congo itself and not from outside interference, or be hampered by the interference of other African nations.[108] With Soviet support, however, the African and Asian states held their ground. Between 9 and 17 December, an increasing number of African nations were invited to participate in the discussion (without the right to vote) on the Security Council. Among them were some of the loudest critics of British and American policy, including Algeria, Guinea, Ghana, Uganda, Tanzania and the UAR. During one meeting, the Algerian representative surmised the general view of the African states when he declared the illegality of the military action which had been 'aimed at repressing the insurrection of the Congolese people against a government which was merely an agent in the hands of the old colonial powers'.[109] By the time of the vote on 30 December twenty-one states in the Afro-Asian bloc considered the arguments of humanitarian intervention as a pretext for neo-colonialism.[110] The Security Council legitimised these views, roundly condemning the Stanleyville intervention with the final vote. Resolution 199 '*deplored* the recent events', reaffirmed the sovereignty of the Congo and called for 'all States to refrain or desist from intervening in the domestic affairs of the Congo'.[111]

The resolution was highly significant for the Afro-Asian bloc as it was the first time it had succeeded in using both moral and legal arguments to condemn Western policies in the Congo and in Africa as a whole. The violation of the international norms regarding the use of force and the contravention of Congolese sovereignty indicated the extent to which both the US and Britain were willing to go in pursuit of their neo-colonial agenda in the Congo. Crucially, the intervention revealed to other African states the hegemonic nature of Anglo-American internationalism in Africa, and the willingness of London and Washington to use humanitarian reasoning as a pretext for intervention. There were long-term effects for the relationship with African states, as the validity of arguments about rescuing nationals abroad became shrouded in ambiguity until the end of the Cold War. In addition, the once sacrosanct nature of sovereignty had now been converted into an increasingly nebulous idea in the context of Africa.

The Mobutu coup

Throughout most of 1963, although the UN was in control of Elisabethville and simultaneously providing social and economic support to the Central Government in Léopoldville, behind-the-scenes negotiations were taking place between the State Department and General Mobutu, which would produce one of Africa's longest-serving dictators and profoundly influence the development of the Congolese state for decades to come. From the beginning of the crisis, the US had found an ally in Joseph-Desiré Mobutu, the Chief of Staff of the ANC. He maintained good relations with the US in particular due to his determination to stamp out all Soviet influence in the country and his cooperation with CIA Chief Larry Devlin in doing so. In a conversation with the General on 31 May 1963, Kennedy thanked Mobutu for his efforts in reintegrating Katanga, remarking: 'General, if it hadn't been for you, the whole thing would have collapsed and the Communists would have taken over.'[112] There were plenty of early signs of Mobutu's eventual second successful coup which would to bring him to power in 1965 as a military dictator, a position he would hold until 1997, in the process bleeding the country dry of most of its wealth and natural resources. By the end of December 1964, rumours were already rife among Congolese politicians about what the US would do next in the Congo.[113]

Elections in March 1965 produced a majority for an alliance of Congolese parties led by Tshombe, referred to as the Congolese National Convention. In spite of this result, however, Kasavubu appointed Evariste Kimba, a critic of Tshombe, as his Prime Minister. The largely pro-Tshombe parliament refused to ratify the selection of Kimba, landing the Central Government once again in a political vacuum similar to that which had existed in September 1960.[114] The Department of State was concerned that the election would return of some of the rebel leaders, such as Gbenye and Soumialot, to power and therefore that the paralysed situation would lead to further uprisings or, worst of all, that the rebels would be adopted into the Government.[115] In the run up to the coup, there was a fluster of negotiations between Kasavubu, Mobutu and Tshombe, and rumours circulated once more that Mobutu was 'planning a new edition of his 1960 exploit'.[116] These fears proved correct on 25 November when Mobutu seized power in a bloodless coup, following which he declared an end to all party political activity in the Congo for at least five years.

Godley immediately advised the State Department that it was important that the US should not give the impression that it had anything to do with the coup.[117] He stressed that American prestige in Congo and in Africa would now be linked to the success of the Congo under Mobutu as more than any of his predecessors, he was known to have strong ties with the US. He emphasised, 'We have good chance of influencing Mobutu ... Without giving his regime a "made in America" label ... we must set to work to influence and form policy in pro-Western but non-aligned and pro-African direction'.[118] He also stressed that he had no objection to Mobutu working 'hand in glove' with the Belgians.

The result of the clearly orchestrated American–Belgian coup was quickly greeted by 'relief and satisfaction' among Belgian politicians including Spaak and the Belgian business community.[119] On explaining their privately warm but publicly distant position to Mobutu he apparently burst out laughing. He told the Belgian Ambassador De Kerchove that he intended to establish the same type of relationship between Léopoldville and Brussels as that which existed between ex-British and French colonies and their respective former metropoles.[120] Tshombe and Kasavubu and other politicians such as Victor Nendaka generally responded positively to the coup but expressed concern over the five-year term of office. Indeed, the announcement allegedly came as a shock even to his Prime Minister designate Mulamba, and although it was welcomed as a method of stabilising the country, it proved to be the ideal foundation for the establishment of Mobutu's thirty-one-year dictatorship.[121] For their part, many other African countries immediately viewed the coup with well-founded suspicion.[122] For the US and Britain, however, the kaleidoscopic Congo finally seemed to have settled on a political constellation favourable to their interests.

The Stanleyville intervention, the violation of Congolese sovereignty, and the sanctioned use of mercenaries and military and political support of Tshombe was considered by many African countries an act of imperialist aggression. It was regarded a breach of the prohibition to use force in international relations, which could barely be justified by the mere acquiescence of the Congolese Government.[123] Indeed the Security Council and twenty-one African states condemned the actions of Belgium, Britain and the US in Resolution 199.[124] The debate signified the extent to which the Afro-Asian bloc could dominate international discussions and represents their increased recourse to the UN in pursuit of their agenda. In seizing upon the organisation as a means to wield legal and racial arguments against Western powers, African states also had an opportunity to create consensus and cohesion with regard to the question of when humanitarian intervention was justified.

For Britain, fears that instability created by the Congo crisis would spill over and damage relations with other African states were realised on 11 November 1965 when Rhodesia, led by the white minority leader Ian Smith, issued a unilateral declaration of independence. Throughout the crisis Rhodesia had threatened independence as the best way to safeguard the white minority regime.[125] The declaration was unprecedented for a British colony and provoked further criticism of British African policy. Denouncing it, Nkrumah even called on other African states to unite and lead an armed force against Smith's regime. The UN further condemned the unilateral declaration of independence and imposed sanctions on Rhodesia in two Security Council Resolutions in December 1965.[126] The declaration threatened the stability of other former British colonies, including Zambia, which supplied 40 per cent of British copper requirements. The question of whether or not to impose sanctions on Rhodesia also presented another problem in that it might set a precedent for similar actions against South Africa in retaliation for the policy of apartheid, which would be very damaging to Britain's total overseas investments.[127] It also negatively affected Commonwealth relations, when Britain failed to pursue sanctions against Rhodesia as vigorously as other members demanded.[128] The illusion of a Commonwealth of equal members, as commonly promoted by British Governments during this period, was gradually exposed as being increasingly at odds with their African policies. At the same time, the utility of the Commonwealth at the UN was becoming negligible and ties with African members faced increasing strain. As the State Department reflected internally on the matter, 'In handling the Rhodesian affair, Britain's main problem continues to be that of maintaining the existing multi-racial Commonwealth. Those Commonwealth ties are weak and becoming less meaningful'.[129]

As Britain sought to protect the Commonwealth by directing efforts towards managing relations with South Africa, Rhodesia and Uganda, the US turned its focus to waging war in Vietnam. Anglo-American cooperation on African issues such as the wars in Algeria, Angola and later the struggle against apartheid in South Africa, did not have the same prominence in relations between Washington and London as the Congo crisis. In addition, the nature of Anglo-American cooperation in Africa had subtly changed. In January 1966 the State Department took stock of its relationship with Britain vis-à-vis America's policy towards Africa, recognising that 'No longer is the UK the "workshop" of the world'. As the Congo experience had shown repeatedly, Britain's ability to wield influence among former colonies was increasingly limited. The US now sought to assess whether Britain's declining role in Africa would create new opportunities or new burdens for American policy. Policy-planners advised that 'the US should develop for itself an independent and more flexible role in British Africa'.[130] 'Britain's difficulties at home and abroad are not only economic and politico-military, but psychological as well. She may also move toward approving or tacitly condoning greater involvement of the UN in African affairs than she has previously been willing to accept.'[131]

The Congo experience highlighted the important role of the UN in Africa and the limitations of Anglo-American cooperation on colonial issues to both the US and Britain. The UN political and military operation revealed the problems inherent in managing a large peacekeeping force, preventing the eruption of a full-blown Cold War conflict and simultaneously balancing Western objectives with the aims of the Afro-Asian bloc, on whose support ONUC relied so heavily. The State Department's efforts to build relations with the Congo and other Afro-Asian leaders, alongside its programme of bilateral aid and interference in internal Congolese politics, ultimately served to reify its Cold War objectives in Africa. For the Foreign Office, however, the Rhodesian unilateral declaration of independence had demonstrated the extent to which the Congo crisis spilled over into other areas of decolonisation policy and the revelation of diminishing British influence at the UN showed how much the organisation had been changed by the crisis. At the root of their reflections on the Congo crisis, their visions of the role and utility of the UN in managing the decolonisation process and ordering the world remained fundamentally different.

Notes

1 GPL, BAA/RLAA/691, 'Republic of Congo': Newspaper Clippings (Congo), Jan 1963, Bureau of African Affairs, 'Wire report', *Reuters* (18 January 1963). Agreement handing over the last remaining bases in Katanga signed by Tshombe, George Sherry, the UN Civil Chief in Elisabethville and Major Prem Chand, Commander of UN forces in Katanga.
2 NAL, FO 371/167314, Copy of records of a Meeting of the Congo Advisory Committee, 20 March 1963.
3 NAL, FO 371/167314, Comments of Ralph Bunche to Sir P. Dean, United Kingdom Mission to the United Nations in New York to the Foreign Office, 22 March 1963.
4 NAL, PREM 11/4084, Telegram from Riches in Léopoldville to the Foreign Office, 9 January 1963.
5 NAL, PREM 11/4084, Telegram translating the note from the Congolese Ministry of Foreign Affairs in Léopoldville to the Foreign Office, 10 January 1963.
6 NAL, FO 317/167311, C. Brady, 'Wreckers storm embassy', *Daily Mail* (16 January 1963).
7 NAL, PREM 11/4084, Draft message from the Prime Minster to Kennedy, 11 January 1963.
8 GPL, BAA/RLAA/691, 'Republic of Congo': Newspaper Clippings (Congo) 1963, Bureau of African Affairs, 'Wire report', *Reuters* (23 January 1963).
9 GPL, BAA/RLAA/690, 'Republic of Congo': Newspaper Clippings (Congo) 1963, Bureau of African Affairs, 'Wire report', *Reuters* (4 March 1963).
10 NAL, FO 141/6935, Letter from the British representative in Kampala to the Governor of Kenya, Nairobi, 2 January 1963.
11 NAL, PREM 11/4084, Letter from the Ugandan Prime Minister in Entebbe, to the British Secretary of State, 7 January 1963.
12 NAL, PREM 11/4564, Report from Patrick Dean on Commonwealth consultation at the UN, 25 September 1963.
13 GPL, BAA/RLAA/690, 'Republic of Congo': Newspaper Clippings (Congo) 1963, Bureau of African Affairs, 'Wire report', *Reuters* (8 February 1963).
14 NAL, PREM11/4564, Note from the Foreign Office to the Prime Minister, 27 September 1963.
15 For more on this see Holt, 'Lord Home and Anglo-American relations', 706.
16 NAL, PREM 11/4584, R. Crossman, 'Mr Macmillan snubbed by Mr Kennedy', *Sunday Mirror* (19 May 1963).

17 NAL, PREM 11/4586, White House Press Conference with McGeorge Bundy and Pierre Salinger, 4 July 1963.
18 NAL, PREM 11/4563, Personal letter from Philip de Zulueta to McGeorge Bundy, 23 July 1963.
19 NARA, Subject Numeric Files, State Department, RG59, Central Foreign Policy Files, 1963, Box 4066, File: POL 27-3 Military Operations The Congo, File Political Affairs and Rels, POL 27-4 Military Operations, 3/1/63, Telegram recounting discussions between Stevenson and Duncan Wilson, Assistant Under Secretary UK Foreign Office, London, to the State Department, 30 March 1963.
20 Memo from Williams to Rusk, 7 March 1963, Schwar, *FRUS, XX, Congo*, p. 840. Williams points out that the Cleveland Report indicated that the Congolese economy should be encouraged to be self-sustaining, given the amount of resources in the Congo and that this could take place within the next two years.
21 *Ibid.*
22 NARA, Subject Numeric Files, State Department, RG59, Central Foreign Policy Files, 1963, Box, 4065, File – Pol 22, Military Operations, The Congo, Report 'Proposals for U.S. Policy in the Congo', by a mission headed by Harlan Cleveland, Assistant Secretary for International Organization Affairs, 20 February 1963. The so-called 'Cleveland Report' was a policy planning document for further US policy in the Congo, produced by Harlan Cleveland after his visit to the Congo in February 1963.
23 *Ibid.*, p. 81.
24 *Ibid.*, p. 103.
25 NARA, Subject Numeric Files, State Department, RG59, Central Foreign Policy Files, 1963, Box, 4065, File – Pol 22, Summary of US Recommendations for a programme of international assistance to the Congo, 1 March 1963.
26 Conversation with between Thant, Stevenson, Yost and Cleveland as detailed in Memorandum from the Assistant Secretary of State for International Organization Affairs Harlan Cleveland to the Undersecretary of State George Ball, 16 December 1962, Schwar, *FRUS, XX, Congo*, p. 742.
27 NAL, PREM 13/16, Record of a Conversation between Under-Secretary of State Harriman and the Foreign Secretary at the State Department, 26 October 1964.
28 NAL, PREM 11/4565, Note from Harold Macmillan to the Secretary of State for Foreign Affairs, 13 February 1963.
29 NAL, PREM 11/4565, Private note from de Zulueta to the Prime Minister, 25 July 1961.
30 NAL, PREM 11/4565, Confidential telegram from the Foreign Office to the UK Mission to the UN, 8 March 1963.
31 Namikas, *Battleground Africa*, p. 186.
32 Memo from the Assistant Secretary of State for African Affairs, Williams, to the Secretary of State Rusk, Washington, 7 March 1963, Schwar, *FRUS, XX, Congo*, p. 841.
33 NARA, Subject Numeric Files, State Department, RG59, Central Foreign Policy Files, Box 3874, File: POL 27, Military Operations Congo, 2/1/1963, Telegram from the American Embassy in Quito to the State Department, 10 October 1963.
34 NARA, Subject Numeric Files, State Department, RG59, Central Foreign Policy Files, Box 4065, File: POL 26, Rebellion, Coups, Insurgency, Telegram from Elisabethville to State Department detailing the death of eighty-four individuals in a massacre in Jadotville, 20 April 1963.

35 GPL, BAA/RLAA/690, 'Republic of Congo': Newspaper Clippings (Congo) 1963, Bureau of African Affairs, 'Wire report', *Reuters* (12 February 1963).
36 NARA, Subject Numeric Files, State Department, RG59, Central Foreign Policy Files, Box 4065, File- POL 26, Rebellion, Coups, Insurgency, Ambassador Guillon, American Embassy Léopoldville, to Secretary of State, 30 October 1963.
37 NARA, Subject Numeric Files, State Department, RG59, Central Foreign Policy Files, Box 3874, File: POL 27, Military Operations Congo, 2/1/1963, Telegram from Brazzaville to State Department, 16 November 1963.
38 NAL, PREM 13/16, Telegram from Brussels to the Foreign Office, 30 November 1964.
39 Namikas, *Battleground Africa*, p. 191.
40 NARA, Subject Numeric Files, State Department, RG59, Central Foreign Policy Files, Box 2721, File: POL 23-9 Rebellion, Coups the Congo, 6/8/64, Telegram from American embassy in Kampala to State Department recounting discussion with Odaka, 7 August 1964.
41 NARA, Subject Numeric Files, State Department, RG59, Central Foreign Policy Files, Box 2721, File: POL 23-9 Rebellion, Coups the Congo, 8/8/64, Telegram from CINCAFSTRIKE to Department of State, 10 August 1964.
42 NARA, Subject Numeric Files, State Department, RG59, Central Foreign Policy Files, Box 2721, File: POL 23-9 Rebellion, Coups the Congo, 6/8/64, Telegram recounting a discussion with British Embassy Officer Neilson in which he showed American Embassy official Godley the details of a letter received from Millard, recounting the details of Colvin's interview of Soumialot, 7 August 1964.
43 LOC, Averell Harriman Papers, Subject Files, Congo, Special Files: Public Service, Kennedy/Administrations, 1958-1971, Box 448, Folder 5, Subject File Congo (1), Memorandum on Chinese Communist involvement in the Congo, undated. A memorandum on Chinese Communist involvement in the Congo noted that Mulele had 'received training in communist China itself'.
44 PRAAD, RG 17/2/232, Political Reports from Léopoldville, 8/1/64-7/3/64, RG 17/2, Special Collection Bureau of African Affairs (SC/BAA) RG 17, Memo for Osagyefo, Mutiny in the freedom fighters military camp, Kinkuzu, Congo from M.F. Dei-Anang.
45 NARA, Subject Numeric Files, State Department, RG59, Central Foreign Policy Files, Box 2714, File: POL 23-9 Rebellion, Coups The Congo 2/1/64, Telegram from Ambassador Guillon, American Embassy Léopoldville to State Department, 31 January 1964. Although curiously this invincible quality did not extend to bullets from the air, which the Jeunesse accepted would still kill them. See also F.R. Villafana, *Cold War in the Congo: The Confrontation of Cuban Military Forces, 1960-1967* (New Brunswick: Transaction Publishers, 2012), pp. 69-70.
46 NARA, Subject Numeric Files, State Department, RG59, Central Foreign Policy Files, Box 2729, File POL 23-9 the Congo 11/30/64, Memorandum of Conversation, Department of State, November 30, 1964. The rebels believed that a 'magic medicine' could be bestowed upon them by their witch doctors and would protect them from bullets as long as they remained celibate, honest and were not touched by anyone who was not. Evidence of the rebels' belief in witch-doctors, magic potions and the reports that Congolese soldiers fled in fear from them comes from a statement of a Methodist medical missionary, Dr William S. Hughlett, who was evacuated from Northern Congo on 15 October.

47 NARA, State Department, Subject Numeric Files, RG59, Central Foreign Policy Files, Box 2714, File: POL 23-9 Rebellion, Coups The Congo 2/1/64, Telegram from the American Embassy in Brussels to the State Department, 19 February 1964. Augueste Gerard, a high-ranking official from the Societe Generale, conducted a fact-finding mission to Congo in January 1964 and presented his results including this characterisation of the rebellion to the American embassy in Brussels.

48 NARA, State Department, Subject Numeric Files, RG59, Central Foreign Policy Files, Box 2714, File: POL 23-9 Rebellion, Coups The Congo 2/1/64, Memorandum for the Secretary of Defense, Subject: Retraining of the Congolese National Army, 30 January 1964.

49 'The Americans wanted the Belgians to take the lead in the Congo–the lead, that is, in executing Washington's policy. Belgium cooperated.' P. Gleijeses, ' "Flee! The white giants are coming!": the United States, the mercenaries, and the Congo, 1964–65', *Diplomatic History*, 18:2 (1994), 226.

50 NARA, State Department, Subject Numeric Files, RG59, Central Foreign Policy Files, Box 2721, File: POL 23-9 Rebellion, Coups the Congo, 6/8/64, Telegram from Rusk in the State Department to the American Embassy in Brussels with instructions for communications with Belgian officials, 6 August 1964.

51 NARA, State Department, Subject Numeric Files, RG59, Central Foreign Policy Files, Box 2721, File: POL 23-9 Rebellion, Coups the Congo, 6/8/64, Telegram from the Department of State to the American Embassy in Léopoldville, 7 August 1964.

52 NARA, State Department, Subject Numeric Files, RG59, Central Foreign Policy Files, Box 2721, File: POL 23-9 Rebellion, Coups the Congo, 16/8/64, Memorandum for McGeorge Bundy, The White House, from Averell Harriman, State Department, 17 August 1964.

53 *Ibid*.

54 NARA, State Department, Subject Numeric Files, RG59, Central Foreign Policy Files, Box 2721, File: POL 23-9 Rebellion, Coups the Congo, 16/8/64, Telegram from Rusk in the State Department to USUN, New York, 17 August 1964.

55 NARA, State Department, Subject Numeric Files, RG59, Central Foreign Policy Files, Box 2722, File: POL 23-9 Rebellion, Coups the Congo, 23/8/64, Statement of the Somali Government's position on the Congo situation, from US Embassy Mogadiscio, 25 August 1964.

56 NARA, State Department, Subject Numeric Files, RG59, Central Foreign Policy Files, Box 2722, File: POL 23-9 Rebellion, Coups the Congo, 23/8/64, Telegram from Leonhart, American Embassy Dar-es-Salaam, recounting conversation with Nyerere on Congo, 28 August 1964.

57 NARA, State Department, Subject Numeric Files, RG59, Central Foreign Policy Files, Box 2722, File: POL 23-9 Rebellion, Coups the Congo, 23/8/64, Telegram from Loure, American Embassy in Conakry, to State Department, 26 August 1966.

58 Namikas, *Battleground Africa*, p. 194.

59 *Ibid*., p. 198.

60 NARA, State Department, Subject Numeric Files, RG59, Central Foreign Policy Files, Box 2721, File: POL 23-9 Rebellion, Coups the Congo, 16/8/64, Telegram from American Embassy in Lusaka to State Department, 1 August 1964.

61 Gleijeses, ' "Flee! The white giants are coming!" ', 227.

62 UNA, S-0888-0006-08, U Thant Secretary-General Files, Records of the Office for Special Political Affairs, Report by the Secretary-General on the withdrawal of the United Nations force in the Congo and of Other Aspects of the operation there.
63 NARA, State Department, Subject Numeric Files, RG59, Central Foreign Policy Files, Box 2721, File: POL 23-9 Rebellion, Coups the Congo, 16/8/64, Telegram from Rusk to the American Embassy in Léopoldville, 6 August 1964.
64 For example, the selection of a Belgian diplomat to serve as the Head of the Bureau for Economic Affairs in Léopoldville drew widespread accusations of neo-colonialism from the anti-Tshombe politicians. Kent, *America, the UN and Decolonisation*, p. 201.
65 J.H. Michaels, 'Breaking the rules: the CIA and counterinsurgency in the Congo 1964-1965', *International Journal of Intelligence and Counterintelligence*, 25:1 (2012), 148.
66 One official of the American embassy in Léopoldville, as quoted in Gleijeses, ' "Flee! The white giants are coming" ', 211.
67 NAL, PREM 13/16, Conversation between the Prime Minister and Mr Botsio, the Foreign Minister of Ghana at 10 Downing Street, 23 November 1964.
68 NARA, State Department, Subject Numeric Files, RG59, Central Foreign Policy Files, Box 2727, File: POL 23-9 The Congo, Telegram from American Embassy in Léopoldville, recounting the telegram they received from Hoyt in Stanleyville, 20 November 1964.
69 NARA, State Department, Subject Numeric Files, RG59, Central Foreign Policy Files, Box 2727, File: POL 23-9 The Congo, Telegram from Godley in the American Embassy in Léopoldville to State Department, 20 November 1964.
70 NARA, State Department, Subject Numeric Files, RG59, Central Foreign Policy Files, Box 2727, File: POL 23-9 The Congo, Joint message from American and Belgian Embassies in Léopoldville, 21 November 1964.
71 NARA, State Department, Subject Numeric Files, RG59, Central Foreign Policy Files, Box 2727, File: POL 23-9 The Congo, Telegram from Ball in the State Department to the American Embassy in Brussels, laying out the precise instructions for Dragon Rouge, 20 November 1964.
72 NARA, State Department, Subject Numeric Files, RG59, Central Foreign Policy Files, Box 2727, File: POL 23-9 The Congo, Telegram from Godley in the American Embassy in Léopoldville to the State Department, 23 November 1964.
73 NARA, State Department, Subject Numeric Files, RG59, Central Foreign Policy Files, Box 2722, File: POL 23-9 Rebellion, Coups the Congo, 23/8/64, Telegram from the American Embassy in Léopoldville to State Department, 23 August 1964.
74 NARA, State Department, Subject Numeric Files, RG59, Central Foreign Policy Files, Box 2727, File: POL 23-9 the Congo, Letter from Tshombe to Godley, 21 November 1964.
75 NARA, State Department, Subject Numeric Files, RG59, Central Foreign Policy Files, Box 2727, File: POL 23-9 the Congo, Incoming telegram from the American Embassy in Léopoldville to the State Department, recounting a discussion with Kasavubu and Mobutu on the wording of the official letter, 21 November 1964.

76 NARA, State Department, Subject Numeric Files, RG59, Central Foreign Policy Files, Box 2713, File: POL 23-8 The Congo, Letter from President Johnson to Kwame Nkrumah, 7 October 1964.
77 NARA, State Department, Subject Numeric Files, RG59, Central Foreign Policy Files, Box 2727, File: POL 23-9 the Congo, Telegram from Attwood in Nairobi to Secretary of State, 21 November 1964.
78 NAL, PREM 13/16, Telegram to the Commonwealth Relations Office from Nairobi, 13 November 1964.
79 UNA, S-0279, Box 3, File 19, Congo_ Stanleyville Incidents - Missionaries, November 1964, African Group Press Conference, 25 November 1964.
80 LOC, Averell Harriman Papers, Box 448, Subject Files, Congo, Special Files: Public Service, Kennedy/Administrations, 1958-1971, Folder 5, Subject File Congo (1), Telephone conversation between Harriman and Rusk, 20 November 1964.
81 NAL, PREM 13/16, Record of conversation between Dr Kaunda, the President of the Republic of Zambia and the Prime Minister, at 10 Downing Street, 13 November 1964.
82 NAL, PREM 13/16, Note for the Record, 'Trouble in Stanleyville', 12 November 1964.
83 LOC, Averell Harriman Papers, Box 448, Subject Files, Congo, Special Files: Public Service, Kennedy/Administrations, 1958-1971, Folder 5, Subject File Congo (1), Telephone conversation between Harriman and Williams, 24 November 1964.
84 NARA, State Department, Subject Numeric Files, RG59, Central Foreign Policy Files, Box 2731, File: POL 23-9 the Congo 12/30/64, Telegram from Attwood in Nairobi to Secretary of State, 30 December 1964. In it he recounts an interview with Thomas Kanza in the *Nairobi East African Standard* on 28 December in which Kanza describes that Carlson's death occurred during the landing of the paratroopers when the European hostages started running to the airport. According to him, 'Bullet that hit him could have been Belgian or Nationalist'.
85 L. De Witte, 'The suppression of the Congo rebellions and the rise of Mobutu, 1963-5', *The International History Review*, 39:1 (2017), 107-125.
86 NAL, PREM 13/16, Confidential note for the Prime Minister outlining the British position on the Stanleyville intervention, 25 November 1964.
87 NAL, PREM 13/16, Telegram from the British Embassy in Algiers to the Foreign Office reporting the statement of Ben Bella, 25 November 1964.
88 NARA, State Department, Subject Numeric Files, RG59, Central Foreign Policy Files, Box 2728, File: POL 23-9 the Congo 11/24/64, Telegram from American Embassy in Léopoldville, to Department of State, 24 November 1964.
89 NARA, State Department, Subject Numeric Files, RG59, Central Foreign Policy Files, Box 2728, File: POL 23-9 the Congo 11/27/64, Outgoing telegram from Department of State to all diplomatic posts, 27 November 1964.
90 NARA, State Department, Subject Numeric Files, RG59, Central Foreign Policy Files, Box 2729, File: POL 23-9 the Congo 11/25/64, Stevenson in New York, to Secretary of State, Washington, 25 November 1964.
91 NARA, State Department, Subject Numeric Files, RG59, Central Foreign Policy Files, Box 2729, File: POL 23-9 the Congo 11/30/64, Memorandum of conversation at USUN between Secretary John Dorman, Bureau of African Affairs, State Department

and Joseph Anthony Zuzarte Murumbi, Minister of State, Prime Minister's Office, Kenya, 30 November 1964.
92 NARA, State Department, Subject Numeric Files, RG59, Central Foreign Policy Files, Box 2728, File: POL 23-9 the Congo 11/27/64, Telegram from State Department to the American Embassy in Algiers recounting the statements of views of the Algerian Charge d'Affaires, 27 November 1964.
93 NARA, State Department, Subject Numeric Files, RG59, Central Foreign Policy Files, Box 2729, File: POL 23-9 the Congo 12/09/64, Press conference given by Congolese Ambassador to Nigeria, Mr Gervais Bahizi, 26 November 1964. Among those killed was Jason Sendwe, the Governor of North Katanga.
94 NARA, State Department, Subject Numeric Files, RG59, Central Foreign Policy Files, Box 2729, File: POL 23-9 the Congo 11/25/64, Outgoing telegram from Department of State to American Embassies in Brussels and Léopoldville, 25 November 1964.
95 NARA, State Department, Subject Numeric Files, RG59, Central Foreign Policy Files, Box 2728, File: POL 23-9 the Congo 11/27/64, Incoming telegram from Godley in Léopoldville to the Department of State 27 November 1964.
96 NARA, State Department, Subject Numeric Files, RG59, Central Foreign Policy Files, Box 2729, File: POL 23-9 the Congo 12/09/64, Telegram from the Department of State to USUN, 9 December 1964.
97 NARA, State Department, Subject Numeric Files, RG59, Central Foreign Policy Files, Box 2728, POL- 1 General Policy Background, the Congo, 1/1/64, Telegram on 'GOIC Views on the Congo problem' from Leslie L. Rood, Counselor of American Embassy in Abidjan, 21 November 1964.
98 NARA, State Department, Subject Numeric Files, RG59, Central Foreign Policy Files, Box 2731, File: POL 23-9 the Congo 12/26/64, Telegram from Department of State to American Embassy Léopoldville, 28 December 1964.
99 NARA, State Department, Subject Numeric Files, RG59, Central Foreign Policy Files, Box 2730, File: POL 23-9 the Congo 12/15/64, Telegram from Charles P. Howard to President Johnson, 30 November 1964.
100 NAL, PREM 13/16, Confidential telegram from Washington to the Foreign Office, 11 December 1964.
101 NAL, PREM 13/104, Record of meeting between British and Canadian officials at the Canadian Parliament which included Commonwealth Secretary Arthur Bottomley and Canadian Secretary of State for External Affairs, Paul Martin, 9 December 1964.
102 *Ibid.*
103 NAL, PREM 13/16, Telegram from the UK Mission to the UN in New York, to the Foreign Office, 2 December 1964. NAL, PREM 13/16, Confidential telegram from New York to the Foreign Office recounting discussion with U Thant, 3 December 1964.
104 NAL, PREM 13/104, Record of a Conversation between the Foreign Secretary Gordon Walker and Mr Gromyko, the Foreign Minister of the USSR at the Soviet Embassy in Washington, 9 December 1964.
105 NAL, PREM 13/16, Telegram floating the idea of approaching U Thant, from the Foreign Office to Washington, 30 November 1964.
106 NAL, PREM 13/16, Confidential telegram from New York to the Foreign Office recounting discussion with U Thant, 3 December 1964.

107 NAL, PREM 13/104, Record of a Conversation between the Foreign Secretary Gordon Walker and Mr Gromyko, the Foreign Minister of the USSR at the Soviet Embassy in Washington, 9 December 1964. For more on the Chinese role in supporting the Stanleyville rebels and the effect of the Sino-Soviet split, see Namikas, *Battleground Africa*, pp. 194–196.

108 NAL, PREM 13/16, Text of a speech delivered by the UK permanent Representative at the UN, Sir Hugh Foot, to the UN Security Council, 15 December 1964.

109 Algerian representative speaking at the UN Security Council, 1183rd meeting, 22 December 1964. As quoted in N. Ronzitti, *Rescuing Nationals Abroad Through Military Coercion and Intervention on the Grounds of Humanity* (Dordrecht and Boston: Martinus Nijhoff Publishers, 1985), p. 83.

110 See S. Chesterman, *Just War or Just Peace? Humanitarian Intervention and International Law* (Oxford: Oxford University Press, 2001), p. 69.

111 Emphasis in the original. Security Council Resolution 199, [S/6129] 30 December 1964: 'Requests all states to refrain or desist from intervening in the domestic affairs of the Congo; Appeals for a cease-fire in the Congo in accordance with the resolution of the Organisation of African Unity dated 10 September 1964; Considers, in accordance with that same resolution, that the mercenaries should as a matter of urgency be withdrawn from the Congo; Encourages the Organisation of African Unity to pursue its efforts to help the Government of the Democratic Republic of Congo to achieve national reconciliation in accordance with the above-mentioned resolution of the Organisation of African Unity; Requests all states to assist the Organisation of African Unity in the attainment of this objective; Requests the Organisation of African Unity, in accordance with Article 54 of the Charter of the United Nations, to keep the Security Council fully informed of any action it may take under the present resolution; Requests the Secretary-General of the United Nations to follow the situation in the Congo and to report to the Security Council at the appropriate time.' *Resolutions and Decisions of the Security Council 1964, Security Council, Official Records: Nineteenth Year* (New York: United Nations Press, 1966), pp. 28–29.

112 Remark from President Kennedy to General Mobutu during his meeting with the Congolese Commander-in-Chief of the Congolese National Army, Memorandum of Conversation, Washington, 31 May 1963, Schwar, *FRUS, XX, Congo Crisis*, p. 861.

113 NARA, State Department, Subject Numeric Files, RG59, Central Foreign Policy Files, Box 2731, File: POL 23–9 the Congo 12/26/64, Telegram recounting discussion of resolution with Tshombe over lunch in Léopoldville, from American Embassy to State Department and USUN, 31 December 1964.

114 See Young, *Politics in the Congo*.

115 NARA, State Department, Subject Numeric Files, RG59, Central Foreign Policy Files, Box 2736, POL 23–9 Rebellions, Coups the Congo 11/01/65, Telegram from Rusk, Department of State to the American Embassy in Léopoldville, 3 November 1965.

116 NARA, State Department, Subject Numeric Files, RG59, Central Foreign Policy Files, Box 2736, File: POL 23–9 Rebellions, Coups the Congo 11/01/65, Article from 30 October edition of *Le Depeche* as quoted in Telegram from American Consul in Elisabethville to American Embassy in Léopoldville, 2 November 1965.

117 NARA, State Department, Subject Numeric Files, RG59, Central Foreign Policy Files, Box 2736, File: POL 23–9 Rebellions, Coups the Congo 11/01/65, Telegram from Godley in the American Embassy in Léopoldville to the Department of States, 25 November 1965.
118 NARA, State Department, Subject Numeric Files, RG59, Central Foreign Policy Files, Box 2736, File: POL 23–9 Rebellions, Coups the Congo 11/26/65, Telegram from Godley to the Secretary of State, 27 November 1965.
119 NARA, State Department, Subject Numeric Files, RG59, Central Foreign Policy Files, Box 2736, File: POL 23–9 Rebellions, Coups the Congo 11/26/65, Telegram from the American embassy in Brussels, to the Department of State 26 November 1965.
120 NARA, State Department, Subject Numeric Files, RG59, Central Foreign Policy Files, Box 2736, File: POL 23–9 Rebellions, Coups the Congo 11/26/65, As revealed in a conversation with Davignon, Telegram from American Embassy in Brussels to Department of State, 26 November 1965.
121 NARA, State Department, Subject Numeric Files, RG59, Central Foreign Policy Files, Box 2736, File: POL 23–9 Rebellions, Coups the Congo 11/26/65, Telegram from American Embassy Bukavu to State Department, 27 November 1965.
122 NARA, State Department, Subject Numeric Files, RG59, Central Foreign Policy Files, Box 1873, File: POL – Political Affairs & Relations, AFR- T, Telegram from State Department to the American Embassy in Tunis, 21 December 1965.
123 Article 2(4) of the Charter of the United Nations states: 'All members shall refrain in their international relations from the threat or use of force against the territorial integrity or political independence of any state, or in any other manner inconsistent with the Purposes of the United Nations.' Simma et al., *The Charter of the United Nations*, p. 106.
124 Albrecht Randelzhofer, commentary to Article 2(4), in Simma et al., *The Charter of the United Nations*, p. 113. Emphasis added.
125 R. Coggins, 'Wilson and Rhodesia: UDI and British policy towards Africa', *Contemporary British History*, 20:3 (2006), 363–381.
126 S/Res/216 (1965), 12 November 1965, Security Council Official Records, www.un.org/en/ga/search/view_doc.asp?symbol=S/RES/217(1965). UN Security Council Resolution 216 was adopted by ten votes to none on 12 November 1965. The resolution condemned the unilateral declaration of independence from the racist minority in Southern Rhodesia. Resolution 217 further requested all states to withdraw economic relations with Southern Rhodesia.
127 Coggins, 'Wilson and Rhodesia'. One-third of British overseas investments were in South Africa in 1964.
128 M. Ford, 'Building stability overseas: three case studies in British defence diplomacy – Uganda, Rhodesia-Zimbabwe, and Sierra Leone', *Small Wars & Insurgencies*, 25:3 (2014), 584–606.
129 NARA, State Department, Subject Numeric Files, RG59, Central Foreign Policy Files, Box 1873, File: POL – Political Affairs and Relations, AFR-TS/P Assessment on British Commitments in Africa, William R. Duggan, Policy Planning Council, 25 October 1966.
130 NARA, State Department, Subject Numeric Files, RG59, Central Foreign Policy Files, Box 1873, File, POL – Political Affairs & Relations, AFR- T, Telegram

entitled: 'Britain and Ghana: Comments on S/P Assessment of British Commitments in Africa' from American Embassy in Ghana to Department of State, 18 December 1966.
131 NARA, State Department, Subject Numeric Files, RG59, Central Foreign Policy Files, Box 1873, File: POL – Political Affairs and Relations, AFR-T, All from S/P Assessment on British Commitments in Africa, William R. Duggan, Policy Planning Council, 25 October 1966.

Conclusion

The formal condemnation of American, British and Belgian actions during the Stanleyville intervention represented the zenith of the influence of the Afro-Asian bloc at the UN on the Congo question. Indeed, such a critique would have been unimaginable in previous years and was secured only because of the experience of the crisis and the exacerbation it produced among African and Asian states at what they perceived as the imperialist policies of America, Britain and Belgium towards the Congo. The crisis had served as a lightning rod for the interaction of decolonisation with the Cold War, revealing the important role of the Afro-Asian bloc in shaping UN policy and revealing how they used the UN as a platform to challenge Anglo-American liberal internationalism in Africa. By instrumentalising the organisation and enhancing its agency and potential in a variety of ways, the Afro-Asian bloc enhanced the role of the UN in accelerating decolonisation across Africa. The reverberation of the Congo problem in wider debates on colonial issues also showed its symbolic importance for newly independent states and granted them an opportunity to create a generally coherent anti-colonial internationalism, which impacted both on Western unity and on the UN itself.

The UN was transformed by the Congo experience in a variety of ways. On the first level, while the structure of the organisation was dramatically altered by the impact of decolonisation in producing many new members, the crisis had highlighted not just the perils of peacekeeping, but also the opportunities and limitations of UN agency, both on the ground and in the Secretariat. The activism of officials within the Secretariat, particularly the Secretaries-General Hammarskjöld and Thant in creating mechanisms such as the CAC and the 'Congo club' and activating other channels of influence such as the Fourth Committee, served to increase the role of the Afro-Asian states in devising and effecting the formation of UN Congo policy. Moreover, their interpretations of the Charter and the function of the office signified the agency the UN wielded in directing the Congo operation and generally supporting the wider anti-colonial campaign. As the crisis evolved, ONUC policy and its implementation came to increasingly reflect the Afro-Asian view of how the crisis should be managed and, by extension, enhanced the role of the UN in overseeing decolonisation and challenging the discriminatory, racist and imperialist policies of Britain and Belgium, and to a lesser extent, the US.

On the second level, the organisation provided a public platform for the campaign against colonialism. In the General Assembly and its associated committees, not only did the Afro-Asians have a vehicle for their objectives but they also had an opportunity to maximise the benefits of their numerically dominant position. The Congo debates frequently served as a microcosm of the wider issues that were at stake and were often used as a foil with which to attack Western policies in Africa and Asia that were commonly perceived as neo-colonial in nature. These public debates served to launch a wider discussion about the manifestations of neo-colonialism in the post-colonial world and increasingly highlighted that the North–South divide was more important to newly independent nations than the East–West conflict. Efforts to rebalance this relationship continued well into the 1970s as the Afro-Asian bloc, in cooperation with Latin American states, used UN public platforms as a means with which to reshape the global economic system through the campaign for the New International Economic Order. It was the Congo crisis, however, with its Cold War dimensions and internationalisation through the intervention of the UN, which served as the starting point for their agency.

On the third level, the UN served as a forum in which actors became socialised by engaging with different interpretations of sovereignty and self-determination. This was particularly important in turning the Congo crisis into a watershed moment for decolonisation. The engagement of Western statesmen and women, particularly American and British representatives, in direct dialogue with African and Asian leaders about the format of decolonisation and the varying understandings of self-determination and sovereignty which emerged during the debates on the Congo and colonialism, was important in reifying and legitimising non-Western views. Coupled with the difficult experience of the crisis, this process produced a shift in the position of both the US and Britain on colonial questions; the State Department moved from a position of passivity to declare a more forthright condemnation of all forms of colonialism by abandoning its traditional policy of abstention in voting on colonial issues. The Foreign Office overcame earlier resistance and agreed to supply information to the UN on how British colonies were progressing towards independence. Moreover, British officials gradually moved from the idea of a long road towards independence for many of its remaining colonies, to rapid decolonisation as the Congo had proven the difficulties of maintaining colonial networks of power and protecting economic and political interests in the context of poor relations between colonial powers and their former colonies. As this process of socialisation took place, both the US and Britain shifted their perceptions of the importance of the Third World as a sphere of foreign policy, and most importantly, of the utility and role of the UN in the process of decolonisation. During the crisis, across these three separate but mutually enforcing dimensions, the UN functioned to constrain the policies of both the US and Britain towards Congo and decolonisation, and changed the dynamic of Anglo-American cooperation on colonial issues.

By 30 June 1964, US technical and economic assistance to the Congo totalled $243 million, significantly ahead of the $0.4 million the British contributed in 1965.

The disparity between their contributions points to the deeper division that existed between London and Washington on policy towards the Congo. The crisis exposed the limitations of Anglo-American cooperation on colonial questions. Despite numerous efforts to coordinate strategies throughout the crisis, the US and Britain remained divided over the use of force by the UN, as Britain sought to consistently reign back the organisation whereas the US facilitated the speedy implementation of resolutions, acting under the impression that Congo could at any moment ignite into a 'hot' Cold War conflict. The failure to cooperate effectively at the UN served to reveal to both London and Washington the extent to which Britain had a much-diminished influence with former colonies and even Commonwealth states. The inability of the Foreign Office to prevent the crisis from affecting British plans for decolonisation and relations with Commonwealth members was indicative of the lack of influence of British officials both in New York and in various regional capitals. From New Delhi to Lagos, former and remaining British colonies roundly condemned British Congo policy and the neo-colonial guise of London's approach to Africa. Numerous British attempts to use Commonwealth connections and former colonial networks to coach moderation on the Afro-Asian group at the UN during Congo debates ultimately failed. The increasingly marginalised position of Britain at the UN was spelled out very clearly by British representatives such as Dean, who even questioned the usefulness of coordinating with the Americans and raised doubts about the utility of the Commonwealth voting bloc as a whole.

This lack of British influence with African and Asian leaders, and their continued criticism of British neo-colonialism, was viewed with unease in the State Department. Far from being a useful ally at the UN, the association with Britain actually served to undermine the American position as it publicly linked the US with the policies of a former colonial power. It also revealed to American officials that the utility of the alliance with Britain was severely limited as its connections and influence over African and Asian officials was increasingly tenuous. This realisation changed the dynamic of Anglo-American relations at the UN as the US gradually sought to assert a more anti-colonial stance and disassociate itself from the European colonial powers in public. This was most clear in the debates that took place on colonial questions, where the US voted against the former colonial powers, in the process fundamentally rupturing the agreement of tacit support for Britain's colonial policies. The Congo in fact marked the last coordinated effort to assert an Anglo-American position on decolonisation. Other crises in Angola, Algeria and later in South Africa were reflective of a different Anglo-American dynamic. Both countries opted to work outside the UN as much as possible and tackle successive conflicts in Africa through bilateral aid or subversive tactics, which began with the Stanleyville operation. Only on South Africa was there an increased effort to coordinate British and American policies once more, but again, as in the Congo, differing perceptions of the role of the UN persisted between London and Washington. The Congo crisis had served to subtly shift the dynamic of Anglo-American relations on colonial issues, as reflected in the State Department's report of 1965.

The crisis also produced different impressions of the UN itself. The State Department henceforth sought to reassert authority within the UN and reviewed USUN policy in a number of areas as understandings of the 'problem-solving' utility of the UN changed. The crisis had shown that an activist UN could pose a challenge to the execution of American policy, especially when the Secretary-General had the support of the Afro-Asian bloc. American officials had found, for the first time, that their ability to influence the Secretary-General and Congo policy was limited when there was a broad agreement between the Afro-Asians and the Secretariat. In addition, the public fora of the UN had served as a battleground for influence among newly independent states, as American officials sought to dilute the criticism of the USSR. In this contentious atmosphere, the State Department openly criticised the Secretary-General, splitting with Hammarskjöld publicly in an unprecedented move in 1961. The impression of the UN amongst American policymakers shifted during the early years of the Congo conflict from being a tool of American power to being overly activist and run by the Afro-Asian bloc, which, at times, constrained American policy. In this way the UN functioned as a valve for American power in the Congo during the crisis, leading directly to a revision of policy on colonial questions and altering views of the UN and its utility in this area amongst policymakers. The later development of the functions of the organisation in negotiating settlements, producing broad-based resolutions on colonial questions and managing the decolonisation process, gradually led to it becoming regarded as a more useful organisation towards the end of the crisis.

This perception of the UN was directly opposed to that of the Foreign Office. From 1962 onwards, Britain had an increasingly marginalised position on security matters relating to decolonisation and on colonial issues in the General Assembly and associated committees. Not only did the British resist UN policy in Congo, they sought to undermine the efforts of the organisation as a whole throughout Africa in order to dismantle the Afro-Asian bloc, protect their interests and split the 'unnatural alliance' between Africans and Asians on colonial issues.[1] The Afro-Asian bloc had consistently used the Congo crisis as a way to demonstrate a wider critique of British colonial policies, which increased the oversight role of the UN in managing the decolonisation process in Africa. As the crisis spilled over into wider debates about decolonisation, it posed a broader dilemma for British officials who remained opposed to increasing the role of the UN in managing decolonisation through the Trusteeship Committee, the Fourth Committee and the Committee of 24. By 1968, such was the damage to the British position that the Foreign Office even internally discussed withdrawing altogether from the Committee of 24.[2]

The Congo operation revealed both the potential of the Charter and the limits of its operation. There was no other peacekeeping mission on a scale comparable to the Congo until the end of the Cold War. Beyond peacekeeping, the experience also began a longer debate about forms of development and the project of state-building in post-colonial societies. The crisis proved to be an attempt to amalgamate different, complex visions about how to order the decolonised world. The Cold War caused the US and Britain to securitise the challenges of decolonisation and African nationalism in different ways, in the process exposing their various approaches to post-colonial development and security. To the US, the Congo had shown how efforts to perpetuate old colonial networks actually served to destabilise newly independent regimes as it drew accusations of neo-colonialism from other states. But the American preference for directly influencing African politics in order to foster the creation of Western-friendly Governments, to Britain and Belgium, constituted a heavy-handed role that complicated the process of quietly winding up their empires. In addition, it threatened to incite outbursts of anti-colonial violence that were directed at white minorities, European settlers and, most importantly, Western companies, whose business was often disrupted. The crisis had revealed how quickly the lack of a coherent strategy in these areas could produce a serious conflict with the Soviet Union as the Cold War ignited regional insecurities. With one stroke, Africa had been transformed from what had been perceived as mainly a European sphere of influence into a new battleground for ideas and power. The Congo in many ways demonstrated the worst-case scenario for decolonisation and showed how explosive the situation could be when a civil war became embroiled in the superpower conflict and was internationalised through the UN.

The Congo crisis served as a lightning rod which ignited these wider debates and in the process required the US and Britain to engage directly with African and Asian interpretations of statehood and self-determination in the wider nexus of decolonisation. It is framed here as a moment of resistance by the Afro-Asian world against the enactment of Anglo-American internationalism in the Congo and a challenge to American and British ideas of how to order the world. It was also an important moment of cohesion among African, Asian and Latin American states that was the first expression of a longer dynamic of cooperation and consolidation at the UN. Into the 1970s the Third World emerged as an important force that sought to redress North–South inequality in a number of areas, crucially by seizing upon UN structures and systems. With a longer perspective, therefore, throughout the Congo crisis the UN can be viewed as a space where African and Asian countries began their attempt to change the international order. In the process, the agency of the organisation, in combination with the emerging role of the Third World, served to alter the enactment of American and British imperial internationalism towards Africa. The crisis ultimately served as a moment which illuminated these perspectives and the role the UN could play in shaping world order.

Notes

1 NAL, PREM 11/4978, Secret memo from Philip de Zulueta to the Prime Minister, 19 January 1962.
2 W.R. Louis and S.R. Ashton, *East of Suez and the Commonwealth: British Documents on the End of Empire* (London: The Institute for Commonwealth Studies, The Stationery Office, 2004), pp. 147–149.

Index

ABAKO *see* Association des Bakongo pour l'Unification, l'Expansion et la
Addis Ababa Conference of African States 40
Adoula, C. 12
  government of 115–121, 129–130, 139–140, 144, 173–176
  as Prime Minister 82–97, 101, 119–120, 123–124, 127–130, 142–147, 152, 157, 170–172
African Group 40–56, 154, 180–181
Afro-Asian Bloc 2–7, 29, 38, 40–54, 55–60, 62, 73–91, 114, 119–130, 138–149, 152, 166, 181–186, 197–200
Afro-Asian Group 83, 89, 153, 199
Afro-Asian People's Solidarity Organization 138, 180
aircraft 117, 120–123, 139, 154
Algeria 5, 13, 22, 38, 46, 60, 86–87, 138–139, 147, 173, 180–186, 199
All-African People's Conference 13
Alliance for Progress 121, 147
AMAX mining company 26
American Committee for Aid to Katanga Freedom Fighters 126
ANC 44, 47, 49, 61, 74–79, 138, 144, 166, 170–184
Anglo-American Corporation 18–19
Anglo-American relations 2–7, 23, 73–88, 127–128, 145, 154–158, 167–169, 199
Angola 5, 13–19, 43, 86–87, 139, 150, 172, 186, 199
anti-colonial(ism) 4–7, 12, 19–26, 28–29, 41–57, 62, 83–88, 130, 149, 158, 197–201
Argentina 180
Ascension Island 178–179
Association des Bakongo pour l'Unification, l'Expansion et la (ABAKO) 13, 14, 17
Attwood, W. 177–178

Balewa, A.T. 52
Ball, G. 27, 76, 97, 119–127, 141, 153, 177
baluba 13, 15, 99, 172
Balubakat 59
Banana 79–81
Banda, H. 21
Baudouin, King 16
Belgium 1, 6, 11, 14–17, 27–28, 42–44, 49, 60, 74–82, 92–95, 99, 114–124, 128, 140–145, 151, 168–177, 180–185, 197–201 *passim*
Bermuda meeting 126–129, 139
Binza Group 18, 93, 172
Bomboko, J. 18, 45, 60
bombs 122–127
Botsio, K. 171
Bowles, C.B. 24–27, 76
British Guiana 168–169
Bruce, D. 140
Bunche, R.J. 40, 47, 120, 157, 166
Bundy, M. 27, 124, 144, 169, 174
Burden, W. 74

CAC *see* Congo Advisory Committee
Caccia, (Sir) H. 45, 85, 149
CAF *see* Central African Federation
Cameroon 13, 51, 53, 56
Canada 52, 182
Carson, P. 177–179
Casablanca Group 47, 61–62, 74, 138
Casement, R. 11–12
CDC *see* Commonwealth Development Corporation
Central African Federation 19, 95, 126, 152, 157
Central Government
  aid to 28
  authority of 17, 43–50, 59, 88, 93–94, 95–96, 137, 140–147

relations with 79, 82, 92, 99–101, 115–119, 121–125, 127–128, 156–158, 166, 172–174, 184
Central Intelligence Agency (CIA) 25–28, 45, 50, 58–59, 73, 82, 124, 177, 184
Ceylon 53, 56, 60, 76, 119, 121, 151
Chile 116
China 39, 60, 173
 debate over representation at the UN 89–90
Christmas Island 126–129
Church, committee 45
Churchill, W. 23, 29, 89
CIA *see* Central Intelligence Agency
civil rights 24, 27, 75, 175
Cleveland, H. 83, 91, 97–98, 120, 121, 126, 129, 148, 154, 170
CNL *see* Conseil National de Liberation
Cohen, (Sir) A. 55–56
Cold War 2–6, 12, 23–28, 38, 43–49, 53–62, 73–75, 80–88, 121–122, 129, 130, 138–139, 147–149, 182–187, 197–201
College of Commissioners 47, 50, 58–59
Committee of Twenty-Four 2, 55, 84–89, 149–151, 157–158, 168–169, 200
Commonwealth 4, 19–22, 52–53, 84–85, 88–91, 122, 130, 150–155, 167–168, 175–179, 182, 186, 199
Commonwealth Development Corporation (CDC) 19
Commonwealth Relations Office (CRO) 52, 94, 149
Communism 21–22, 26–27, 44, 139, 147
Conan Doyle, A. 11
Confederation of Katanga Associations (Conakat) 15, 17, 93, 99
Congo Advisory Committee (CAC) 41–43, 45, 49, 76, 82, 120, 126, 143–144, 154, 166, 197
Congo-Brazzaville 22, 45, 50, 172, 174, 180
Congo Club 40–41, 197
Congo Free State 11–12
Conrad, J. 11
Conseil National de Liberation (CNL) 172–176
Conservative Party (Britain) 18–20, 92, 123–130, 142, 171

copper 11, 12, 15, 17–19, 140–141, 186
Cordier, A.W. 45, 53
credentials debate 50–53
CRO *see* Commonwealth Relations Office
Cuba 29, 138, 147–150, 157

Dahomey 22
Dayal, R. 60–61, 75, 80–83
Dean, P. 26, 74, 78, 88–89, 96, 120–125, 127, 129, 145, 166–168, 199
Delvaux, A. 79
Devlin, L. 45, 184
Devlin, P. 21
De Zulueta, P. 144, 150, 169, 171
diamonds 11, 17, 18, 26, 28, 44
Diefenbaker, J. 146
Dirksen, E. 96, 126
Dodd, T. 96, 97, 126
Dodson, D. 166–167
Dragon Noir 181
Dragon Rouge 176–177, 179, 181
Dulles, A. 26
Dulles, J.F. 26, 29
Duncan-Sandys, (Lord) E. 169
Dunnett, D. 97–101, 114, 120, 128

Economic and Social Council of the United Nations (ECOSOC) 40
Economist, The 1, 39, 130
Ecuador 180
EEC *see* European Economic Community
Egypt *see* UAR
Eisenhower, D.D. 6, 23–24, 26–29, 57–58, 61–62, 82, 89
Elisabethville 6, 14, 17, 20, 46, 47, 59, 61, 82, 88, 92, 96, 97, 98, 99, 100, 114, 115, 118, 128, 140, 141, 152, 154, 166, 167, 184
Ethiopia 13, 40, 42, 46, 48, 61, 125, 155, 156, 174
European Economic Community (EEC) 151, 170
Eyskens, G. 15, 16, 79

February Resolution 7, 76, 79–80, 83, 92, 93–94, 114–119, 123, 144
Finletter, T. 153, 155

Foot, (Lord Caradon) H. 89, 98, 183
Force Publique 1, 16, 28, 44
Fourth Committee 2, 55, 84, 87, 150, 151, 197, 200
France 22, 23, 24, 61, 77, 79, 86, 88, 99, 116, 121, 124, 145, 149, 151, 168, 171
Fredericks, W.J. 26, 153
Front de Liberation Nationale (FLN) 40, 41

Gbenye, C. 172, 184
gendarmerie (of Katanga) 44, 46, 60, 94–95, 99, 100, 114, 128, 139, 144, 154, 174
Ghana 13, 21, 25, 38, 40, 46, 48, 49, 51, 53, 56, 58, 59, 60, 73, 80, 91, 120, 122, 125, 138, 151, 171, 179, 180, 183
Gizenga, A. 59, 60, 79, 93, 97, 120, 138, 172, 173
Godley, M. 177, 179, 185
Goldwater, B. 96, 175
Green, C.H. 52, 154
Grinwis, D. 177
Gromyko, A. 183
Guatemala 28, 139
Guinea 13, 40, 43, 46, 48, 49, 50, 53, 56, 60, 80, 138, 177, 178, 180, 183
Gullion, E. 97, 101, 118, 128

Hambro, C. 19
Hammarskjöld, D. 1, 2, 38, 50, 53–60, 73–83, 114, 129
  alleged assassination of 115–120
  relations with Lumumba 51, 61
  vision for the UN 3, 7, 39–45, 86–101, 148, 197–200
Harriman, A. 58, 78, 171–179
Herter, C.A. 28, 54, 73
Hoare, M. 175, 177
Home, A.D. 18, 52, 58, 88, 90, 100, 114, 124, 127, 129, 142–145, 150–157, 167–169, 171

ICJ *see* International Court of Justice
Illeo, J. 12
India 21, 25, 41–42, 48–49, 53–56, 73, 84, 101, 116, 120, 122, 123, 139, 149, 151–153, 180

Indian peacekeepers in Congo 38, 76–81, 95, 143–145, 154
Indonesia 48, 53, 56, 126, 181
International Committee in Defence of Africa 182
International Court of Justice (ICJ) 146, 168, 171
Ireland 38, 116
Ivory Coast 181

Janssens, (General) E. 16
Jeunesse 173
Johnson, L.B. 25, 27, 171, 174–175, 182

Kalonji, A. 80, 99, 172
Kamitatu, C. 15
Kanza, T. 13, 46, 50, 59, 61, 62, 177–178
Kasai 13, 17, 44–48, 79–80, 99, 147, 172
Kasavubu, J. 1, 13–15, 60, 76, 79–81, 84, 88, 90, 128, 130, 176–178, 184–185
  relations with Lumumba 38–45, 47–59
Katanga 3–7, 22, 26, 48, 59–60, 130, 153–157, 166–167, 172, 174, 176, 184
  economic interests in 12–20, 26
  sanctions against 140–147
  secession as a political problem at the UN 29, 43–48, 62, 73–79, 88, 91–100, 114–129
Katanga Baluba Association 15
Kennedy, J.F. 6, 24–27, 58–62, 73–78, 82, 85, 88–90, 101, 120–128, 140–145, 150–157, 167–171, 184
Kenya 13, 21, 22, 49, 57, 139, 175, 177, 180
Kenyatta, J. 177–178, 180
Khiary, M. 99
Khrushchev, N. 44, 54, 57, 61, 90, 116, 146–148
Kitona (accords) 127–129, 138
Kivu 18, 147
Kongo, Kingdom of 13, 17
Korea 39
Kuznetsov, V.V. 53
Kwilu 173

Laos 124, 139
Latin America 24, 51, 53, 87, 121, 147, 169, 172, 198, 201

League of Nations 5
Lennox-Boyd, Alan 21–22
Leopoldville 1, 6, 13, 15–18, 25, 28, 38, 41,
    49, 50, 58, 82, 97–101, 115–118, 138,
    155–158, 166–167, 170–177, 180,
    182, 185
  government in 14, 45–48, 59–61, 75–79,
    88, 91–94, 124, 128, 129, 140–177, 184
Liberia 13, 40, 48, 77, 80, 114, 119, 120,
    121, 140, 174, 180
Libya 13, 21, 40, 60
Linner, S. 74, 94, 97, 98, 116, 125
Lloyd, S. 20
Lodge, H.C. 23, 53
Loi Fondamentale 92
Lumumba, P. 1, 12–18, 38–41, 44–50,
    51–56, 80–82, 93–99, 138, 172, 177,
    179, 183
  assassination of 58–62, 74–79, 92

MacLeod, I. 100
Macmillan, H. 6, 20, 23, 51, 54, 78, 85,
    88–89, 92, 114, 145, 150–151,
    154–156, 167–171
  government of 20–21, 97–98, 123–130,
    139–142
Malagasy 22, 153, 174
Mali 22, 38, 48, 53, 56, 60, 85, 138
Mauritania 22, 180
Mboya, T. 13
McGhee, G. 27, 29, 96, 141
Menon, K. 56, 120
mercenaries 46, 94, 95, 97, 100, 120, 123,
    139, 140, 173–178, 182, 185
mining 15, 18, 19, 26, 121, 140, 155, 156
MNC *see* Mouvement Nationale Congolais
Mobutu, (Colonel) J.D. 18, 45–47, 50, 58–59,
    60, 80, 170, 172, 178, 181, 184–185
Monrovia Group 47, 62, 74, 76, 152
moratorium, on Congo debate 3, 78–79
Morel, E. D. 11–12
Morocco 13, 38, 40, 46, 48, 53, 56, 60, 166,
    173, 181
Mouvement Nationale Congolais (MNC)
    12, 14, 15, 18, 59
Mpolo, M. 60
Mulele, P. 138, 172–173, 176

Munongo, G. 95, 96, 99, 101
Mwamba, R. 59

Nasser, G.A. 51
NATO 27, 43, 79, 86, 127, 153
Ndele, A. 18, 81
Ndola 97, 115, 116, 128
Nehru, J. 41, 49, 81, 82, 101, 139
Nendaka, V. 18, 185
New Deal 25
Nigeria 22, 52, 53, 56, 84, 120, 122, 123,
    171, 174, 175, 180, 181
Nkrumah, K. 13, 41, 44–52, 80, 82, 114,
    122, 125, 178, 186
Norway 116
Nyerere, J. 13, 175, 176
Nzonzi, E. 59

OAU *see* Organization of African Unity
O'Brien, C. 77, 92–101, 116, 118–125, 141
Okito, J. 60
Olenga (General) N. 174
Operation Morthor 95, 98–102
Operation Rumpunch 94, 95–99
Operations des nations unies au Congo
    (ONUC) 3, 7, 38, 41–49, 50–51, 56,
    59–61, 73–81, 88, 91, 94, 95, 100,
    114–118, 120–130, 143–151, 152–157,
    166, 180, 186, 197
Operation UNOKAT 7, 152–158, 166
Oppenheimer, H. 18
Organization of African Unity (OAU)
    172–175, 177–181
Orientale 14, 58, 181
Ormsby-Gore, D. 127–129

Pakistan 55, 76, 139, 144, 146
Pan-African Freedom Movement of East
    and Central Africa (PAFMECA)
    155, 167
Pan-African(ism) 13, 22, 47, 155
Parti Solidaire Africain (PSA) 14, 15
Paulis 181
peacekeepers 38, 39, 77
peacekeeping 2–3, 29, 38–40, 44, 49, 77,
    142, 146, 154, 157, 170, 186, 197, 200
Peru 147, 172

Polaris missiles 156
Portugal 86–88
PSA *see* Parti Solidaire Africain

Quaison-Sackey, A. 46
quiet diplomacy 39, 54, 74, 82, 118

rapporteurs, use of at the UN 148–149
rebels 80, 147, 172–184
Rhodesia 19, 20, 95, 97, 114–117, 120–123, 139, 150–152, 155–158, 168, 175, 185–186
Riches, D. 166
Rostow, W. 25–26
rubber 11
Rusk, D. 26–27, 74, 76, 81, 83, 85, 88, 115, 127, 129, 148–149, 174–179

Sangwa, J. 59
Santo Domingo 180
Satterthwaite, J. 23
Scott, I. 60, 100
Secession (of Katanga) 3, 17–18, 20, 44, 46–47, 92–97, 100–101, 114, 115, 119–121, 123–129, 140–146, 152–158, 166–171
  of South Kasai, 44, 47, 48
Second World War 23
Secretary-General 1–3, 7, 29, 38–51, 54–59, 60–62, 74–83, 90–99, 114–130, 142–154, 157, 172–178, 200
  good offices of 39, 76
  see also Hammarskjöld, D.; Thant, U.
Sendwe, J. 15
Senegal 22, 174
Shell 18, 19
Sierra Leone 22, 180
Simba (rebels) 173, 176–177, 179, 182
Sino-Indian War 139
Skybolt 155
Slim, M. 47, 49, 87, 116
Smith, A.H. 143, 155
Smith, I. 185–186
socialist 25
Societe Generale de Belgique (SGB) 17
Somalia 21, 174, 180
Soumialot, G. 172–173, 184

South Africa 18, 19, 22, 57, 87–88, 117, 139, 150, 152, 158, 169, 186, 199
South Kasai 44, 47, 48, 80, 172
  see also Kasai
Soviet Union 3, 6, 27–28, 43–44, 57, 122, 138, 146, 171, 173, 201
  see also USSR
Spaak, P.H. 175, 178, 185
Special Committee on Decolonisation *see* Committee of Twenty-Four
Special Political and Decolonization Committee *see* Fourth Committee
Stanleyville 1, 7, 14, 58–61, 79, 93, 120, 138–158
  hostage crisis in 166–185, 197, 199
Stevenson, A.E. 25–27, 62, 75–79, 81–83, 88–89, 96–97, 116–118, 121–122, 127, 129, 144, 146
Struelens, M. 97
Sudan 21, 22, 40, 61, 79, 138, 180

Tananarive meeting 79
Tanganyika 19, 22, 51, 86, 151, 176
Tanganyika Concessions Limited (TANKS) 17–19
Tanzania 13, 22, 117, 174, 176, 180, 183
Telli, D. 177–178
Tempelsman, L. 26
Thant, U. 2, 3, 7, 83, 116–121, 123–129, 141–143, 148–152, 153–158, 166–171, 174, 180–183, 197
  plan for the Congo 143–147
Third World 5–7, 24–27, 147, 150, 198, 201
Timberlake, C. 28, 50, 76, 80, 82
Tory *see* Conservative Party (Britain)
Toure, A.S. 13, 46, 80, 175
troika proposal 53–58, 91, 116, 120
Tshombe, M. 15, 20, 60, 91–92, 96–98, 182
  British support for 122–124, 151, 166–167
  leader of Katanga secession 17, 43, 46–47, 77, 95, 100–101, 114–121, 138–147, 152–157
  negotiations with 79, 88, 90, 93–94, 99, 125–130
  as Prime Minister of the Congo 172–179, 184–185

Tunisia 13, 40, 46, 47, 48, 80, 116, 166, 180
Twain, M. 11

UAR *see* United Arab Republic
Uganda 19, 22, 151, 167, 172, 183, 186
UMHK *see* Union Miniere de Haut Katanga
UNEF *see* United Nations Emergency Force
Unilever 20, 143, 155
Union Miniere de Haut Katanga (UMHK) 17–20, 43, 140–144, 155–156, 166–167
United Arab Republic 51–54, 56, 60, 80, 119, 121, 122, 144, 183
United Nations (UN)
  Charter 39, 83, 90, 94, 146
  financing 152, 155
  General Assembly 3–5, 28–29, 38, 40–42, 48–58, 73–79, 82, 87–91, 94, 97–98, 120–121, 131, 139, 144–151, 154, 157, 170, 198, 200
  secretariat 2, 9, 7, 39–43, 60, 83, 86–87, 90–94, 114, 116, 118, 120, 122, 129, 149, 199–200
  Security Council 1, 27, 38–44, 47, 49, 51–56, 60–61, 73–77, 79, 86, 90, 93–94, 118–128, 138–149, 151–155, 168, 170, 180–186
  Trusteeship Committee 100, 200

United Nations Emergency Force (UNEF) 41, 42
United States Agency for International Development (USAID) 26
uranium 3, 12, 18, 27, 145
US Mission to the UN (USUN) 75, 83, 148, 174, 199
USSR 12, 23, 60, 61, 77, 82, 83, 89, 90–91, 114, 121, 129, 147, 180, 183, 200
  see also Soviet Union
U Thant Plan *see* Thant, U.

Van De Walle, F. 175, 177, 178
Venezuela 116
Vietnam 28, 29, 115, 121, 124, 139, 147, 171, 175, 186
Volta River 125
Von Horn, C. 59

Wachuku, J. 52–53, 171
Walker, G. 182, 183
Waterhouse, C. 17, 18
Welensky, R. 20, 97, 123, 126, 142, 151
Western bloc 2, 3, 43, 62, 79
Williams, G.M. 54, 57, 76, 78, 96, 97, 120, 153, 170, 178
Wilson, H. 175–176
Wisner, F. 52

Zambia 13, 186

Lightning Source UK Ltd.
Milton Keynes UK
UKHW021257011219
354565UK00012B/336/P